D1163791

WHITE
SILENCE

SYLVIA E. CRANE

WHITE SILENCE

GREENOUGH, POWERS, and CRAWFORD

American Sculptors in Nineteenth-Century Italy

UNIVERSITY of MIAMI PRESS *Coral Gables*

Copyright © 1972 by
University of Miami Press
Library of Congress Catalog Card Number 79–156141
ISBN 0–87024–199–0

All rights reserved, including rights of reproduction
and use in any form or by any means, including the making
of copies by any photo process, or by any electronic or
mechanical device, printed or written or oral, or recording
for sound or visual reproduction or for use in any knowledge
or retrieval system or device, unless permission in writing
is obtained from the copyright proprietors.

Designed by Bernard Lipsky
Manufactured in the United States of America

NB
236
.C 72

WITHDRAWN

E. M. CUDAHY
LOYOLA
UNIVERSITY
MEMORIAL LIBRARY

TO

THE THREE MEN OF MY FAMILY,
JOHN, CHARLES, AND THOMAS,
WHOSE ABIDING DEVOTION
AND SYMPATHETIC
UNDERSTANDING
THROUGHOUT
THE
PROTRACTED
EFFORT ARE
DEEPLY APPRECIATED

Contents

Illustrations

Preface

The post World War II wave of Italophilia not only attracted a fixed American population of some 10,000 to Rome but has directed attention to the English-speaking colony resident there and in Florence throughout the nineteenth century. Earlier, notice centered on such renowned literary figures as Shelley, Keats, and Byron in Rome, and Robert and Elizabeth Barrett Browning in Florence, while the Americans who went in quest of the artist's life were largely overlooked.

The English and Germans virtually monopolized the art history of this period and gave the Americans short shrift, undoubtedly still viewing them as barbarous colonials even though the American group was numerous and as distinguished as the British. Perhaps the oversight was due to aesthetic bias but in any case the prejudice persists. Some literary biographies of these artists have appeared, but in the light of the group's size, the historic record is pitifully lean. Among the memoirs published in the nineteenth century were John Galt's biography of Benjamin West, Horatio Greenough's *Letters* with appended biographical notes, Henry T. Tuckerman's short memorial to Horatio Greenough and other slim biographical essays, Clara Erskine Clement's sketchy compendium of nineteenth century artists, George Washington Greene's *Biographical Studies*, Thomas Hicks' and Samuel Osgood's memorials to their colleague Thomas Crawford,

Louis Noble's book extolling Thomas Cole's allegorical paintings, James E. Freeman's Roman recollections, Charles E. Lester's remarks about Hiram Powers and his colleagues, Samuel I. Prime's *Life of Samuel F. B. Morse*, James Douglas Breckinridge's *Memorial to Joel T. Hart*, G. P. A. Healy's *Reminiscences*, Thomas Ball's autobiography, Jared B. Flagg's *Life and Letters* of his uncle, Washington Allston, Charles Bullfinch's *Life and Letters*, edited by his daughter; and Henry James' authorized biography of *William Wetmore Story and his Friends*. The five books last named did not appear until the nineties. They all have some value as source materials, but they lack historical accuracy or objectivity, among other requisite qualities of history. This is understandable as they were not intended as historical accounts but were primarily designed to record the memory of a famed personality. Of textbooks, William Dunlap's history of American art, published in 1834, supplies information about an earlier period, the writings of James Jackson Jarves are superficial, as are Tuckerman's and Clement's, and Lorado Taft's *History of American Sculpture* (1903) leaves the subject incomplete.

After the turn of the century it seemed dutiful to descendants and intimate friends to collate the letters and spin out brief biographical sketches of the illustrious artists who were cose to them. Owing to such efforts, we have *The Life and Letters of Christopher Pearse Cranch* edited by his daughter, *Harriet Hosmer, Letters and Memories* by Cornelia Carr, and *George Inness's Life, Art, and Letters* by his son. It wasn't until 1914 that the Massachusetts Historical Society published the *Letters and Papers of John Singleton Copley*, and it was 1931 when the Boston Athenaeum issued the journal of Amasa Hewins.

Giuseppe Prezzolini focused attention in 1933 to the nineteenth century American group in Italy in his *Come Gli Americani Scoprirono L'Italia*. It gave rise to some modern scholarly works about the artists of this period, notably by Talbot Hamlin, James T. Flexner, Edgar P. Richardson, Otto Wittman, Oliver Larkin, Albert Ten Eyck Gardner, Howard Marraro, Elizabeth McCausland, Carleton Mabee, William Sener Rusk, Paul Baker, Nathalia Wright, and Robert Gale. Although some American literary critics wrote more generally of the group (such as Van Wyck Brooks and Francis O.

Mathiessen, followed by Italian writers like Giuliana Artom Treves and Silvio Negro), the field has not been intensively mined. The foremost American art historian of our time, Bernard Berenson, although enamoured of Italy to the extent of living his adult years there, completely ignored the early American artists who were similarly captivated. Barbara Novak's *American Painting in the Nineteenth Century* is a splendid modern contribution, but the sculptors still await adequate treatment. The letters of the period have been hard to come by, underrated until recently when the archivists began to display appropriate interest.

While a few painters and writers visited and lingered in European capitals to improve their technique and imbibe the cosmopolitan atmosphere, a group of sculptors settled in Italy, expressly to learn and pursue their art. Among these were Horatio Greenough, Hiram Powers, Thomas Crawford, Randolph Rogers, William Wetmore Story, William Henry Rinehart, Chauncey B. Ives, Shobal Vail Clevenger, Henry Kirke-Brown, and Harriet Hosmer. This study of the first three of these sculptors, who spent their active years in Italy during its mid-century Risorgimento, explores their experience from the dual perspective of the American backdrop and the extended Italian residence. The objective is a composite account of their careers and their goals and contributions within the context of their times. The text has been constructed upon strict adherence to the contemporary record, comprising chiefly letters, but including periodical articles, journals, and books.

These American sculptors in Italy set the precedent for the inundation of their country with Italian artistic productions and native works in the Italian style, a trend that prevailed during the major part of the nineteenth century. They were responsible for the transmission back home of the Italianate neoclassical aesthetics of their epoch.

Their active lives coincided with the period in America of the Classical Revival, a glorified concept of the Roman republic and the Greek city-state, epitomizing the highest level of known civilization. Ancient Rome and Athens were exemplars of the democratic state. The new republic, auspiciously launched and successfully defended against mighty, imperial Britain, was characterized in classical terms.

Justice, liberty, art, poetry, history, and constitutionalism were favored subjects, symbolized by the Greek muses. Public figures were clad in Roman togas and often unclad in busts. They were even represented at times nude as Apollo. Although the classical references and symbols were familiar to a handful of the literary elite, they were alien incongruities to the untutored and puritanical populace.

Sculpture in Western Europe was the laggard among the arts both in initiating and perpetuating the neoclassical style. During the nineteenth century, poets and novelists had already progressed into a romantic phase. Since the Renaissance, sculptors plied their customary craft within a spectrum of tastes until the dramatic transformation was exerted in Paris by Auguste Rodin, who distorted the human figure to heighten its emotional impact.

The neoclassical scene was laid chiefly in Italy where it was presided over by Flaxman, Canova, and Thorwaldsen; its influence was diffused throughout the Western world. Occasionally, romantic poetical abstractions were rendered in the classical mold. Generalizations were rampant in the artistic idiom of the time, as was rhetoric in the public discourses; artistic and literary criticisms were promotional eulogies. Literature was steeped in chivalrous flourishes, sentimentality, and prudery. The novels of James Fenimore Cooper's European period, as exemplified in *The Bravo*, were intellectual delineations of political and social criticism at the expense of individualized character development and interaction. A generation later, Ralph Waldo Emerson still sought the meaning of truth in abstractions of the "good" and the "beautiful."

Italy made her mark on almost every major literary figure in nineteenth century America. It is difficult to name one writer of consequence who has not written either a memoir, travel book, or novel as a result of that experience. James Fenimore Cooper, Francis Marion Crawford, Louisa May Alcott, and Mark Twain were foremost among the novelists who set their tales in Italian cities. The works of Nathaniel Hawthorne and Henry James set in Rome, Florence, and Venice pronounced nostalgic yet often acerbic judgments upon life in those places.

The landscape, cities and mores of Italy were described in travel books and memoirs for American readers by most of the peripatetic literati, including Catherine Sedgwick, Margaret Fuller, Washington Irving, Herman Melville, Charles Sumner, George Stillman Hillard, William Ware, William Cullen Bryant, Horace Greeley, James Russell Lowell, Charles Eliot Norton, William Wetmore Story, Cornelius C. Felton, and William Dean Howells.

Florence still bears the traces of this incursion. In the small square of Bellosguardo, there is a granite monument that bears the inscription "James Fenimore Cooper, Nathaniel Hawthorne, Louisa May Alcott, and Henry James loved this place."

Since art mirrors its contemporary scene, this glimpse into our cultural history through the sculptors' experience ought to be relevant. It is hoped that this account of the first three American sculptors, who were selected from the standpoint of their diverse origins, adopted cities of work, and their various artistic trials and productions, will illumine something of the broader canvas of their pre-Civil War setting in America.

Acknowledgments

Without the cooperation of numerous librarians and archivists whose primary occupation is to provision researchers, the author of a historical work would be thwarted. The assistance of these dedicated public servants is vital to such an enterprise; to them I tender my sincere appreciation for their unstinting help.

I credit my inspiration for the subject of my study to my mentor, Henry Steele Commager. Oliver Larkin and James Marston Fitch, whose own works and judgments I esteem, both read the manuscript at an early stage and gave me sustaining encouragement, as did other sympathetic friends. Foremost among these are Helen Lamb Lamont, Barrows Dunham, Barbara Guest, Chang Hsin-hai, Virginia Peters, and Philip Goodheim. Their encouragement and their perceptive suggestions for improvements were essentially supportive.

Among the archivists, I am particularly grateful to Mrs. Carolyn E. Jakeman, assistant librarian for reference in the Houghton Library at Harvard University; John D. Cushing, librarian of the Massachusetts Historical Society; Adolph K. Placzek, librarian of the Avery Library at Columbia University; and David McKibben, who, as Fine Arts Director of the Boston Athenaeum, gave me access to the invaluable archive of that institution. Mrs. Lillian Kessler, who directed the reference library at the office of the Architect of the Capitol in

Washington, D.C., was assiduous in ferreting out for my attention pertinent materials buried in that immense archive. I had solid help as well at the Cincinnati Historical Society under the directorship of Louis L. Tucker, where I worked at length; the New York Historical Society under the guidance of Dr. James J. Heslin; and the Virginia State Library, whose director, Randolph W. Church, state librarian, and assistant librarian, Dr. Ray O. Hummel, Jr., invariably extracted precisely the material I would require for my hurried visits. It was a distinct pleasure to spend the requisite weeks at the Yale University's Beinecke Rare Book and Manuscript Library, directed by Herman W. Liebert. My work was similarly expedited. and aided at the Boston Public Library, the Library of Congress, the Pennsylvania Historical Society, and the Maryland Historical Society·

Unusual generosity and cooperation was extended at the Accademia di Belle Arti in Florence under the aegis of its director, Dr. Luigi Biaggi, whose enthusiasm for the discoveries I unearthed from his repository almost rivaled mine.

Throughout the years of this work's progress, my constant sustainers were the men of my family, my devoted husband, John O. Crane, and my two understanding sons, Charles and Thomas, who stalwartly withstood my frequent absences from home, especially during family outings and holidays. Their patience and forebearance were remarkable.

For its generous support of the publication, which allowed the price of the book to be within normal bounds, I thank the Friendship Fund of New York. The substance is entirely my own responsibility.

WHITE
SILENCE

Introduction

FOR THE AMERICAN ARTISTIC NEOPHYTE IN THE LATE TWENTIES OF
the last century, ties of family and country paled before euphoric
dreams of art and poetry in the classical land of sunny Italy. "The
country which could then boast the names of Dante . . . of
Petrarch . . . of Boccacio, stood high in the scale of intellectual
refinement."[1] Donatello, Brunelleschi, Ghiberti, and Michelangelo
conjured visions of magnificence. The unrivaled cadences of Ovid
and Tasso and the soaring imagery of Goethe and Shelley were enhanced in their Italian setting. Touring Americans shared the artists'
romantic sighs in response to their first views of ancient palaces and
more ancient ruins. The cost of living in splendid residences was so
low that it challenged credibility, and the abundance of artistic models, ancient and alive, provided further enticement. The combination
of the "Utile with the dulci" was irresistible.[2] Italy was the world
mecca of sculpture.

At the close of the Napoleonic wars, the Continent reopened
to tourists and Europe's nobility once again converged at the Italian
art centers, joined now by America's commercial princes, who were
quite willing to embellish their own lives with art productions at
bargain prices. In Italy, the wealth of Europe's art and history was
available for the looking. Much of it could be shipped home for a
price. The British were setting the standard,[3] the Russians were repre-

sented in numbers and distinction, and the Americans were aware of their late arrival.

The James Fenimore Coopers wrote that Florence was "the cheapest place we have lived since being in Europe," although their Yankee morality and thrift were initially offended by what they referred to as society's "constant round of dissipation." Mrs. Cooper wrote:

> Mr. Cooper almost affronted the Lords, the Dukes, and the Princes by declining their invitations—but after satisfying Curiosity, we thought it quite wise to stay at home, and save our Purse, for other purposes. But, there are many pleasures here to be enjoyed without incurring any additional expense to one's ordinary style of living. Their Magnificent Galley of Antiquities, Collections of Paintings, Libraries, are exposed on the most liberal plan, and present a constant source of Improvement and delight.[4]

Cooper was captivated by the artistic splendor and his puritanism was mellowed by the warmth and geniality of the Italians. After a while, he began to envy their "singular indolence," and their capacity "to make a siesta of life." He reported that they seemed "too gentlemanlike to work, or to be fussy," and they could "enjoy the passing moment."[5] To Cooper this was a refreshing contrast to the driving pace of life at home.

The early American expatriates yearned for the art life of Europe. It became fashionable at the turn of the last century for educated young Americans to make the Grand Tour of Europe's art world. It was equally modish for the intelligentsia at home to deplore the cultural barrenness of the domestic soil and denounce the prevailing mercantile values that denied recognition for creative efforts. At the commencement of his career, one young American asserted caustically: "Let us see if we can show Jonathan that art is a noble vehicle of national gratitude and glory and that a man may be an artist without being ergo a blackguard and a mischievous member of society. Allston and Morse, they say, are exceptions of a high order. I can tell them that Allston and Morse have made the rule."[6]

After attaining his first artistic success, which met with popular resistance at home, this same artist elaborated: "America has always acted toward her artists like a hen who has hatched ducklings. She cannot understand why they run to the water instead of thriving upon the dunghill—which has only to be scratched in order to feed them all. She will learn better but not yet. . . . If you could but see the career of a high artist here . . . you would understand why I grieve."[7]

Paradoxically, these self-styled iconoclasts brought with them into exile many of the stigmata of the culture against which they railed and fortified their sense of nationalism. At a safe distance, they had the best of both worlds. Despite the sympathetic warmth of their reception in stratified European society, they resisted total conversion. In Italy, the artists had no need to justify themselves by conventional standards of success. The creative effort was appreciated for itself. They were thus induced to trade their persistent nostalgia for home for commodious studios, palatial residences, a retinue of trained servants, and a respected, even honored, position in society. Being American, however, they were relentlessly pursued into the heart of the "dolce far niente" by the demon of Yankee industry and the rigor of Calvinist morality. Neither the fertile, sun-drenched soil, nor the pervading warmth of the climate, nor the breadth of Italian tolerance could soften their fiber. Their lives were brightened, their sights enlarged, and their understanding deepened in response to the moderating influence of their foreign environment, but they were substantially undeflected from their course, as if directed by some inner force toward their artistic objectives.

America's second victory over England generated a wave of nationalism that stimulated a widespread desire to memorialize the victories and heroes of the young Republic. Public buildings and monuments mushroomed. The burning of the Capitol at Washington dramatized the need for sculptors. American artists responded by adorning the squares of the expanding cities, the new statehouses, and the United States Capitol with works made in Italy.

This nationalistic sentiment spurred sculptors to give form to noble conceptions for public works. Patronage was forthcoming when sought, both public and private, coming chiefly from the newly acquired commercial and infant industrial fortunes. One commentator observed, "The East was discovering its Utopia in an industrial capitalistic order," while witnessing the "emergence of a new middle class."[8] New England had recovered sufficiently from the commercial paralysis of "Mr. Jefferson's Embargo" and "Mr. Madison's War" to accumulate a reserve available for artistic patronage. Boston was the principal center, but New York and Philadelphia did not lag notably.

Just as the Grand Tour was deemed a fitting culmination to the education of any cultivated young American making his way in the east coast's Europe-oriented society, so it was the essential commencement of his artistic training. Native American painters were plentiful along the seaboard for portraits and they eked out an itinerant existence. More evolved interior compositions, landscapes, or historical subjects were beyond the usual scope before Benjamin West charted the pilgrimage from America to artistic Arcadia in 1760. It is reported apocryphally, that when West first saw the Apollo Belvedere in the Vatican Galleries, he startled Rome with his exclamation. "How like a Mohawk warrior he seems." West was followed to Italy by John Singleton Copley, John Vanderlyn, Samuel F. B. Morse, Rembrandt Peale, Washington Allston, and later by John Gadsby Chapman, Francis Alexander, Thomas Cole, Asher B. Durand, Christopher Pearse Cranch, James E. Freeman, John Gore, Emanuel Leutze, John Kensett, William Page, Henry Inman, Thomas Doughty, Jaspar Cropsey, and others too numerous to mention. Virtually every prominent member of the first American school of painters, the famed Hudson River School, received his training in Italy.

In the early years of America's independence, she had no choice but to turn to the Italians for her public sculptural adornments. American art was in its infancy. There were few skilled workmen, but there were some native stonecutters of talent, such as Hezekiah Augur at New Haven and John Frazee and Robert Launitz at New York. Whether these men could be entrusted with the important task of decorating the public buildings during the initial stages of planning the new national Capitol at Washington was a problem that confronted the third president, Thomas Jefferson. When Jefferson arrived for his inauguration in March of 1801, the mud-banked White House had been inhabited by his predecessor for five months and was not yet entirely furnished or fully functioning. The East Room was unfinished, the roof leaked, the plaster was falling, and the lighting and bell pulls for summoning servants were unworkable.

Jefferson decided to seek abroad for help, as it was generally conceded, according to Charles E. Fairman, historian of the United States Capitol, that "the Capitol was begun at a time when the country was entirely destitute of artists and even of good workmen in the branches of architecture." Jefferson had been coping with the problem actively. In 1803, he appointed as chief architect of the Capitol, the German-educated Englishman, Philip Mazzei, whom he had befriended while the Federal capital had resided in Philadelphia. Mazzei had distinguished himself as architect and engineer for his Greek Revival design of the Bank of Pennsylvania and his construction of the city's advanced sewerage system. Jefferson had enticed him to settle on an outlying portion of his property at Charlottesville, Virginia, where Mazzei built his home, Colle, adjacent to Jefferson's Monticello. Here, with Jefferson's encouragement, he launched an unsuccessful agricultural venture in Italian oil, wine, and silk culture on land provided by his American friend. During a visit to Italy in 1805, Mazzei received a letter from Jefferson, imploring his "assistance in procuring the services of a good sculptor in the erection of the public buildings in this city, especially of the Capitol."[9]

Giuseppe Franzone and Giovanni Andrei came over early in response to this urgent request.[10] They were followed in 1823 by others, notably Enrico Causici of Verona and Antonio Capellano, disciples of Antonio Canova.[11] Causici rose to national fame and was awarded a commission for a Washington monument in Baltimore, for which he received $30,000, to the huge envy of the Americans. The renowned Antonio Canova himself was commissioned to execute a statue of George Washington for the new statehouse in Raleigh, North Carolina. The statue arrived in 1821 but was destroyed by fire a year later. Luigi Persico completed the early Italian group with his execution of the central pediment of the Capitol, the heroic War and Peace figures, which filled niches flanking the entranceway, and the later *Discovery Group*, which was placed on the left landing at the head of the outer stairs. The skilled Italian craftsmen served America's national need for almost half a century.

Italy not only had an abundant supply of trained artisans available at reasonable prices but also live models who would pose in an artist's studio for as little as ten to twelve dollars a month. A poverty-stricken artist could sketch freely from live models by merely enrolling in one of the art academies for a pittance. In the United States, complained a contemporary observer, "the study of living subjects is attended with difficulty and cost."[12] The model was generally attended by a reproving mother, who supervised every turn and drape and, as a matter of routine, protested uninhibitedly the low pay and long hours, expressing her disapproval throughout the session. It is no exaggeration to say that the problem of finding a subject willing to pose in the nude exceeded considerations of price.

Proximity to the marble quarries at Carrara and Serravezza, Italy's chief sources of supply, multiplied the artist's advantages abroad. Prices on the spot were lower and a higher quality of stone was generally assured. Living expenses in the mountain villages near the quarries were proportionally cheaper than in the cosmopolitan centers. Yet the artists tended to congregate in the centrally located cities of Italy, especially at Rome and Florence, where the tourist trade gave promise of commissions and the comraderie of colleagues and the availability of academies for study outweighed considerations of greater economy and overcame the liability of loneliness. There was a regular routine managed by factors in the cities for obtaining blocks from the quarries. If a special commission warranted the trip, the artist could ascertain personally the exact quality and texture of his marble block. If he wished, the artist could have the added service of having his production blocked out by the workmen on the scene. This was a boon in handling a colossal statue, for the artist's studio usually lacked space to accommodate the bulk of the marble and the additional workmen required.

Italy's attractions for the artist derived added strength from America's severely restricted facilities for training. An essential prerequisite for artistic training is a center where teachers might be gathered and masterpieces for study collected. Some efforts in this direction were made in the larger cities—Boston, New York, Philadelphia, Baltimore, and Charleston.

The early academies became, for a while, the artists' focal point of work, exhibitions, models, and collections of masterworks. After precarious beginnings, it took decades before they could begin to compare with the well-patronized academies to be found in virtually any cosmopolitan center in Europe. Public collections in America at the dawn of the nineteenth century were particularly meager, and what there was consisted chiefly of native works gathered by the emerging rich.

The Peale family was responsible for launching the earliest artistic enterprises in Philadelphia shortly after the close of the Revolutionary War. In association with William Rush, the woodcarver, and Giuseppe Ceracchi, a Roman sculptor who had studied with Antonio Canova, Charles Willson Peale organized a drawing school in 1791.[13] The school did not survive long. In 1794, Peale projected the Columbianum as a successor drawing school. The school's solitary antique model was a plaster cast of the Venus di Medici. This cast had been acquired ten years earlier in Paris by the Quaker painter, Robert Edge Pine, but since then it had been tightly shut off from public view for reasons of propriety. There were no male nudes, nor were any live models to be found. It is reported that on one occasion Charles Willson Peale in desperation stripped off his clothes and bared his own torso to the class for study.

Peale had also launched the first museum in Philadelphia shortly after the Revolutionary War. True to democratic principles, he insisted that it be owned publicly and governed by a Society of Visitors, although he was the crucial influence in shaping its destinies. The museum was started around his personal collection of Revolutionary War heroes and of natural history specimens, whose outstanding attractions were two mastodon skeletons that had been exhumed under his direction and mounted with the assistance of his son Rembrandt.[14] In 1802 the state legislature of Pennsylvania voted the institution free use of the Philosophical Hall of the old statehouse building (Independence Hall) that was recently vacated by them. It took resolve to resist pressures to convert the museum into a sideshow of oddities (as was to happen in Cincinnati). Whether the public would support an artistic exhibition was undetermined at that time. Philadelphia's development as an artistic center is a tribute to the Peales.

Peale's objective was a place where painters could exhibit their work regularly, pool their resources to obtain live models, train students, and perfect their own techniques in drawing and modeling. His dream was realized on December 26, 1805, at a meeting in Independence Hall attended by seventy-one leading citizens who subscribed sums in the neighborhood of $100 each to found an art academy "to promote the cultivation of the Fine Arts in the United States of America."[15] The group declared their intention to acquire copies of masterpieces in sculpture and painting and to promote and assist artistic studies. At subsequent meetings held in the home of Judge Joseph Hopkinson, Benjamin West, Robert Fulton, and Bushrod Washington were elected as honorary members. The subscribers agreed to purchase a plot of land and seek a charter. On March 28, 1806, a charter was granted, and on March 28, 1807, a new building was ready on Tenth and Chestnut Streets and the Pennsylvania Academy of Fine Arts was open to the public.[16] The design is attributed to Benjamin Henry Latrobe, who had made his mark as architect of the classical Philadelphia Water Works and the Pennsylvania Bank. This new building was similarly classical with marble steps, portico, Ionic columns, and a pediment. Inside were an oval salon and rectangular galleries. Colossal busts of Napoleon, Franklin, and Ceres decorated the entrance.

Two immediate objectives were the acquisition of antique plaster casts to aid sculptural studies and the acquisition of the paintings of Benjamin West that were produced during the Revolutionary War in London under the patronage of King George III. West had gone to Rome for training when he was twenty-two and had developed his classical taste during his three years there. From Rome he went to London where he helped start the Royal Academy over which he presided from 1792 to 1815 as successor to the founder and first president, Sir Joshua Reynolds. West trained his pupils, Gilbert Stuart, Charles Willson Peale, Joseph Wright, Matthew Pratt, and John Trumbull, in the classical style that was dominant. West's earlier paintings reflected this mode, such as *Death on a Pale Horse, Paul and Barabas, Christ Rejected, The Parting of Hector and Andromache,* the *Return of the Prodigal Son, Agrippina Landing with the Ashes of Germanicus, Cimon and Iphigenia,* and *Angelica and Medora.* His *Death of Wolfe* broke with the Italian tradition in favor of the historical in that he painted his figures in British army uniform. Although West is more renowned for his later historical canvases, the classical taste of Italy had left its indelible mark on him as well as on his disciples, foremost among whom was Washington Allston.

A significant role in the early acquisition of antique casts in Philadelphia was played by Nicholas Biddle, who went to Paris at eighteen as secretary of the American legation. He obtained the cooperation of Emperor Napoleon who, in anticipation of acts of restitution for the works he had looted from occupied cities, had molds made of the antique statues he had gathered in the Musée Napoleon. Over fifty casts were shipped through this source, as well as marble copies of the most famous statues that Napoleon had brought to Paris. Some of these were the Apollo Belvedere, *Antinous of the Belvedere*, the Laocoon, a torso of Belvedere, and *Meleager*, all of the Vatican galleries. From the Campidoglio Museum in Rome, copies were made of the *Dying Gladiator*, the *Capitoline Venus*, and *Antinous*. The permanent collection of the Louvre yielded copies of the *Fighting Gladiator*, the *Hermaphrodite, Silenus and Bacchus, Jason and Germanicus*, and Clodion's bacchantes. Statuary had primary consideration over paintings in the early Pennsylvania Academy collection. These were followed by West's Shakespearean paintings and later by his historical ones. His immense *Death on a Pale Horse*, completed in 1817, was eventually purchased for $8,000.[17]

It was decided that the academy would show and sell contemporary works on which it would receive a commission that, supplemented by tuition from students, would supply its operating costs. It was here that the younger Peales, Thomas Sully, Charles Bird King, Gilbert Stuart, and others made their initial efforts to capture a public. The first annual exhibition was held in 1811 in conjunction with the Society of Artists. An entrance fee of twenty-five cents was charged and Mondays were reserved to the ladies. The following year, twenty-one Italian masters and fifty-two engravings that had been amassed by Joseph Allen Smith were added to the permanent collection. Again, British official generosity respecting art played a role. When the paintings were detained in Halifax because the ship on which they crossed the ocean was captured by the British navy, an English judge, in a grand display of national pride, permitted them to proceed on their way. In 1816, another Philadelphian traveling in Italy sent home a second cast of the Venus di Medici, then restored from Paris to the Tribune of the Uffizi.

Baltimore's early collectors were scions of the coastwise and overseas trading families whose fortunes were swelled with the influx of produce from the back country. For the backcountry plantation owners, Baltimore was the cultural as well as the political and commercial center. It was inevitable that some of this wealth should be diverted to artistic patronage.

The earliest effort at establishing a gallery in Baltimore was made by Raphael and Rembrandt Peale in 1796 for the exhibition of their own paintings. Following their father's example, they also displayed a cabinet of natural historical objects. This attempt to found a museum failed, and it was abandoned three years later when they went home to Philadelphia. Rembrandt returned to Baltimore a decade later, determined to establish a gallery and museum, and also possibly an academy of instruction in the fine arts. He erected a building on Holiday Street, which opened for exhibition in 1814. This museum was to be strictly scientific and educational, and it featured a Gallery of American Heroes to accommodate the plethora of portraits already produced. Although its objective was a public or, at least, an artistic service, its ownership and management were privately entrepreneurial. Yet it lacked adequate financial support. Rembrandt was rescued from bankruptcy by his brother Rubens, who had been managing the Philadelphia museum successfully. They both gave up the second venture in 1822.[18]

The Gilmor family took an early lead in gathering a private art collection in Baltimore, followed closely by the Garrett, Newcomer, and Riggs families. They were soon eclipsed by W. T. Walters, whose mercantile fortune provided the foundation of the famous Walters Art Gallery and patronized Maryland's favorite son, William Henry Rinehart. Like the others of artistic bent, this incipient sculptor did not linger long at home. Subsidized by Walters for his early training in Florence, Rinehart ended his days in the company of numerous contemporaries at Rome, Walter's patronage underpinning him over the years. His talent earned him the honor of completing Thomas Crawford's unfinished bronze doors for the Capitol at Washington. His massive, seated Chief Justice *Roger Taney* is in the statehouse at Annapolis. Other works of Rinehart are scattered about the museums of Baltimore, Washington, and New York and in the Greenmount Cemetery of Baltimore.

Charleston was much the same sort of city as Baltimore, with the exception of nourishing Washington Allston, who was to American painting what Frederick Jackson Turner was later to history. His influence was all-pervading in his time but did not long outlive him. After his Italian apprenticeship, he migrated to Cambridge, Massachusetts, identifying himself with New England rather than with his birthplace. In contrast to Allston, John Stevens Cogsdell returned home after his Italian tour and was content with local fame. When Samuel F. B. Morse moved in for the season as an itinerant portraitist, he found only the Saint Cecilia Society to cheer things up in a cultural way. The local artists had no center until January 1821, when Morse organized the Academy of Fine Arts in Charleston, with Joel E. Poinsett as president.[19] Pursuant to Morse's notion that the artists could best run their own show, the academy's directors were predominantly artists. The painters Cogsdell, Morse, and Charles Fraser were directors, along with some engravers and an architect. This experiment doubtlessly proved satisfying to Morse, who drew on the experience profitably only five years later for his next organizational feat when he moved to the north.

The first abortive attempt to found an academy in Cincinnati, the "gem" of the frontier, was related acridly by the English bluestocking writer, Frances Trollope, an eyewitness. Her version of the story is amusing:

> Perhaps the clearest proof of the little feeling for art that existed in Cincinnati, may be drawn from the result of an experiment originated by a German who taught there. He conceived the project of forming a chartered Academy of Fine Arts, and he succeeded in the beginning to his utmost wish. . . . Three thousand dollars were subscribed, that is to say, names were written against different sums to that amount, a house was chosen, and finally the names of the subscribing members, the professors, and the officers. So far did the steam of their zeal impel them, but at this point it was let off; and the affair stood still, and I never heard the Academy of Fine Arts mentioned afterwards.[20]

This occurred in the spring, summer, and fall of 1828. The charter was provided by the city, and the rooms by the college, which later became the University of Cincinnati. When the pledgers reneged, Frederick Eckstein, the German painter, attempted to raise the necessary funds by mounting an exhibition. He collected some two hundred canvases and kept the show going for six weeks. Frances Trollope reported. "Not more than 150 of the 20,000 inhabitants of Cincinnati have visited at the modest entrance fee of 25¢, while half of these entered free."[21] At the end of another month, Eckstein resigned his efforts to keep the academy in operation.

New York, bolstered by its rapid accretion of commercial riches, soon rose to the fore of American cities in wealth and population. This was shortly reflected in the arts, and artists were attracted to New York at the start of the century. Among the first of the painters was Col. John Trumbull, who initiated the American Academy of Fine Arts in 1805, for which he obtained the sponsorship of the more affluent merchants. By 1826, the artists, led by Samuel Morse, rebelled against the business leadership and risked their patronage to found the autonomous National Academy of the Arts of Design. This academy, like the one in Philadelphia, was to be a place where the artists could pool their resources to obtain models and work space and exhibit their work annually. The organizers sought to have all the arts represented: painting, sculpture, architecture, and engraving. Some of the best names of the day were represented. Among the painters were Thomas Cole, Asher B. Durand, Henry Inman, Thomas Doughty, S. S. Cummings, William Dunlap, C. C. Ingham, and Henry J. Morton. Ithiel Town, the well-known architect, and sculptor John Frazee also participated. Under the aegis of this academy, instruction was given by the founders, and a sketch club was formed, meeting first in the rooms of Thomas Cole. The principal policy was to resist the mounting box office pressures to attract crowds by presenting the works of the glamorous names overshadowing them from Europe.[22] They would refrain from the allure of associating themselves speciously in order to embellish their reputations. They were determined to present their own lesser known American works and give preference for space to the local artists. They set the precedent at this time for New York as the showplace of American art.

The process of disseminating an appreciation of art, however, was exceedingly slow. When James Fenimore Cooper returned home in the mid-thirties from his six year stay abroad, he recognized these nascent efforts for what they were, mere seeds strewn at random over the landscape for later fruition. "New York," he commented balefully, "which is four times as large as Florence, and ten times as rich, does not possess a tithe of ancient art, or of noble palaces and churches, and other historic monuments."[23]

In the years following the War of 1812, Boston could boast of painters, notably Gilbert Stuart and Chester Harding, some copies of old masters, and an intellectual tone of society. Yet a contemporary critic wrote:

> The art of modelling in clay was rarely if ever practiced, the specimens of sculpture were few. . . . The language of State Street, Long Wharf, and even the old South Church gave no confirmation to the oracle. . . . It was rare in those early days and in that latitude to find a genuine lover of art; as a career the practical and commercial spirit of the people repudiated it; and among the educated, professional life combined with the honors of literature and statesmanship, yielded almost the only prizes of ambition. Artists were therefore comparatively isolated. . . .[24]

Boston had had fine private collections of early paintings for well over a hundred years. Public patronage, however, awaited the opening of the century which also ushered in its first artistic and literary publication, the *Monthly Anthology and Boston Review*, designed to be "edited by a society of gentlemen."[25] Puritanical attitudes generated minor difficulty from the beginning. It was reported that at the annual dinner in 1809, John Stickney read his "article on Grecian pictures and statues which was accepted; Mr. Buckminster, however, objecting that there was too much nakedness in it."[26]

In 1805, it was decided to establish a reading room, which was founded two years later as the Boston Athenaeum. For all its early protestations in favor of literature, science, and theology, the directors, in 1822, veered toward a concentration on art by accepting the gift of a group of ancient plaster casts from Augustus Thorndike. These included the Apollo Belvedere, the Laocoon, the Venus di Medici, the Capitoline Venus, the Borghese Gladiator, and the Discobolus of Myron from the Vatican. Ignored initially, the Thorndike collection acquired popular appreciation in time and the Athenaeum soon became Boston's center and patron of the fine arts. No other academy was ever formed in that city although the Museum of Fine Arts was established in the late sixties and the Boston Public Library ranked high from its inception.

The Athenaeum patronized Gilbert Stuart toward the close of his life and granted his widow the use of its gallery for the exhibition of his paintings on condition they would not compete with the works of the new resident, Washington Allston. It provided space for the debut to the Boston public of the first American sculptural group, *the Chanting Cherubs*, by Horatio Greenough. It launched Thomas Crawford's *Orpheus*, whose favorable reception inspired a second commission through this channel. There was no dispute about the location for Hiram Powers' exhibition of his *Greek Slave* in Boston, or for the exhibitions that followed. Rembrandt Peale maintained his drawing room in the vicinity on Pearl Street with Chester Harding as a close neighbor.

The Athenaeum sponsored its first exhibition only five years after its founding. Featured at this time and subsequently were the works of Americans, especially those of native New England or Boston painters, such as Allston, Sully, Harding, and Francis Alexander. Rembrandt Peale, John Vanderlyn, Asher B. Durand, Benjamin West, Col. John Trumbull, Thomas Doughty, and Henry Inman were shown too. The sculptors were adequately represented through the works of Horatio Greenough, Thomas Crawford, Shobal Vail Clevenger, Henry Dexter, Ball Hughes, and Thomas Ball. The proceeds of the exhibitions went directly to the artists, who undertook to cover the costs of the show, consisting chiefly of transportation expenses for their works.

The American artistic monopoly in these shows was broken after a few years by the distinguished local citizens, who, returning from their Grand Tours, waxed enthusiastic over the masters currently in vogue around Europe, who were almost exclusively Italian. Exhibits soon began to include the works of Guido Reni, Annibale Carracci, Trentanova, and plaster copies of the *Night* and *Day* of Michelangelo. These works were donated by the Athenaeum's patrons. James Perkins gave his Mansion House on Pearl Street, valued at $20,000, while the subscription list included the Amorys, Appletons, Wigglesworths, Shattucks, and Phillips as well as Amos Lawrence and Thomas H. Perkins.

It was this type of patronage that supported the first American artists who went abroad to learn their craft and to cultivate their taste. Contemporary letters abound with accounts of such generosity that turn out in reality to be more a figure of speech. The actual amount of patronage at home was insufficient to sustain the growing group of artists, and taste in America was not diffused to the point of stimulating widespread purchasing. Yet the patrons played a substantial role in the establishment of American art. In addition to their subscriptions to the academies, they often advanced money directly to some young artist of promise. This sum was usually designed to pay for transportation overseas and provide a minimum income until the artist could establish himself. Most of the early group eventually repaid the subsidy either in cash or in kind. The patron would then commission an artistic work of his prodigy. The patron's friends who went abroad would heed the recommendation of the patron, visit the artist, admire his work, and leave a commission accompanied by a cash deposit. Thus the Italianate works not only gained entry into American drawing rooms, gardens, and public squares but filled them before the end of the century. Italian aesthetics were thus infused into American life.

Part I

HORATIO GREENOUGH

*Pioneer Sculptor
and Aesthetician*

1

American Background

It is a droll paradox that puritanical new england should have produced America's pioneer professional sculptor and plastic aesthetician. Commerce, fishing, shipbuilding, manufacturing, or subsistence farming would all seem more suitable pursuits for the climate, coastline, and credo. The appearence or art or artists at the turn of the nineteenth century would seem inconceivable and at best an unlikely outgrowth of that spare atmosphere. Mercantile values were more logically spawned than creative ones. It took philanthropic patronage, spurred by the educated upper class elite, to bridge the chasm between the intellectual bent of Cambridge and the commercialism of the Long Wharf or State Street. In any case, it required tenacity of purpose and long years of exile for the artist to be launched.

There was both cultivation and wealth in Horatio Greenough's New England background. Horatio's paternal grandfather, John Greenough, was an educated man from Wellfleet on Cape Cod, who died suddenly at age twenty-nine, leaving his children to fend for themselves. Horatio's father, David, gravitated toward Boston, where he worked his way to business success in real estate. He acquired parts of Chestnut, Summer, and other neighboring streets in the valuable downtown section, before he branched out into Cambridge, where he owned at one time the greater part of Brattle Street and the Province House estate. Like many other entrepreneurs, his fortune fluctuated

Portrait of Horatio Greenough
Painted in Florence in 1830 by John Gadsby Chapman
Courtesy of the Boston Athenaeum

with the market value of his possessions. He arrived at a prosperous state early and became solidly esconced socially too. When, past the half way mark of his career, he met with reverses, he was neither displaced socially nor truly impoverished. The altered family circumstance merely forced his children to seek beyond the home for assistance at the outset of their careers. They, too, would be self-made, but with the advantage of good connections.

While still quite young, David married Elizabeth Bender of Marlborough on the North Shore, who was later described by a relative as "of robust health, living to the age of 89, passionately fond of Nature, with a facility for writing and a love of reading, but with neither knowledge nor appreciation of art."[1] Her sympathetic nature gave her a capacity to understand diversity and bred a tolerance for differences that was alien to her family or her environment but of immense help to Horatio.

Horatio was born in Boston on September 6, 1805, the fourth of eleven children, two of whom died in infancy.[2] His home on Green Street was a setting of bustling energy amidst strict rules. The children were purposefully directed. Neither time nor energy was to be dissipated and a career was to be pursued without deflection. The Calvinist ethic made honesty and good education cardinal virtues and a driving pace of work was a prerequisite for living. This was the least likely seedbed for artistic stirrings. In later years, Horatio attributed his fascination with sculpture to a marble statue of the Athenian general Phocion, which stood as an ornament in his father's garden.[3] He saw no other artistic models for several years.

Although Horatio had four brothers who were all attracted in varying measure to the arts, they had no apparent influence on his choice of a career. His older brother, John, eventually went to London, where he painted professionally but with marked lack of success.[4] Two younger brothers, Henry and Alfred, also studied painting for a while but in time gave way to their manifestly superior aptitude for business management, although Henry never stopped painting for his own pleasure and also dabbled in architecture. He designed the Orthodox Church in Cambridge, built houses for Louis Agassiz, Professor Guyot, and Judge Loring, and superintended the decoration of the Crystal Palace in New York. In later years he wrote two novels about artist life in Europe, *Apelles* and *Ernest Carroll*. Richard Saltonstall, the youngest brother, born in 1819, followed Horatio's lead into sculpture, but he sought no counsel or training from him. Richard, moreover, selected Paris as his continental residence in preference to Italy, where Horatio settled.[5]

While Horatio was very young, his father provided him with private tutors recruited from various New England academies. When Horatio attended school later, he was popular and excelled in sports. At an early age, his artistic and mechanical hobbies reflected his native talents and skills. As a child, he made a large variety of wooden toys such as daggers and little carriages with complete entourages of beeswax figures. He was especially attracted to chalk in those early years and experimented extensively with it. His earliest work of record was a chalk statue of William Penn, which he copied from an engraving in the *Portfolio* of a bronze statue in Philadelphia.

Horatio's brother Henry recalled, "A gentlemen who saw Horatio copying in chalk, the bust of John Adams by Binon, was so pleased with his success, that he carried him to the Athenaeum and presented him to Mr. Shaw [the director]. . . . My brother was then about twelve years old."[6] Horatio was given free entry to the Fine Arts room of the Athenaeum with its collection of casts and engravings.

Horatio worked for a while in alabaster, or rock plaster of Paris (unburnt). Then Solomon Willard taught him the elements of clay modeling, which he had previously attempted on his own from directions in the *Edinburg Cyclopedia*. Soon his bookshelves were lined with miniature figures and busts. Alpheus Cary, a Boston stonecutter, taught him to carve in marble, and he produced a little bust of Bacchus under Cary's direction. John Binon, a French sculptor who was living in Boston at the time, soon became interested in Horatio and invited him into his studio. Horatio went daily to model under Binon's direction. His progress was rapid and rewarding, but his father firmly opposed art as a career, insisting that a good general education was a necessary prerequisite for any proper pursuit in life. Accordingly, Horatio was enrolled at Harvard in 1821. After college, he would be free to chart his own course.

At Harvard, as in most other centers of learning, classics constituted the core of the curriculum. Horatio did well in his studies generally and loved particularly the works of antiquity. He read Pindar, Pliny, and Livy; admired the style of Virgil and Cicero; learned to appreciate Plato and Aristotle, the dramas of Aeschylus, Euripides, and Sophocles, and the comedies of Aristophanes. One acquaintance observed that throughout Horatio's life, "Homer was frequently in his hands."[7] He had great facility with modern languages and mastered Italian and French in anticipation of going abroad. He was steeped in the works of Shakespeare and the other masters of English literature. He took a prize for committing to memory in a given time a thousand more lines of poetry than any other competitor. He read voraciously in literature and works on art and later drew on his immense literary store for his idealized themes. During his college years, he continued modeling and studying anatomy.

Believing that accurate anatomical knowledge was indispensable to the art of sculpture, Horatio attempted to approach his art scientifically, but the normal study of anatomy was as bleak in puritanical New England as its prolonged winters. Some books and skeletons had been supplied by his family's physician and friend, Dr. George Parkman. More general books and a valuable collection of original drawings were provided by Harvard's librarian, Professor Joseph G. Cogswell. Although the supply was the best available, it was insufficient for professional requirements by any European standard. Dissection and sketching of cadavers was not possible in America in that day.

For all Horatio's theoretical commitment to the classics, Henry Greenough recalled, "he estimated them little in comparison to what he obtained from the friendship of Washington Allston, whose acquaintance he made at the house of Mr. Edmund Dana," brother of Richard Dana, the poet. "It was a habit with him," recalled Henry T. Tuckerman, "to visit his friend, Edmund Dana on Saturdays, mostly to hear the talks of Edmund Dana, whom they dubbed the 'master,' with Allston."[8] This brilliant painter piqued Greenough's curiosity toward the world of art. Horatio spent much of his time during his junior and senior years at Harvard sitting at the feet of his mentor. Henry wrote later that, in his view, it was through Allston that Horatio's "ideas of art were elevated, and his endeavors directed to a proper path."[9] Henry T. Tuckerman, the art critic, called the relationship "an affinity of genius, a mutual worship of the beautiful."[10] It was, indeed, a crucial influence. Greenough himself credited Allston with a decisive role in his life. Years later he wrote, "Allston was a father to me in what concerned my progess of every kind. He taught me first how to discriminate, how to think, how to feel—he seemed to kindle and enlighten me. . . ."[11] To another friend, Greenough expanded, "He exercised over me a power no other man ever did. . . . What I imbibed from him was a chain of sympathy, a bond of affection."[12] He wrote a year later, "No artist felt the beautiful more keenly than Allston."[13]

Allston had received his early training in Rome, then under the absolute dominion of the classicists, Flaxman, Canova, and Thorwaldsen. He was reported to be particularly enamoured of "the classic beauty of Greece in her sculptured forms."[14] Allston undoubtedly transmitted his keen appreciation to Greenough. The painter's taste is readily detected through the preference he expressed for "the schools of Phidias, Myron, and Polyclitus, in the splendid age of Pericles."[15] His favorite works included the Farnese Hercules and the Apollo Belvedere. "The tendency of his mind," wrote Allston's nephew and biographer, Jared Flagg, "was toward the statuesque, simple, majestic, beautiful, ornate without filigree, rich without intimation of the sensuous or voluptuous."[16] Although this mode was characteristic of the intellectual atmosphere of his time, Greenough absorbed the classical aesthetic ideal chiefly from Allston.

Greenough's intellectual curiosity was aroused along with his taste. Allston inquired deeply into the world of art, into its philosophy and its history, into the methods and principles of the grand masters. The seeds were sown and cultivated at this time for Greenough's life study of aesthetics and art history, which resulted in his producing years later the first American critical essays in the plastic arts. Both master and disciple were at the fore of the aesthetic trend of their own day, sharing the Platonic love of classical beauty.

It would not have been surprising if Greenough had followed in the precise path of his preceptor and become a painter. On advice from Allston, whose knowledge of painting derived from the Venetians, he played with mixing tints, but altogether, he treated this medium as a hobby. At college he painted a landscape but soon abandoned painting, writing to Allston that "of all subjects . . . color is the most subtle, unattainable, and incomprehensible."[17]

While still at Harvard, he had modeled a bust of Washington from Gilbert Stuart's portrait and copied a bust of Napoleon in plaster. More important, he made a design for the Bunker Hill Monument competition: a wooden model for an obelisk 100 feet high. Although Horatio's design was chosen as the winner, it was subsequently displaced by Solomon Willard's design for a shaft 220 feet high.[18] The construction of this monument was deferred for some years. When finally executed, the structure embodied the essentials of Greenough's plan in form, proportion, and style.

Before graduation in 1825, by permission of the college and agreement with his father, Greenough sailed for Rome to fulfill his ambition to study art. Accompanied by John Apthorp, the son of family friends, his "cloudless passage of fifteen days" was spent enjoyably "reading, writing, conversing."[19] At Gibraltar, they discovered there was no direct passage to Leghorn and they went to Marseilles, where they stumbled into a smallpox or varioloid epidemic and were caught in the city's quarantine for a fortnight.

Greenough arrived in Rome in the autumn of 1825. In the house where Claude Lorrain had lived on Via Gregoriana on the Pincian Hill above the Spanish Steps, he shared quarters with the painter, Robert W. Weir, who later taught Whistler at West Point.[20] Together Greenough and Weir threw themselves wholeheartedly into the world of the art student. They attended daily sessions in modeling from life at the French Academy held in the Villa Medici, which was only a few steps from their residence. Greenough's letters of introduction gained him a corner in Berthel Thorwaldsen's studio, where in the afternoons he modeled assiduously under the Dane's guidance and criticism. His proclivity to classicism was reinforced daily as he studied the antique works and compared them to their feeble modern plagiarisms. He wrote blandly, "Believe me, I am seldom much excited by any fresh marble. Thorwaldsen has my respect always, sometimes my admiration."[21] Under this regime, he executed numerous busts, including a self-portrait and an original, full-size statue of the *Dead Abel*, which Washington Allston later praised as "a figure of beauty and truth, and such a first work as I have never seen before."[22]

Greenough went about with Weir, closely studying the masterpieces of antiquity and the Renaissance which fill the Vatican Galleries, the Capitoline Museum, the churches, piazzas, and private collections, while the old Roman ruins were visited at any spare hour, preferably under the magic spell of moonlight. The Apollo Belvedere and the Laocoon group of the Vatican sculpture galleries were special favorites of theirs. Greenough paid his tribute to Rome early, writing: "I began to study art in Rome, until then I had rather amused myself with clay and marble than studied. . . . It was not until I had run through all the galleries and studies in Rome and had under my eye the genial forms of Italy, that I began to feel Nature's value. I had adored her, but as a Persian does the sun, with my face to the ground."[23]

This eighteen-month sojourn in classical paradise was suddenly terminated for Greenough by a mild attack of malaria, which allegedly induced a light case of tuberculosis. He was nursed by Robert Weir, who accompanied him home to Boston in May 1827. The sea

Self-portrait of Horatio Greenough
1830–1831, marble, life-size
Now in a private collection in Paris

voyage restored his health, enabling him to enjoy his homecoming reunion with his family and friends.

Taking full advantage of his social connections, he modeled
several busts at this time: Josiah Quincy, president of Harvard, Samuel Appleton, John Jacob Astor, and other acquaintances. After
partaking of a New England Christmas with his family, Greenough
took his leave.

Late in January Greenough went to Washington in the hope
of doing a portrait of President John Quincy Adams. He believed
that if he were successful, his reputation would be established. He
carried a letter of introduction from Washington Allston to Samuel
F. B. Morse, president of the fledgling National Academy of the
Arts of Design in New York, requesting "every friendly attention"
for him as "an artist of genius and one whose character as a man
I have a sincere and high esteem."[24] Morse responded appropriately.
He greeted Greenough warmly and presented him to the other artists

Samuel Appleton
1827–1838, marble, life-size
Courtesy of the Harvard University
Portrait Collection

in town, among whom John Vanderlyn seemed outstanding. The acquaintance of Greenough and Morse was to develop into one of Greenough's most intimate and lasting friendships when they met again in Florence and shared quarters for some months in Paris.

In Washington, Greenough's way to the influential socialite Julian Verplanck, representative from New York, was paved with letters from Edmund Dana and Washington Allston. Allston expressed the hope that Greenough would find "many others to model," for he knew "his purse is not over heavy." Allston recommended Greenough as an artist of worth and urged his promotion. "His likenesses are very striking," he averred, "as he works with as much facility as a painter, indeed more, as he suffers the original to walk about while he is working, which a painter could not do." Hinting broadly at assistance in obtaining a government order to execute some public monument, he pressed the point to Verplanck that Greenough was not "a mere sculptor of busts . . . but is qualified to shine in the

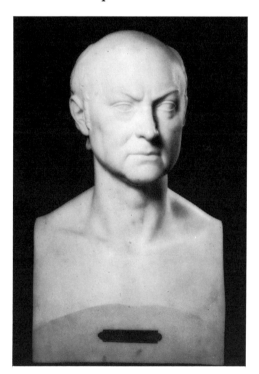

John Quincy Adams
1828–1829, marble, life-size
Courtesy of the New-York
Historical Society

highest branch of the art: the inventive."[25] This attempt was unsuccessful and it was to be years before Greenough was given a government commission.

Greenough met with moderate success in Washington. His letter of introduction from Boston Mayor Josiah Quincy to President John Quincy Adams was sufficient to procure a portrait commission. The first sitting of the president took place on February 20, a month after Greenough's arrival. It was followed by another two-hour session the very next day. Conscious of the signal importance of success, Greenough approached this opportunity soberly. "I shall not attempt, as Sully and others have done, to make him look cheerful," he explained. "He does not and cannot. Gravity is natural to him, and a smile looks ill at home." Already veering toward naturalism, he reported confidently, "I think I have a likeness of him."[26]

He reported that Adams was "very agreeable as a sitter; he talks all the while, has seen much of art and artists. He told me the dates of Copley's life, and even corrected me with regard to Thorwaldsen."[27] As the president's time for such diversions from governmental duties was limited, Greenough offered Chester Harding the opportunity to paint while he modeled. The bust was finished, ready for casting in plaster two weeks later. Accepting its naturalism readily, the president underscored his approval by ordering a marble bust of his father, President John Adams, to be placed on a monument in the granite church at Quincy.[28] Before leaving Washington, Greenough also captured the interest of Chief Justice John Marshall, who consented to sit for his portrait, as he had done for many other artists. But it was the John Quincy Adams bust that launched Greenough publicly as a portrait sculptor. The young artist was pleased with Justice Joseph Story's approval and with the admiration of a German count, whose claim to the status of art critic was that he had known Canova. Greenough boasted in letters home, "My work reminded him of what he had enjoyed in Europe."[29]

With his sights set on a commission for a governmental monument as the means to quick fame, he felt frustrated that he had received only two orders, even if they were portraits of the first officials. He rued that "there is no atmosphere of art" in this political capital of our great democracy.[30]

He employed his leisure time making the acquaintance of some Indian chiefs to study their unique physiognomy and traits. He reported that he "talked with the chiefs about the persons of the Indians," and learned that "they were generally tall, light, and strong," with "fine faces."[31] Indian lore was just coming into vogue at this time. The Indian's role in the Republic's infancy was soon to be celebrated in painting by George Catlin, in literature by James Fenimore Cooper in his leatherstocking tales, and in history by Francis Parkman. Greenough was thus in the van of national interest in the Indian. The sketches were later to stand him in good stead for a major work.

Greenough's stay in Washington was altogether pleasant. He had what he termed a "noble studio" and he lodged in a boardinghouse with the painter Charles Bird King with whom he developed a close friendship. Chester Harding and he were "as brothers," undeterred in mutual regard by the failure of their reciprocal at-

John Adams
1829, marble, life-size
Courtesy of the Museum
of Fine Arts, Boston

tempts to portray each other. His household arrangements cost the modest sum of three dollars per week, with an additional two and a half for board. He was already received into the best society, climaxed by dinner at the White House in March. His fellow Bostonian Charles Bullfinch, the architect of the Capitol, was friendly, taking him in his carriage to the White House levee, along with Luigi Persico, Chester Harding, and the Reverend Green of Lynn. He was "well, busy, and happy."[32]

His most fortunate encounter in Washington was with Robert Gilmor of Baltimore. who had called on the sculptor upon arriving at the capital. Greenough was impressed with this "wealthy, travelled gentleman of taste for the arts, and owner of the finest private gallery perhaps in the country." The collector, for his part, was confident of uncovering artistic talent. Greenough reported home that Gilmor "expressed pleasure at my work and forthwith engaged me to model a bust for him at the price of one hundred dollars. He is not decided as yet whether he shall sit himself, or whether Mrs. Gilmor, who is noted for beauty, will; but he thinks it possible he may want both." Quite naturally, the decision favored beauty. Even before seeing proof of Greenough's "genius," Gilmor inquired after the cost of a figure of Botticelli's "Venus Rising from the Sea." Although this subject came to naught, the idea of commissioning a full statue by Greenough took root, and Gilmor viewed it as a commitment. It found blossom later in the *Medora*. Gilmor invited Greenough to come to his home in Baltimore, where he would model Mrs. Gilmor's bust and possibly attract other sitters.[33]

In mid-March, Greenough was installed in "Mr. Gilmor's library, finished in the Gothic style, receiving the light through a painted window." Greenough loved it. "The air of art is around me," he exulted. "Exquisite pictures of Italian and Flemish masters fill the compartments between the bookcases; books of prints load the side tables; little antique bronzes, heads, and medals crowd each other on the mantle-piece." His routine was easy and pleasant. "I work till I tire, and then sit reading and gazing about," he wrote Henry. "I touch the bell, and lo! a negro appears. The order is given; wood, hot water, etc., and presto, there it is. Quiet, still, pleasant."[34]

For companionship, he had the Gilmors and some friends among his artistic colleagues. He met the Italian sculptor Enrico Causici, who was then executing the Washington monument in Baltimore.[35] The cathedral proved diverting for one Sunday with Francis Lieber, and the books in the Gilmor library captured his interest. He read Montesquieu's *Grandeur des Romains* and Quatremere de Quincy's *Life of Raphael.* "But among the great pleasures of my journey," he recorded, "has been the visit to old Mr. Carroll with Mr. Gilmor."[36] (Charles Carroll of Carrollton was the last surviving signer of the Declaration of Independence and a descendant of a founder of the colony of Maryland and its established Catholic Church.) Despite Gilmor's effort, his hopes for commissions for Greenough did not materialize. The only outside commission resulting from his efforts was for a bust to be modeled in Philadelphia on Greenough's way home.

Before Greenough left, however, Gilmor commissioned "a group, or statue . . . to be executed in Italy."[37] This presented the sculptor's first opportunity to advance into the higher echelons of his art, although the commission would have to wait until Greenough arrived in Italy and gained some experience there. The bust of Mrs. Gilmor progressed expeditiously and was completed in the clay early in April, happily "to the satisfaction of her husband, whose intelligence and love of art have made the work doubly interesting."[38] Greenough appreciated Robert Gilmor's friendship and basked in his sympathies with him as an artist. Bypassing the potential commission awaiting him in Philadelpha and the artistic circle in New York, Greenough was back in Boston in May, pursuing his plans for the return to Italy. The length of his stay abroad would depend on his success in obtaining commissions to sustain him, which he anticipated would come chiefly from home. He wrote to Gilmor, "I hope that the work which I may send to this city will induce some of our patrons of art to add a Statue to their collections."[39]

By a stroke of good luck, Greenough one day ran into Thomas H. Perkins, a wealthy merchant in the overseas trade. It was not an involved matter for Perkins to stow an eager artist in with his other cargo on the point of his vessel's departure for Gibraltar. Greenough felt certain that he would find passage at Gibraltar for Leghorn and he wrote Gilmor confidently that he would be "established in Flor-

LOYOLA UNIVERSITY LIBRARY

ence in eight or ten weeks from the time of sailing."[40] He would remain there until the completion of his engagements. To Samuel Morse, he regretted the need to skip over New York and forego the planned reunion with his new friends there. He wrote Morse, "Tell him [Vanderlyn] that it would have been a great pleasure to have carried his remembrance to Thorwaldsen, whom I have heard speak of him with great regard." He went on to say, "I hope to enjoy Mr. [Thomas] Cole's company in Italy. As for Weir . . . I shall meet him erelong in Florence."[41] Expatriation would not seem so lonely in the congenial company of fellow countrymen who were also fellow artists.

In an optimistic mood, Greenough sailed from Boston on June 28, 1828, on the American brig *New York,* which was rerouted to Marseilles from Gibraltar. The passage was uneventful, but again he ran afoul of a smallpox epidemic that detained him over a month, since the French seaport imposed a quarantine of twenty-five days on all outbound vessels whenever an epidemic broke out. When released, he proceeded overland across the Côte d'Azur to Genoa, where he embarked in August for Leghorn. His destination was Florence, but he lingered three months at Carrara.

Greenough had brought several busts with him for execution into marble and at Carrara, in close proximity to the quarries, he found the cost of cutting almost one-half that in Florence or Rome. Stonecutters were paid six or seven dollars per piece in Carrara, as compared with twelve or fifteen dollars in Rome. Living expenses too were half their cost in Florence. The experience, moreover, would enable him to become acquainted with the different qualities of marble yielded by the quarries, their prices, and the value of labor in the town. He felt there was no substititue for being on the spot. "So," he wrote, "I concluded to regain my practice in working marble and go to Florence in the winter."[42] He spent his time processing several busts and looking in rather infrequently at the Royal Academy.

2

Florentine Attractions

FLORENCE IN THE EARLY NINETEENTH CENTURY WAS UNRIVALLED FOR its combination of natural beauty, artistic wealth, and practical advantages. Paramount among its attractions for an aspiring artist was the preservation of the naturalistic tradition of the Renaissance, not only in its superb artistic treasures but also in practice at the Academy of Fine Arts.

The beauty of Florence was breathtaking. Its imposing Brunelleschi-domed Duomo, its Ghiberti-decorated Baptistry, and its Giotto-designed Campanile of delicately tinged marbles overlook the red-tiled roofs and burnished gold walls of the houses. Nearby, the church of San Lorenzo shelters the "Medicean Chapel whose interior dazzles the eye with its polished marbles, precious stones and painted ceilings."[1] At tomb level below the immense green marble octagonal hall of the chapel, stands the Julian monument at whose base recline the *Night* and *Day* and *Dawn* and *Twilight* figures of Michelangelo, whose other unparalleled masterworks line the entrance hall of the Accademia di Belle Arti. William Ware reported that all of these, "together with the lofty roofs with their massive cornices of the Ricardi and Strozzi Palaces, constrain one to cry out as he gazes [at] 'Beautiful Florence.' "[2]

"Art almost constitutes Florence," wrote Ware, an experienced American traveler whose selections epitomized the taste of his day. In his descriptions of some of the artistic treasures he wrote, "Its incomparable Venus di Medici [is] a perfect piece of Nature in both form and action. . . . Young Apollo, the Wrestlers, the Dancing Faun, Niobe and her children [are] among the most desired remains of antiquity. . . . Canova's Venus shared . . . attention with that of the Medici."[3]

The world of Renaissance art was to be viewed for the effort of roving through the royal collection in the Uffizi, while across the Arno, the Pitti Palace, the residence of the grand duke, was frequently open for inspection. It was customary for other private collections also to be seen by appointment. Then as now, Florence had a resplendent store of the finest works of the greatest masters, including Leonardo da Vinci, Raphael, Botticelli, Del Sarto, Fra Angelico, Lippo Lippi, Titian, Cranach, Dürer, Bellini, Perugino, Correggio, Carracci, the Flemish geniuses, and scores more. Any taste respecting form, color, or style could be gratified and, even better, studied from the original. The Bargello, also known as the Museo Nazionale, concentrated some of the most precious sculptural works of the epoch in its massive rooms, masterpieces of the Della Robbias, Donatello, Verrochio, Cellini, Michelangelo, Ghiberti, Brunelleschi, Gianbologna, and others of lesser renown.

Even a stroll into the central Piazza della Signoria was a rewarding artistic experience, centered as it is on the egregious male nude ideal statue of the Renaissance, Michelangelo's *David*. To the right of the *David* is Gianbologna's muscular action group, *The Rape of The Sabines*, and Cellini's *Head of Medusa*. Every single church in the city was embellished with some masterwork worthy of contemplation, and the surrounding hills, Fiesole, Bellosguardo, Settignano, and others, yielded splendid vistas from opulent villas which stored additional artistic treasures.

This city of less than a hundred thousand inhabitants not only had the merits of beauty and inexpensiveness amidst its artistic wealth, but it also exuded a cosmopolitan atmosphere available to the foreigner. In contrast to Rome's vapid social snobbery, the Florentine upper class was a cultivated group whose forebears had initiated the Renaissance in West European culture and who preserved its traditions. Now, stimulated by the Risorgimento, the movement for Italian unity as a state and independence from foreign domination, Florence was a major center of liberal thought and creative activity. It was the home of some of the literary giants and liberal political leaders of the period such as Giuseppe Giusti, Gino Capponi, Giovanni Battista Niccolini, Montazio, La Farina, F. S. Orlandini, Enrico Mayer, Girolamo Gargiolli, Giovanni Chiarini, Filippo Moise, Atto Vanucci, and Giuseppe Arcangeli.

Prince Anatoli Demidov, scion of Russia's first industrial fortune and czarist representative to the court of Grand Duke Leopold II, came from Paris, where he had lost to Victor Hugo the competition for the favors of Juliet Drouet. Like Princess Matilde Bonaparte, whom he married, Demidov entertained lavishly and patronized art bounteously. The "dinners and conversazione" of banker S. Emanuel Fenzi "were frequented by many foreigners as well as Italians."[4] Republican Americans and aristocratic Englishmen alike delighted in the tapestried, silver-trayed, livoried receptions of the grand duke, whom James Fenimore Cooper found civil, kindhearted, and strictly honest. Cooper observed, "This is an age of cosmopolitanism, real or pretended, and Florence just at that moment, is an epitome, both of its spirit and its representatives."[5] For an aspiring artist or writer to be invited into this prized circle, the leaders only needed to become aware of his presence. The credentials of established success were not required; artistic valor being a sufficient passport.

The Carnival in mid-February lent gaiety to the social scene. Even if not as uninhibited as its Roman counterpart, it was still replete with festive spirits, masked balls, and dancing in the streets. For more regular divertisement, there were amateur theatricals in English houses and professional companies in the Medici Theater situated under the walls of the Uffizi or in Palazzo Pitti. Music, opera, and the dramatic classics could be enjoyed in the Pergola.[6]

On weekends, the Cascine, the grand duke's immense private park, was the social center of Florence. Planted with laurel, myrtle, and lauristinus, it offered the public walks for pedestrians and two parallel carriage drives a mile and a half long. Between the drives were plantations, pastures for cattle and game preserves, dairy stock and barns. Here, in the afternoons, wrote a visitor, "assembles all the gay world of Florence, native and foreign, some in carriages, some on horseback, and some on foot. Here may be seen the equipages and the manners of all Europe." Italy, England, Russia, and France were all conspicuously represented in high fashion in the promenades and processions. "This is the resort of the flower girls for whom Florence is so well-known," the visitor recorded. He also noted that Florence, with "its clean, quiet streets, its lovely environs, its incomparable Cascine . . . and its cheapness, presents an aggregate of attractions hardly to be met elsewhere."[7]

The overriding attraction, however, for a dedicated student of sculpture like Greenough was the presence of Lorenzo Bartolini, the "fashionable and grand sculptor" of his time, the former director of the School of Imperial Works at Carrara and currently Master of Sculpture in the Royal Academy in Florence.[8] In due time, in the early forties, Bartolini would succeed Stefano Ricci to the directorship.[9]

Bartolini was said by an eyewitness to have "taken possession of the school with the air of a conqueror . . . he prohibited all study from statues, and restricted the whole system of teaching to an imitation only of nature."[10] Some of the more conventional students thought he went to excessive lengths when he introduced a hunchback into the school one day for copying. One account of this event reports: "This daring novelty raised a shout of indignation. They cried out against the profanation of the school, of the sacred principles of the beautiful."[11]

As a student in Napoleonic Paris, Bartolini had commanded imperial attention by winning the bronze medal at the Academy of Fine Arts and tossing it into the Seine to protest its lack of nutritional value. When Antonio Canova was in Paris in 1802 to execute the colossal nude statue of Napoleon, Bartolini was personally presented to him by the art-snatching Emperor, who ignored the offense of the youthful artist's loud opposition to the static, mechanical reigning school of David. Canova responded graciously and invited Bartolini to work under his tutelage at Rome. This would be the sure making of a career, but to Bartolini's credit, he declined the offer.

"Let us remember how sculpture was then studied," recapitulated a younger contemporary of Bartolini:

> Only a long and tedious exercise of copying wholesale the antique statues, good and bad; and what was worse, the criterion of Greek

art was carried into the study of nude life—characteristic forms of the antique statues supplanting those of the living model. The outlines were added to and cut away with a calm superiority, which was even comical. The abdominal muscles were widened, the base of the pelvis narrowed in order to give strength and elegance to the figure. The model was never copied; the head was kept smaller, the neck fuller.[12]

It was against this mode of distortion, distinctive of the school of Rome, that the formidable Bartolini battled. He later boasted that he had never "been to Rome and [that he] despises the idea of following the antique, whilst he has eyes to see nature."[13]

After his prolonged Roman experience, Greenough understood the disparity between the sculptural methods practiced there and in Florence, and he sought out the fresh approach for his training. Justifying his choice, the American affirmed that his new instructor "counts more able men among his pupils than Canova or Thorwaldsen."[14] From Bartolini, "his favorite pupil" learned the necessity of modeling from nature and the desirability of having a live model for his statues. Greenough thus attained distinction "as the first and only American who had studied sculpture scientifically."[15]

In accord with this "scientific" approach to his art, Greenough dissected cadavers. "In a couple of hours," he reported, "one sees more of the why of organization and form than in days of lectures, reading, or examining the living model. . . . This dissection will hereafter be my constant study in the winter."[16] Greenough learned his anatomy well in the mortuary as he meticulously sketched the various muscles and joints which he dissected to gain an intimate knowledge of their structure.

"The ground aim of my studies since my return to Italy," he wrote to Richard Henry Dana, "has been the formation of a method both in drawing and modelling which shall enable me to pay in the future, my whole attention to form and expression without continual interruption."[17] Six months later Greenough was still steeped conscientiously in the quest for proficiency in technique. He detailed his method to Dana:

> I copy what I see before me . . . whatever the object be, whether naked—drapery—hair or even animals and vegetables, 'tis soon rendered by a hand schooled to obey an eye practiced in scanning

geometrically its outline and dissecting its variety of surface from light to shade. This security of method I owe to the study of drawing. 'Twas drawing that taught me that the planes of a form are shaded in proportion to the obliquity to the source of light. The foundation of my system of modelling lies in this fact.[18]

The habit of drawing from minute observation had already been inculcated into him by Washington Allston, who shared the judgment that placed drawing at the base of technique in any of the plastic arts. Bartolini's strictures to idolize nature and "to imitate her exactly" were not, however, to be confounded with photographic reflections of reality in Greenough's opinion. This brand of naturalism was not the objective. On the contrary, wrote Greenough, "Truth I consider necessary in a work, but by possible truth I mean not reality. I love reality dearly," he continued, "and when I want to enjoy it I go into the marketplace, the church, the wharf."[19] In his view, the artist's conception was obliged to transcend the commonplace. The heart of creative merit was to be found in that element which the artist supplied in his interpretation of external reality.

Greenough had been indoctrinated by Washington Allston with reverence for the ancient classical aesthetic ideals, and he sought to express these in his sculpture. "Sublimity—majesty—truth seem," he said, "the only true elements of any art either in conception, composition, or form," He elucidated, "Beauty is always truth. . . . Truth is not always beauty. . . . A work merely true, I consider the lowest in the order of works of sculpture."[20] For Greenough this disparaged category of realism included portraiture, as he interpreted it as involving merely precise copying of facial lines and cavities and the rendition of a characteristic expression. "Instead of attempting to convey trivial detail," he explained, "we should seek to ennoble our works by breathing into them all that we can conceive to move the mind—all that I can in beauty, all that's moving in passion, all that's grand in thought."[21]

Animated by his theories and ambition, Greenough came to his first commission through the intercession of his friend, Ambrosi, United States Consul at Leghorn, upon whom he had called in August when he arrived at Carrara. Ambrosi promptly decided to help the artist at his first opportunity, which he detected when he greeted the Fenimore Coopers and helped to settle them for the fall and winter season into an apartment in Casa Ricasoli. Ambrosi talked of Greenough with enthusiasm and broached the proposal of a possible portrait commission. Cooper was not averse to the project as he had come to Italy for the sake of imbibing art. Ambrosi alerted Greenough to hasten to town and Greenough responded quickly. Since he had come abroad to complete his studies on a quite slender purse provided on loan by Robert Gilmor, the prospect of a commission in Florence had an instantaneous magnetic effect. He left his studio in Carrara for Florence toward the end of October 1828.

The pair met, took to each other spontaneously, and a bust of Cooper was commissioned. The clay portrait was begun promptly and was completed in January 1829, the copying in marble followed immediately. The two Americans toured the galleries together and daily grew closer in their friendship.

On going through the Pitti collection one day, they stopped before Raphael's *Madonna del Trono*, long a favorite of Greenough's. Cooper was fascinated with the children in the lower end of the canvas and returned repeatedly to see them. Eventually he asked Greenough "if a subject like this was not well adapted to sculpture."[22] They studied the question and requested Cooper's eldest daughter, handy with a brush, to sketch the excerpted figures. Seeing them independently encouraged them in the notion that they would make a splendid subject for a group, and Cooper unhesitatingly commissioned the work to be done in marble. Cooper agreed to pay $250 to the artist for his labor, exclusive of the cost of the marble block and its cutting, which eventually came to $1,500. This was enough money to sustain Greenough modestly for a year in Florence. Viewing himself as an untried student, Greenough "consented to undertake the task on condition that unless both were pleased, the order should be null and the work considered merely as one of his studies."[23] Cooper appreciated Greenough's honesty, stating that his "diffidence . . . did as much credit to his principles as his modesty."[24] Greenough was content that Cooper's "conditions to the bargain of the group [were] marked by the same liberality" of a true patron.[25]

With genuine gratitude for the opportunity, Greenough later

confided to Cooper his deeply depressed state of mind when they had first met. "That group was ordered," he confessed, "at a moment which was a crisis in my life, when, wearied with bustmaking, I began to think that there was no hope for one of my turn of thought in America."[26] For years, Greenough insisted that Cooper had saved him from despair at the dawn of his career. "He employed me as I wished to be employed, and . . . has been a father to me in kindness."[27] To Greenough, Cooper remained "the noblest patron," endowed with "the broadest ideas on the subject of art."[28]

In reality, only one month had elapsed since the completion of Cooper's marble bust when Greenough was thus given the opportunity to produce a creative work of art through which he could prove his mettle and come to public notice.

It was an artistic challenge historically, too, for no sculptural group had yet been wrought in America by a native artist. James Jackson Jarves, the American sculptor turned art critic, recorded the state of artistic taste in Greenough's day. "A marble figure by an American was in itself," he wrote, "strange and curious."[29] Having participated in the selection of the subject, although "the suggestion was Mr. Cooper's," Greenough set about the task of rounding out his conception of the composition and planning its execution.[30] He wrote Gilmor that he had hoped to capture in his marble the "angel beauty and infantile form which are so charming combined in the original."[31]

He decided to represent the figures as "two cherub boys chanting."[32] Greenough planned to make them "30″ high with the arm of one thrown negligently over the shoulder of the other . . . with the head bowed," adding wings to "give them an ethereal look."[33] Unaware that Greenough "had recourse to Nature for [his] forms" and that he "not only modelled, but chiselled every part of them from life,"[34] Cooper was keen enough to detect "a great deal of nature in their postures, and as much distinctness and diversity in expression as the subject requires."[35] He rhapsodized that "nothing can be more beautiful than the infantile grace, the attitudes, and character of their expression . . . in short, taking the beauty of the design and the execution together, I scarce know a more pleasing piece of statuary for the size. . . . I confess I am delighted."[36] His judgment was reinforced by the "high approbation" of Bartolini and many other artists and connoisseurs. The approval seemed unanimous. "I hear but one opinion of its beauty," wrote Cooper triumphantly, vindicated in his layman's judgment and his generous impulse to art patronage.[37]

Vastly encouraged by spring that his "prospects were cheering," Greenough enclosed a gift of five dollars in his letter to his brother John, who was painting in London without recognition. He reported that he was heartened "to secure as great a portion of praise at the hands of [his] brother artists as one so inexperienced has a right to hope for."[38] To Cooper he wrote, "The work pleased generally and that highly."[39] Above all was the flattery of Bartolini's praises. Incredulous over his good fortune, Greenough wrote, "Bartolini . . . expressed much pleasure and did me the honor to offer me the advantages of a pupil in the use of his studios, the loan of instruments, and workmen and the sight of his pensioned models, in a way which will save me much money."[40]

Artistic recognition for a meritorious work was ample reward for a fledgling artist laboring away from home, but it would be quite another thing to gain public recognition at home, the source of potential largess. To Richard Henry Dana, Greenough wrote: "I am the pioneer of a band which I doubt not will hereafter enrich and beautify the cities of the Republic. I am warmed with the thought that if I seize on the path, they will do me the honor of having begun well. I do my countrymen the justice to believe that I have but to place myself on a level with the sculptors of Europe and I shall be preferred to them."[41]

The subject of public decoration of the buildings and squares of the cities of America must have stirred the imagination of Greenough's entire circle as they all wrote and spoke of it at length. When Bartolini himself visited Greenough in his studio to see the acclaimed group, he assured his younger colleague "that his conscience would never permit him to accept a commission from [the American] government until [Greenough's] hands were full.[42]

Cooper retained an objective measure of the situation, from the dual vantage point of appreciating both Greenough's capabilities and America's want of handsome public works. Why should the

Americans be put to the necessity of travel through Europe for artistic pleasures? Was not the young republic vigorous enough to create its own cultural taste and satisfy it? He intended to play a significant role in the development of American art. He explained his intention to friends at home early in the maturation of this initial project.

> I intend to send these cherubs home, as soon as finished, and I hope they may be a means of bringing patronage and encouragement to the artist. I have no more doubt, in my own mind, of his ability to do that which I know he has done. It would cost him time, and study, and great labour, but his chance of success would be equal to that of artists whose reputations are being established here.
>
> It is time that delusions on the subject of Europe had an end on our side of the Atlantic. . . . It is my intention to have these little angels exhibited for the benefit of the artist. . . . In a country like ours, the acquisition of good sculpture is no trifle. Of all the arts, that of statuary is perhaps the one we most want, since it is more openly and visibly connected with the tastes of the people, through monuments and architecture, than any other. . . . If we wish to compete as artisans with the manufacturers of Europe, we must get taste.[43]

Through the fall and winter of 1829, Greenough concentrated his attention on casting his figures in plaster preparatory to cutting them in marble. He curtailed his social life and increased his working hours. He filled his leisure hours reading on art or studying the masterpieces in the well-stocked galleries. Greenough's abiding interest in art history and criticism, already aroused by Allston, deepened during this time. "I have met with a very interesting and valuable book entitled *Lettere Sulla Pittura, Scultura Ed Architettura*," he wrote Robert Gilmor. "The work (7 volumes) consists of letters of artists or relating to the arts from the dates of the age of Michelangelo to that of Poussin. These letters contain much good sense and good criticism."[44] He read widely in several languages, gathering amorphous bits of observations which gestated over a dozen years, maturing into his later published critical essays.

He used live models for both the modeling and the chiseling of the group and all the work was wrought by his own hand. This personal application may have been a matter more of necessity than of deference to technique, due to his shortage of cash for outlay on stonecutters. In any case, it proved a most salutary effort for him. He reported to Cooper, "The group was commenced in ill health and melancholy. It was chiselled amid some difficulties. I found both health and spirits in the task."[45] While still in Florence Cooper watched the development with interest at close range and encouraged Greenough with "praise and flattering attention throughout the work."[46] He followed its course even from the south of Italy after he had left Florence for the summer and fall seasons. "I am glad to hear that our young gentlemen turn out so proper," he wrote from Sorrento.[47] He waxed lyrical in his praises of the work to their mutual friends.

The group was completed in plaster in May 1830 and in marble before the year was out. Greenough marked the occasion by his inscription on the front of the plinth, "GLORIA IN EXCELSIS DIO," and on the back, "SCULPTURED IN FLORENCE FOR JAMES FENIMORE COOPER, 1830." The work proceeded rapidly considering the excessive hardness of the marble, and Greenough reported "it has turned out exquisite both for texture and for tint."[48] Not one internal flaw emerged. Greenough acknowledged that there was immense difficulty in the mechanical execution but he reported proudly that "the wings are wrought so light and thin that they are quite transparent as drawing paper. In this form, I am confident of having surpassed the model."[49] Cooper did not dispute the verdict but rather joined the chorus in his accolade, writing Greenough, "In your works, the purity of the marble has the effect which is produced by beauty in style and composition. They are both mistresses of the ideas."[50]

Greenough's talk of melancholy at the outset had much to do with money, as well as depressed energies. He had come abroad with a modest stipend and for some months had earned nothing. His expenses for food, lodging, studio, and materials were a constant drain. In the fall of 1829, at the completion of his first year abroad, he had $200 and calculated that "$108 will be exhausted by board and lodging for the coming year."[51] He certainly was operating on a close margin. He could hardly afford to wait overlong for the recognition and sizable commission he craved.

Immediately, Cooper set about to introduce the work in America. He had agreed to lend the work to Greenough for three months for the purpose of its being exhibited for the benefit of the artist, who would, of course, be responsible for its management, the expenses of transport, and so on. Cooper would help from the distance of his continued residence in Europe. He sent advice unremittingly and his judgments were cannily unerring. He displayed appropriate concern over Greenough's dwindling funds. "If you have need of money, tell me without reserve," he urged in a letter from Sorrento during the winter of the statue's carving. "And if you have not, keep the payment before you so long as there is a blow to be struck with a chisel. The belly and the bank are two tyrants who must be kept in good humor."[52]

Greenough expressed his gratitude in more than words. He rendered numerous reciprocal services. After Cooper left Florence for points south in March 1829, Greenough undertook to supervise one of the writer's books through the printing. This task entailed his coping with typesetters and his dealing at length with the censors and the translators. The next spring still saw the sculptor busy with these chores.

While he was entrepreneur of the exhibition, Greenough delegated arrangements in America to the charge of his brother Alfred in Boston. Although he was anxious about money he merely expressed the pious hope of realizing some profit, without which he would be seriously embarrassed. He restricted his instructions to details for the group's placement and lighting. It was to be "placed on a pedestal high enough to raise it to the level of the eye, with a dark crimson curtain behind."[53] Instead of New York, practical considerations of transportation and exhibition space caused the group to be shown first in Boston in the spring of 1831. The group excited controversy, as Cooper had apprehensively prophesied. He argued consistently against its prior exhibition in Boston, urging a New York debut instead. "You will be covered with twaddling criticism in Boston, which is no better . . . than a gossiping country town though it has so many clever people. The tone of criticism is essentially narrow and vulgar."[54]

Cooper's concern was hardly neurotic for the time. On the

contrary, it was solidly founded. There was another inherent dilemma for the sculptor in that day. The nude form was the prescribed mode in fashion emanating from Italy and reigning on the Continent under the dominion of Antonio Canova.[55] The puritanical New Englanders, however, would not countenance such "immorality" as represented in the nudity of these youthful figures. It was suggested in some newspapers that the figures should be draped. Whether the resistance to the classical style and nude representations derived from innocence, prudery, pragmatism, or simple antiforeign bias, it was stubborn and pervasive. Only the elite cosmopolitan set on the east coast appreciated the classical feeling and understood the symbolic references.

Cooper issued warnings to the last moment, to protect the work from this irrevelant abuse. "I would they were in New York," he wrote Greenough, where there are as "good judges of their merits among their 230,000 souls, as Boston among her 80,000 college included."[56]

The damage turned out to be relatively inconsequential, chiefly because Greenough's friends rallied to the defense. They were an articulate lot. Washington Allston, Edward Everett, and Richard Henry Dana wrote ecstatic reviews, the latter bursting into verse in their plaudits. Cornelius C. Felton wrote a eulogistic piece for the North American Review, claiming for the group "the highest excellence of soul and sentiment."[57] Another American spoke of "the celestial yet infantile beauty of these exquisite statues."[58] Greenough's sister, Elizabeth, proudly gathered the comments in her circle at home to cheer her brother. "Mother admires them . . ."; she wrote, "R. H. Dana seemed delighted. Mr. Allston . . . thought them admirably well done. He had no idea Horatio could do anything like this, though he expected something very fine. This is high praise and most gratifying."[59]

The charge of plagiarism was another critical barb. The Americans failed to appreciate the wide currency given in Europe to the age-old practice of artistic repetition of any familiar subject. It was the vogue from classical times, as witness the proliferation of Venuses and Apollos alone. Were it not so, would any sane aspirant make his initial stand for public recognition with a derivative composition? The master Bartolini himself was at that very moment "bringing to a close his copy of Titian's Venus in marble for Lord Londonderry," a work which was reported to have "occupied him for a long time."[60]

Instead of taking offense at the added calumny that focused on those irrelevancies, Greenough probably considered it only a reflection "of the infancy of sculpture in America" at that time.[61] Years later James Jackson Jarves used the incident to illustrate the primitive artistic taste of Greenough's day. "At that time, we had so vague a notion of aesthetic enjoyment that even the cold purity of the marble could not protect these little children from the reproach of immodesty."[62] Bearing out Cooper's forecast, it took a New York reviewer to silence the carping: "Perhaps the authority of Raphael was necessary to render such a representation of the subject palatable in our day. . . . I hope that the peculiarity of its being the first work of the kind which has come from an American chisel, as well as the rare merit of the artist, will be found to interest the public at home."[63]

The New York exhibition which followed was arranged by Horatio's brother Alfred, through Col. John Trumbull, to take place in the late fall and winter of 1831 in a room engaged for the purpose at the American Academy of Fine Arts. As if by some providential hand, the group seemed destined to run into petty blunders. Obviously, Alfred lacked the worldliness in the artistic ambience to have realized that Greenough's closest artistic friend in New York, Samuel F. B. Morse, was president of the National Academy of Design, the rival of Trumbull's American Academy of Fine Arts. Quite naturally, Morse was ruffled by the gaucherie. News of the incident reached Cooper in Paris, who relayed it tactfully to Greenough. "I see that the boys are exhibiting in New York," he wrote, "and to the scandal of the President."[64] Greenough, a partisan of Morse's coterie of artists in their earlier rebellion, now protested that he was in complete accord with Morse's charge that "the Academy of Fine Arts was only an "association for the discouragement and the humiliation of artists." He apologized further, "I regret most sincerely that my group has been exhibited in New York in a manner directly or indirectly unfavorable to the National Academy. . . . Had I been aware of it, I should have countermanded the arrangement. My brother had the entire arrangement of the thing."[65] No hard feelings were harbored over the episode.

From Paris, Cooper watched the proceedings with deep interest. When the New York exhibition was well along, he wrote Greenough, "I am glad to hear of the success of the group, though I never doubted it. I have set $1,000 as your lowest net receipts. It would not surprise me were they to near $1,500 or $2,000."[66] Then he pressed the next logical step in the advancement of Greenough's career. "It must go to Washington next winter by all means. It must be seen in the Capital, after which leave it to your friends who have the ear of the government. . . . I shall move in the matter at the proper moment."[67] By the end of the year, Cooper's ambition for the artist ranged even further afield. He urged, "You must send the boys to Charleston, New Orleans, and Cincinnati. You may not gain in the way of money, but you will gain enormously in making yourself known, and you will get orders in consequence."[68] Cooper ignored completely the three month limit he had placed earlier on his loan of the group.

He behaved with similar magnanimity regarding the various queries for copies too. "I hear you are asking only $400 for copies of the Cherubs," he wrote. "Your price should be 6 to 8 hundred."[69] This seems to be a high valuation to give a work that cost Cooper only $250 to purchase. It can be supposed he was estimating an inflated market value with Greenough's rising fame. There is the outside chance that Cooper was prompting Greenough to stiffen his prices so as to restrict the number of reproductions, but this less generous motive seems unlikely in view of his consistent magnanimity throughout the relationship.

The exhibitions did not get beyond Boston and New York but still yielded a profit in the neighborhood of $400. Although the figure fell short of the mark set by Cooper, the sum was welcome at a moment when Greenough had "but 2 Napoleons in [his] purse" and was forced to increase his already sizable loan from Cooper.[70]

The *Chanting Cherubs* altogether fulfilled their promise. They affixed Greenough's reputation as a talented American sculptor in Florence. They brought him dramatically to the attention of Bartolini, who directed the completion of his training and took pride in Greenough's accomplishments. This esteem in turn advanced him in Italian circles and led him eventually into the sacred precincts of the faculty of the Academy of Fine Arts in Florence. They gained him a reputation at home on a national scale to the point of obtaining a commission from the Congress of the United States for a monumental public statue. They stimulated private orders for his works. And in their execution, they obliged the artist to settle definitively on his style of sculpture.

3

Poetry and the Bread
and Butter Staple

GREENOUGH'S DEVOTION TO DOCTRINAL EXPLORATION DID NOT PRECLUDE his attention to works of cash value. Circumstances provided constant pressure. The bread and butter staple of the artist, that "lowest branch" of art, the portrait commission, was his only means of sustenance. While modeling the *Cherubs*, Greenough grudgingly diverted countless hours to supervising the carving in marble of the numerous busts he had modeled in the States. He processed a new order from the Boston Athenaeum that offered $200 for a marble copy of his bust of John Quincy Adams, which he managed to deliver in October 1829. In the same season the Athenaeum also acquired a marble copy of his bust of President Josiah Quincy of Harvard. The likeness of Dr. John Thornton Kirkland, another former president of Harvard, was commissioned for later presentation to the Athenaeum by a small group of wealthy New Englanders resident in Florence at that time. It was completed two years later in a marble copy of colossal size and is still lodged in the Athenaeum.

Greenough now began to retain stonecutters for the routine tasks. His own time was to be preserved for the creative effort. He applied all of his talents to the execution of the *Cherubs*, but they were the last work to be chiseled by his own hand. For them, he craved the level of perfection on which he would stake his public debut.

In keeping with the Napoleonic cult then modish in Florence, the sculptor modeled a bust of Napoleon taken directly from the death mask. The Bonaparte family then living in Florence thought it a fine likeness but failed to commission it. Greenough himself rated it lowly and rarely alluded to it. On his permanent return to the States years later, he deposited it for safekeeping with many other busts in the Boston Athenaeum. It was subsequently presented to the Boston Museum of Fine Arts where it now stands.

After some unaccountable delays, the plaster cast of Greenough's bust of Mrs. Robert Gilmor arrived from Baltimore in February 1829. This was the work which catalyzed Greenough's relationship with his affluent patron. Quite by accident the work became enmeshed in a web of circumstances strictly Italian. On second viewing, Greenough disapproved of "the drapery which surrounds the

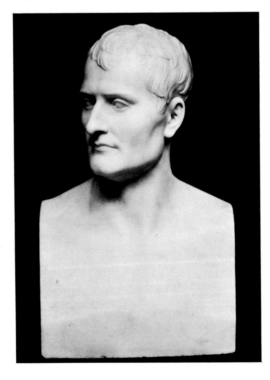

Napoleon I
1832, marble, life-size
Courtesy of the Museum
of Fine Arts, Boston

shoulders and determined to spare no pains to make the merit of the whole equal to that of the head."[1] He promptly sent word to his agent at Carrara to cease carving pending these desired changes.

Meanwhile, the agent had quarreled with Bartolini, whose association with Greenough was well known. Fearing dismissal also by Greenough, the craftsman made haste to get on with the job. When Greenough arrived at Carrara he found the bust far advanced and, from his revised view, ruined. Intent upon perfection at any cost, he decided to send the head minus the drapery to Gilmor as a gift, appending another design which he now preferred. Drawing on Gilmor for "$50 on account of the expense of marble and preparation," he took consolation for the cost exceeding the stipulated price in having "done [his] utmost to please the employer."[2] The marble cutter demanded full payment. Greenough balked. They bargained and arrived at a settlement through the intervention of Greenough's friend, Ambrosi, with the payment of half the price, twelve francesconi.[3] After all the fuss, the bust was shipped home only six months late, unchanged from its original design.

Gilmor was so pleased with the marble bust that he asked for a cameo of his wife's profile to be taken from it. He asked Greenough to see to this, intending that it be made by G. A. Santarelli of Florence, whom he had met on an earlier visit. But the artist had died, and with him went the art of cameo making in Florence. The work could only be done in Rome, now the center of this craft. Greenough dragged his feet on the request, being loathe to risk harm to his precious bust if shipped to Rome and to incur the expense involved. Add to this his bias against the School of Rome generally and the dim view he took of cameos in comparison with marble busts and his procrastination becomes understandable. "I think those workmen feebler in particular than in ideal heads," he explained.[4] Gilmor persisted and prevailed. The cameo was cut in Rome in 1831 through the intercession of Horatio's colleague and housemate of the previous year, Thomas Cole, the landscape painter, also a friend of Gilmor's.

The Baltimorean's insatiable desire to enlarge his collection gave Greenough the opportunity to indulge vicariously his penchant to play the collector, to outwit the tourist competitors, notably the

British, who were outpricing the others. The incentive gave spice to Greenough's artistic meanderings. If a gem should turn up in a pile of worthless objects, he would acquire it. The game challenged his taste as well as his knowledge. So proud was he of the bargains and the discovery, it seemed to matter little that they all went to his patron. In the spring of 1829, Greenough sent as a gift "a salver and vase cast in Scagliola from a piece of plate by Cellini, the greatest genius. . . ."[5] The next year he picked up an Albano (*A Repose in Egypt*) for 112 francesconi and a copy of a Salvatore Rosa painting that he had acquired for ten dollars. He spurned a portrait of Rosa for the "outrageous" sum of $100 but sent Gilmor a portrait of Michelangelo that had cost a mere seven dollars.

Long unsettled between them was the subject for the statue which Gilmor had ordered in his enthusiasm over the bust of his wife. Suggestions were shuttled back and forth in their letters, but they were ignored or discarded. An interpretation of Sandro Botticelli's *Birth of Venus* was Gilmor's first notion, to which Greenough countered with offerings of a "Shepherd Boy," "Sappho," "Jacob," and "Rebecca," "all," as he put it, "first thoughts made after dinner with the cigars."[6] The subject waned awhile with both of them, until revived when Alfred gave Gilmor an exclusive preview of the *Chanting Cherubs*, who were uncased especially for this purpose before their New York exhibition. The patron reacted as anticipated. "I have received a letter from Mr. Gilmor," reported Greenough to Cooper, "in which he speaks in raptures of the group—declares that he envies you the idea, as well as the possession."[7] Whether he was truly covetous of Cooper's "Cherubs" or was goaded by guilt over his promise to the artist, Gilmor reverted to the search of an appropriate subject for an equally original and beautiful work.

Thinking more of the dimensions of his drawing-room's display niches than of the requirements of art, Gilmor asked for a smaller than life-size partially draped female figure. This idea received short shrift from Greenough, chiefly on account of its size. Greenough's objection rested on classical ground. He contended, "Adult forms on a small scale produced but a mean effect unless decidedly in miniature."[8] He offered the compromise suggestion for a girl of nine, whose proportions would meet Gilmor's curtailed specifications. This proposal seemed uninspired and vanished in the shuffle. Gilmor then asked for a boy supporting a lamp or vase, for which Greenough worked up a model, if only to demonstrate that despite "its pleasing expression, being obliged to make it serve to bear a vase of flowers cramped very much the attitude in composition."[9] Morse and other friends would attest to the "thoroughness of the trial," wrote Greenough. "Many were highly pleased," he continued, "but I remembered how different was the sensation produced from that of Mr. Cooper's group."[10] Greenough was loathe to jeopardize the standard he had set with his "Cherubs," and expressed "his determination to outdo all his previous efforts at creativity."[11] Grateful for the liberty which Gilmor finally extended him regarding the theme and "determined to make another trial," he began a study of a figure out of Byron's poem "The Corsair." Deciding on this first nude female form, he realized that it was exactly the sort of subject that he had been seeking for months. It would be the vehicle to test his craftmanship by Italian standards. Schooled by New England's deprecating view of nudity, he declared that in this subject he would "attempt to interest and charm the eye and mind with a female form without appealing to the baser passions, what has not been done in Italy for many years."[12]

The "Medora" conformed to his purpose to perfection. She embodied all the classical virtues. She was cold and dead, consequently tranquil and beautiful; her literary creator was the incomparable romantic Lord Byron, whose popularity in Italy had outlived him by years. Thorwaldsen had executed an impressive statue of the poet and Bartolini had also made his bust.[13] "The Corsair" was familiar to readers of English poetry and contained in Canto III a reverential description of the Medora.

> In life itself she was so still and fair,
> That death with gentler aspect withered there,
> And the cold flowers her colder hand contained,
> In that last grasp as tenderly were strained
> As if she scarcely felt, but feigned a sleep,
> And made it almost mockery yet to weep;
> The long dark lashes fringed her lids of snow,
> And veil'd—thought shrinks from all that lurk'd below—

Oh! o'er the eye Death most exerts his might,
And hurls the spirit from her throne of light!
Sinks those blue orbs in that long last eclipse,
But spares as yet, the charm around her lips—
Yet, yet they seem as they forbore to smile
And wish'd repose—but only for a while;
But the white shroud, and each extended tress,
Long—fair—but spread in utter lifelessness,
Which late the sport of every summer wind,
Escaped the baffled wreath that strove to bind
These—the pale pure cheek became the bier
But she is nothing—wherefore is she here?[14]

This work rolled along easily for Greenough after having produced the Cherubs." "Hitherto," he wrote, "I have been obliged to spur myself to the task, in modelling the 'Medora' I had but to *laissez aller*. I trust it will be the same with the marble."[15] The *"Medora"* emerged from Greenough's workshop a recumbent, seminude idealized female figure, nearly life-size. According to an observer, the face was an idealization of the sculptor's.[16] His first poetical work, pretensions aside, was a typical neoclassical figure of the period.

Completing the model detained Greenough in his studio through the worst of the summer's heat, until late August. The rest of the work, casting in plaster and copying into marble, was a matter of technical details which could be easily delegated to his skilled assistants. They could proceed in his absence, and they did. The marble cutter took over shortly. Inevitable technical delays occurred before Greenough applied "the finishing touches" in June 1832.[17] Happily the *Medora* "pleased many in [his] studio and attracted many Englishmen,"[18] still the most avid and affluent purchasers on the Continent.

Again, the inexperienced sculptor, overanxious to please, had underestimated both his time and expense. The original price had been set at $500. Realizing his mistake, he attempted to raise it to $550 but failed. Confiding his embarrassment to a Boston intimate, he wrote, "For Mr. Gilmor's statue, I have received $700 of which I am to repay $200 on its being exhibited."[19] More accurate accounting revealed that the total cost including shipping charges came to $775.75. He concluded ruefully, "You will observe the production of my statues has more than consumed the prices paid for them."[20] The transaction ended with Greenough's absorbing the loss, receiving from Gilmor, 475 francesconi, the equivalent of $500. The lesson gained. Greenough announced that his fees for statues would henceforth be $550. This was hardly insurance against profitless pursuit, but he felt dependent on the patronage of traveling Yankees who were innately thrifty. He increased his price for busts to 100 Tuscan crowns (approximately $100), which he hoped would be just enough to save him from what he "endeavored not to deserve—Debt."[21]

Months went by before the *Medora* arrived in Boston. It was exhibited from October 24 through the end of the year, once more under the management of Alfred. It could be seen in the rooms of Chester Harding from nine in the morning until ten at night. Tickets sold for twenty-five cents with a season ticket costing fifty cents. One newspaper reported that 2,000 persons had attended by December 1. If true, this represented egregious success.

The enthusiastic critical reception reduced considerations of mundane finances to insignificance. In the *North American Review* Cornelius C. Felton delivered the typical panegyric: "Mr. Greenough . . . has shown a high creative genius, set off by the graces of refined taste. . . . He has a correct eye for form, a skillful hand for drawing . . . the highest excellence of soul and sentiment. With such gifts of genius . . . Mr. Greenough's prospects are more flattering to his ambition."[22] Leonard Jarvis sang his praises from Washington about the "beautiful work of art."[23] Richard Henry Dana once again composed a poem in welcome, hoping thus to advance the fortunes of his friend.

Despite the *Medora's* favorable reception, the joint efforts of Alfred and Gilmor to arrange further exhibitions were fruitless. Alfred could not neglect his business affairs in Boston to make the trip to New York which seemed essential, and Gilmor did not stir out of Baltimore. Having failed to obtain space at long distance for a spring showing in either New York or Philadelphia, Alfred resigned the search and dispatched the statue to its owner in Baltimore after a delay of some months "on account of the continuation of stormy weather."[24] The summer season being deemed safe for oceanic transportation, the statue was sent aboard a coastwise vessel in charge of the captain himself, who undertook the full responsibility for his valuable cargo and discharged his obligation without incident.

Baltimore had its public glimpse of the *Medora* probably in the fall, the receipts being divided between patron and sculptor. After the exhibition, the *Medora* came to rest in the Gilmor home, where, surprisingly, it was stored in the basement for lack of suitable space in the inhabited quarters. However, Mrs. Gilmor must have thought well of it, because she attended a fancy ball during the winter of 1837, clad as "Medora," in a white muslin dress.[25]

That spring of 1830 was a fairly bright one for the artists gathered in Florence. They had gained social footing and were invited to the soirees of the international set. The ducal balls and receptions at the casino were held weekly; Joseph Bonaparte, ex-king of Westphalia, entertained the Americans at his exclusive parties, as did the Polish Prince Poniatowski, who favored them socially. The British were friendly and their entertainments were lavish. The Carnival was "in its glory" that year; the operatic season at the Pergola featured Giulia Grisi, whose debut "in the early flower of her beauty and wonderful voice" created a stir.[26] The admission fee, set at one paul, was within easy reach, and the Americans were regular patrons, especially Greenough, who thought the soprano "the loveliest woman I ever set eye upon."[27] Glamor-struck to the point of gossip by his friends, he modeled her bust, but the affair apparently ended there. He dressed Morse down in this connection, bristling at the intimations of intimacy. "You do me the honour to think with Mr. Gore, that I'm in love with an opera singer, the hackneyed mistress of God knows how many innamorati. I've pilot enough aboard to save me from all that, I assure you, though I don't navigate with exactly your chart."[28]

Horatio was "intoxicated by the arrival in Florence of [his] younger brother" Henry, who, he proclaimed, "put the finishing touch to [his] good fortune."[29] Horatio reported that he was pleased to be able "to contribute to his instruction in the art" and to receive "assistance from him in such of [his] studies as have hitherto occupied him."[30] At home, the family understood Henry's value to Horatio and concluded it was probably the "wisest course" for both. Advancing himself in the arts, studying drawing as well as painting, Henry's utility to Horatio was manifold. "While managing his [Horatio's] financial affairs," for which he was better fitted in Alfred's opinion than Horatio, Henry would free the sculptor "to concentrate upon his creations" and, moreover, "would cheer him with his company."[31]

There were several other American painters to complete the circle, and Horatio's apartment and studio were the foci of the group. Living with the brothers under the same roof were Christopher Pearse Cranch, son of Judge Cranch, whom Greenough had met in Washington; Thomas Cole, the landscape painter, and Samuel Morse, who stayed the season. Not far off lived Horatio's future brother-in-law, John Gore of Boston. John Gadsby Chapman of Alexandria painted a fine portrait of Horatio and Rembrandt Peale and Morse followed suit.[32] Greenough reciprocated by modeling busts of Cole and Morse. Henry joined a class with this group of American painters at the Academy of Fine Arts, then headed by Bezzuoli. Together, they enjoyed the art life and eagerly pursued the work it entailed. They suffered in unison the dejections of frustration in the creative process and in mutual criticism, and they found encouragement in reciprocal praise.

Through all this busy time Greenough, with the help of Cooper, had been charting the course to wider fame at the earliest opportunity. A good portrait bust of a world famous personality was almost as advantageous to reputation as a well-wrought creative work. The previous December, Greenough had broached the subject to Cooper, now installed in the Rue St. Dominique 59, near the Invalides in Paris, of the possibility of his interceding with General Lafayette for "sitting for his head. . . ."[33] He averred, "His portrait would be worth a fortune to me hereafter."[34] Not feeling importuned, Cooper had replied promptly, "His sitting at present is out of the question. It is difficult to get two minutes conversation with him. He has also given a pledge to a French sculptor never to sit again for his bust, but as he says, how can I refuse an American sculptor. If your friend should be here in the spring, we will see what we can do. . . ."[35] In February, Cooper wrote encouragingly, "I think Lafayette would now sit to you."[36]

Spring and early summer still saw Greenough laboring away

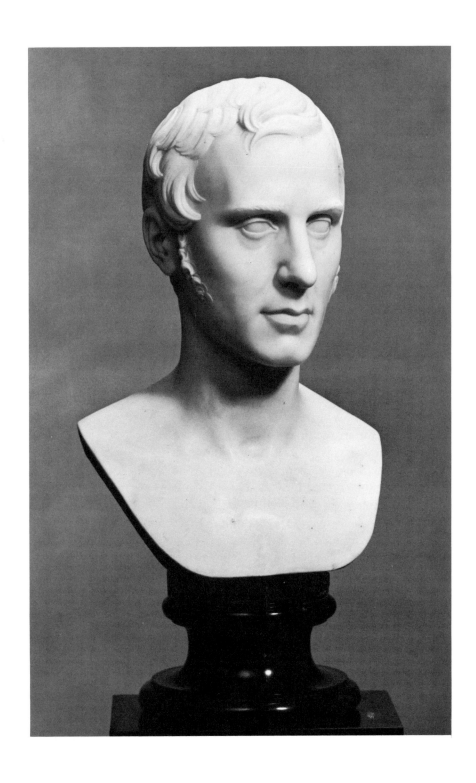

Thomas Cole 1831, marble, 17″
Courtesy of the Wordsworth Atheneum, Hartford, Connecticut

Samuel Finley Breese Morse 1831, painted plaster copy, 21½"
The Metropolitan Museum of Art

in his studio. It was not until quite late in the summer, on August 24, 1831, that Greenough broke away for his trip to Paris. With his *Medora* casting and his busts being cut, he felt free to leave. He boarded a steamer at Leghorn for Genoa, where he looked over the Academy of Fine Arts, took in the theater, explored palaces, and discovered some "glorious" Van Dykes. Then he proceeded overland via Turin and Lyons. Although he stated he saw "nothing of art in two days," he said he was overwhelmed with the beauty of the Savoy countryside.[37]

Arriving in Paris on his twenty-sixth birthday, Greenough took rooms near the center of town. He reported to Rembrandt Peale that he was located "within a few doors of the good General."[38] The area was distinguished and a likely habitat for poets and philosophers. Following his own detour through Switzerland and Germany, Samuel Morse visited Greenough some days later, and once more they delved energetically into the art life. It took Greenough but three days to call on the well-known Italianate painter, Dominique Ingres, at his atelier in Place Furstenburg, and Ingres offered him "any assistance."[39] He was dazzled to meet the poets Alphonse de Lamartine and Victor Hugo and he reported to Washington Allston that he was struck with the "magnificence and luxurious gayness" of Paris.

He commenced modeling almost immediately and made five busts in short order. He remodeled that of Cooper and fashioned those of Lafayette, Princess Christina di Belgioioso, Brisbane of New York, and an anonymous Italian lady. Mr. Kinlock, an old acquaintance from the Carolinas, likewise commissioned a bust. Heartened by this auspicious beginning, Horatio wrote Henry a few weeks later that "Two French ladies desire their busts, in plaster merely. It will not do to hurry away. I am getting pluck."[40]

The Lafayette bust was not accomplished without the trial of waiting upon the harried old general. Since Lafayette was a key political figure in the July Monarchy, he was under severe pressure of the business of state. Then an English painter, Pickersgill, sent over by a committee from London, nabbed him first. Greenough persevered and related the episode.

Circumstances required that I should be on the alert for more than a fortnight to seize such pitiful quarter of an hour afforded by the pressure of General Lafayette's affairs. . . . I have finished, however, and they say it's like him—thanks to Cooper who pinned the old gentleman to his chair one morning for two whole hours with stories and bon mots. I believe that was the saving of my bust for I have become out of humour with it and you know how fatal *that* often proves.[41]

The fortnight easily stretched into a month. The American circle was saddened early in October when Cooper's nephew, William, died of lung inflammation. Cooper was also preoccupied with finishing *The Wept of Wish-ton-Wish*. Although anxious to commence the Lafayette bust, Greenough passed the month of waiting busily and pleasantly enough. There were many hours devoted to viewing Paris and her art treasures, and Greenough reported that he enjoyed the communion of friendship "for hours at a stretch, seated in a little chamber with Cooper [and Morse]—now talking seriously and now letting ding [sic] anyhow."[42]

The American triumvirate attended with particular interest the morning "conversazioni" of Princess Belgioioso, a socialite with political proclivities who is renowned for having suffered con-

Marquis de Lafayette
1831, marble, 25¾"
Courtesy of the Pennsylvania Academy
of the Fine Arts

fiscation of her estates near Milan in reprisal for her support of Mazzini and his stand for militant Republicanism in the Risorgimento.[43] Because of her recent impoverishment, Greenough was commissioned to model her head only in plaster.

The innocent Yankees were subject to proselytizing by disciples of the utopian French socialist, Count Claude-Henri Saint-Simon, who won Brisbane as a sole convert. It was a novel intellectual excursion for Greenough to probe into political economy with the Saint-Simonians. Liberal ideas and the Polish Committee saturated their ambience, which centered in the salon of Lafayette where ideas circulated freely and the expounders and auditors were received with equal hospitality. Greenough reported, "The old man [was] in glorious health."[44] At the wedding visit of his granddaughter, "there were deputies, generals, Poles, Italians, Yankees . . . all in harmony, all liberal, all grieved for Warsaw."[45] Morse actually became secretary of the American Committee for the Assistance of the Polish Liberation, on whose mission of mercy Samuel Gridley Howe was arrested in Berlin, held incommunicado for some weeks, and then released through the intercession of the sympathetic American minister in Paris, William C. Rives.[46] Rives had been alerted by Brisbane who had stumbled into Howe accidentally in a Berlin hotel lobby the evening before the latter was spirited off by the police. It was a minor international scandal at the time and rather titillating to the group.

Greenough's three-month stay in Paris was pleasant. "I had been so long living secluded amid those who cared not for me, that I was prepared to relish every comfort of intercourse and of kindness," he wrote upon leaving.[47] The Parisian interlude was too gratifying "to leave it without regret."[48] Three years later his appreciation of Paris was vitiated by the dispersal of his friends—Cooper and Morse had returned home and Lafayette had died. Then he recalled almost defiantly, there is nothing in Paris to "regret [leaving] save the Théâtre Français and the Burgundy wine, which is really Christian."[49] His serious reservation about Paris now hinged on his antipathy to modern French art, which seemed to him "at a pretty low ebb here just now," with "clever men employed in twiddle-twaddle."[50] Upon reflection, however, he conceded, "I have

been less disgusted at the modern French pictures than I anticipated."[51] He attributed "great cleverness" to the famed David and
found much to his delight in the Louvre. "I didn't know Poussin
until now," he affirmed appreciatively of the great neoclassicist. "He
felt the Italians to the core as well as the Greeks."[52] The public
statues, however, seemed grotesque, and he resented particularly the
generally deprecating tone in Paris toward Italian sculpture.

Although it was work which had brought him to Paris, the
excursion seemed more like a protracted holiday. Now it had to end.
He left early in December and returned to Florence by way of
Lyons, Marseilles, and Leghorn.

Homecoming on December 14 evoked appreciation for the city
of his first choice. "I go to Florence," he wrote, "convinced that
there is no spot on earth equal to that for what I want. . . . Dear
compact, bird's eye, cheap, quiet, mind-your-own business, beautiful
Florence, how does my heart yearn for you! There stand your bell-
tower and your Palazzo Vecchio. What care I for those who inhabit
you? There will I build my Church."[53]

He found his brother Henry "well and established in new
lodgings" in Casa dei Frati in Via San Sebastiano.[54] Money to cover
household expenses during his absence had come from the windfall
of a commission for a Washington bust modeled as a study the
previous spring (1830) from a Commodore Biddle, whose representative, Mr. Murtrie, offered assurances "that the Commodore intends
ordering two other busts and he hopes to effect a subscription for
a statue among the officers of the squadron at Makon this winter."[55]
Fortunately Murtrie understood the Italian practice of sending a
check to accompany the order. It apparently made no difference
that this bust would be a copy of one already commissioned by a
Mr. Roosevelt of New York, whose confirmation awaited Green-
nough as he passed through Marseilles homeward bound. The double
order was a particular boon because it entailed no extra work for
the sculptor. He had made the study undoubtedly with a view to
demonstrating his capacity to execute a public monument around
the popular theme of the Founding Father. The bread and butter
recompense of bust making arrived in good time.

Although Alfred had arranged the New York exhibition of the

"Cherubs" and prospects were generally auspicious, Greenough faced the reality of having a virtually empty purse. His slender earnings in Paris had been consumed by the journey. Apprehensions overwhelmed him concerning "the spectre Debt" leaning over his pillow, asking if they were not intended as companions through life. He announced his determination to "make uncertain hopes fight certain fears,"[56] and turned once more to Cooper, despite his indebtedness for 500 francs. His embarrassment was compounded by the lack of prospects for immediate cash income beyond the dubious proceeds from the anticipated show or a possible commission from Col. Perkins of Boston. Apparently undismayed and with appropriate detachment, Cooper gave assurances of his pleasure to continue to serve as patron and friend. He wrote that he loved art and Greenough personally and that he had respect for and faith in his talents and was intent on stimulating American art and cultivating American taste. Beyond these personal considerations, he could easily afford to be generous as his income for that year was in the neighborhood of $20,000. The coincidence of these factors was most fortunate for Greenough because 1832 was a time of stringency. By August, Greenough owed Cooper 1,100 francs, and in September he drew another 500 francs "to keep along above water."[57]

Lowered resistance induced by strenuous work and nervous strain brought on an attack of ague in January after Greenough "remained in the cold study after exercise."[58] In this sorry state, he lamented his condition to Morse.

> Poor, very poor, stung by ambition, overwhelmed by obligation, encumbered with duties that tax . . . to the utmost . . . all hopeless —all mere brainwork. . . . I have been in some distress since my arrival here—and am at the moment waiting and hoping, but thank God at work and therefore easy through the day. I pass some nights a little poetically to be sure. . . . Nothing shall ever force me to regret my choice of profession though I starve for it.[59]

His depressed mood drew heavily on his reserve of physical and psychological energy, but a counterbalance was provided by the fierce ambition which fired him. He had come abroad with it. After his first season in Florence, he had complained self-reproachfully,

"Not one solid blow struck for a name—at an age when Michelangelo had nearly finished his colossal David, the grandest presentation of the naked that the Christian world has seen done."[60] Now, out of the depths of debt and depression, his vaulting aspiration sustained him. He confided to Cooper, "I would fain do something in the large, before habit shall have cramped my hand to the little . . . while I'm young."[61] Horatio's ambition was consistent with the aesthetic taste of the time which favored colossal size to express grand or noble subjects.

Bust making, the sure source of income, was tainted with artistic inferiority and indelibly sullied a priori. The true artist was expected to depict nobility and sublimity on a grand scale. This was the only way an artist could establish himself and gain public notice. The paradox went further; as Greenough put it to Cooper, "I came abroad to make myself known and respected in my country."[62]

Similarly, he had gone to Paris for the accretion of his continental prestige, which would reverberate in Washington. He decried his country's employment of what he considered inferior Italian craftsmen for the decoration of its national Capitol and other public buildings. He deplored America's general lack of taste and her overseas cultural orientation which alienated her from her own culture. He pleaded with Rembrandt Peale, who was just returning home, to enlist in his crusade.

> Convince them that one American work is of more value to the United States than three foreign ones even of superior merit . . . Let them employ us manfully and not tell us to learn to swim before we venture into the water. . . . I had been hoping that they had made some progress since I left America. . . . Mr. Peale, the scholars of America have looked so much abroad for salvation in letters, arts, and manners that they have not only overlooked home but have unfitted all under their influence for judging impartially of anything American. They have carted sand in upon a fine soil and nothing but a flood of satire can remove it and bring to light the fertile bottom which they have encumbered.[63]

Greenough was not thrashing about aimlessly. He had a plan to attain the highest rung of success and had taken steps to effectuate it.

George Washington 1832–1840, marble, 136″
Courtesy of the National Collection of Fine Arts, Smithsonian Institution

4

George Jupiter Washington

GREENOUGH'S AMBITION TO PRODUCE A NATIONAL MONUMENT FOR THE Capitol at Washington coincided with popular demand. Toward this end he had the support of a number of highly placed friends. A few months after arriving in Florence, he had already disclosed his plan to Richard Henry Dana, "Mr. Cooper thinks I ought to get a commission from the government, which will enable me to take a stand as an American sculptor."[1] During the summer of 1829, Greenough undertook to model a figure of Washington, for which he garnered advice from Cooper. "Make the figure as servant and simple as possible," Cooper counselled, "for these two qualities contain the essence of the imaginative with such a man. It will also suit our [national] idea of his character. Aim rather at the natural than the classical; this can always preserve the dignity of the man and his stature."[2] Cooper had his ear cocked close to native soil. If only Greenough had heeded.

A year later Greenough had modeled the bust and incorporated the figure into a model for a monument commemorating the revolution. This version of the figure was integrated some months later into an intricate design centered around the figure of Washington holding a scroll. The small subordinate figures were Columbus gazing at the globe, an infant cradled protectively by a mother who is menaced from behind by a stealthy Indian figure,[3] and "King Philip

Bust of George Washington
1830–1832, marble,
smaller than life-size
Courtesy of the Museum of Fine Arts,
Boston

[who] is seated amid the bones of his fallen brethren." The design soon changed to focus on the contrast between barbarity, symbolized by the Indian, and civilization, represented "as a female, seated with the implements of industry in her hands, while [a] boy is represented at her side reading."[4] Bas-reliefs around the sides would represent "Oppression," "Independence," "Remonstrance," and "Resistance." In this rendition, the whole would be surmounted "with a Statue of Washington in the act of resigning his authority as General-in-Chief."[5] These were Greenough's own descriptions of his early plans for the monument. Convoluted, muddled, and pretentious, nevertheless they comprised the germs of two mature productions. Greenough's rationalization for his grandiosity was candid and disingenuous. "I like to think about great works," he confessed. At twenty-six, his ambition was protean.

The assault on Congress in behalf of a statue by Greenough

began as early as 1830, when Allston had interested himself in promoting a statue of Washington and had written to Daniel Webster, senator from Massachusetts, recommending Horatio Greenough to execute the statue as "the only person capable" of this undertaking. It was to be a major commemorative monument. Cooper did his stint to advance the project. He had urged Greenough to send the successful "Cherubs" for exhibition to Washington so as to spark his fame at the hub. He had written Secretary of the Treasury Louis M. Lane, and even "King Andrew" himself on the subject.[6] Edward Everett claimed his share in furthering the plan in Congress, having gone so far as to have "interceded with Mr. Livingston [secretary of state] for liberal terms," and suggested "$10,000 for the principal figure, and as much more for the pedestal with its reliefs, and that a fourth part of the whole sum ought to be paid . . . in advance."[7]

The lobbying effort was eventually successful. A government commission, which proved the turning point in the sculptor's career, was awarded by House Resolution on February 14, 1832. It read: "Resolved, that the President of the United States be authorized to employ Horatio Greenough, of Massachusetts, to execute, in marble, a full length pedestrian statue of Washington, to be placed in the centre of the rotunda of the Capitol; the head to be a copy of Houdon's Washington, and the accessories to be left to the judgment of the artist."[8]

Greenough's friends were jubilant over the notable honor that the award signified. "What an opportunity," wrote Cole to Morse, "for an artist to immortalize himself to make the statue of the greatest man to be placed in the most conspicuous situation in the country or where it will be gazed upon by thousands unborn. Greenough feels the weight of his subject, but I do not fear him."[9]

The unofficial notification, dispatched on February 23 by the secretary of state, Edward Livingston, contained a plan and description of the rotunda and suggestions for the design. In a letter to Greenough the secretary admonished that "no appropriation was at that time made by Congress for compensation." He stipulated "that the expense should not exceed that which has been paid for similar works, executed by artists of the first reputation."[10] Greenough could feel quite safe. He never hoped to exceed the sum paid Luigi

Persico of $10,000 per figure, and could hardly hope to attain the $30,000 paid to Enrico Causici by Baltimore. The secretary requested that Greenough send an estimate of cost to accompany his acceptance. In July 1832, six months later, Greenough officially undertook the work for $20,000, to be executed in four years and compensated in annual installments of $5,000 each. The first appropriation of $5,000 was made by Congress on July 14, 1832; the others followed regularly.

As in other pioneer efforts, Greenough had to overcome a variety of difficulties in the production of his "Washington." The first cause for perplexity turned on the question of Greenough's location during the execution of the work. Greenough wrote Cooper that he was deciding whether he "ought to fix" himself in Florence throughout the completion of the work, which he estimated would require a minimum of four more years of exile.[11] Using Cooper as a sounding board, he analyzed the problem:

> I fear I may become anchored for life. Still I see many obstacles to the study and exercise of my art in the States. The choice of country in this case amounts to a choice of life. . . . I cast my eye from continent to continent and sigh that I can't plant one foot in the states and the other on the boot—chisel here with one hand and hold up to the christening font there with the other. . . . I have reached one of those cross roads of life.[12]

The discussion was entirely theoretical. There was no real choice. He undoubtedly could not have earned a livelihood at home, nor could he obtain the supply of marble or have the assistance of his skilled workmen. Washington Allston was certain on the first point, as he reviewed the situation with a friend.

> It has often been doubted by Greenough's friends here, notwithstanding the high and general esteem in which he stands, as well for his private character as for his talents, whether he will be able to support himself in Boston from private employment alone. And if Boston cannot afford him sufficient, I know not in what other city of the Union he can expect it. His resources, they think, must be at Washington, in works for the government, or in Europe. . . . The interest taken in sculpture is by no means so general as that taken in pictures. Then the prices which a sculptor must

charge, even to defray his expenses, are such as very few in our country are either able or willing to give for works of art. So I do not see much prospect even of a bare support, unless he is content to confine himself to busts that are portraits.[13]

Here was a keen estimate of the American scene. There was no viable alternative to expatriation. Greenough relished neither starvation nor restriction to the "lowest branch" of the art.

Florence, on the other hand, was the inevitable location. Its proximity to the quarries was a cardinal consideration in view of the enormity of the block required, besides the other practical considerations. An added advantage was the presence of the Baptistry, whose proportions resembled the rotunda so closely for size, height, and shape that it could substitute as a testing place. Socially too, Greenough was entrenched and the "Americano-Italian colony . . . was still flourishing, providing companionship and entertainment almost at will."[14]

The *Washington* statue demanded Greenough's complete attention. Authorized by Congress to choose his own design, Greenough determined it would be a masterpiece in the grand style on which he would stake his artistic reputation at home. The father of his country deserved representation in superlative terms: lofty, heroic, and ideal, to signify the highest and noblest virtues. This was to be the first American-made public monument, and Greenough resolved to set a precedent of perfection. He wrote Morse:

> I have made up my mind on one score, namely, that this order shall not be fruitless to the greater men who are now in our rear. They are sucking now and rocking in cradles, but I can hear the pung! Puff! Puffety! of their hammers, and I am prophetic, too. We'll see if Yankee land can't muster some ten or a dozen of them in the course of as many years.[15]

Unhappily, but inevitably, the grand style bore the seeds of the statue's eventual failure at home. Greenough stubbed his toe on the root of the neoclassical aesthetic. The classical treatment, which alone could yield the "noblest" representation, implied the use of classical drapery and some degree of nudity, too alien for acceptance in America. Moreover, Washington's reputation for austerity conjured the feeling for one wag that the founding father had been so proper as to have been born fully clothed, making a stately bow upon his first appearance.

Greenough sought a resolution of the dilemma and courted advice from all quarters. The intellectuals plumped for an idealized, classical interpretation; the politicians veered toward a more popular, historical, and realistic rendition. Edward Everett compared Greenough's task and responsibility to that of Phidias in the creation of his "Olympian Jupiter, the object of general worship of all Greece."[16] He counseled Greenough, "Have that immortal work ever before your mind. It will deserve your profound consideration whether you will not have your Washington seated. I like the Jupiter, and as near colossal as modern taste permits. . . . The vastness of the hall . . . and the absence of other furniture will require you to go to the utmost limit of size. . . . The rotunda is so lofty . . . I want a colossal figure."[17] On another occasion, Everett counseled more moderately, "Your Washington must after all be the statue of a man and in dimension, as in all other things, the truth of nature . . . must not be departed from."[18]

In regard to Washington's costume, Everett vacillated between his personal preference for the classical and the manifest necessity of accommodation to popular taste which favored contemporary dress. At the outset, he observed, "What artist who had a grain of taste would submit to make Washington in the old contemporary uniform, his weary boots and clubbed hair and a three-cornered hat. Canova boldly defied the popular prejudice . . . Chantrey compromised the matter by resorting to mantles, cloaks, gowns, etc."[19]

After sounding prevailing opinion, however, Everett proceeded to hedge. He wrote Greenough that he feared the "Washington's shock to the prejudices of those for whose edification the work is made. A figure as naked as your Washington appears to our people just as an Apollo would be to the Ancient Grecians if draped in Persian Pantaloons." Mustering evidence to justify his about-face, he added, "It appears from a letter of Jefferson, that Washington, himself, expressed a decided preference of the modern costume for his own statue."[20] Everett's sly corralling of Jeffersonian precedent to bolster his retreat conveyed a note of desperation. At this point, he was convinced that a classical interpretation would fail at home and would frustrate his ambitions for Greenough's success. He elucidated, "I want you to make a popular, as well as a good Statue of Washington; because I want to have you employed to execute a series of Presidential Statues to adorn the Rotunda."[21] He shifted ground once again, suiting his own predilection for the classical and later shed his misgivings to defend unreservedly Greenough's portrayal when it appeared.

Cooper, too, favored a modified classical costume. "Of course, your costume will be elysian," he ventured in reply to his friend's query, "as to prevent us from thinking of tailors and breeches."[22]

After comprehensive consideration, Greenough decided upon a classical representation of George Washington. It conformed to his intellectual orientation and training and it suited his taste. He refused to single out one distinctive characteristic of Washington for portrayal and was thus forced to forego the technique of naturalism which he had imbibed from Bartolini. In a personal letter Greenough disclosed that he chose to "address himself to a distant posterity" by creating a timeless "poetical abstract" of Washington's whole career.[23] He wrote that since the statue was "intended to fill a central position in the Capitol of the United States," it would be appropriately majestic. He explained that his interpretation of Washington "as a conductor between God and Man," godlike but not celestial, human yet heroic, would allow him to effect the Greek ideal of sublimity.[24] He elaborated, "I have made him seated as first magistrate and he extends with his left hand the emblem of his military command toward the people as the sovereign. He points heavenward with his right hand. By this double gesture, my wish was to convey the idea of an entire abnegation of self."[25]

The symbolism for the entire monument was intricate. Every single item had allegorical reference in the classical lexicon. Greenough explained the various devices incorporated in the monument in a letter to Lady Lytton Bulwer:

> Though the Presidential chair is very like any other chair, I have thought it my duty to make that on which Washington is seated mean something with reference to the country. It is appointed with acanthos and garlands of flowers, while the body is solid and massive.

By this I mean to hint at high cultivation as the proper finish for sound government and to say that man when well planted and well tilled must flower as well as grow.

By the figure of Columbus on the left side, I wished to connect our history with that of Europe. By that of the Indian Chief on the right to show what state our country was in when civilization first raised her standard there. The bas relief . . . on the left side, I have represented the Genii of North and South America under the forms of the infants Hercules and Iphictus—the latter shrinking in dread while the former struggles successfully with the obstacles and dangers of an incipient political existence.[26]

Greenough thus projected an inordinately abstruse, ambitious, and complex undertaking. The dilemma in which it was caught was intrinsic, fating the work to failure. The style was Italian, the symbolism, classical, both elements inapplicable to the historical American theme. The statue was guaranteed from its inception to elude popular comprehension, yet it was intended for placement at the cynosure of the national scene.

Aware of the statue's significance and conscious of its unique, precedential character at home, Greenough applied himself to its execution unsparingly for eight years. At each stage of the execution, he was to withstand challenging criticisms at home, which were counterbalanced by the constant encouragement of his sophisticated friends. From time to time he became apprehensive about the reception the statue would receive at home. He wrote Lady Bulwer, "The Italians have been indulgent in their opinion of the sort, but I am not the less anxious of its fate in my own country. Here it has been like an opera of which they do not understand or see the words. . . . There it will be the words that are thoroughly examined, for of music they have less knowledge."[27]

It took Greenough two years of application to complete the drawings for the design. When they arrived in Washington the secretary of state, Louis M. Lane, feeling unsure to judge their merit, invited Washington Allston to consult with him on changes suggested by President Jackson. Illness, which might have been more diplomatic than physical, prevented Allston from traveling to Washington, whereupon Leonard Jarvis agreed to pursue the matter for the administration. He wrote Allston bluntly, summarizing popular attitudes and Congressional sentiment on the subject: "Greenough's design does not satisfy me. He has undertaken to idealize Washington and to make an emblemical Statue. It is not *our* Washington that he has represented. He has evidently taken the ideal of his Statue from that of Jupiter . . . As a work of art the design is worthy of praise. . . . But I object to the absence of drapery on the upper part of the figure. . . ."[28]

Allston conferred in Cambridge with both Edmund and Richard Henry Dana, who conceded to the objections so far as to join in taking exception to the "inappropriateness of the raised arm" and "the idealizing of Washington."[29] The Danas argued loyally that "competent judges" in Boston, with whom Allston talked seemed to be "pretty nearly balanced on the subject of the costume . . . as many preferring the ancient as the modern."[30] Allston concluded his ambiguous reply to Jarvis' inquiry, acceding weakly to the argument. "The character of the *man* is, and should be the principal."[31] The classicists at home fought to stand their ground with Greenough against the artistic Philistines. No one would commit himself definitely either for the classical or the more popular treatment. The final decision reverted to Greenough, who held uncompromisingly to the classical conception.

Like Everett and Cooper, Charles Sumner, a personal acquaintance of Greenough from the Florentine winter of 1838–1839 when the *Washington* was nearing completion, interested himself in the problem and made numerous suggestions Sumner wrote Morse that he was most favorably impressed with Greenough's "remarkable character," his "practical knowledge of his art, and the poetry of it," his "elevated tone of mind," and "all his conversation."[32] He described the *Washington* as "truly great,"[33] although he cautioned Greenough to "keep clear of debatable ground."[34] Sumner foresaw that Americans, ill-educated in art, would not hesitate to criticize and consequently make inevitable "a disagreeable ordeal." Pursuing his crystal gazing, he prophesied cannily, "Some will, perhaps, complain that Washington is naked, that he is not standing, etc. These loungers in the Rotunda . . . many never before having seen a statue in marble—will want the necessary knowledge to enable them to appreciate your Washington."[35] He concluded his advice with an astute, practical suggestion which Greenough should have taken seriously. "You should prepare them," Sumner cautioned. "Publish some of the papers you read me during my visit to Florence—particularly that on the Nude; for there, I think, you will encounter a deal of squeamish criticism. It will give you fame."[36]

Sumner served Greenough further in discussing at great length a variety of ideas for the accessories of the *Washington* statue. Greenough ranged through the gamut of prosaic American themes for the subsidiary figures in his monument, which he tested on Sumner, for example Columbus versus the Negro; the Indian versus Virgin America; Columbus versus the Indian, and so on. There was much comment back and forth. Sumner consistently selected severely classical representations, such as symbols for Commerce and Agriculture. Of the accessories, he wrote that he "would have all pure, harmonious, classical," resorting as "much as possible to the actual antique."[37]

Greenough thought to cushion hostility to classicism by introducing a more characteristic American subject for a subordinate theme, like that of a "girl spinning, emblematic of manufactures," which he would execute in classical style for the sake of unity.[38] But Sumner stood firm: although the girl was "very pretty," he was still partial to the classical figures of Ceres and Neptune.[39] He approved Greenough's sketches of "the strangling of the serpent, the rising of the Sun, and the bird of Jove," the first two of these being incorporated in the monument. As for the chair, Greenough settled on a massive one as symbolizing the solidity of the nation.[40] He then selected figures of Columbus and an Indian with which to flank his seated *Washington*, of a size so diminutive by contrast with the colossal central one as to become adumbrated.

Despite the discord on the subject in Washington, Greenough's design was approved by the secretary of state, acting for the president, and the green light was beamed across the ocean. As the face was directed to be made "after Houdon," it was imperative for Greenough to obtain a copy of the illustrious bust. Delays of work and lack of solid cash detained him in Florence for two years before he could go to Paris "to secure a cast of the [Houdon] model of Washington which [was] in General Lafayette's possession."[41] Greenough left Florence in mid-August 1834 for a brief visit to Paris. The arrangement to borrow Lafayette's bust miscarried, and Greenough reported to his brother Henry that although the search for another cast of Houdon's work was a matter of "the greatest difficulty," he found "what would serve" at Fontainebleau.[42]

The principal business at hand accomplished, he saw to the printing of a reproduction of his own bust of Lafayette and indulged in the purchase of "a lot of books, Latin, Spanish, etc."[43] He also found time to call on Dominique Ingres, who had just been appointed to succeed Horace Vernet as director of the French Academy at Rome. Although he attended the Théâtre Français with "lasting pleasure," Paris had changed essentially for him.[44] Neither Morse nor Cooper was present. "You can't think how flat Paris is," he wrote. "I find the society in which I lived when here before threw a charm over everything. The very Louvre seems mediocre and [the] Luxembourg makes me laugh—that ever I should have thought so highly of it."[45] Confirmed in his impression that "the French are not a people of *genius in art*," but only "slaves of fashion," his leave-taking of Paris on September 6 tugged at no heart strings and Florence positively beckoned.[46] He wrote Morse almost defiantly:

> There is more beauty and more art in Florence than in Paris in spite of all this show. I shall return to Florence with an unwillingness to leave it again but for my own home. I prefer the Italians with all their faults to any other people. I thank God I've seen people that can beat them all hollow at cheating. . . . I want to get back to my own nest—my own clay—and my own hammer.[47]

He did not speed home quite as rapidly as before, taking the time now for a detour with his traveling companion, Jonathan Mason, to explore the art treasures and sights of Milan and Venice which he had not yet seen. On his return home he found the *Washington* intact with all its problems, with which he was to wrestle until the statue's completion at the end of 1840. Numerous technical difficulties accrued from its colossal size and bulk. Greenough had taken soundings in advance on this score too with Cooper, Morse, and Edward Everett. Cooper and Morse had been opposed at the outset to the colossal, considering twelve feet as too large. Their preference had run to some modified enlargement of the natural figure, ranging from about nine to nine and a half feet. Everett had consistently championed the colossal, while Greenough agreed, his proportions running from twelve to fifteen feet as most suitable to express the majesty of the subject and sufficiently eye-filling for the center of the lofty Rotunda. When finished in marble, the statue weighed "somewhat under 20 tons"; it stood ten feet, six inches high, was the same length, and measured six feet, six inches in width.[48] Greenough found it necessary to lease a special studio in Florence and have it enlarged to receive the statue for its completion, after its blocking at Carrara. Transporting the statue from the quarry to the studio took eleven yoke of cattle and fifteen men and cost over $300.

A Congressional Resolution of May 27, 1840, directed "that the Secretary of the Navy be authorized and instructed to take measures for the importation and erection of the statue of Washington by Greenough."[49] Accordingly, the secretary of the navy directed Commodore Isaac Hull, commanding the Mediterranean station, to "furnish any aid and assistance Mr. Greenough may deem necessary."[50] The navy sloop *Preble* was sent to Leghorn on this mission, but it was quickly discovered that its hatches were inadequate. After irksome delay, the commodore, having received authorization to charter a mercantile vessel, found the merchant ship *Sea* at Marseilles with Captain Delano in command. The *Preble*, commanded by Captain Voorhees, was ordered to stand by and assist. The contract that was executed on April 23, 1841, gave the captain the privilege of touching at one or more ports in the Mediterranean to complete his cargo; after which he was allowed to discharge such cargo at any port in the United States north of Norfolk, Virginia, before landing the statue at the Washington Navy Yard. The original price of $5,000, exclusive of other cargo, was thus cut to $3,500. To this price would be added the cost of any postvoyage restoration in the *Sea*, plus reimbursement for any labor beyond fifteen days for the loading and landing.

Greenough was outraged by the proviso to include other cargo with his statue and protested vigorously to Washington, going so far as to offer personally to make up the $1,500 deficit in order to insure utmost safety for "the flower of [his] freshest days."[51] Not hearing from Washington in time and anxious to guarantee a direct and secure voyage, he advanced the difference, which he later recovered from the government.

Further delay in shipment was occasioned by Greenough's insistence on awaiting the return to Florence of the engineer Misuri, who was the only person to whose skill and experience he would entrust the movement of the statue. The trip overland to Leghorn was tedious and heavily damaging to the trees along the narrow road.[52] Greenough followed to witness the loading and to dispatch his detailed instructions for its placement, elevation, lighting, pedestal, and so on at its destination. The *Sea* sailed from Leghorn June 8 and arrived in Washington on July 31. Thirteen days later, on August 13, the statue was unloaded at the Washington Navy Yard.

Although Greenough's out-of-pocket disbursement in the execution exceeded $10,000, for which he billed the government, the figure did not disclose hidden expenses, as reflected in increments in his style of living. No longer an obscure artistic aspirant, he was now the executor of a national monument of paramount importance. "My position has increased my private disbursements to a degree that would have made it impossible for me to fulfill my contract," he wrote, "had I not possessed other means than those furnished by the contract itself."[53] The sum was not unreasonable in view of the extenuating circumstances attending a colossal statue, "in which, indeed, the expenditure increased in geometrical ratio with the increase of weight."[54] Moreover, justified Greenough, "great as has been the expense, . . . there is scarce an item in the account which is not 50% lower than the work or the article charged could have been had in the U.S."[55] On September 9, 1841, Congress appropriated $8,000 to pay Greenough's itemized bill for expenses and cover the cost of an iron railing to protect the statue.

On the same day, Congress authorized the expenditure of $6,500 to pay for the voyage of the *Sea*. Actually, the cost came to $7,700, including freight and demurrage. An additional $5,000 was required immediately to transport the statue from the navy yard, place it in the Capitol, and provide it with a marble pedestal. A further unforeseen complication developed when the statue was placed in the center of the rotunda. The floor began to give way, requiring reinforcement with concrete piles built up from below and adding another $2,000 to the cost.

Greenough's presence in Washington was desirable to handle the problems attending proper elevation and lighting of the statue. Again, there were delays before his departure in June 1842. Then, in celebration of the end of the long period of concentrated labor, he spent a summer's holiday of three months in Paris. Once more he protested that he found Paris "a thorough trial" due to "the hurry and rush of business—the overwhelming interest of politics—the ten thousand clever and amusing nothings in the shape of theatrical entertainments . . . [which] leave but little taste or disposition in the public for the quiet and proper appreciation of art."[56] Sailing from Le Havre on the ship *Emerald*, he arrived in New York October 22, 1842. He stayed a few days before going to Boston for a reunion with his family and friends.

By the first of December, he was settled in rooms taken for the season in Washington. He plunged directly into his dual business. His attempts to clear up his financial differences with the government took him immediately to the office of the secretary of state, where he dealt amicably if unsuccessfully with Daniel Webster.

Greenough then turned to the problem of lighting the Washington, which was sitting in the dim center of the vast rotunda as if "in a cave" even in broad daylight.[57] Greenough began experiments in lighting with flares and torches, at one time causing a fire with "lamps melting and exploding" and igniting the wooden casing that held them.[58] Emerson was one of the few witnesses to the fire and he tried to encourage Greenough in his trials, but the primitive methods of lighting in those pre-electrical days proved inadequate.

Conceding failure, Greenough petitioned Congress late in January for the removal of the statue to the ground in front of the western facade of the Capitol, to be covered by a temporary shelter until the treasury could provide for an appropriately elegant one. Emerson argued to retain the statue in the rotunda "in the worst light" rather than expose it outdoors, but Greenough insisted on the change. His request was approved on February 22 by the Joint Committee on the Library. The committee recommended "a position . . . in the green space in the eastern grounds lying directly in front of the main entrance to the rotunda, and between the two gravelled shaded walks leading eastward from the Capitol . . . [where] it will be at once accessible and conspicuous in harmony with the general plans of the grounds, and a source . . . of added beauty."[59] This change was not effected for yet another year. In August 1846 the wooden building sheltering the statue was removed and an iron railing was substituted for the statue's protection.

The dire prophecy of Charles Sumner came to pass. The statue was vituperatively assailed for all the conventional reasons: its nudity, its Roman drapery, its idealized conception, its seated posture. This popular reaction was epitomized some years later by a reviewer who charged "the extraordinary effigy of George Jupiter Washington" with the base fault of "utter confusion of ideas. Nobody can get from it any notion of Washington as he was."[60] Ex-Mayor Philip Hone of New York noted in his diary:

> It looks like a great herculean Warrier—like Venus of the bath, a grand Martial Magog—undraped, with a huge napkin lying on his lap and covering his lower extremities and he is preparing to perform his ablutions in the act of consigning his sword to the care of the attendant. . . . Washington was too prudent, and careful of his health, to expose himself thus in a climate so uncertain as ours, to say nothing of the indecency of such an exposure on which he was known to be exceedingly fastidious.[61]

The doughty Mrs. Trollope, although respecting Greenough's erudition and accomplishments and generally deeming the statue to be "noble," posited, "there is much about it that justifies this description."[62]

Edward Everett defended the monument "as one of the greatest works of sculpture of modern times." He extolled its "purity of taste, . . . loftiness of . . . conception, truth of character and . . . accuracy of anatomical study and mechanical skill."[63] He argued that if it had been found among the ruins of Rome, it would certainly have been placed in the Vatican Gallery or Tribune among the masterpieces of antiquity. On the other hand, had the dress been contemporary, it would have reflected "only mechanical imitation" rather than a creative production.[64] In Everett's view, the work had "dignity, afforded refined pleasure, and was timeless. It represented Washington in the aggregate of his qualities . . . of a whole life, not of any one moment."[65] As if to vindicate his own classicism, Everett evoked all the favorite neoclassical cliches, typical of the rhetorical cant of the day. It might have constituted poor art criticism, but the public relations were excellent.

Fortunately, Greenough's articulate friends could be mobilized to activate their pens as much in the cause of "art" as for educational and political reform or personal loyalty. Their active support could be assumed. While other eulogists composed the defense poetically, Alexander Everett, brother of Edward, did his stint, prosaically, yet unreservedly.[66] In a popular magazine published in June of 1844 he wrote, "Without pretensions to connoisseurship in the art of sculpture, Greenough's great work has surpassed my expectations, high as they were. It is truly sublime. The statue is of colossal grandeur. This magnificent production of genius does not seem to be appreciated at its full value in this metropolis."[67]

Once the *Washington* went outdoors, Greenough quickly realized his imprudence in having rushed at this makeshift solution to correct the problem of lighting. His perfectionism proved a snare. Possible as the statue was in the center of the rotunda, it was entirely inappropriate to its location out-of-doors, half-nude, exposed to summer sun and winter frost. In a desperate reach for a cure to this situation, he wrote to his old New England acquaintance, Robert Winthrop, who was presently the Superintendent of Buildings and Grounds of the Capitol.

> Had I been ordered to make a statue for any square or other similar situation at the Metropolis, I should have represented Washington on horse back and in his actual dress. I should have made my work purely a historical one. I have treated the subject poetically and I confess, I should feel pain at seeing it placed in direct and flagrant contrast with every day life. Moreover, I modelled the figure without reference to an exposure of rain or frost so that there are many parts of the statue where the water would collect and soon disintegrate and rot the stone if it did not, freezing, split off large fragments of the drapery, which indeed it would be almost sure to do. . . . I think it would perish in the open air.[68]

Greenough petitioned for a handsome colonnaded structure to be erected for the statue's protection, but the plea came to naught.

In 1905 there was a new superintendent and he recommended to the Joint Committee on the Library that the statue be moved indoors for protection against the ravages of weather. As predicted, the marble was chipping and breaking off because of the collection of water in the folds and joints. A low pedestal in the center of the rotunda was suggested, but previous failures there provided a conclusive deterrent to this plan. Three years and another $5,000 appropriation later, in response to the prodding of Professor Amateis of the National Art Society to avoid the onslaught of cold weather, the statue was relegated on November 21, 1908, to virtual storage space in the Smithsonian Institution, an ironical switch of fate indeed, in view of Greenough's intense dislike of the building. After costing the public an aggregate sum exceeding $50,000, this monument, which was never widely understood or popular in its time, was foredoomed.

The statue has now attained historical perspective. Retrieved in the spring of 1958, it was wedged into the head of the newly decorated Graphic Arts Room of the Smithsonian Institution. Now it is more appropriately lodged in the place of honor in the western corridor of the new Museum of History and Technology in Washington. There it looks very well in its position on the main floor leading to the major exhibition, "The Growth of America."

Head of Christ 1837, 21½″
Courtesy of the Fogg Art Museum, Harvard University

5

Prolific Years

ALONG WITH THE OPPORTUNITY TO PRODUCE A MASTERWORK, THE
Washington commission gave Greenough a national, even an international, reputation of distinction well before its execution. The very
recognition of his talent by the American Congress catapulted him
into a higher price category for choice privately commissioned compositions. He was freer than before from the necessity of the portrait
trade. He was also more attractive prey of the social lions and their
mates, both in residence and on tour.

The Anglo-Americans were still his mainstays for social relaxation, especially since the departure for home in June 1833, of
his brother Henry, who followed on the heels of Cole and Gore.
Complaining of loneliness and depression, Greenough took comfort
in his "constant companion," a fine English greyhound sent to him
at his own request by his brother Alfred as a model three summers
earlier.[1] It must have been a spirited charmer, for Greenough commenced a model of him. The execution lagged so long that in the
middle the dog died. There was some trouble about finding a replacement, as just at that time, the two other dogs of Greenough's acquaintance, those of Madame Catalani and the grand duke, followed
suit into oblivion. His pet's successor was a frolicking white greyhound that cost five dollars. Horatio credited him with "$55 worth
of pleasure."[2] The arrival of Arno filled the lonely gap at home for

Greenough and solved the problem of completing the statue. Edward Everett acquired the statue and displayed it in his library at Cambridge. It was admired by Colonel Perkins, who commissioned another statue of a dog. For Perkins, Greenough modeled a figure of a Saint Bernard that subsequently was placed on the family plot in the Mount Auburn Cemetery in Cambridge.

Greenough was now on friendly terms with Walter Savage Landor, the successful English writer to whose villa in Fiesole he often brought Emerson during his Florentine visit. The quiet exchange of ideas on these occasions initiated an increasing intimacy among the three men. Subsequently, Landor brought his English guests to the studio, broadening Greenough's contacts and enlarging his business potential. Greenough reported frequenting the home of another Englishman "who took the trouble of making his acquaintance," and that he soon was being received by Madame Murat, the widow of the ex-King of Naples.[3] He wrote that Madame Murat "receives every evening in a way which I think agreeable. There are commonly four or five rooms open; in one are card tables; in another billiards; in a third tea is served throughout the evening."[4] It took no great effort to acclimate to this aristocratic elegance. Greenough slid easily into identification with it, augmenting his own sense of luxurious living.

The pleasant round of diversions continued through the following season and thereafter without interruption, despite Greenough's continued protestations of preoccupation with work. He was participating zestfully and he reported the "carnival celebrations gayer than ever. I might have danced and frolicked to my heart's content if I had had a mind," he boasted to Henry. "I was at a masked ball at Countess Orloff's lately," he went on. "I was to have gone to another at the Anderson's tonight, but am fagged out, and must go to see Dr. Codman of Dorchester."[5] It created a stir when Madame Catalani came to his studio, but he soon grew accustomed to his acceptance into the higher echelons of society.

Although Greenough enjoyed both work and social events, the combination must have taxed him to the edge of exhaustion. Occasionally, he confided to his intimates that he had to struggle "to prevent melancholy from getting mastery over [him]."[6] If his health could stand the strain, the social life had uses beyond diversion. There was hope for practical advantages in getting around. For protection against the incursions of increasing numbers of visitors to his studio, "to the great interruption of [his] studies," he sought insurance for the privacy of his working hours by posting a notice on his door instituting regular visiting hours "in the summer after 6 o'clock P.M. and in the winter after 4 P.M."[7]

His *Washington* held the center of his stage of operation, but it was not preclusive of other work as he often claimed. While pondering the design, he modeled a bust of his friend Miles and supervised the cutting of those of Cooper and Lafayette. More important was his latest private commission from a Mr. Hoyt of New York, who desired two companion pieces to stand only two and a half feet high. Greenough's prices were still modest, $500 for the pair. Hitting quickly on the theme of the Genius of America for the first, he was modeling it within a month. For the second he decided to symbolize Italy.

Searching beyond the confines of the classical world for subjects, he began to explore the Bible at this time and came up with a study of David, "singing to Saul in his frenzy," representing "the crazy king, his noble son . . . the young poet and warrior."[8] In this group, he explained to Morse, he would attempt a study in contrast, "afford a variety of character and expression while the tender daughter will come in as a relief and fill the void which the absence of the petticoat interest makes us feel in all the works that address the heart."[9] There was no simplicity in Greenough. As in his *Washington* statue, his intellectuality embroidered everything. He overlaid each concept with a multiplicity of ideas, which extended his time schedules and accentuated the difficulty of expression. Frequently the execution of a work would be delayed for years. This was the fate of the *David*, which awaited reworking to completion for ten years.

The poetic concepts were displaced momentarily by a more practical matter that presented the prospect of earning 700 francesconi from the Perkins family of Boston, who ordered a group resembling the *Cherubs*. Fascinated by the notion of studies in contrast and in the mood for a religious subject, Greenough devised a subject coupling both themes. It has been called variously *The Ascension of the Infant Spirit*, the *Angel and Child*, and *The Infant and Cherub*.[10] He decided to "represent a young angelic figure conducting a babe to the other world. The points of expression," he said, "will be the contrast between the ideal forms and face of the cherub and the milky fatness [of the] baby, [the] half doubting, half pleased look of the child."[11] He was soon reporting with pride. "My journey to Heaven groupe is far advanced, I feel confident it will take quite as well as the former one."[12]

His optimism for this work of Italian style and form disposed him to overlook the problem of nudity that remained a liability at home. It reappeared like a recurrent plague, threatening to discredit his works and undermine his reputation. In the running contest, Greenough stood his ground stalwartly for the classical style, describing his triumph mischievously for Cooper.

> I make 'em both start naked. The conversation that passed between me and the gentleman who ordered the group was a scene. I fought hard and carried the day—the little fellows are to be provided with alabaster fig leaves which shall fall at a tap! of the hammers when the discerning public shall have digested the fruit of the knowledge of good and evil.[13]

When the work was completed in marble, it was received in Boston early in 1835 with accolades of praise. Washington Allston composed a sonnet in its honor. Deeply appreciative, Greenough commented, "Your verses were as far from being addressed to the mind of the many as my composition was from being adapted to their tastes." Wistfully, he added, "I have made up my mind to look for the approbation of a few."[14] Given his aesthetic bent, he had no choice but to innure his ego from the inevitable popular slings at home in favor of composing for his elite friends, who were all devout classicists as well as faithful supporters.

George S. Hillard wrote an extravagant review of this latest work.

> We hail with pride and pleasure this new proof of the genius of our countryman Greenough. . . . It equals the *Medora* in beauty and finish of execution and surpasses it in originality of conception. . . .

Angel and Child
1835, marble, life-size
Courtesy of the Museum
of Fine Arts, Boston

The cherub . . . is the purity of a divine essence . . . has that calm and pensive beauty. . . . It is a great merit in this group, that tells its own story so plainly . . . it speaks at once to the heart and soul of the natural man. . . . It is a fine poem in marble—an idea embodied in a material form. . . . [The] execution equals the conception.[15]

The glow of its reception by the cognoscenti was tempered for Greenough by some questions about its price that were posed by the Perkins family, probably after having learned through the grapevine about the sum that Gilmor had paid for the *Medora*. Greenough responded self-consciously. Feeling "under obligations to the Perkins family and . . . very unwilling to have the charge appear extortionate," he reduced his fee by $200, letting it stand at only $500, barely covering the cost of the marble and its cutting.[16]

Greenough's finances had attained a fair balance, and he could afford to indulge his pride. He had repaid Cooper's loan of 1,600 francs in May of 1833 and he had squared his account with Gilmor that July.

With the *Medora* gone in the spring of 1833, he proceeded to "put up an Achilles 7 feet high" to fill the gap and stave off his recurrent melancholia.[17] Greenough liked his colossal nude male figure, despite its "nailing him for the summer."[18] "He's a whacker," he wrote Cooper.[19] Emerson thought so too, having been attracted by both the artist and his work. "His face was so handsome and his person so well formed," affirmed Emerson about the sculptor. He went on to call him "A superior man, ardent and eloquent, [whose] opinions had elevation and magnanimity . . . an accurate and a deep man."[20] Emerson gave it out that the *Achilles* was an idealization of Greenough's figure, as the *Medora* had been of his face. Emerson's admiration of the artist's personality deepened a friendship which was to flower later on home ground. Emerson and Greenough shared ideals of public and personal freedom that brought them ever closer over the years.

Greenough's labors on his latest colossal statue were interrupted early that summer by a mild attack of smallpox that exacerbated his tendency toward melancholia. After rallying, he suffered a minor crisis. Thereafter, to stay relapses, he took regular exercise outdoors, long walks either alone or with colleagues, or riding horseback. Florence was ideally suited for these pastimes; the Cascine provided gorgeous walks, as did the bank of the Arno, and one could get to the lovely country beyond the city by horse in a few minutes.

The season of 1834–1835 reflected his growing fame. He was busier than ever. "I have made fifteen busts this winter," he informed Washington Allston.[21] Among these was one of his painter friend, the painter Francis Alexander, one of Madame Para, and another of the son of Mr. Griffith of New York, modeled the previous winter from a print and a mask. He completed this last one in marble by order of Colonel Thorn and made a copy for the family. With so many cash orders, Greenough's finances began to move toward security.

These bust commissions were a boon once more in the face of the government's constant delinquency in its payments for the *Washington* model, which was still in process. Yet Greenough continued to resent the menial labor upon busts, always preferring to spend his time more artistically.

Creative employment came in the form of an order from Mr. Sears of Boston for a cherub-like portrayal of his two children at play. Greenough's first sketch of the little daughter teaching her brother to read, was rejected for being too matter-of-fact. Sears wanted something of the whimsical touch which he had detected in the *Cherubs*. A satisfactory revision depicted "the daughter [with] a squirrel held by a string" while her younger "brother is trying to make it play about."[22] Once accepted, the artist rushed its execution, nearing the completion of the model in four months. This group was finished in marble at the close of 1837 and was received with delight by the family.

Sears Children 1835–1837, marble, life-size
Courtesy of the Massachusetts Historical Society

As if not to be outdone, friends of the Sears named Thomson, nabobs from Boston who were enjoying the social life of Florence for a spell, commissioned statues of their boys. They also requested a playful theme. Greenough hit upon the novel device of having the boys face each other with one "standing with a shuttlecock ready to let drive at his brother, who is standing ready for it."[23] This idea pleased Greenough "for the novelty and the expressive action," and his colleagues also approved the design.[24] The pair, completed in marble in the summer of 1837, turned out most successfully, fulfilling the family's expectations as well as the artist's. Shortly afterwards, an order was placed for a bust of Colonel Thomson himself.

Desiring a change in subject from children at play, before the year was out Greenough was "finishing his figure of *Love Captive*," an idealized young boy which he had contrived years earlier from a sonnet of Petrarch in *Trifono Della Castita*.[25] He sought to depict a "Goddess chained to a rock where a bird of wisdom (symbolic of Minerva) stands sentinel—hands crossed behind [signifying] helplessness. [In the] face mingle lurking mischief with shame."[26] The goddess of love was prisoner to wisdom, with his feet chained to earth, inhibiting flight into happiness. Surely there was some element here of self-justification for his own Victorian comportment as a thirty-one-year-old bachelor. The statue was changed into a representation of Cupid. Characteristically, Greenough proceeded to overburden the conception which was not too simple to begin with. Elaborating on the theme to Washington Allston, Greenough averred, "I have tried to represent that twisting impatience which a boy manifests at restraint in his form and an expression of treachery and mischief in his face."[27] Perhaps he hoped to deflect attention from the unmistakable romantic note that he had struck in an earlier version. It is no wonder that this complex composition was never commissioned. Not only were the intrinsic contradictions difficult to render, but Greenough's circumstances were rapidly altered. Within another year, he would be married.

Meanwhile, the focus of his attention was directed to Washington, where there was continuous discussion throughout the spring of 1836 on the feasibility of commissioning "two groups of statues to complete the ornaments on the east front of the Capitol."[28] The representatives vacillated in their choice of sculptor, leaning at first in the direction of Luigi Persico, who had already executed the central pediment of the eastern front of the Capitol and completed his model of the *Columbus* group, which one protagonist in the debate called "one of the happiest, noblest, grandest, conceptions of genius."[29] If the language was hyperbolic, the message was effective propaganda. Persico's reputation was enhanced by the arrival in December 1834 of his *War* and *Peace* figures from Italy, where they had been cut. As with the *Washington* commission, Greenough's powerful political friends pressed for the choice of an American. It was urged that Greenough be given the opportunity to submit a design; that he be selected in preference also to Hiram Powers who still lacked Greenough's Italian training and experience.

Magnetized by the dual goals of greater fame and remuneration, Greenough thought it politic to attend to this business personally and planned a trip to Washington. He had spoken hopefully of such a trip home for several years. But delay followed delay. In the spring of 1833, he had speculated optimistically to Cooper, that "five months more will see me free of all small jobs. . . . I had . . . made all preparations for decamping myself but was prevented."[30] His commissions, the impetuous, unplanned *Achilles*, and his shortage of cash were all contributing factors to his procrastination. Now the incentive was overpowering, and his finances were solvent. In March, he wrote his brother, Henry, "I have plans of great moment, which depend partly on my getting there when Congress is sitting. He cautioned his family that he was bent on business. "I come home not to lionize," he wrote, "but to work and attend to my own affairs."[31]

By April he was in Paris, and he arrived in New York early in June "in fine health and spirits" by all accounts.[32] Despite his father's grave illness, Greenough declined all side trips. He was bound directly for Washington. He stayed in New York only long enough to renew his slight acquaintance with Vanderlyn and see something of the other painters, especially his old friend Morse who awaited him cordially. They reminisced sentimentally on their good times together in Paris, recalling how one solemn evening there huddled in their cold, fireless room five years earlier, they had mutually pledged "In the year 1833, S. F. B. Morse and H. Greenough will be in the city of New York decidedly the merriest and the best fellows in the place."[33] Now, three years behind schedule, they enjoyed a curtailed reunion, which, though friendly enough, lacked the spirit of gay fellowship and intimacy of the earlier days. Time had sobered both young men. A similar estrangement occurred in his relations with Cooper. Greenough's long planned trip to Cooperstown, deferred until the business in Washington could be completed and his family in Boston visited, failed to materialize. He never saw Cooper again.

The mission to Washington produced no immediate reward. Hobnobbing with the influential Congressional leaders might have brought results during that session if continued a bit longer, but another illness struck that debilitated him. The climax of ill-luck arrived with the fatal turn of his father's health. Greenough rushed home, and fortunately found his father still able to converse, cheerful with his family gathered around. Greenough reported that his father died peacefully July 27. As might be expected from the anticlericalism he acquired among the liberals in Florence, Greenough vented his spleen on the officiating clergyman, whose "duty it was to console the family," but instead, employed "mannered jargon . . . helter-skelter quotations from the Old and New Testament to prove [the family] should rejoice in the event."[34]

There was, however, little time for grieving. The family estate, which "proved a very valuable one," required settling, especially in behalf of the female members.[35] David Greenough had been a major real estate dealer, the only one in Cambridge. A few years before his death, he had sold $13,000 worth of the Washington gardens to a Masonic Lodge" and proceeded to build "at the corner of Sumner and Washington Streets" in the heart of the business section of Boston.[36] This represented enterprise of considerable size. Greenough was pleased to inform Cooper of this sharp upswing in his financial affairs. He declared himself to be "in a very prosperous state."[37]

The next two months passed in a constant flurry of modeling portrait busts for execution in marble on his return to Italy. Among these was one of Carlo Botta, the historian, "of which the Marquis Capponi is to have one copy and Niccolini the poet another," Greenough reported later. Mrs. Samuel Appleton was memorialized this way at the request of her niece, and Mr. Thomas, of Baltimore, at his own.

Mr. Thomas also commissioned an ideal figure, for which Greenough selected a head of *Heloise*, based on Alexander Pope's characterization. Of Heloise "two marbles are to be wrought," reported Greenough, "one for Baltimore, and one for Philadelphia."[38]

Conditioned by his residence in Florence and regular talks with Greenough, Mr. Frances Calley Gray, another Boston patron, ordered an idealized head of *Psyche* and "a copy of young Augustus, of Roman days who lodges in the Vatican sculpture galleries."[39] Another pair of statuettes, only two feet high, was commissioned by a Bostonian named Halsey. He also asked for a copy of the statue of Aristides which was found at Herculaneum and taken to the Royal Bourbon Museum at Naples, where it was much admired by Cooper in 1829 and commended to his disciple for study. Greenough had made the model at that time and now had it cast.[40] The companion piece requested by Halsey was to be a Washington in modern dress.

Greenough must have worked with inordinate speed for he was squared away for departure in two months' time. Leaving his brothers to manage the estate, Horatio prepared to resume hammer and chisel, "more convinced than ever that there's no place for an artist like his

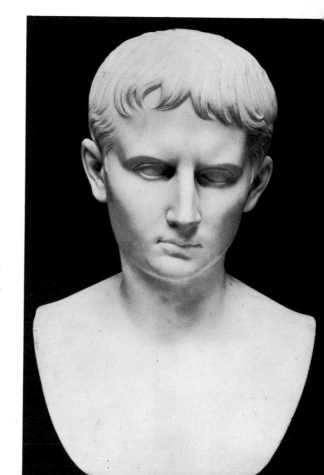

Young Augustus
c. 1836, life-size
Courtesy of the Museum of Fine Arts, Boston

own studio."[41] Accompanied by his eldest sister, Louisa, whose precarious health required relief from the dreary cold of a New England winter, he left for New York at the end of September and embarked on October 10 for England. His reunion there a month later with his older brother John was more than cordial. For some months they explored London together, studying especially its architecture, which they found handsome. They also toured the historic sites and the splendid country homes and enjoyed the scenery in the vicinity. Their explorations contributed to crystallizing Greenough's aesthetical criticism.

Horatio returned with Louisa to Florence toward the end of the winter, guilt-ridden over his protracted absence. With a burst of vigor, he attacked the execution in marble of the commissions that he had gathered, and in a few short months he was able to report their completion to his family. A prodigious number of pieces was represented in the lot, five portrait busts, three ideal ones, and two statuettes, and all were paid for. As the marble cutting was now routinely left to the skilled artisans, the system thoroughly suited Greenough's predilection for speed in production.

He decided now to try his hand at an ideal portrayal of an essentially Catholic subject, that of Jesus Christ. Although commonplace in Italy and in the European artistic tradition, it was an iconoclastic act for an American Protestant. But Greenough was free of native prejudice and reinforced by his liberal anticlericalism. With full realization of the unconventionality of this step, he wrote in justification:

> I am not aware that any American, has until now, risked the placing before his countrymen a representation of our Saviour. The strong prejudice, or rather, conviction of the Protestant mind has, perhaps, deterred many . . . [and] deprecates the abuse of images in places of public worship. I think nevertheless, that the person and face of Our Saviour is a legitimate subject of art . . . as a fervent aspiration after the good and beautiful.[42]

Although artistically valid, Greenough's logic failed to allay the bias of his predominantly Protestant clientele despite their European cultural proclivities. With Christ's head, slightly larger than life-size, "fixed upon a coiled serpent, whose head is bowed in front," obviously to signify Christianity's triumph over the forces of evil, Greenough attained an effect scarcely at variance with Canova's.[43] It was, indeed a perfect subject in conformity with the grand style as decreed by Winckelmann. As Henry Tuckerman interpolated the work, the sculptor wanted to portray an expression of profound calm; to achieve "a sublimity of effect . . . a serenity . . . of conscious power tempered with a touching benignity . . . at once holy, pure and majestic," in a style at once "chaste and noble."[44] Tuckerman understood the composition perfectly. In view of its modish form, it seems strange that this rather pleasing neoclassical composition remained in the studio almost a decade before a couple of marble copies were commissioned.[45]

The summer of 1837 saw a marked change in Greenough's life. For once, he indulged himself in a ten day holiday. To escape the worst of the heat of Florence, he sought "the finest air and scenery of Italy" in the verdant mountainous fairyland which is Bagni di Lucca.[46] There, he mingled with families like the Demidovs and the Bacciochis who summered there. It was the chic summer spot also for the expatriated intellectuals who resided in Rome and Florence.

His artistic colleagues being absent, he found relaxation in the war tales, horse talk, and otherwise sophisticated conversation of Colonel Sisted, who some years before had been head groom in the stables of the duke of Lucca. Having fought with Wellington at Waterloo, Sisted had been elevated by the eccentric duke to ennoblement, riches, and the position of intimate friend and advisor. Greenough could associate freely with the native social leaders not only because of his artistic station and genteel background, but even more because of his cultivation and fluency in both French and Italian.

With his reputation and finances on the upswing, there were no practical considerations now against marrying. He could not be expected to remain a bachelor. His growing success must have been mirrored in an optimistic mood, enhancing his normal ebullience and native powers of attraction. Ralph Waldo Emerson had said that Greenough possessed the face of a *Medora* and the figure of an *Achilles* and that he was a witty and intellectual conversationalist. There was no dissent to this eloquent appraisal of Greenough among the Anglo-American expatriates.

Moreover, his living standards now reflected his prosperity. He had added to his studio a regular shop where the carpenter's work could be done, eliminating the constant hammering from his living quarters. He had written to Henry that he had acquired a carriage and a fine horse, which he "bought cheap, and another which matches him for the ladies, who go trundling around the Cascine to their great satisfaction." He added: "I drive them myself on Sundays. The two, with the man who takes care of them, stand me somewhat short of a dollar a day, which, I think cheap for a luxury which insures me two hours' amusement per diem."[47] By this time he had also acquired a more relaxed attitude, allowing himself two hours daily for diversion and exercise.

He had long since been disposed to marriage. Years earlier, he had at once jokingly and seriously implored Morse, then contemplating his return to America, to "Pray, advertise for me when you get there.—Wanted a young woman of knowledge without being aware of it—very humble at finding herself proud—a blonde and inclining to the petite—not slothful . . . [with] fervent spirit. . . ."[48]

He was drawn to these qualities upon meeting Louisa Gore that summer in Florence. She was an old acquaintance from his own Boston set who was traveling with her mother in Europe.[49] Charles Sumner spoke of her literary interests and shared her admiration for Wordsworth. An intimate friend of Edward Everett, who found her "a charming lady, with a little more warmth and tenderness than propriety admits on daily intercourse . . . [possessing an] angelic temper," she immediately interested Horatio seriously.[50] She was nineteen, youthful and attractive.

After a brief courtship, Greenough declared his intention to marry Louisa. By way of preparation, he quickly found a thirteen room apartment in Palazzo Bacciochi, which he described as both spacious and "very compact." This belonged to Marquis Bacciochi, a descendant of the Corsican officer who married Napoleon's sister Elisa and became Prince of Lucca and Piombino. The house was situated on Via Borgo Pinti, in the center of town, some five or six blocks from the Duomo, almost directly behind the Pergola which its garden faced. "I shall move into it about the first of October," he informed his brother, "and be married to Miss Gore, I trust, by the 15th."[51] Arrangements were in the charge of his friend Richard Henry Wilde, a lawyer who had turned to poetry and was then living in Florence in retirement from a political career. The marriage contract was drawn in Italian, but they were wed by an English clergyman at the request of the bride. It was a happy union despite her ailing health in the beginning, which resulted in childlessness for eight years.

Greenough's life at thirty-two was now rounded. "The prospect of a pleasant evening circle," he declared, "carries me through the toils of the day."[52] His social life also received added impetus as befitted a newly married man. Friends called upon them to greet the bride and these visits had to be returned. The popularity of Florence itself was growing with the Americans, a trend which swelled their circle of acquaintances naturally. The Cabots were present that fall, when Horatio made a bust of "Madame." No sooner had these friends moved on to Rome when the Warrens of Boston came to Florence for a couple of months to occupy themselves "agreeably."[53] The available pastimes attracted everyone who thus shared "la vita far niente," a novel experience for the Yankees. One slid painlessly into

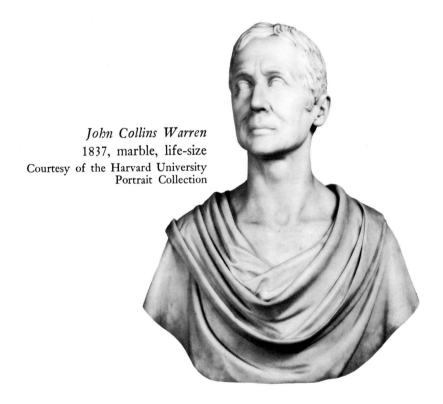

John Collins Warren
1837, marble, life-size
Courtesy of the Harvard University
Portrait Collection

the routine. The Warrens were a distinguished family. Dr. John Collins Warren gained fame for being one of the first to perform an operation in the United States upon an anaesthetized patient.[54] The physician ordered a bust of his father for the family and a medallion for his mother. The bust turned out so well that Dr. Warren was persuaded to sit for his own bust.[55]

The critic Henry T. Tuckerman joined the group that season, and John Gibson, the renowned English sculptor, sought refuge there from the cholera epidemic in Rome. Gibson was bent on seeing Marquis Capponi's collection of beautiful drawings by Sabatelli, and Greenough arranged this. Greenough received the visitors and served them all in countless ways. Occasionally a commission resulted, but usually Greenough's acquaintances merely provided companionship and a social outlet for Louisa

Hiram Powers arrived with his family during the winter of 1837 and was greeted by Greenough with characteristic cordiality, recalling their previous meetings in Washington and Boston. Overlooking the implicit potentiality of Powers' rivalry, Greenough had encouraged Powers to choose Florence over Rome because of its lower costs and artistic superiority. Ensconced in first position among foreign sculptors in Florence, Greenough could easily afford this degree of generosity. How keenly he perceived Powers' character is revealed in his offhand remark to his brother Henry, "The east wind has dealt hardly with 'honest Jack.' "[56] Out of the uncultured, poverty-ridden frontier "Honest Jack" was a simple man, admirably fired with ambition, and endowed with a mechanical rather than creative turn of mind. He could hardly have kept pace with Greenough's ranging interests. Powers' forte was accuracy in busts. With just a few exceptions, Greenough denigrated the busts for their lack of creativity or challenge although he admired Powers' technical ingenuity.

Shortly after his arrival, Powers gave Greenough some of the American clay that he had found while working in Washington and judged far superior to anything in use in Italy. Greenough experimented with it forthwith in an ideal head and announced ebulliently "at four paces' distance you would pronounce it a highly wrought marble, such is the degree of finish of which it is susceptible."[57] Greenough encouraged Powers to devise a new plaster of paris that would eliminate the initial step of modeling in clay. When Powers attempted the construction of an improved machine to block and carve more efficiently, Greenough encouraged him with abounding interest. In the spring he sat to Powers for a bust which Greenough pronounced "admirable." He grew to like "honest Jack" and esteemed his talent in portraiture.

Although he had his hands full of work on the *Washington* monument and the numerous busts, Greenough now received the unexpected dividend from his last trip to the capital, Congress' award of a second major commission. It was for a group that would adorn the east front blocking of the entrance to the Capitol. This work evolved over a period of thirteen years into the *Rescue Group*. As it did not befit a good Puritan to trumpet his windfall, he broke it ever so blandly to his family at Boston, writing, "You will perhaps have seen in the papers that I accept the new order which the President has offered me."[58] A couple of years passed before Greenough even considered the theme for this work and many more before his ideas jelled into a unified concept.

He was concentrating on his *Washington*, disrupting the work only for cash orders from glamorous personages whom he could not refuse. He would not make a bust for less than "one hundred napoleons" and declared he didn't care if he never had another portrait commission.[59] He often deferred work on these in preference to his more creative ideal subjects. The year of 1838 seemed to him his "most productive," and he asserted that "no man since Canova has undertaken more."[60]

He was overburdened with work in spite of his advanced prices, and this bread and butter stuff had become anathema to him. The portraits diverted his attention from the creative compositions, which required time for reflection and application. He confided to Washington Allston his grim "determination . . . hereafter [to] make fewer works and spend more time in preparing them."[61] His tendency toward selectivity was pronounced socially too. There was no longer any need for him to curry favor for potential business.

While his marital state brought "new cares and the increase of old ones," he was living comfortably but felt pinched for time.[62] He vowed to "set [his] face against promiscuous society in this country,—

a society of which some vapid Yankees, who pass a month or two perhaps, are sure to be enamoured." He now looked to a "proud and savage concentration" on work as being "sometimes necessary."[63] To minimize his social entanglements and escape from ready availability to touring Yankees on holiday, he moved his residence late in 1838 out of the center of town. Two miles from the studio, the new home was in Casa Lablanc on Via Bardi across the Arno just beyond the Ponte Vecchio. The distance did not isolate him but did provide him with the desired insulation. Moreover, he appreciated the exercise of walking to and from the studio each day, ascribing to it his good health. It was in his studio at the center that his energies were concentrated. He increasingly resented being "obliged to be civil to persons of respectability, for *definite objects*."[64]

The move increased the privacy of his family life into which he enjoyed including his intimate friends. He had not turned recluse or misanthrope and he reassured his brother Henry on this score. "I see a few friends in my own house and am rarely without a visitor in the evening," he wrote.[65] He still reveled in the thoughtful conversation permitted by a limited number of guests, but he disliked even more intensely the banalities imposed by the larger scale entertainments that epitomized Italian society.

Greenough made a fine bust at this time of a friend, Marquis Gino Capponi. Capponi was an intellectual engaged in the political leadership of the Risorgimento, and he was to become prime minister of the short-lived Florentine Republic. Through tomes of correspondence, he maintained legions of contacts abroad, including some of the outstanding members of the Boston intelligentsia, such as George Ticknor and Ralph Waldo Emerson. Capponi was joined by his daughters in admiring Greenough's work, especially the *Washington* model, and he yielded to their prompting to have Greenough make them a miniature copy. With this gesture, the Capponis could at once commemorate their favorite American statesman and national founder, the vaunted Republican prototype for Florentine and other Italian liberals, and show their esteem of Greenough's own talent. This acquaintance blossomed over the years through unforgettable "conversazioni" into an intimate friendship.

At Capponi's, Greenough again broadened his connections in

the foreign set, which led to additional commissions. Outstanding in this group were Lord Holland, the Ruspoli family, Count Seristori, Colonel Sisted, the chamberlain of the duke of Lucca, and several celebrated writers of various nationalities. Court Mournieff and his family became household "staples."[66] Greenough was made to feel at home by this Russian nobleman, whose entertainments were frequent and sumptuous. One evening Greenough "entered the lists" to defend America from a "most unseemly diatribe" launched by a Russian diplomat, Count Galoskin, who thought England superior. The colloquy ended in triumph for Greenough who had the count "quoting De Tocqueville and eulogizing Washington."[67] Mournieff's interests were primarily literary, and at the time he was helping a bookseller to prepare a new edition of the works of Channing, the American Unitarian minister, for which they wanted a good portrait by Greenough. As none could be had from America, Mournieff elicited a bust by Greenough to be fashioned from an available photograph.

The Greenoughs attended receptions at the homes of Lord Fox, the British minister, the banker Fenzi and at the ducal court. Count Ruspoli became one of Greenough's closest Italian friends. Several times the Greenoughs went to the parties of Mrs. Thomson, which were declared to be generally "the pleasantist in town."[68] It was in this circle that they met the minister of the Austro-Hungarian Empire, a Hungarian nobleman named Count Revicksky, who later that season commissioned a statue of his three-year-old daughter. Although it was to be a portrait, its saving grace for Greenough was its being a life-size statue. He described his conception of it to Henry:

> The little girl is represented as seated on a bank of flowers contemplating a butterfly, which has just lighted on her raised forearm. The intentness with which she regards the symbol of the immortal soul, happily indicated the awakening of an infant understanding. So entirely absorbed is she in contemplation of the object which has attracted her attention, and so complete is her repose, that a lizard creeps fearlessly from his hole in the bank of flowers. The gaze of the child is full of that mixture of simplicity and thought. . . .[69]

The Revickskys placed the statue "in the center of their salon, in a fine light," where it elicited comments from all who entered.[70]

Edward Everett thought it "among the most charming creations of Mr. Greenough's chisel," a judgment roundly joined.[71] Reinforced by this generous reception the family soon had Greenough "making a bust of the mother, who is very beautiful."[72]

Although Greenough was now entrenched in his career, he never lost his feelings of obligation to his patrons, well after he had repaid their initial loans. Nor did he shed his old, pleasurable habit, begun in their behalf, of bargain hunting for art treasures for trans-Atlantic shipment. Friends and acquaintances respected his knowledge of the art market and appreciated the opportunity to embellish their homes. Greenough was not averse to enriching the cultural texture of his native Boston. He purchased several masterpieces for American owners from the sale of the Cellestini collection which were acclaimed at home as "the best pictures that had been brought to this country." He felt this expression of gratitude for his effort was ample compensation for the "vexations resulting from this deal."[73]

He detected a lucky strike when a molder sent by Louis Philippe arrived in Florence to copy the figures by Michelangelo in the Laurentian Chapel. By careful maneuver, Greenough was able to obtain proof casts of the lot, excepting that of Lorenzo Medici. He made a gift to Colonel Thomas N. Perkins of the *Night* and *Day*, as "the best return [he] could make for that gentleman's kind offices in having given [him] a free passage to Europe in one of his vessels."[74] These figures became a symbolic gift to Boston when Perkins passed them on to the Athenaeum. Greenough retained the other three figures comprising the Julian monument as decoration for his studio. The Athenaeum was deprived of these additions years later by their loss at sea.

Greenough had for five years wanted to fashion a nude classical female figure; a Venus, as an ideal of female beauty. Cooper jocularly attributed this notion to his marriage. He bantered, "I take it for granted the Venus Victrix is a homage to your wife . . . a votive offering to propitiate the goddess."[75] Florence lent itself to this subject as Venuses abounded and were constantly admired and discussed. Foremost among these was the Venus di Medici, generally deemed the most perfect female nude. Canova's Venus did not lag far in public esteem, while the curvaceous Venus of Botticelli dominated a central room in the Uffizi. Greenough was impressed when he learned that Bezzuoli of the Royal Academy "sold his Venus for one thousand frances-coni."[76] Fired by the beauty of still another *Venus*, owned by a Mr. Derby, Greenough determined to attempt his "first female figure entirely naked."[77] Apprehensive of its success, he called it an experiment. He was vastly encouraged in his pursuit of the subject when the figure was commissioned by his old friend, John Lowell of Cambridge, the father of James Russell Lowell.

He fixed on an interpretation of Venus as Victrix, holding her golden apple. Conceived to embody all the elements of the classical grand style, Greenough proposed "to combine symmetry with expression and beauty with innocence taking the more poetic sense of the character, and considering the matter of Beauty, and the patroness of the graces."[78] Choosing to adjust his technique to the classical subject, he consciously departed from Bartolini's stricture to follow nature assiduously and to reject the study of antique casts in preference to live models." In making this study," explained Greenough to Washington Allston, "I had occasion to conceive Nature pretty widely and to scrutinize the . . . models of antiquity very closely."[79] It was an understandable stylistic switch.

Venus turned out after the typical delays of nine months at Carrara "owing to the press of work and scarcity of fine pieces of stone," smaller than life-size, highly finished in "a good piece of marble," and truly classical.[80] It was unfortunate that Lowell died in February 1842, so soon after her arrival. However, the public was heir to his generosity for he had willed the *Venus Victrix* together with another of Greenough's classical works, a bas-relief depicting the *Judgment of Paris*, to the Boston Athenaeum, where they were exhibited annually for many years.

Greenough was hitting his stride in these classical ideal works. Having "always thought it best to aim at what we dream of in our warmest aspirational [moments]," as he had long ago confided that lofty thought to Washington Allston, he was delighted now to find a market for them.[81] Greenough appreciated his good fortune when the wealthy art collector, Edward Salisbury of Connecticut, came along at the culmination of his grand tour. He sought Greenough out directly and selected from the studies in the studio a figure of "the

faithful Seraph . . . Abdiel walking through the rebel host of angels, described in Milton's Paradise Lost."[82] The subject had been suggested by Allston years earlier and Greenough had modeled it and set it aside awaiting a commission.

Abdiel is illustrated "just as he concludes his speech to Satan and is turning to leave him" in the company of the assemblage of rebellious angels.[83] Smaller than life-size he is described by Charles Sumner as "a winged, heaven-born Achilles."[84] He was probably summarizing Greenough's explanation during their long talks together during Sumner's extended visit in Florence. Another writer described the statue as "uniting the expression of tender compassion with just indignation, formal beauty . . . blended with intense ugliness of expression."[85] It was clear that Greenough was still trying to portray a combination of conflicting emotions within one subject. By contemporary standards this work was a huge success.

Greenough apparently agreed wholeheartedly with his patron's selection of the *Abdiel* because he made a copy of it in an enlarged bust to fill an old order from a Mrs. Bartol, who had left the subject to him and then waited patiently six years for its arrival. This was a perfectly acceptable way of solving the problem of his time pressures in that day of the proliferation of copies. The bust, in turn, inspired another, by way of counterpoint, an idealized interpretation of *Satan*. Like its predecessor, this figure stands thirty-three inches high, and the head rests on a coiled serpent with its mouth open. Above the head are two winged and chained demons. Thoroughly satisfied, Greenough thought it was his "highest effort in that ideal line."[86] It was well received at Boston, where it forms a pair with the *Christ* figure at the entry to the public library. Similarly satisfied, Salisbury commissioned a second work, a bas-relief of the *Angel Forbidding St. John to Worship Him*, with the admonition to direct the prayers to God.[87]

It was too bad, but inevitable that Greenough could not have it all his own way with idealized subjects. He could not avoid making some busts, either out of personal or family friendship, prestige, or money. One of these turned into a classical idealization, that of Mrs. Emily Marshall Otis which he had modeled during his last trip home. One of Mrs. Samuel Appleton was more realistic. These two were

Venus Victrix   1839, marble, smaller than life-size
Courtesy of the Boston Athenaeum

now accorded priority for completion after their delay in shipment because their cases had been carelessly left behind. Mrs. Otis had died meanwhile, causing Greenough more than normal anxiety about the likeness. He finished it in marble in 1839 but retained it in his studio five years longer for fear of not satisfying her husband with it. Like so many of the others, the bust eventually made its way into the Boston Athenaeum. During the execution of these, he also worked on the portrait bust of his old Boston friend Jonathan Mason, which he reported was "coming on rapidly and without a stain."[88]

More important than any of these was his colossal bust of Benjamin Franklin. The great inventor-statesman's personality presented the complexity of attributes that Greenough liked. Although he began this study without a commission in view, it was not an unreasonable speculation. Portraits of the founding fathers were in general demand at home. Upon its completion in 1839, Greenough pondered on the best place to offer it, vacillating between Philadelphia and New York. He bypassed Boston in his speculations, explaining "I find Bos-

Emily Marshall Otis
1839, marble
Courtesy of the Boston Athenaeum

tonians are not fond of the colossal."[89] He turned out to be right, not only for Boston but elsewhere. The work did not sell. When Greenough returned to the states to stay in 1851, he placed it in the Athenaeum where it was exhibited in the fall. A local reviewer described it as "crowning the entrance, flanked by Houdon's *Washington* and Ball Hughes' *Bowditch*."[90] The colossal bust of *Benjamin Franklin* never left the Boston Athenaeum.

During these years of the late thirties, Greenough allotted the major portion of his time to his monumental works. By the end of 1839, he had cast the figures of his *Rescue Group* in plaster, so they could be examined critically. He fussed considerably over finding accessories pertinent to Indian physiognomy and life, such as skulls, dresses, embroidery, drawings, to fit notions about racial features that were prevalent at the time. Meanwhile, he gained enough confidence to show the *Washington* group in his studio to a select local audience. It was their positive response which finally encouraged him to complete it according to his original conception, overcoming his continuing apprehensions over the American reaction to its nudity.

Early in July of 1840, Greenough went for a spell to Carrara, where he could oversee the blocking and cutting of his colossal statues while at the same time taking relief from the debilitating heat of Florence. He loved the greenery of the vicinity, the majesty of the mountain peaks, the variety of line in the undulating hills, the brisk atmosphere, and the rapidly changing moods, which were as variable as his own. He walked a great deal, fifteen miles not being excessive in one day. He was restored by the feeling of tranquility which overtook him in the mountains.

On his return to Florence, he was met with the most treasured artistic prize of his career, an honor not attained hitherto by any other foreigner. For five years he had worked intermittently at the Royal Academy of Fine Arts, which outshone the Academy of Saint Luke at Rome in its faculty for sculpture. His knowledge of Italian, assisted by his charm and brilliance, had enabled him to ingratiate himself with his Italian associates. In recognition of his major productions in progress, he was now proposed not only to membership in the academy, but also as professor of sculpture. His nomination was sponsored by his famous Italian colleagues, Emilio Santarelli, Luigi Pampaloni, Emilio Demi, and Francesco Pozzi. Oddly enough, Bartolini had nothing to do with any of this. The vote on July 30 was unanimous. Greenough expressed his profound gratitude for this unique honor as "the only American ever to have been voted into the Academy in either capacity of membership or professorship." He compared it with "stumbling upon water in a desert."[91]

With this honor, Greenough reached the summit of artistic success in both his native and adopted lands. He could climb no higher. He could only work to improve his art, teach, found a school, or publish his critical notions on art and architecture.

By the following spring, Greenough was so renowned that it didn't take more than one day for the English blue-stocking writer Frances Trollope to make her way to his studio. The Greenough's gave her a dinner party, Horatio's way of showing "marked attention . . . the only mode of receiving a clever person."[92] Edward Everett attended, having spent the season in Florence upon his retirement as governor of Massachusetts and before taking up his post as U.S. minister to England. It must have been a notable evening for the English writer, who discriminated between chatter and conversation, chose to record it. She wrote:

> The conversation at table deserved the name much better than is often the case, particularly when several of the party are entirely strangers to each other . . . and among other theses we had an extremely interesting discussion on the subject of Art in general, and Sculpture in particular. . . . The question so often mooted as to the source of the superiority in ancient over modern art, was long dwelt upon, and handled with considerable taste and savoir. There was general agreement on the superiority of classical productions, but disagreement as to why. Were their "almost miraculous" productions due to imagination, or to "faithful accuracy," the minutest truth of their imitations . . . together with able handicraft?[93]

Greenough's interest in and broad knowledge of literature, history, and art and his earnest, well-turned arguments had long made him a highly prized dinner guest. He more than held his own in those circles, especially when espousing his original, provoking theories on art and architecture. As a host at his own dinner table, where he could more easily dominate the conversation, he must have set a formidable standard.

6

Sculptural Hiatus

GREENOUGH'S ARTISTIC SUCCESS WAS NOT UNTRAMMELED DURING THE ensuing decade of the forties. One exigency followed on the heels of another, conspiring to remove him physically from his studio. The underlying thread of his interest during these imposed absences revolved, unsurprisingly, around intellectual matters. He read, studied, and theorized incessantly. Actually, he never relinquished these habits that he had formed during his Harvard days when he sat so often captivated at the feet of Washington Allston. He continued his discussions on art and aesthetics with Allston by trans-Atlantic correspondence after settling in Florence. He pursued such talk at closer range with Ralph Waldo Emerson, Henry T. Tuckerman, Walter Savage Landor, and others in his proximity whenever the opportunity arose. When Charles Sumner visited Florence in 1839, Greenough read to him for criticism a paper he had written on "The Nude." Sumner returned to the theme frequently in his letters to Greenough after quitting Rome, making numerous observations about the sculpture and architecture he saw in various cities he visited as he continued his grand tour.

In 1843, Greenough published his first critical essay, "Aesthetics at Washington," the pioneer paper in aesthetics by an American, in the *United States Magazine and Democratic Review*. The essay sparked national attention and was the beginning of Greenough's campaign against the American practice of plagiarizing the Greeks.

This ruffled his sense of nationalism. He wanted his native country to improve in all conceivable ways, especially culturally, where he considered her sadly deficient. He not only intended that public buildings and squares be adorned with the best productions of the arts, but he also desired that the buildings be beautiful. He decried the want of an American art. He wanted sculptural subjects and paintings to deal with American themes, and he wanted architecture to conform to uniquely American needs or conditions, reflecting American traditions and aspirations. In this crusade he antedated (by a few years) John Ruskin, who concerned himself with similar problems from the English standpoint.

Some work proceeded in his studio during his long absences, but it was mechanical, such as bust carving or checking on the supplies at Serravezza. The quest for a suitable block of marble was more time-consuming than one would suppose. The search for suitable pieces and the difficulties encountered contributed to the delay in completing the *Rescue Group*.

In June 1842, Greenough left for his trip to Washington. His primary business there was to place and light the *Washington* statue. The problem not only consumed much time but proved insoluble and ended in frustration. It detained him overseas a year, until July 1843. It was not until early the following year that he returned to his studio, and then it was only for four or five months, because he felt obliged to take his ailing wife off to Graefenberg, in Austrian Silesia, in pursuit of the highly touted water cure for her undiagnosable ailment.[1]

Greenough regretted leaving his work, but he saw no alternative as it was presented to him as a matter of Louisa's survival. He wrote a friend, "I had to go on consulting the most eminent physicians in order to see my wife go down to an untimely grave."[2] He was outraged by the quackery of "bleeding" and wrote, "I am sure that her body has been injured by impertinent, ignorant, and presumptuous interferences" by those dabblers.[3]

At Graefenberg, he was profoundly impressed by Dr. Priessnitz, the founder of hydrotherapy, whose method effected the almost miraculous cure of his wife. They had expected at the outset to stay some two months but lingered for eighteen.

The cure was based on a regime of regular exercise in the open air, drinking pure water, and a simple diet. All stimulants, including coffee and tea, were strictly forbidden and infractions were reported by the servants, who functioned simultaneously as police agents for the director. It was reported that Dr. Priessnitz "found amusements valuable aids in restoring a healthy state of mind and body, and encouraged shooting-matches, outdoor fetes, dances,—ending at an early hour,—and bands of music."[4] The patients rented cottages for their families at Freiwaldau, a picturesque mountain village. The outdoor life was to Greenough's liking and culture was not entirely wanting, for efforts were made in this direction. "Ideas were exchanged in many languages," and "noblemen could be seen chopping wood, leaping, and jumping to quicken their circulation, and highborn women sawing logs together with double-handed saws."[5]

Louisa rallied into a hale and hearty female. Under this system, she conceived and gave birth to their first son, Henry, on May 11, 1845. Toughened by regular exercise during pregnancy, she came through her ordeal without undue stress or debility. Dr. Priessnitz was in the next room supervising the application of cold water stimulation throughout the confinement. The happy aftermath converted Greenough resolutely to this natural method of health cure. He was grateful to Priessnitz for Louisa's life and for the joys of fatherhood, which he relished in every spare hour. Moreover, the routine at Graefenberg was hardly disagreeable.

During this second exile from Florence, Greenough made frequent brief sorties into Vienna to study art and architecture and to purchase books. Endless nuisances cropped up in his increasingly complicated family life to sap his energy and consume his time. His wife's condition held top priority in his concern and attention, but he also had to deal with all the irksome household details, such as the delay in obtaining the passport for their maid.

These annoyances at Graefenberg had to be balanced against the urgent matters in Florence that would not yield to ready solution at long distance. The worst of these was the neglect of the United States Consul to issue the progress report on the *Rescue Group*, without which the annual installment from Washington would be withheld, possibly forcing suspension of operations in Greenough's studio.

The situation seemed sufficiently threatening to demand his presence. Realizing the necessity of putting off his return at least until the arrival of the child, he advanced some money to Powers early in May for transmission to the marble merchants at Serravezza to guarantee his supply. He then waited a respectful time beyond Louisa's confinement before going to Florence at the end of June. He would now deal with the progress report and check on the actual work on his group. The trip coincided with the arrival in Florence of his brother Henry and his family. Horatio did his share to entice Henry to join him in the arcadian mountains, but the lure was not taken until the following spring. Their reunion gave them all a pleasurable summer.

In the autumn of 1846 the Greenoughs left Freiwaldau with reluctance. Having become parents and experiencing excellent health during their stay, they were naturally loathe to leave, but studio and home beckoned. They returned by way of Munich to give Horatio an opportunity to examine the store of Bavarian art, particularly the colossal fifty-four foot high statue of *Bavaria* which was then nearly completed and which he found impressive. He was excited at his discovery of a new book on architectural precepts, *The Secrets of the Proportions, Attitudes, and Compositions of the Ancients*.[6]

At Florence they returned to the Casa Bacciochi, where Greenough had retained his lease. Greenough reported to Henry that they found Arno (the greyhound) "as large as life" and "William [the coachman] at his post."[7] That winter was "cold as Greenland," and there was "sleighing in the streets," but the Greenoughs were inured to the discomforts better than their neighbors and they resumed their normal activities.[8] Horatio reported, "We have had lots of brother Yankees here and done the amiable by them, giving six or seven tea-parties."[9]

A strange fever scourged Florence that winter and the entire family fell prey. It was so endemic and devastating that Greenough suspected it was the dread cholera, but they all survived, and by late spring, Horatio was on the road to recovery. Resolved not to risk another hot summer in Florence, they moved out into the suburb of Pratolino, about eighteen kilometers north in the hills. They began to doubt the prudence of spending the following winter in town, but that mood was soon to be dispelled.

Greenough's resilience was remarkable and he was eager to return to his work. He soon finished the model of the *Genius of Italy*, an Apollo-like figure in bas-relief to stand between the priest and the soldier in the monument of the poet and lawyer, Giuseppe Giusti, which was never completed. At the same time, he designed a companion classical ideal bas-relief to symbolize the muse of poetry for the same monument. He called it the *Genius of Poesy* but apparently never completed it beyond the sketch and clay model, probably for lack of a commission.[10] When the weather moderated, the family returned to Florence, and Greenough concentrated on finishing his *Rescue Group*. Friends passing through reported on its progress with approval. Two of the original four figures contemplated for the work had progressed almost to their completion in marble that season.

Once more misfortune hampered Greenough's work, for revolutions occurred throughout Europe in the spring of 1848. Metternich was driven from Vienna in April, but the eighty-three-year-old General Radetsky rallied the forces of the Austro-Hungarian Empire and mounted an offensive to check the nationalist republican movements. The Italian hymn of liberty could be heard in the streets of Florence. The event was described sympathetically: "One beautiful June morning thirteen hundred youths marched out of the Pratogate, with bouquets on their bayonets. . . . Most of them, apparently, were under twenty years of age and they looked as if bound on a pleasure party. Their lives were sold dearly, and gave an effectual though short-lived check to the Austrians."[11]

A handful of dusty, worn-out stragglers returned from the unequal battle. The grand duke, after his earlier protestations and pledges of Tuscan loyalty, lost courage, defected, and fled in 1849, leaving the government and any resistance to the Austrians. No revolution had been more bloodless. Marquis Gino Capponi, almost blind, became prime minister, and the poet Niccolini joined the cabinet. Giuseppe Giusti participated unofficially. Greenough, identifying throughout with the Italians and republicanism, was hardly neutral. Louisa had sewn the flag under which the American group had appeared in the earlier demonstration of 1847 to show sympathy and support for the Italians, when the grand duke had granted the populace its own Civic Guard. Now, the Civic Guard mobilized its meager forces against the advancing Austrians, led personally by the wily General Radetsky, but it was soon dispersed like thistledown on a brisk breeze. In no time at all, Florence billeted 20,000 Austrian troops.

The events of 1849 were disturbing to Greenough. "His love of freedom and education in a land of liberty made foreign despotism in his second home a daily annoyance," and he remarked that he found "the study of Austrian character in Italy far less interesting than in Austria."[12] The officers and soldiers behaved as gentlemen, however, even making overtures to win over the populace. Their fine bands of music were generally appreciated, and the Americans were exempt from the quartering of troops. But the Greenoughs were too Italophile to adjust pragmatically to the foreign occupation. In their antipathy to the Austrians, they were joined by most members of the American colony. The Powers family declared themselves for liberty and professed their dislike of the unpopular Austrians but lived through the entire episode without overt protest. Hiram had participated with his colleagues in the demonstration of 1847 before the revolutionary movement had progressed to republicanism. At the other end of the spectrum, the intrepid Margaret Fuller and her husband, Marquis Ossoli, were forced to flee Rome with their child and seek refuge in Florence because of their activity in behalf of Mazzini and the abortive Roman Republic. Thomas Crawford manned his post bravely on the walls of Rome, too, but escaped reprisal during the general repression which ensued.

In the midst of all the excitement of political upheaval, Louisa Greenough was delivered of a second child on July 25, 1848. This time there was no cause of worry for Horatio. Louisa fared well and the baby, a girl who was named Mary Louisa, thrived.

Not long afterwards, Greenough moved from the Palazzo Bacciocchi to the northern end of the city on the Fiesole side of the Arno "between Porta al Prato and the Porta San Gallo," toward Monte Morello, where a new square was laid out, named after the grand duchess, Piazza Maria Antonia, now renamed Piazza Indipendenza. He purchased the corner lot at one end of Via di Barbano, where it converged with Via San Francesco Poverino and Via San Caterina. There he erected an ultramodern studio of his own design according to his principles of functionalism, with all the rooms on one floor. Henry T. Tuckerman called this studio "a monument of Greenough's intelligent taste and aesthetic culture," and he reported that the studio was "built with great strength and fine ornamental stone work . . . having in the center the cypher G. Attached to the structure [was] a beautiful garden; within [was] a spacious and admirably lighted exhibition room—nearby the sculptor's private studio, a large apartment for the workmen, a gallery of plaster casts, a vestibule hung with pictures, a noble rotunda, leading by a short flight of steps to the garden, and a charming library."[13]

When he had settled into the new studio Greenough completed a bas-relief that had been on his mind for years. In 1833, when he had just gotten free of debt, he had thought to inquire after the names of the patrons in Boston who had contributed to the fund gathered to pay his way abroad. The loan had been arranged anonymously through Harvard University and the names withheld. He had harbored "hopes to pay a part if not the whole of the amount" that year.[14] Now Greenough decided to execute a work to commemorate the event. He deliberated over a suitable subject and eventually conceived a theme for a bas-relief that represented the artist as a female figure in a dejected mood, "while a hand, unseen by him pours oil into his expiring lamp."[15] This concept may seem to express more sentimentality than sentiment, but it conformed to the style of the day. Greenough had no order for the work but he decided to complete it anyway and send it as a gift to George Ticknor as a representative (and very likely the largest) benefactor of the group. The work was dispatched in October 1849 and although delayed at sea reached Boston in time for Christmas. Ticknor was genuinely grateful and placed it in the entrance hall of his magnificent home on Beacon Hill, where Greenough, upon returning home for the last time, could satisfy himself about its placement and lighting.

For all the beauty and elegance of his newly appointed studio, Greenough could not escape the pervasive feeling of oppression. Censorship, espionage, and the quartering of troops, age-old grievances against tyranny against which the Americans had waged their own revolution, were regular occurrences of the Austrian occupation. Greenough returned home one day to find several cavalry officers quartered on his own premises. He protested through the

American Consul at Leghorn, who gave him a minor diplomatic appointment, United States Vice-Consul at Porto San Stefano, which carried diplomatic immunity and consequently exemption from such embarrassment.

To make matters worse, the precarious state of political unrest had kept travelers at home; business lagged for the artists, and Greenough cast about for alternatives. He wrote home, "I hope you will give me some idea of how things are going on at home. . . . I am sorry to say it, but for the present Florence has lost much of its charm for me, perhaps a season at home would restore it."[16] He was assailed with doubts. "I look forward with anxiety to the future," he wrote, "partly on account of the complications of European politics and partly for the fear that my being too long out of sight will put me equally out of mind with the public in America."[17] He continued candidly to express his principal reservation: "After being so long employed on works of a high order, it is not possible for me to play the shopman and cut fancy work for furniture or cultivate the vogue of the day. I have chosen my path and if the state of national taste does not afford me support I must wait and arm myself with courage for the consequences."[18]

Lacking assured status at home, he dallied in Florence, where he was widely recognized. Was he not the only foreigner to have been granted the honor of a professorship in the Royal Academy? Was he not here, underpinned by his private income supplemented by the government's generous payments for its major commissions, free to live with his family in comfort without wasting excessive time on portraiture? His way of life suited him. His studio was glamorous and his home stylish and staffed with servants. His family prospered and grew. On September 10, 1850, his third child and second daughter, Charlotte, was born. A fortnight later Horatio proudly reported "both she and infant are doing well."[19] Greenough's professional stake in Italy was solid and business soon improved.

After the revolutionary crisis subsided in the fall of 1850, visitors returned in droves from all over Europe, especially from England, France, and Russia. His studio filled once more to overflowing with these aristocratic dilettantes. In one week, he reported four English lords appeared to admire his "genius."[20] He even acquired a talented pupil named Falcini, who worked "like a Trojan" to prove his worth.[21]

Greenough's work progressed with momentum. The *Rescue Group* was "nearly done after the most tormenting delay [at Serravezza] for marble owing to contracts with the Emperor of Russia."[22] Greenough drew a sketch of *Apollo, the Avenger*, which he forwarded to Henry for criticism, and made a bas-relief of *Castor and Pollux*, which he intended to complete quickly. Unlike his other two ideal reliefs, the *Genius of Italy* and the *Genius of Poesy*, the *Castor and Pollux* composition in bas-relief was finished in marble and joined his numerous other works in Boston.[23] It was also successfully lithographed by an able French draftsman.

Several eyewitnesses attested that his finest work of this period was another *Venus*, one contending for the golden apple, which he modeled in Powers' new plaster of paris. The advantages of this material were manifold and fed Horatio's love of the functional. He

Castor and Pollux 1850, marble bas-relief
Courtesy of the Museum of Fine Arts, Boston

had already experimented with this material early in 1844 when he had erected a statue in it nearly six feet high. He had used it also in his revised model of *David*, which he deemed deficient by his perfectionist standard and never completed. Using a tool that was another Powers' innovation, this *Venus* was "stippled . . . till the surface was of the finest finish."[24] She was oversized like the Venus di Milo in the Louvre. In September 1850, Greenough said he was "anxious to put [her] into marble."[25]

Later that year Greenough could finally announce, "I am about to finish a colossal work for the government which has almost exclusively occupied me for thirteen years past."[26] Taking encouragement from the approval of his endless visitors, he planned to petition Congress "for leave to exhibit the group at New York" and London on its way home.[27] He would have casts made which he would tour more extensively. The *Venus* would accompany them. President Millard Fillmore denied the permission that Greenough requested for a private showing of the group. Greenough grumbled that Trumbull and Weir had received such permission for their paintings that were destined to adorn the rotunda of the Capitol. His reasoned argument was of no avail and he lacked the confidence to show the *Venus* alone, as Powers had done with his *Greek Slave*. The debate was terminated abruptly when this "latest and most perfect work" was broken into fragments during its shipment to America, making her restoration impractical.[28]

The plan for the exhibition of the group was designed to revive his reputation in America as a forerunner for his return. He feared his name had been undermined by the popular reaction against the *Washington* or possibly even forgotten because of his prolonged absence. He wanted some new and favorable publicity to precede his arrival, which might conceivably also gain him another important commission from the government. Such good luck would solve the practical problem of underpinning his subsistence during the transition from Florence and his installation at home. There had been talk at the capital over a period of years of commissioning an equestrian statue of Washington, and Greenough had drawn plans and made sketches for such a statue. He wanted to demonstrate publicly that he could execute an appropriate outdoor version of Washington.

Further delays in the completion and shipment of his group caused the studies for the equestrian *Washington* to be temporarily relegated to his files, but they were to serve him well later.

Meanwhile, for greater political and personal security he moved his family at the close of the year out to Villa Brichieri at Bellosguardo on the outskirts of Florence. He was sorry to leave the genial companionship of the Trollope family who had recently moved next door. The hill area of Bellosguardo was just then beginning to be developed as an exclusive residential area, covered with lavish villas each having a more magnificent view of the city than the next. Greenough said officially that his "principal aim in withdrawing from the city was to assure his family the benefits of fresh air and the healthy exercise of walking."[29] Perhaps fresh air was his cautious euphemism for a freer atmosphere. In Italy in those days, however, there was little freedom or security.

In the spring of 1851, Greenough added a fifth figure to the *Rescue Group* at the last moment. Then, satisfied that he had done his utmost for the realization of his theme, he made tentative arrangements for the group's transportation and turned his attention to summer plans and the family's move to the States. For the hot summer months of July and August, they migrated to the Canton de Vaud, in the Swiss mountains just above Geneva. While there news reached them of the death of Horatio's brother Alfred. Horatio sank into a deep depression, compounding the normal anxiety that inevitably accompanied his inactivity. All "the tranquilizing effect" of the splendid scenery was of no avail, and he sped his journey homeward.[30]

They steamed down the Rhine late in August, arriving in Brussels early in September. Greenough indulged himself one brief detour "to run up to Paris for two or three days . . . to see Lamartine and Victor Hugo. I admire and love these men," he explained unabashedly.[31] Had he come along one year later, he would have found both these stalwart republicans right there in Brussels at the beginning of their years of heroic exile from the new repressive Bonapartist empire.

7

Untriumphant Return

GREENOUGH DID NOT RECEIVE A POPULAR HERO'S WELCOME WHEN HE
returned home for what proved to be his last years. The family
sailed from Liverpool the first of October 1851 on the S.S. *America*
and arrived in Boston without fanfare on the seventeenth. They
carried with them two young Italian household servants, a nurse
and a maid, and the three children, who were then six, three, and one.

Their Boston friends had kept in touch with Greenough in
Italy and took pride in his attainments. There were many welcoming
dinner parties, but Greenough was too apprehensive about his career
to enjoy these pleasures just then. He felt pressed to get on with
the task of finding a monumental commission somewhere to buttress
his return home.

Rumors were relayed to him from Washington of a monument
being planned to honor James Fenimore Cooper, who had died only
a few months before. Greenough was determined to be the artist
selected to execute the memorial. He hastily devised a plan for it
that centered on a seated statue of the writer. "The base [would]
be flanked by two figures" "to recall his greatest triumphs as a writer
of fiction—Leather Stocking and Long Tom Coffin."[1] He told
William Cullen Bryant that he wanted the memorial to be incorporated "in a facade or in the court of some literary institution.[2]
He was unsure about the city of its placement. Not having heard

of any rival plans, he would prefer New York, but if that was precluded by others, he would try for Philadelphia or Baltimore.

Armed with his sketch and holding in reserve his completed
design for an equestrian statue of Washington, he felt equipped after
a couple of weeks' dallying to face the capital city. Yet he did so
tentatively, "with a feeling akin to dismay."[3] He still recoiled from
the memories of his embarrassing failure with the lighting of the
Washington and with its subsequent popular ridicule. Lodging Louisa
and her entourage of children and servants temporarily with the
family, he traveled southward.

The legislators gainsaid his uneasiness with their warm reception of him. They apparently harbored no prejudices against him
over the *Washington*. He now reported, "With one accord I was
looked to as the sculptor of the Cooper monument. Glorious
Cooper!"[4] Even in death, Cooper was his solid supporter. Exactly
what went wrong with this commission is obscure, but soon Greenough's tone changed to talk about the corrupt atmosphere in Washington that repelled him, and he wrote Henry, "I will never make
it for this town."[5] He agreed with Edward Everett that "Everything
is carried on [there] by personal solicitation . . . which shuts out
at once those artists who have any pride of personal character."[6]

Greenough then prospected possibilities in New York. He
moved into 98 Chambers Street, with luggage intact, including his two
major designs. The Cooper design, being original and topical, seemed
more readily viable, and he applied himself to its elaboration. As the
plan matured, it took the form of a classical rectangular building of
twenty-four by forty-eight feet, raised three steps and enclosing a
room twenty feet high, to be lighted from above and placed at the
center of a "noble square," hopefully that of the recently founded
New York University. It would have an external frieze carved with
illustrations of Cooper's favorite literary themes. The internal walls
would be adorned with paintings executed by the best landscape
and historical painters in the land who would derive their compositions from the author's books. The center opposite the entrance
would be dominated by a colossal bronze statue of Cooper, represented as "the abstract type of the American ideal man," having his
effect "upon the soul of the people and upon the world."[7] Shades

of the old *Washington!* Outside at the corners of the steps, he would erect statues on pedestals portraying four leading characters created by the novelist.

Horatio's brother Henry balked and undertook a corrective "at the risk of being tiresome, not to say impertinent." Granting Horatio "a great triumph in overcoming the great attack," he pointedly reminded him "it has taken 10 years to effect it." Henry was thoroughly "convinced that a horse by Phidias of twice the size of life would not be appreciated by 10 men in America." He recalled the bust of Franklin "was viewed with utter indifference by everyone here [because of its colossal size] until it was placed by me at a height where the eye was accommodated to its size." Ultimately, he conceded "the only proper situation for colossal statues to be on the top of hills or in large squares or buildings where the *only entrance* is at such a distance as to make it necessary to increase the size *to compensate for the distance* at which the artist wishes his work to have an effect." He twitted his brother at the conclusion of his lengthy unsolicited discourse, "If you make a colossus, I shall insist on it you are like a scholar who makes all his lectures in Latin."[8]

Horatio's direct response to this adroit manipulation of his own precepts is unrecorded. Although the project failed to materialize, he did bring the plaster model of the colossal Cooper statue, untrimmed, to completion by August 1852, whereupon he informed Susan Cooper that it would be "cast in bronze in a few weeks."[9]

There was a rival project afoot in New York that deflected Greenough's attention. Upon arriving in town, he found that a committee of prosperous public-minded merchants had been formed to raise a subscription for an equestrian Washington statue for Union Square, and that $15,000 had already been raised in denominations of $500. Greenough took his design from his portfolio and entered the competition. The commission was awarded to him with the stipulation that he collaborate with a younger colleague, Henry Kirke-Brown, who had been a novice when they had met some years earlier in Italy. From Florence, Kirke-Brown had gone to Rome for three more years of study before returning to Albany and New York. Kirke-Brown's upstate friends had wielded political pressures successfully and New Yorkers could not ignore their native talent.

A joint contract was signed for the work to be executed in bronze and the two sculptors took a studio together in Brooklyn where Kirke-Brown installed two French bronze workers to assist them technically. Greenough promptly asserted his seniority by taking the dominant role in the collaboration. The initiative hardly seemed unreasonable in view of Greenough's seniority of age and training. It was, moreover, vital for Greenough to utilize this opportunity to demonstrate his ability to portray Washington in contemporary uniform. He would overlook his aversion to sculptural tailoring details.

The matter of the statue's size was next to be decided. In view of the enormity of the square and Greenough's classical bias favoring the colossal, it is not surprising that the sculptor contended that "it would look mean if not of the heroic size."[10] Greenough proceeded with dispatch, and after a brief holiday with his family in Newport, he said he expected to complete his model of the horse by the early fall. His efforts soon came to a halt, however, due to a petty misunderstanding that arose with the committee. Greenough explained the dispute to his family as follows:

> They wanted me to finish the work first and then go to the public afterward, if they could not furnish money enough. I insisted upon making every thing known *beforehand* and so they cooled off. I had received my right to do as I pleased in a clause of the contract; but they squealed so hard that I proposed to destroy the agreement and they consented. I have now asked the Common Council [of New York City] to allow me a square where I can set up such a statue as I can make, with means that I can command and thus far I get no answer.[11]

In his confrontation with the affluent mercantile committee in charge, Greenough insisted on the customary terms that he had obtained abroad.

He withdrew from the partnership in midsummer, and Henry Kirke-Brown, who was still without a major monument to his credit, completed the work on those disadvantageous terms. He was in no position to strike a better bargain.

Greenough ventilated his anger unreservedly against the merchants. He decided to appeal over their heads directly to the public to raise a purse for a "colossal equestrian statue of Andrew Jackson . . . [to be] commemorative of his military, civil, and private career." He would "collect 25¢ a head from those who are able and willing to spare it for this object . . . [and] to be accountable to a committee for the outlay on the work."[12] He would take up his collections as he toured from lyceum to community center, spreading his artistic gospel among the common folk. This utopian dream came to no better pass than did Robert Owen's experiment in communal living at New Harmony or George Ripley's experiment at Brook Farm.

Reservations toward commercialism aside, Greenough was positively impressed with the city of New York. "The spectacle of this vast activity excites and pleases me beyond measure," he declared.[13] The intellectuals were begining to take notice of him and befriended him because of his introduction by Samuel F. B. Morse, who enjoyed an entrenched position in these circles. Greenough began to feel acclimated and pleased with his decision to turn his back on Europe. "I thank God from the bottom of my heart," he wrote ardently, "that I have once more put my foot on *my own native soil* and I hope, though now arrived to the mezza del cammin di nostra vita, to be of some use here both in illustrative art, and in structure, for here I mean now to stay."[14]

Not that Greenough went overboard in his refreshed view of his homeland. He detected many faults, but in general he was glad to identify with his native country despite its pronounced mercantilism. He expounded on his reaction to Morse.

> I find a certain creed that seeks rather to carve private welfare out of the commonwealth than to seek private weal in the general wellbeing. This has gone very far and is on the increase unless I err. . . . I see symptoms also of loose organization in society from an ignorance of the limits of private liberty and this is reacted against by the abuse of legislation. Still we drown and burn less than they shoot and hang in Europe nor do we do it altogether on purpose, which is a very great consolation. I would rather perish on a railway or steamer than be shot by a ragamuffin at the word of command or swung off at a given hour in the morning because of my opinion.[15]

Although his artistic career seemed to have foundered stateside on the reef of commercialism, his patriotism, natural exuberance, and the recognition of his colleagues gave reason for optimism. In the spring of 1852, he reported an encouraging offer. "Some of the leading men of letters in New York," he wrote, "have whispered to me of a professorship of Art in a university on a grand scale, which they would like to have me take. I was invited to meet a committee on the subject, but was out of town."[16]

In Boston too, during his frequent visits home, he was enveloped with the warmth of the comraderie of his old friends. The Boston crowd continued to receive him as if he had never been absent. He was invited to numerous dinner parties which were primarily intellectual feasts for him. One evening in January 1852, recounted Henry Wadsworth Longfellow, "Horatio Greenough came in, and we had a long chat about politics and art."[17] A few evenings later, Longfellow hosted Greenough at dinner, this time with Emerson and Ticknor, "very pleasantly, with some chat about art."[18]

In the spring of 1852, Greenough's endeavors were once more interrupted by family illness. This time it was "the health of an invalid child."[19] Horatio took a house for the family in Newport to expose his ailing daughter to the salubrious sea air, and they were all relieved to watch her steady progress. In those years Newport was already a fashionable summer resort for the Boston set and the Greenoughs' social life maintained its brisk pace. For a mountain-loving city dweller, Greenough was remarkably adaptable. "God is great and Newport is His abode," he explained exultantly one sunny day late in May.[20] He swam and romped with his children and enjoyed the company of his wife. When he wasn't conversing, he was reading, or reflecting at length.

This interlude allowed him the time to collate his numerous critical essays for publication. They were issued in August by Putnam's of New York, under the title, *The Travels, Observations, and Experience of a Yankee Stonecutter*, and he used his maternal family name to supply his pseudonym, Horace Bender. This work was his principal occupation that season while he awaited word from the City Council in New York or some other civic body to proceed with an equestrian *Washington* or *Jackson*.

In September and October, he busied himself in preparation of a series of community lectures, two of which he wrote and delivered in Boston the following month. Failing to attract much of an audience, it became apparent that he would never raise the sum he had envisioned to finance the equestrian monument he had in mind. He was no greater popular success as a lecturer than as a sculptor. There would not be enough money forthcoming from this source to publish the lectures. For all the complexity and profundity of his notions or even their revolutionary quality, his style was ill-organized and prolix—the sole unifying thread being his functionalism. These lectures and some of his essays and articles were eventually edited and published by Henry T. Tuckerman with the assistance of Louisa in *A Memorial of Horatio Greenough*.

Greenough scurried about in his usual energetic fashion that fall upon the resumption of Boston's social season. He courted the advice of his literary friends, using them again to test his prolific ideas. He sought Emerson's support in particular to bolster his own confidence. Emerson's judgments were his most accurate barometer because of the affinity of the pair on the subjects of art, beauty, and nature. Their differences over slavery and the Negro failed to mar their essential rapport. The best party of the season was arranged by Emerson at Tremont House in Boston late in November. The guests included Greenough, Charles Sumner, James Russell Lowell, Nathaniel Hawthorne, Samuel G. Ward, and Theodore Parker. After dinner, they all attended a concert in the new music hall.

Working at home in Newport on the evening of December 4, Greenough was suddenly stricken with a mysterious ailment that gave rise to a dangerously high fever and produced a state of violent agitation. Louisa sent for Henry, who rushed Horatio in a closed carriage in the middle of the night to the nearest hospital, which was MacLeans Asylum for the insane in Somerville, near Boston. The diagnosis was "brain fever."[21] After lingering two weeks in a state ranging from delirium to unconsciousness, he died suddenly on December 18.

Because of his agitated condition and the nature of the hospital, some friends attributed the cause of his death to mental derangement. Speculation began to circulate that he had suffered spells of insanity before. Richard H. Dana wrote to Charles Sumner two days after his death about Greenough's "nervous excitability" as having been constitutional and hereditary. He then noted his surprise at the report of his friend's death, asserting, "I never knew the case of a man so full of health and vigorous manly beauty so soon struck down."[22] Thomas B. Curtis is said to have been convinced that Greenough was mentally disturbed. Hiram Powers fed the rumors effectively. Upon learning of Horatio's death, he reported to Edward Everett that he was not surprised at the news, adding as if it were common knowledge that "his mind had been affected more or less for years." The evidence he adduced was his recollection of Greenough's confession to him years ago during one of their peripatetic talks in the Cascine at Florence of a momentary hallucination.[23]

A recent biographer of Greenough reported that "there is no doubt he evidently suffered at this period recurring attacks of dementia."[24] She based her judgment on an observation by Henry and a couple of friends that fall that Horatio had been "under a little too great nervous excitement," and she concluded that "the fact was evidence of his increasing instability."[25]

In the light of modern medical knowledge and the scant evidence regarding insanity or mental derangement, this conclusion seems not only highly questionable but implausible, founded more upon rumor than fact. An evaluation of the evidence is warranted.

It is now established that high fever from any cause or type of infection produces either a state of agitation or delirium, or, occasionally, a catatonic reaction. In that period of primitive knowledge about mental disease, an agitated state may have been interpreted as insanity, warranting the consignment of such a patient to MacLeans, which was then but a branch of the Massachusetts General Hospital.

It is true that Greenough's moods oscillated considerably in direct ratio with his energies, the ebb generally coincident with a physical ailment such as influenza or varioloid. When he was immersed in a large work and its related problems, Greenough often overtaxed his strength, doubtlessly sapping his abundant vitality and exposing himself to infection. This range of moods seemed in no way extraordinary for an ebullient artist either to this reader of his letters or to his friends in his voluminous correspondence, including

Hiram Powers, who saw him almost daily after his arrival in Florence at the end of 1837. Powers' report of Greenough's alleged hallucination was made post hoc, as were the similar assertions by other friends, upon learning of Greenough's death in a mental hospital, following a prolonged state of high fever and agitation. There is no mention of such an episode in Powers' or other contemporary letters, nor is there any record or suggestion of Greenough's having been disabled at any time due to mental derangement. This would surely have occurred had he been a victim of dementia praecox.

"Brain fever" is an obsolete euphemism for a fever of unknown origin. In Greenough's case, it could have derived from a neurological disorder or any other violent physiological disorder producing extremes of temperature. There seems to be little question that it was the undefined attack and the resultant high fever that caused Greenough's death, so unexpected at the premature age of forty-seven, at the height of his creative powers and intellectual maturity.

The funeral service in Cambridge was conducted on December 21 by the Reverend Dr. James Walker, It was a private affair and poorly attended. Horatio's body was interred in Mount Auburn Cemetery in Cambridge. A memorial meeting for him was held in Rome on Saturday, January 15, 1853, at the home of his colleague, Thomas Crawford, who delivered the usual eulogy, followed by an oration by William Wetmore Story. This was well attended by the Anglo-American artistic circle. They voted Greenough the title of Pioneer of American Sculpture, took cognizance of his accomplishments in both sculpture and scholarship and pledged to wear the black crepe armband of mourning for thirty days and transmit their expressions of sympathy to the family.[26]

The Rescue Group   1837–1850, marble
Courtesy of the National Collection of Fine Arts, Smithsonian Institution

8

Rescue Group and
Summation of Influence

IT WAS NOT UNTIL AFTER HIS DEATH THAT GREENOUGH'S SECOND monumental work for the Capitol was erected. Commissioned in 1837 it took thirteen years to complete and three years longer before it arrived at its destination. After its erection, it engendered controversy for over half a century.

The subject for this monument had been left open by President Martin Van Buren when he signed the contract with the sculptor on October 22, 1838.[1] It was simply stipulated that the group was to consist of "two statues, 9 feet high," in accordance with proposals and designs submitted by Greenough in his letter of November 15, 1837. This group was designed to adorn the east landing of the entranceway to the Capitol, as a companion piece to the group by Luigi Persico, which had been commissioned the previous February. Pressures had been mounting at the capital for the second group to be given to an American for execution, and Greenough was the obvious candidate as the best qualified American sculptor.

The government agreed to pay Greenough $4,000 annually for four years, upon certification of progress by the U.S. Consul at Leghorn or Rome, with a final payment of $5,000 upon completion, also properly certified (this last sum included $1,000 for the six-foot base). The total amounted to $21,000 for the group, prorated originally in accordance with the scale set at $10,000 each by Persico's *War* and *Peace* figures. Although a four-year term was stipulated for the group's completion, Greenough had learned better than to take the limitation seriously. He felt he had arrived at the happy juncture of indulging "the love of seeing things done as they should be" without compromising "the satisfaction for any money."[2] When writing to Henry of his private reservation respecting the fixed deadline, Horatio declared he would undertake the second monumental work "only on condition of having my own time to do it in."[3] The inefficiencies of Italian daily life alone would create unpredictable delays even if his work roster were less encumbered.

In contrast to his earlier poetical abstractions, Greenough resolved in this work to produce a realistic historical interpretation. This time he would conform to the popular idiom in his subject as well as style. Depicting the aboriginal Indian was generally in vogue at home. It was further settled that the group would be placed outdoors.

With these considerations in mind, he selected the theme of white civilization crowding the Indian from his soil, portraying the Indian as epitomizing a "barbarous race" in contrast to the "white" settler and his wife, representing the "virtuous Caucasian civilization."[4] His theme is that of the backwoodsman's triumphs through his "superiority" over the Indian, who menaces the white settler's wife and child. As related by a close friend of Greenough:

> The mother and child were before the Indian and she, in maternal instinct was shielding her child from his grasp, to prevent which the husband seized both arms of the Indian, and bears him down at the same time; so the group told its story of the peril of the American wilderness, the ferocity of the Indians, the superiority of the white man, and how and why civilization crowded the Indian from his soil, with the episode of woman and infancy and the sentiments which belong to them.[5]

At the design stage, Greenough had already increased the number of figures originally planned from two to four; the Indian, the white settler, and the settler's wife and child. Toward the end, when these were cast in plaster, it occurred to him to add a fifth figure, that of the household dog, for its "excellent effect" in filling out the group.[6]

Although Greenough completed his models by 1839, he was not satisfied with them and kept them in the studio. He made good use of the sketches he had made of Indian physiognomy in Washington years earlier. He reworked the figures, particularly the mother and child subgroup, more than once. In 1847, he remodeled them completely in the new plaster. Again the cutting into marble was delayed until the spring of 1851, when they were completed in beautiful white Serravezza stone, to the delight of the sculptor, who thought the tint of the marble a "perfect match," and of superior quality.[7]

If there were delays in the group's execution, they were matched by the government's dilatoriness in its payments. There was no getting around inevitable human delays, as when the witnessing consul absented himself for weeks, or perhaps months, or the official in Washington neglected this business in deference to more pressing matters closer to home. Greenough was caught in such circumstances throughout the entire execution of the group. He took advantage of the strategic position of his sympathetic friend Edward Everett as U.S. minister to London. Everett reported on his efforts; "By the last steamer, I wrote a strong letter to Mr. Webster [secretary of state] on the non-payment of your drafts."[8] Two weeks later, he reassured Greenough that "another appropriation is asked for, for your group. They have no idea of breaking your contract."[9] In June of 1842 the sum was still unpaid, and in December, when Greenough confronted Webster personally in Washington, the situation had not been altered. The extended delays compounded Greenough's financial problems, especially when he was forced to leave his studio to take Louisa to Graefenberg.

The final bothersome episode had to do with the transportation home of the completed figures. Just before leaving Florence in 1851, Greenough had met Commodore Morgan of the U.S. Navy, who happened to be in town, and made a tentative plan on the spot for the shipment, providing the cases would go down the hatches. The arrangement had only to await authorization from Washington. The last remaining detail, getting Mr. Binda, the United States Consul at

Leghorn, to execute the document of certification, seemed a super-fluous triviality at point. But protocol would be served and Gree-nough felt satisfied that all necessary items had been attended.

After those long years of exercising *pazienza* on Italian soil, of parrying daily with *subito* and *domani*, Greenough should have known better than to trust the Italians to adhere to a fixed schedule.

In Washington that fall his first errand was to check on the progress of the transportation. He learned that orders from Wash-ington to ship the group had been sent as requested to Commodore Morgan. Six months later Greenough was vexed to discover that the naval commander was still not under way despite having been ordered home "peremptorily with the group."[10] In August 1852, $9,000 was appropriated by Congress to cover these shipping charges from Leg-horn to Washington and the cost of placing the group on a pedestal. The total cost now stood at a minimum of $30,000.[11] The group ar-rived at its final resting place only after Greenough's death and was erected late in the fall of 1853 under the supervision of Clark Mills, then superintendent of buildings at the Capitol.

When placed, the group stood eleven feet, nine inches high, ten feet, two inches wide, and seven feet, three inches deep. The main figure was nine feet, one inch high, as stipulated in the contract, and it reposed on a base measuring three feet, five inches high, instead of the six feet specified in the document. There was no caviling about these small discrepancies, but a few years later an extraordinary ques-tion arose.

In the spring of 1859, a letter was directed to Senator James Pearce, chairman of the Joint Committee on the Library, which had charge of Capitol decorations, from Judge Edward G. Loring of Boston, a friend of the Greenough family. Judge Loring insisted that the position of the figures had been transposed and the signifi-cance of the group had been distorted. Greenough's emphasis on the ferocity of the Indians and the superiority of white civilization seemed perverted charged Judge Loring. "The mother and the child are removed from the peril, which is the causa causans of the action of the piece, and she is looking unconcernedly away from it."[12] The judge, acting for the Greenoughs, wanted to know what could be done to rectify the "error." This letter was forwarded for explanation by Senator Pearce to Captain M. C. Meigs, the current superintendent of buildings at the Capitol, who essayed a defense of the government's procedures by placing the blame on Greenough.

> How such a mistake could have occurred is very extraordinary. It argues carelessness on the part of the artist for had he sent proper instructions and drawings, they would of course have been followed. The figures, according to my recollection were set up under an appropriation of Congress, by . . . the sculptor of the Jackson statue, Mr. Clark Mills, under the general direction of the Commissioner of Public Buildings.
>
> I do not suppose that there is any money now appropriated applicable to the purpose of changing their position. . . .
>
> Any drawing by the sculptor of the group of Mr. Horatio Greenough, would be sufficient evidence of his intention.[13]

Although it is inconceivable that Greenough had failed to specify the details of the placement of each figure, his overall designs were not to be found at that time either among his personal papers or in the files of the architect of the Capitol. With no records to go by and the artist dead, the protest came to naught. The group has remained as it was placed originally until recently, when in the course of extending the Capitol building's east facade, it was removed (with Persico's work) from the landing of the entranceway.

Another postscript to this group's history must here be recorded. Some thirty years ago, an attack was leveled at the statue because of its racist connotation. The following is an excerpt of a resolution that was introduced into Congress in April of 1939 and died a natural death in the Joint Committee on the Library.

> To remove a monument now standing at the right of the east entrance to the National Capitol, representing the American Indian.
>
> Whereas some 87 years ago there was a monument erected at the right of the east entrance to the National Capitol, representing an American Indian with a tomahawk in hand about to kill a white woman and her child; and
>
> Whereas this monument is a constant reminder of ill-will toward the American Indian, who has now become a part of this Nation and has . . . assumed the duties of citizenship and has become as law abiding, as honorable, and as patriotic as any other race in our complex civilization;
>
> Whereas it is now the duty of all to forget the past. . . .

> Received by the Senate and House of Representatives of the United States in Congress assembled, that said monument known as *The Rescue* be removed, ground into dust, and scattered to the four winds, that no more remembrance may be perpetuated of our barbaric past....[14]

It is fortunate that the petition was ignored, even though its intent has now been carried out. The petition, arguing at least half a century late for the destruction of a bit of our historical record, was a futile gesture to efface an obsolete sin. Greenough was guilty of the Social Darwinian racism that was characteristic of his upper class fraternity up north which also bred enough heretics to place him in the right wing of the spectrum. He carried the racial bias to a point of hostility toward blacks as well. He disliked the black man because he considered him as a member of an inferior race. Greenough wrote:

> I am not partial to negroes. I dislike their neighborhood even in a menial capacity. I prefer doing many tiresome, and some very disagreeable things for myself rather than be very near a black man. . . . Black slavery was morally justified at its institution. . . . We have transferred a portion of the African race from ferocious barbarism to severe bondage. . . . I admit it. . . . We can answer to God for the act under the circumstances. We leave them better than we found them. . . . The free negroes of the north do not prosper, develop, or do good.[15]

It is odd that Greenough should have echoed John Calhoun's hackneyed defense of slavery at a time when a number of his intellectual peers were risking their reputations, perhaps their very lives, to advocate abolition. It perhaps attests to Calhoun's shrewdness of appealing to the ingrained snobbery of the country's intelligentsia, which found ready allies in this cause among the self-serving merchants of the eastern seaport cities, especially New York. Removed by expatriation from the center of the domestic debate over slavery, Greenough was not prone to correctives by his more radical Boston friends. Most of his fellow countrymen abroad shared his opinions. In Europe, the political center of gravity rested on absolute monarchy which the American expatriates opposed in their zeal for republicanism. The thorough classical education of the American artistic enclave predisposed them to such facile arguments as Calhoun employed; were not the Greek city-states, which had produced the Age of Pericles, the apotheosis of Western culture?

On the other side, Ralph Waldo Emerson marshaled his philosophical precepts to rationalize opposition to slavery. Transcendental notions of the divinity of man led logically to the conclusion of universal equality without excepting men of darker color. Greenough contested this view and wrote as follows:

> My adhesion to the South is political and is based on a belief that once a ship is *at sea* whatever else we may do, we must let her timbers alone. I believe that the example of the North and the growth of the Irish and German additions to our populations will put an end to slavery sooner than any [attack] made upon the South upon moral and scriptural grounds. Precisely because northern morality coexists peaceably with greater woes than the woe of Slavery. . . . In vain shall we preach abstractions and perfection to the south while we offer gold for their tobacco, cotton, and sugar. If we are to act upon the south fairly, we must begin by withdrawing the demand for Slave products.
>
> I am a staunch believer in free discussion and have no objections to hear any amount of abuse of slavery and slaveholders—provided there be also a fair hearing for the defense. So far as the negro himself is concerned, I fully believe . . . he can exist here *only as a bondsman.* Are we not a little rash in asserting our own freedom? We are parts of an organization and being such can have no *freedom* but by a dissolution of the system of which we are fractional and functional components.[16]

This rationale epitomizes a belief in republicanism rather than democracy. Emerson's estimate of Greenough as a staunch democrat must be accounted an exaggeration. Although Greenough professed an interest in politics throughout his life, it was quite a simplistic one. He inveighed against unrepresentative governments in Europe and favored republics as opposed to monarchies. He was but superficially read in politics and remained a dilettante in that sphere. He was the artist and critic to the core, however.

When he concluded "that full economic and social equality were the first conditions for the development of his country's art," his paramount concern was the progress of art.[17] Out of his theories of functionalism came the Social Darwinism that led him astray. When he admired the natural adaptation of man to mechanized society, it was not the promised increase of mass consumption that excited his interest, but the rationality of man's ability to adapt to changing conditions. The theory of the survival of the fittest that is imbedded in Social Darwinism fed the admiration of Greenough and his group for people of special talent, or geniuses, as they called them. Their outlook rarely transcended their own middle class outlook upon the impoverished masses. Their democracy was generally restricted to theory.

Greenough's deep-seated respect for women was again not a distinctly advanced social attitude for his time, but a fair reflection of his group in Boston society, where confirmation of this view was exemplified daily. His female friends had literary attainments and education equal to any of their male peers. The women's rights movement was in full swing under the aegis of the militant Peabody sisters, the Sedgwicks, Wards, and Alcotts. Margaret Fuller had played her part earlier. The women were taking to pen and platform whether their husbands approved or not. His own wife was of this group, although not a leader.

His esteem for women was also closely related to his anti-clericalism, which was rooted in the liberal ethos of the nineteenth century. The Catholic Church's imposition of celibacy on its priests was, in his opinion, a perversion of a natural process and to be condemned. He was vehemently censorious of the clergy in Italy for their sensuality, their immorality, their "trampling thus upon the rights of womanhood . . . and cruel as the grave with regard to all those sufferings which he does not share . . . offspring, the family tie, the honor of the house."[18] Accepting the natural bodily functions as aspects approaching the perfection of the "Godhead," he also disapproved of chastity, per se. "If chastity be in itself pleasing to God," he reasoned, "then the means he has chosen for the peopling of the earth are a strange anomaly."[19]

Greenough's anti-Catholicism also derived from the Church's intimate connection with monarchical institutions. Reprehensible enough in the abstract, this tie was regarded by the American residents in Italy as absolutely pernicious because of its active betrayal of the Roman Republic in 1849.

The participation of the Americans in the defense of the Tuscan and Roman Republics gave them and their liberal Italian friends a real stake in both republicanism and anticlericalism. Moreover, the Church countenanced the poverty of the masses in corrupt Catholic countries of Europe, counseling resignation and countering reform or revolution. Greenough disliked priests in general also because their isolation from society "makes [them] a passive tool in the hands of the governing power."[20]

For all his passion against the church, however, Greenough loved Italy too much and understood his adopted land too well, not to moderate his anger and adjust his views accordingly. The Church's lavish patronage of the arts through the centuries was a mediating factor that helped him to bridge the gap. His humanism, molded in the classics and nurtured in Italy, paved the way. Cognizant of the contradictions at play upon him, he wrote, "I should hate the Catholic Church but for the immense love I bear her. . . . If any man will show me a higher civilization in essence than the Catholic, I will seek the place where it is. . . ." He continued rhetorically, "He who can ponder the relation of the Church to humanity without tears of gratitude, is not worthy of the name of man." And he concluded, "For every rotten branch of the Church, I will undertake to find an unsound root in humanity."[21] This is not the language of a political man, but that of a compassionate artist and humanist.

The longer he lived there, the better he understood Italy's mentality. Margaret Fuller had remarked on his depth of insight when she observed "[Greenough is] one of the few Americans who, living in Italy, takes the pains to know whether it is alive or dead, who penetrated beyond the cheats of the tradesmen and the cunning of the mob corrupted by centuries of slavery, to know the real mind, the vital blood of Italy."[22] The aptness of this judgment is borne out by his own perceptive comment, "The low Italian applies foul names to the Virgin Mary when out of humor. This is one form of belief."[23] This scion of New England showed genuine understanding and sensitivity in transcending his native Protestant bias to notice the security which the church offered her true believers in the Holy Trinity.

By and large, Greenough remained in heart and mind singularly American. It would have been a pity if he had not come home to be buried in his native soil. His chief concern was the American scene, and once there, her welfare. His schemes for her improvement were prolific. To him, we are indebted for the first significant voice to clamor for a distinctive American art to keep pace with national need. He was America's pioneer aesthetician in the best sense. Yet paradoxically, he remained neoclassical, hence Italian, in his sculpture. He led the American sculptors to their Italian training ground, setting the precedent for the wholesale flooding of American homes with Italian works of art through the better half of the nineteenth century, thus transmitting the classical aesthetics in both subject and form as it prevailed in Italy. In this respect, Greenough's influence outlived him a quarter of a century, or roughly until the 1870s, when Americans began to turn to Paris as the world sculptural center.

Although Greenough failed to found a school either of art or design, his short range influence on American sculpture was sizable if indirect. In the long run however, his influence dwindled into insignificance. His own aesthetic principles betrayed him. His neoclassical style, being more derivative than creative and altogether foreign to the American scene, was predestined to doom. He failed to overcome the contradiction between his theories and his productions. Ralph Waldo Emerson perceived the problem. Shortly after Greenough's death, Emerson wrote the news to Thomas Carlyle in London employing the same phrase he had jotted into his journal. After accounting Greenough "one product of American soil, as one of the best proofs of the capabilities of this country," he remarked that Greenough's "tongue was far cunninger in talk than his chisel [was] to carve."[24]

Greenough's failure to resolve the conflict between "Ideality and Substance" was shared by most of his contemporaries. An eminent art historian recently stated, however, that Greenough's "effort was mightier than any other. . . . No American has dared to be so monumental in scale or so majestic in pose and gesture."[25] This critic pronounced Greenough praiseworthy from the modern outlook particularly for his significant contribution as "a believer in the organic principle—nearly a century before Sullivan and Wright. . . . His notions on art ranged far beyond his time and his analysis of the art he saw around him was brilliantly perceptive."[26] This judgment we can share heartily.

A portion of responsibility for Greenough's failure to gain recognition during his lifetime must be ascribed to Greenough himself. He dissipated his cascading energies in corrosive talk, burning himself out before he could produce tangible illustrations of his notions, the only possible medium for reaching pragmatic Americans who habitually turn a deaf ear to abstract principles.

Although the welfare of America and a love of humanity occupied a large share of his concern, it was essentially art to which Greenough was dedicated. In the rhetoric of his own time, Henry T. Tuckerman memorialized him aptly.

> Greenough, by his pen, his presence, and his chisel gave an impetus to taste and to knowledge in sculpture and architecture not destined soon to pass away; no more eloquent and original advocate of the beautiful, the true in the higher social economies has blest our day, his Cherubs and Medora overflow with the poetry of form, his essays are a valuable legacy of philosophical thought.[27]

9

Greenough's Aesthetics in Perspective

RALPH WALDO EMERSON POPULARIZED GREENOUGH'S REPUTATION AS a great democrat. Whether Emerson was focused on the pioneer aesthetician's functionalism or the pleasure Greenough took in talking with mechanics and speculating about machinery, the judgment would appear vindicated at first blush. Add to that Greenough's renunciation of his adopted land because of the tyrannical rule imposed by the Austrians after the Italians had welcomed him in their midst, given him requisite training and optimum working conditions, and accorded him unprecedented recognition as an artist.

Yet, Emerson's attribution of Greenough's functionalism to his democratic outlook is suspect. The undeviating neoclassicism of Greenough's sculptural works scarcely catered to the populace. Skepticism is compounded out of respect for Greenough's intellectuality, which could easily have detected the contradiction between his functional theory and his neoclassical artistry. The dilemma is further multiplied by Greenough's impassioned invocation of a distinctive American art at the same time that he not only gave impetus to large-scale importations of Italianate sculptural works but created them also.

To explain the contradiction, another hypothesis seems required for the sake of logic. It turns out upon closer examination that Greenough's functionalism derived out of the very neoclassical Italian school that determined his sculptural style. The apparent paradox can be resolved if viewed dialectically, if Greenough is seen as the quintessential American artist who was entirely "made in Italy" by its classicism and its humanism. His aesthetics as well as his sculptural style had their taproots in Italy.

In his day, the classical ground of Italy was the cynosure of the Western intellectual. Greenough was appropriately attracted. It was primarily in classical doctrine and the Italian writings which perpetuated it that he stumbled upon his functionalism, the essence of his artistic creed, if not his practice. He distilled the principles of Italian aesthetics out of the innumerable books and masterpieces that he encountered on the Continent and aptly applied them to his native scene. His education at Harvard preparatory to this broadening experience was strictly geared to the classics, as was the extracurricular dominating influence of Washington Allston.

"To do justice to Allston," observed Greenough, "one should be familiar with the history of art at that epoch."[1]

> Allston began the study of Art in Rome at a time when a revolution in taste has just been affected throughout the Continent. The works of Winckelmann and Visconti were but symptoms of the sensation which pervaded the cultivated classes, a reaction whose first wave swept away the puny relics of Bernini and whose second placed Canova on the pedestal of Phidias, and David on the throne of painting. . . .
> We should know how exclusively Roman history occupied public attention as a subject of Art. . . . We should be aware how fully Michelangelo had fallen into disrepute, how the simpler and earlier masters were laughed to scorn. . . . In our day, Canova turned to the Greeks, satiated by the extravagance of Bernini's school.[2]

Allston returned from Italy to spread the new gospel and was the aesthetical dean of his group of intellectuals at Cambridge. Greenough literally sat at his feet.

Educated at Harvard and oriented by Allston in appreciation of the "beautiful," Greenough arrived in Italy adequately armed. He soon came to know "the glories of Schiller and Winckelmann, of Goethe and Hegel."[3] Italy was the meeting place of German idealism and classical humanism, here Plato and Aristotle had been prized particularly by the humanists of the Renaissance and were rediscovered by the liberal nationalist leaders of the Risorgimento whom Greenough had befriended in Florence.

Uniquely significant in recapturing classical values and formulating principles upon them was the German scholar, Johann Joachim Winckelmann, who had come to Rome half a century earlier to study the antique sculptures excavated at Herculanaeum and Pompeii and preserved in the Royal Museum at Naples and the Vatican. In 1758 he became librarian to his patron, Cardinal Albani, who was dedicated to the new art and had amassed an important collection of such works and books. In 1763 Winckelmann was nominated Inspector General of Roman Antiquities and began frequent trips to Pompeii, Herculanaeum, and Naples. He studied, classified, and became the father of modern archaeology, publishing his observations as *Rapporti, La Storia Dell' Arte presso gli Antichi*, and *Monumenti Antichi Inediti* over the ensuing years. The "Storia," appearing in Rome in 1764, was chiefly responsible for the reversal of taste over the baroque trend presided over by Bernini and Borromini. Although Winckelmann was murdered in 1768, only four years later, his work lived on. His influence was pervasive; his conclusions were embodied in the aesthetical writings of every western language.

Winckelmann esteemed Canova for his excellence in the classical form, stating that "Like the Greek, he resolved to begin in the art where the art itself had begun, in assiduously studying and faithfully imitating nature."[4] From the profusion of Greek sculptures available for study, Winckelmann had deduced that "The highest object, after Deity, namely Beauty,"[5] is "the loftiest mark and central point of art."[6] Winckelman inferred from the common source that later also nourished Greenough and the Transcendentalists that "The highest Beauty is in God; and our idea of human beauty advances toward perfection in proportion as it can be imagined in conformity with the highest Existence which, in our conception of unity and indivisibility, we distinguish from matter."[7] This conclusion is logical if Plato's assumption that nature is a reflection of the universal godhead is valid. Plato had defined "true beauty" as "a god-like face or form" and equated "the good with the beautiful."

Greenough found these sentiments congenial and echoed them. "I believe the beautiful to be the promise and the announcement of the good," he wrote.[8] He was not alone. Emerson found a moral element in all high beauty. He was popularly understood when he discussed the eternal trinity of "Truth, and goodness, and beauty," as "different faces of the same All," created by God as a part or expression of nature, the triple face of the Eternal Spirit.[9] In Victorian England, the Utilitarians were demanding the greatest good for the greatest number and condemning in society or architecture, that which was unadapted to human needs. Both Emerson and Greenough saw in the lack of integration between the individual and societal structure selfishness and immorality. The kinship between functionalism and morality was self-evident to these platonic idealists.

The Transcendentalists' interpretation of beauty in moral terms arose also out of their reaction to Calvinism. To these humanist iconoclasts in New England, God was no longer vengeful as decreed by Calvin and interpreted by his puritan followers but was now an omnipotent benign Father. Man's conception became the result of the natural process of procreation rather than the outcome of the sinful act of copulation.

It followed for them that nakedness was closest to godliness: pure, innocent, and good. Before Greenough Winckelmann has discovered the platonic maxim that among the Greeks, "The loftiest aim of art [was] the conformation of the nude."[10] He explained that their familiarity with the nude body was natural in a society that emphasized physical culture in the gymnasiums throughout the land. Greenough arrived at the same conclusion, "In nakedness, I behold the majesty of the essential instead of the trappings of pretension."[11]

If the nude was the noblest form, being closest to nature and to God; then its proximity to perfection was its measure of beauty. By this logic, Winckelmann deduced the quality of beauty in the "Grand Style" as based on portrayals of ideals. At its base was simplicity. "All beauty," he decreed, "is heightened by unity and simplicity . . . for whatever is great in itself is elevated, when executed and uttered with simplicity."[12] He disparaged the "profusion of ornaments" of the Persians, "whereby the members of their edifices, splendid of themselves, lost much of their grandeur."[13]

In elaborating his theory to Emerson, Greenough refined this notion to the extreme. "I beg you to reflect," he wrote, "that this Godlike human body has no ornament for the same reason that men do not gild gold."[14] His admiration for the human body was unbounded, and he considered it the most perfect mechanism conceivable for its habitat. "It is all beauty, its motion is grace, no combination of harmony ever equaled, for expression and variety, its poised and stately gait; its voice is music."[15] The human frame was to him "the most beautiful organization of earth, the exponent and minister of the highest being."[16] In "the many-sided and full and rich harmony of Nature," Greenough found the counterpart of perfection in organization, reflecting "a many-sided response to the call for many functions."[17]

Emerson was persuaded of the validity of this deduction and responded to Greenough's hypothesis as counterpoint to principal theme in a fugue. He wrote: "We ascribe beauty to that which is simple; which has no superfluous parts; which exactly answers its end; which stands related to all things; which is the mean of many extremes. . . . all beauty must be organic; that outside embellishment is deformity."[18]

Greenough considered the essence of beauty as simply "the promise of function,"[19] stating, "If there be any principle of structure more plainly inculcated in the works of the Creator than all others, it is the principle of unflinching adaptation of forms to functions."[20]

The organic principle had roots in several strains of Western culture. Greenough found it in "the men who in Greece and Italy earned a remembrance as creators of the beautiful" because they "were most untiring students of organization."[21]

The new idealists rested their case ultimately on the authority of Plato and Aristotle, who shared a subtle modification of stark functionalism by admitting into the sacred precinct of the beautiful the element of pleasure. As Plato wrote:

> When you speak of beautiful things, do you not call them beautiful in reference to some standard: bodies, for example, are beauti-

ful in proportion as they are useful, or as the sight of them gives pleasure to the spectators. . . .

Laws and institutions also have no beauty in them except in so far as they are pleasant or useful, or both. . . . I very much approve of your measuring beauty by the standard of pleasure and utility.[22]

Aristotle had also hinted at the relation of art to nature, with special reference to adaptation of means to ends. Like Plato, he found fitness the essential component of beauty but not the exclusive factor, acknowledging also the element of pleasure. For proof, he cited varying aspects of comeliness which develop in accordance with the successive stages of man, selecting that element of beauty most appropriate to man's need in any given period. In youth, for example, comeliness consists in

> Having a body useful in enduring toils, whether those of the course, or of personal exertion, himself being pleasant withal to look upon with a view to delight. . . . But the comeliness of one who has attained life's prime is a person adapted to the fatigues of war, with an aspect to be looked upon with pleasure tempered with awe. That of the old, consists in the body being capable of the fatigue which it undergoes.[23]

The midcentury pre-Darwinian evolutionary theorizers gave substance to this idea of functional adaptation in their speculations, culminating with the rule of the survival of the fittest. From these evolutionists, Greenough deduced his organic rule of development. He pared the argument to the next logical step from Plato, denying to pleasure any validity as a component of beauty. Accordingly, he wrote:

> There is no arbitrary law of proportion, no unbending model of form. There is scarce a part of the animal organization which we do not find elongated or foreshortened, increased, diminished, or suppressed, as the wants of the genus or species dictate, as their exposure or their work may require.
>
> The neck of the swan and that of the eagle, however different in character and proportion, equally charm the eye and satisfy the reason. We approve the length of the same member in grazing animals, its shortness in beasts of prey. The horse's shanks are thin,

and we admire them; the greyhound's chest is deep, and we cry, beautiful!

It is neither the presence nor the absence of this or that part, or shape, or color, that wins our eye in natural objects; it is the consistency and harmony of the parts juxtaposed, the subordination of details to masses, and of masses to the whole. The law of adaptation is the fundamental law of nature in all structure.[24]

From this hub, it followed reasonably "that the first downward step was the introduction of the first inorganic, nonfunctional element, whether of shape or color."[25] In the human body, the animal kingdom, indeed, all of nature, Greenough found complete harmony of all parts to the whole and substantial examples of the adaptation of each entity to the grand design of the universe. To him the unrivaled example of this principle was a ship at sea, in which the dimensions of every part are confined and regulated by fitness for sailing. He remarked that when a vessel sails well, the sailors call her a beauty. Greenough marveled:

Observe a ship at sea! Mark the majestic form of her hull as she rushes through the water, observe the graceful bend of her body, the gentle transition from round to flat, the grasp of her keel, the leap of her bows, the symmetry and rich tracery of her spars and rigging, and those grand wind muscles, her sails. . . .
What Academy of Design . . . produced this marvel of construction? Here is the result of the study of man upon the great deep, where Nature spake of the laws of building. . . .[26]

Greenough did detect a flaw—the carved wooden figurehead he considered an impropriety and he demanded that figureheads be discarded as mere embellishment. He wrote: "I was delighted with another proof that I had found of the perfect organization of ships, viz., that the only part of the hull where function will allow a statue to stand without being in Jack's way is one where the plunge bath so soon demolishes it."[27]

Greenough disposed of embellishments as inorganic, nonfunctional encumbrances to harmony and rationality. To Greenough decoration inharmonious with the whole and unsubordinated to the larger purpose of the entire work marked a distinct decline in art. Embellishment of this kind could not avoid the corruption of separating the "sensuously pleasing from its organic relation."[28] Into this trap were snared the rococo painters epitomized by Luca Giordano and Francois Boucher, whom Greenough charged with immorality for being a "chaos of bombast, falsehood, and clogging sensuality."[29]

Greenough believed that the completeness and rational structure of nature showed the accord of truth and one God. Unadapted ornaments Greenough considered sinful, as they were irrational creations in God's rational universe.

Greenough stated, "I cannot accept as a demonstration of embellishment, a sensuous beauty not yet organically explained." This seemed to him to controvert his belief in one God who was both rational and good, he stated, "The advocate of independent beauty" must necessarily believe in a God of evil, or the devil too, for unrelated embellishment is irrational, and refutes its being the "work of a divine hand."[30]

Greenough thus judged "the flying hair and waving draperies of Bernini" as "proofs of ill-judged toil . . . vagaries,"[31] which were no more admissible by proper standards for beauty than "the prolific silliness of Borromini."[32] These were not creative pieces to him but mere displays of craftsmanship representing a "conquest of mechanical difficulty."[33] These baroque works had already been characterized by Sir Joshua Reynolds as "laborious effects of idleness," to be excluded from the compass of art.[34]

The Gothic Trinity Church in New York and Saint Peter's Cathedral were similarly criticized by Greenough. He spoke of Saint Peter's as "that vast aggregation of marble and gilding—of silks and jewels, of glass and metal, of carved and painted embellishment," whose size is a pretension.[35] The excessive adornments and size of Saint Peter's blatantly contradicted Plato's dictum that art must reflect in simplest forms the attributes of "Beauty, Symmetry, and Truth as well as the good."[36] The excesses were also incorrect as symbols to characterize the saint for whom the church is named.

The British art historian John Smythe Memes asserts that the principles of functionalism that Greenough deduced from classical doctrine and Winckelmann's theories were widely disseminated in Greenough's time chiefly through the writings of the Venetian critic, Francesco Algarotti, and the Neapolitan architect, Francesco Milizia.

Smythe described Milizia as "that terrible Aristarchus of the arts, that bitter critic who never ceased to exclaim against modern [baroque] art and artists."[37]

A scholar from a noble Neapolitan family, Milizia had moved to Rome in 1761 where he studied philosophy, admired the venerable antiquities, and devoted himself to architectural history and aesthetics. Four years after the appearance of Winckelmann's study, he published his *Viti degli Architetti piu Celebri,* which was followed by a multivolume analysis of architectural principles, *Elementi di Architetture Civile.* In both of these books, Milizia set forth rules that were steeped in the aesthetical doctrines of the Greeks. He joined with Winckelmann in admiring Canova for his classical works, which represented the most desirable trend away from Bernini. Milizia's influence was significant in Italy and even filtered through the Continent, chiefly by means of the 1828 English translation of his *Viti.* The translator of that volume stated in the preface that Milizia's work "has always been esteemed on the Continent."[38]

A careful comparison of the principles propounded by Milizia with those formulated by Greenough almost a century later reveals an astonishing affinity. While functionalism was the central doctrine for both, the similarity in their reasoning and statements is so striking that Greenough might be suspected of plagiarism.

Milizia spoke of "building [as] the offspring of necessity." Of architectural priorities he wrote "convenience [is] the first consideration, next solidity, and finally beauty." He defined convenience "as the use of reason in the choice and applications of all that is requisite to render the building perfect; that is beautiful, convenient, and strong, according to the various uses for which they may be intended." Having established the use or function of an edifice as its focal point and necessity as the controlling consideration, Milizia advocated simplicity and banished any ornament or element that failed to serve the paramount purpose. If adornment were to be allowed, it must conform, just as "the sculpture of the orders should be conformable to the qualities and conditions of the building." Simplicity, however, need not be carried to the point of dullness. Having in mind a critique of Gothic architecture, Milizia echoed Aristotle in writing, "Without variety, everything is insipid." Deciding that

"Gothic architecture; from being too much loaded with small and different ornaments, destroys the beauty of variety," he confined variety to "a few ornaments well managed."[39]

Milizia was later paraphrased by Hogarth to support his use of the Serpentine line whose variegated curves he considered vital for beauty. This undulating line really characterized the baroque although Hogarth neglected to make the identification. Greenough disposed of it with "the vagaries of Bernini."[40] While agreeing that "fitness of the parts to the design [was] of the greatest consequence to the beauty of the whole," Hogarth insisted that "simplicity without variety is wholly insipid."[41] Milizia had taken the midway position, restricting variety severely so that "variety should not occasion confusion."[42]

Greenough pursued Milizia's argument to its logical conclusion, as he had done with Winckelmann's. He dispelled any possible confusion emanating from variety by excluding it as an element of beauty. Hogarth's serpentine line did not pose any new problem as Greenough argued that the right line is obviously right only in its organic relation. He amplified:

> From its inevitable significance and uniformity of expression it becomes monotonous by repetition, incongruous and impertinent wherever such double action is out of place. Transfer the waving line of a horse's flank to his metatarsal bone, and you have a cripple. Transfer the double curve of a swan's neck to his bell, and you have an impotent and therefore ridiculous arrangement.[43]

Greenough's sole measure of beauty in architecture was relatedness to function and site. All gratuitous adornment was embellishment, and he castigated it as "false beauty." In his essay "Relative and Independent Beauty," he affirmed, "The law of adaptation is the fundamental law of nature in all structure. So unflinchingly does she modify a type in accordance with a new position, that some philosophers have declared a variety of appearance to be the object aimed at; so entirely does she limit the modification to the demands of necessity. . . . [44]

Greenough's standards for beauty were uncompromising, more rigid than Milizia's and unyielding beyond Aristotle's and Plato's. He would not sanction art for art's sake.

With the complete construction in view, Milizia detailed the essential components of good architectural design as follows:

1st, In all its productions, there should be an agreeable relation between the parts and the whole; which is comprehended under the name of symmetry.

2nd, Variety . . . and unity, which prevents disorder and confusion. . . .

3rd, Convenience is necessary, then ornament, which makes a just use of symmetry and eurythny, and of the relation which there should be between an edifice and its destiny, and between the ornament and quality of the building, adopting those most conformable to its magnificence, elegance, or simplicity.

4th, If architecture be the daughter of necessity, even its beauties should appear to result from such. In no part of the decoration should there be any artifice discoverable; hence everything extraneous is a proof of bad taste.

5th, The principal features of architecture are its orders [columns] or, more properly they are the essentials of a building; and are, therefore, considered as ornaments only when usefully placed. . . .

6th, Nothing must be introduced which has not its proper office, and is not an integral part of the fabric itself; so that whatever is represented must appear of service.

7th, No arrangement must be made for which a good reason cannot be assigned.

8th, Every thing must be founded upon truth or its similitude.

9th, Examples and authority, however great they may be should have no effect on that reason.[45]

Milizia considered proportion, the unity of the parts as sublimated to the whole, to be "the most beautiful and principal feature in architecture."[46] In almost the same words Winckelmann had written a few years earlier, "It is impossible to conceive of beauty without proportion."[47]

Milizia went on to observe that "a building devoid of all ornament, and without any other merit than a justness of proportion, will always produce a beautiful effect, and be sufficient in itself."[48] Winckelmann had been satisfied with similar prerequisites, finding the cause of beauty in unity, variety, and harmony. Greenough fell into the same line, requiring the complete harmony of all parts to the whole.

As for his third component of beautiful architecture, solidity, Milizia took a functional stand, as Greenough did later. Not only did Milizia require the size, shape, and weight of a structure to depend on the use intended, but these factors also had to be related to the site. Greenough concurred. Insisting on the same functional features for good architecture as did Milizia, he reduced all construction to bare essentials. He wrote,"To plant a building firmly on the ground [solidity], to give it the light that may, the air that must be be needed [use], to apportion the spaces for convenience, decide their size, and model their shapes for their functions [convenience], these acts organize a building."[49]

Milizia summarized his rules in language already familiar. He declared, "The propriety of every edifice comprehends three principal objects, which are, first, its situation; second, its form; third, the distribution of the parts."[50] Milizia sternly insisted on retaining in an edifice a strict interrelationship between the outside and inside; on conforming its outer appearance to its internal use. He wrote, "The facade is to an edifice what the physiognomy is to man. . . . Various facades should express the purposes of the interior of buildings."[51]

Apropos this proposition, some eighty years later Greenough scorned the appropriation of the Greek temple form for indiscriminate modern commercial purposes. On his return to America he pointed out that a transplanted Greek temple could not efficiently serve in Philadelphia or Boston as a bank or in New York as a merchant's exchange. Believing that the light and spatial arrangements were necessarily foredoomed, he stated that he wanted no sneaking copy of a Greek facade to mask the chaos of "ill-arranged, ill-lighted, and stifled rooms."[52] A bank should have the "physiognomy" of a bank, a church should be recognized as such.[53] In his essay, "American Architecture," Greenough asked, "Is not the Greek temple jammed in between the brick shops of Wall Street, or Cornhill, covered with lettered signs, and occupied by groups of money-changers and applewomen" as ludicrous a sight as an "African King, standing in mock majesty with his legs and feet bare, and his body clothed in a cast coat of the Prince Regent?"[54]

In their own ambience, Greenough did not object to the monuments of Egypt and Greece, stating that the obelisk and the temple were "sublime expressions of their power and their feeling."[55] But modern nations appropriating them out of their native context transformed them into vulgar displays of wealth. Greenough observed at length:

> The mind of this country has never been seriously applied to the subject of building. Intently engaged in matters of more pressing importance, we have been content to receive our notions of architecture as we have received the fashion of our garments and the form of our entertainments, from Europe.
>
> In our eagerness to appropriate, we have neglected to adapt, to distinguish—nay, to understand. We have built small Gothic temples of wood and have omitted all ornaments for economy, unmindful that size, material, and ornament are the elements of effect in that style of building. Captivated by the classic symmetry of the Athenian models, we have sought to bring the Parthenon into our streets to make the temple of Theseus work in our towns.[56]

Greenough had evidently discussed this subject with his friend and patron, James Fenimore Cooper, during their long evenings together in Florence and Paris and had won him over. In his first novel upon returning home, "*Home as Found*," Cooper wrote: "The public sentiment just now runs almost exclusively and popularly into the Grecian school. We build little besides temples for our churches, our banks, our taverns, our courthouses, and our dwellings. A friend of mine has just built a brewery on the model of the Temple of the Winds."[57]

The trend was justified for being "more republican," in that it exemplified the ancient Greek city-states. Before Greenough, the importation was accepted without question. Greenough, however, our first aesthetician, sought a style of American art that would delineate the nation's own character and express its particular outlook. The intelligentsia bemoaned the unquestionable absence of a native culture. From classical principles transmitted to him by the Italians, Greenough found his solution to the problem of developing a true American architecture:

> Instead of forcing the functions of every sort of building into one general form, adopting an outward shape for the sake of the eye or association, without reference to the inner distribution, let us begin from the heart as a nucleus, and work outward.
>
> The most convenient size and arrangement of the rooms that are to constitute the building being fixed, the access of the light that may, of the air that must be wanted, being provided for, we have the skeleton of our building. Nay, we have all excepting the dress. The connection and order of the parts, juxtaposed for convenience, cannot fail to speak of their relation and uses. . . .
>
> So, the unflinching adaptation of a building to its position and use gives, as a sure product of that adaptation, character and expression.[58]

Greenough believed that civil architecture should be based on the same principles of proportion evident in the construction of such things as bridges, scaffolding, ships, and machines. He admired the efficiency of machines and wrote approvingly of their design, noting "how weight is shaken off where strength is less needed, how functions are made to approach without impeding each other, how straight becomes curved, and the curve is straightened, till the straggling and cumbersome machine becomes the compact, effective and beautiful engine."[59]

Greenough studied the substance of every previous style of architecture, especially the Greek, for the guiding rules that would suit the industrial society developing in America. He stated that he would "learn of the Greeks to be American,"[60] and from their philosophy and experience, he would cull the principles of the true and the beautiful and adapt them to home conditions. He concluded, "we learn of them to belong to our day and to our nation, as they to theirs."[61]

The relationship between art and society was considered by Winckelmann as well as Greenough. They both attributed the superiority of Greek art in part to the kind of society that produced it—a competitive, democratic society in which works of art were accessible to all and generally valued. Greece was the "land of art" to Winckelmann, and he believed that everything in that land—from climate and philosophy to constitutional government—conspired to produce that effect.[62] In the days of Phidias when the

Greeks produced their most exalted works, the government sponsored competitions in all branches of arts and sports. "The wisest of
the whole nation in the assembly of united Greece passed judgment
upon and regarded them and their works," noted Winckelmann, impressed that "excellence in art and handiwork of every kind was
particularly prized."[63] According to Winckelmann, in that civilization beauty was "an excellence which led to fame."[64]

After Greenough had turned his back on tyranny in Europe,
he was more than ever the crusading republican, eager to serve his
society in all its facets. He spoke of the American people as "the
advanced guard of humanity."[65] It seemed axiomatic to him that
widespread art education, publicly subsidized, would yield greater
beauty in both public and private architecture. It is the great
multitude for whom all really great things are done, and said, and
suffered," he announced. "The great multitude desires the best of
everything, and in the long run is the best judge of it."[66]

Greenough talked art with mechanics, frequented foundries
and drew practical designs in his last years at home. While Europe
suffered regressive tyranny he was optimistic that American democratic institutions contained greater potentiality for the natural
growth of art than any "hotbed" culture. He wrote glowingly,
"There is at present, no country where the development and growth
of an artist is more free, healthful, and happy than it is in these
United States."[67]

Arguing against the formation of academies, which he believed
inevitably became artistic arbiters, "hostile to artistic progress,"
Greenough called for "working normal schools of structure and
ornament . . . constantly occupied in designing for the manufactur-
ers, and for all the mechanics who need aesthetical guidance."[68]
Greenough made out a persuasive case favoring a congressional subsidy for such a school that would improve our international competitive position, particularly vis-à-vis British textiles. If not from
the national government, then subvention should come from the
states, but he understood the advantages of public patronage and
dangled the obvious benefits that would accrue to the country from
such a program. The boards of trade in England and on the Continent had subsidized artistic training advantageously for centuries, why

shouldn't we. Greenough stated that "the best models of Greece and Italy were placed within reach of every manufacturing population."[69] He added, "High art stands, in relation to manufactures and to the so-called lower trades, where high literature stands in relation to society and to civil life."[70]

Greenough conceived of art essentially as a vehicle expressive of man's personal needs and ideals, his reality and aspiration. "The creation of beauty in art, as in other forms of poetry, is a welling up from the depths of the soul, not a scientific synthesis," he wrote.[71] He had decided this rather early in his career and had remarked, "I look for thought, for imagination, for feeling," when seeking the sources of artistic expression.[72] He observed further, "These beauties [of antiquity], then, have been created by relation in our own minds."[73] In this platonic and Kantian view, the creative process was positive, in contrast to the critical, which is an entirely negative one. "Reason can dissect, but cannot originate; she can adapt, but cannot create," he wrote.[74]

Aristotle had a similar view of the creative act. For him, art encompassed all that constitutes the inward and essential activity of the soul. Art, he thought, "addresses itself not to the abstract reason, but to the sensibility and image-making faculty; it is concerned with outward appearance; it employs illusions; . . . it sees truth, but in its concrete manifestations, not as an abstract idea."[75]

Winckelmann had also dealt with creativity in the same idiom; positing that "many artists are skilled in proportion, but few have produced beauty, because soul and feeling, rather than intellect are required in its creation."[76] He revealed himself as a humanist when he stated that "Beauty in art scaled its highest peak in Athens because of the humanity of the Athenians" and "Athens alone knows the feeling of pity."[77]

Greenough began to dissect the first American edifices at Washington and then to criticize theories of aesthetics which had cropped up abundantly over the past century, chiefly in England. Everything was unsparingly measured by his Procrustean rod. He lopped off any trespass beyond fitness and chastised any permissive genuflection toward Independent Beauty. As Greenough's scholarship was thorough, it must be assumed he read all the pertinent writers from

William Hogarth to Sir Joshua Reynolds and beyond.[78] Sir Archibald Alison, Sir Charles and Lady Eastlake, James Ferguson, and Edmund Burke, all took the Platonic and Aristotelian midway position, admitting both fitness and ornament as elements of beauty.[79] Edward Lacy Garbett arrived later and, like Greenough, emphasized fitness as most essential.[80] Greenough failed to deal with John Ruskin, probably because they were writing contemporaneously, and he concentrated his withering fire on Edmund Burke, giving Burke's categories for the beautiful short shrift.

In his book on the philosophy of beauty, Burke had defined beauty as "that quality, or those qualities in bodies, by which they cause love, or some passion similar to it."[81] He further stated:

> Proportion relates almost wholly to convenience, as every idea of order seems to do; and it must therefore be considered as a creature of the understanding, rather than a primary cause acting on the senses and imagination. . . .
>
> Beauty demands no assistance from our reasoning. . . . Proportion is the measure of relative quantity . . . there is nothing to interest the imagination. . . . That proportion has but a small share in the formation of Beauty, is fully evident among animals. . . . Proportion [is] not the cause of Beauty in the Human species. It arose from the Platonic theory of fitness and aptitude. . . . Proportion and Beauty are not ideas of the same nature. The true opposite to beauty is not disproportion or deformity, but ugliness.
>
> Fitness [is] not the cause of Beauty. . . . Herein is placed the real power of fitness and proportion; they operate on the understanding considering them, which approves the work and acquiesces in it. The passions, and the imagination which principally raises them have here very little to do. . . . Beauty and proportion are not the same; not that they should either of them be disregarded. . . . We find beautiful that which excited in us the passion of love, or some corresponding affection.[82]

Burke had also tackled the problem of adaptation, or the relationship of the parts to their function, which he found reasonable but "contrary to all experience," for he found beauty also where no use appeared.[83] In his view, utility and proportion appealed to the reason, rather than to a sense of beauty. He went on to differentiate between the sublime and the beautiful, which the neoclassicists tended to combine. In this connection, Burke declared: "Sublime objects are vast in their dimensions, beautiful ones comparatively small; beauty should be smooth and polished; the great, rugged and negligent; beauty should shun the right line, yet deviate from it sensibly; the great in many cases loves the right line."[84]

Greenough was repelled. Burke's ideas on the sublime and the beautiful contradicted every neoclassical precept and enraged Greenough. He castigated the Englishman for "a negative examination" of beauty. Burke's demands for smallness, smoothness, delicacy, and gradual variation seemed mechanical, creatures of convention. They must share the fate of Hogarth's "grandeur of the periwig"[85] as irrelevant and ridiculous, because they were unrelated to the "time, place, and circumstances that gave it value."[86]

Greenough disposed of the entire group of English aestheticians with one grand sweep. "There has been in England since 1815 more discussion of aesthetical doctrine, more analysis, experiment, and dogged determination to effect somewhat in art, than attended the birth of the Florentine school; but always in the main, impotent."[87]

Greenough applied his fundamental yardstick intractably as he traveled about his native cities. He decided that the only beautiful architecture produced in America was the "old, bald, neutral-toned Yankee farmhouse," which he praised for being indigenous and for its perfect conformity with the rolling countryside and the extreme vicissitudes of climate.[88] "The men who have reduced locomotion to its simplest elements, in the trotting wagon and the yacht *America*, are nearer to Athens at this moment than they who would bend the Greek temple to every use. I contend for Greek principles, not Greek things."[89]

Greenough found ample justification for his displeasure with the trend in American architecture at Washington, which was indiscriminately reproducing classical patterns. This unadapted use of an alien style contradicted his idea that the nation's capital should be a showcase to reflect the spirit of the world's foremost democracy. Mustering Greek principles, he arrived at essentials, imploring, "Let us consult nature, and in the assurance that she will disclose a mine richer than was ever dreamed of by the Greeks, in art as well as in philosophy."[90]

He saw in the Washington monument with its Egyptian obelisk rising from a Greek base a striking violation of propriety for its incongruous mixture of distinct styles. He criticized heavily the new Smithsonian Institution. Built on the lines of a Norman castle with turrets, Greenough called it "that dark pike—that castle of authority —that outwork of proscription." It defied serious criticism. Looking at the towers and steep belfreys he reasoned, "This is a practical land. They must be for something. Is no coup d'etat lurking there? Can they be merely ornaments like the tassels to a university cap?"[91]

More paradoxical yet was the fact that the chairman of the Building Committee of the Smithsonian Institution, Robert Dale Owen, shared Greenough's sentiments against the unassimilated plagiarism of foreign expressions. In 1849 Owen wrote: "It would undoubtedly be a retrograde movement in civilization if there were to come into fashion among us the gorgeous apparel worn by the great and wealthy 300 years ago; by the nobles, i.e., of the courts of Henry and Francis. . . ."[92] Owen went so far as to share Greenough's preference for the Yankee farmhouse as the structural form most ideally suited to the landscape.

Owen had selected James Renwick, Jr., of New York as the architect for the building, and it was agreed the style would not be Greek. Consciously revolting against the prevailing neoclassicism, these two men, in concert with a few colleagues who joined in Greenough's tirade against bald imitation, fell into the same trap from another direction.

Greenough had thus essayed a resolution of the central problem inherent in evolving an American aesthetic. From the wellsprings of antiquity through his neoclassical experience in Italy, he discovered "the germ of future architecture."[93] Aided by the evolutionists, he found confirmation of his theories in nature through the fundamental law of adaptation. It was his unique contribution to fuse the strands of evolution and neoclassicism into one organic principle of functionalism in architecture. He thus evolved the rockbound law that form should follow function and be subservient to it, nothing more. A building should be adapted first to use, then to site; there should be a harmonious relationship of the parts, and these should synchronize with the unity of the whole structure. Any feature beyond these essentials would be extraneous, false, and illogical, if not to say, immoral.

It was unfortunate that pragmatic America turned a deaf ear until recently to Horatio Greenough's prophetic valuable "legacy of philosophical thought."[94] Tailor-made as his ideas were for the new skyscraping society, they still floundered in the quagmire of Victorian baubles for half a century.

Part II

HIRAM POWERS

Yankee Literalist
in Exile

Hiram Powers Drawing by Peyton S. Symmes
Cincinnati Historical Society

10

Frontier Beginnings

"Make me as I am, Mr. Powers," said President Andrew Jackson as he sat in the White House in 1835 for his portrait bust. The president cautioned, "Be true to nature always, and in everything. It's the only safe rule to follow. I have no desire to look young as long as I feel old; and then it seems to me, although I don't know much about sculpture, that the only object in making a bust is to get a representation of the man who sits, that it be as nearly as possible a perfect likeness. If he has no teeth, why make him with teeth?"[1] Hiram Powers followed Jackson's directions in executing the face, although he draped the shoulders in the orthodox neoclassical Roman toga prescribed for statesmen. This extreme naturalism was a sharp departure from the prevailing aesthetic of generalized prettiness.

The president's ward, Major Donelson, general factotum in the executive mansion, objected to the realistic portrait that clearly showed the president's mouth without the false dentures that Jackson had absentmindedly misplaced. Powers vigorously defended his representation.

> But I liked the expression of his mouth, even as it was, for it's a remarkable fact that when nature is defeated by age, accident, or infirmity, or her original design, she will find some means of reproducing it, and such is particularly the case with General Jackson. The same firmness and inflexibility of character his mouth ex-

pressed in the prime of life, is to be found there still, though the forms are entirely changed. It is an error to suppose that features are accidental, and nature makes them up at haphazard; for the face is the true index of the soul, where everything is written had we the wisdom to read it. People think I am needlessly anxious and careful about the small and fine lines in human faces. It is because I know how much each line represents, and what great distinctions dwell in the small hiding places.[2]

Edward Everett objected to the wrinkles on the grounds that antique statues had none, but Powers insisted that the wrinkles in Jackson's face were important to the likeness. Powers copied the facial lines consciously and conscientiously and he insisted that he would "always do so."[3] He thus expressed the crux of his artistic creed. He defiantly interpreted Everett's criticism flatteringly as an expression of the attention of an eminent man.

Powers was a product of the early American frontier, where man's survival presupposed his conquest of nature through efficiency and ingenuity. This applied both to his tools and his organization of society. The fine trappings of civilization came from afar if at all, and their local manufacture was in the earliest stages when Hiram was born on a farm near Woodstock, Vermont, July 29, 1805, the eighth child in a family of seven brothers and two sisters. "He was slender and feeble at best," we are informed by a contemporary writer.[4] Another related, "He was an active fellow, by all accounts and 'full of queer capers,' always indulging in boyish sports, tricks, and amusements."[5] Until he was thirteen Hiram attended the district school, where he is reported to have learned easily, acquiring a common English education and "no inconsiderable skill in diverse devices of handicraft."[6] This informant added that "he fashioned many things as a boy, such as mill-dams, wagons, and wind-mills" for all the neighborhood. "He also cast pewter guns for his friends" and even before adolescence "demonstrated uncommon technical skill by the feat of devising improvements in casting."[7]

The season of 1817–1818 was one of dire hardship in Vermont. Famine threatened the entire area, and the family survived on the restricted and unvaried fare of milk from their own cows and potatoes from their worn soil. There was a zero cash intake for small

Andrew Jackson 1835, marble, 35¼″
The Metropolitan Museum of Art, gift of Mrs. Francis V. Nash, 1894

farmers like Hiram's father, Stephen, who was also a blacksmith and an ox-yoke maker. Strong-minded and a stern disciplinarian, he taught his children by the rod, imparting fear with every lesson. Hiram learned at the same time to respect as virtues his father's sober, industrious, and economical ways. The mother, Sarah Perry, evidently held the family together by her industry and kindliness, performing all normal maternal functions from spinning the cloth and making the family clothes to meting out justice and charity to all while adjusting their differences. Years later Powers recalled "no rude or unkind, or even hasty word ever passed between" his parents.[8]

To compound their difficulties, his father had become a bondsman for a friend who absconded and the family lost what little property it had owned. At this time one brother was working his way through nearby Dartmouth College while two others, Jason and Benjamin, had migrated westward. Jason kept his hand to the soil, while Benjamin, in partnership with Thomas Penney and Edward B. Cooke, was publishing a newspaper, *The Inquisitor*, at Cincinnati, which was then a newly incorporated city of some ten thousand inhabitants.

That winter the Powers, together with a neighboring family, set out in three wagons in search of richer fields to labor. They stopped for a break over the winter months with brother Jason on his farm near Niagara Falls. In the spring of 1818, they took a flatboat down the Ohio to Cincinnati. They arrived on May 5 and promptly settled on a small farm which Benjamin helped them acquire. All of the family worked in the fields, which were managed by Stephen, Jr., the oldest son remaining with the family, but prosperity eluded their diligent application there too. The farm was located near a marsh and during the first summer, they all succumbed to ague and fever, the scourge of the locality. Their difficulties culminated dramatically with the death of the father on August 29 or 30, 1819. Hiram was sick for an entire year and was incapacitated for the physical work the farm demanded. He went to the city and "read some law and some Latin" with his brother Benjamin, who had become a lawyer.[9] Then, accepting the offer of Col. Andrew Jackson, who managed the finest hotel in town, Hiram became overseer of the reading room until Jackson sold the hotel. Powers quipped, "I was forced to leave as my clothes and shoes were fast leaving me."[10] He next took a job for a year or two in a produce store. His function was to watch for wagons entering town and to direct the wheat and whiskey cargoes to his employer's premises, then to assist in rolling the barrels in and out. He recalled often walking the streets hungry.

"During all these changes," recounted one of Powers' later interviewers, Charles Edwards Lester, "he kept up his mechanics."[11] Powers reiterated, "I always had a mechanical turn."[12] For amusement, he used to draw on the door of the museum opposite the store a caricature of the "peculiar physiognomy" of its proprietor. He became so familiar with the features that he could repeat this in the dark, and did, so that each morning the gentleman would meet this "absurd profile of himself," much to his annoyance.[13] The culprit remained undiscovered. Years later the two men became friends, and Powers could not resist sharing the joke by repeating the cartoon in chalk. "If I had known it at the time," the man retorted, "I would have broken every bone in your body."[14]

Dealing in grain and whiskey for his employer's profit must have been boring to someone as inventive and ambitious as Hiram Powers. "At this time," he later recollected, "no employment would have been more satisfactory to me than something of a mechanical nature and no sight was so beautiful to me as the harmonious movements of machinery. . . . But I could get no employment in any machine shop or manufactory and I wandered about anxious and unhappy."[15]

It wasn't too long before he stumbled into a steady job literally by the back door. Luman Watson, an established clock and organ manufacturer in Cincinnati, employed Powers in 1823 as a collector of bad debts and inadvertently provided the envied opportunity to work with machinery. At the beginning Powers was assigned a broken-down old horse who could barely carry him on level land and up slight inclines, but who needed assistance himself in the descent. Powers traversed the countryside for seven or eight months, charming trusting females and hard-bitten frontiersmen alike into making good their delinquent payments. He was so sucessful at this task that the Watson family took him into their home and gave him a job as apprentice in their factory, polishing brass plates, a highly skilled process in that day. Powers felt he had reached the threshold of a career, and he anticipated no more poverty or famine, or ague or fever on the farm, or dark friendless streets.

Twenty-five years later Powers remembered the six years spent in Luman Watson's clock factory as "some of my happiest days."[16] He enjoyed his work with the intricacies of clock machinery and often reminisced in later years about his love of mechanics. He once confided, "I never, even from the first, saw any difficulty in machinery. I never saw a machine long enough to understand its principles, which I did not believe myself capable of reproducing, without consulting the original a second time."[17]

Watson evidently gave him free reign. Powers polished the brass plates better than the older experienced hands and soon became superintendent of machines. Within a ten-day period, he simplified the implement for cutting watch wheels, a tool that previously had to be imported across the mountains from the traditional clock-making center in Connecticut. Powers' improved machine cut twice as many wheels in a day and twice as well. His attention progressed to the musical instruments, for which he invented a new reed that could be tuned by twisting a screw. His mechanical ability was a boon in that frontier city, poised on the brink of industrial development. Here success hinged on making things work and greater efficiency in production, which would enable the new entrepreneurs to catch up and eventually to surpass the older ones in the established centers.

Early in 1828 a Prussian sculptor named Frederick Eckstein, who had arrived in town three years before, founded the short-lived Academy of Fine Arts. Powers immediately went to him for artistic advice and instruction. Eckstein had attained an American reputation with his busts of Lafayette, General Andrew Jackson, and Governor DeWitt Clinton. Powers later said that Eckstein taught him all he knew about sculpture and his method was apparently as sound as it was unconventional. Eckstein also instructed Henry Kirke-Brown and Shobal Vail Clevenger. He modeled directly from observation of the subject rather than from a plaster cast of the head and face as the others did. Eckstein convinced Powers that the "natural full-ness of the cheeks, lips, and general features were not attainable in those made after the old methods."[18]

Powers said later he was astonished at the simplicity of the operation of modeling. His first attempt was to copy the head of the Venus di Medici, a cast of which had been brought to Cincinnati by an Italian plaster worker. Soon after, Powers related, "I found a sitter in the little daughter [four-year-old Kitty] of Mr. Foote who was willing to come to me at off hours, often early in the morning, but more commonly after the day's work was over. Knowing that my job would be a long one, I was afraid to begin with clay, which was liable to harden or freeze, and I made my first bust in bees' wax—here it is—and so far as the flesh and the likeness are concerned, I don't believe I have done better since."[19] A quarter century later, Mr. Foote was a willing cooperator as president of the board of trustees of the Cincinnati Academy of Art.

Years after modeling the beeswax bust Powers told Nicholas Longworth, "I could not model a better bust now if I were to try."[20] This first success was a crucial point in his life, turning him to sculpture in preference to a more mechanical career. "I found I had a correct eye," he later related, "and a hand which steadily improved in its obedience to my eye. . . . I found early that all talk about catching the expression was mere twaddle; that the expression would take care of itself, if I took care to copy exactly the features. . . . He that can copy a potato precisely can copy a face precisely."[21] He thus arrived at the artistic formula that, fundamentally unmodified, carried him throughout his professional life.

Not long after the budding metropolis of Cincinnati was incorporated, there was a public spirited attempt to import culture with the founding in 1820 of the Western Museum for the display of specimens of natural history and archaeology. Joseph Dorfeuille, a Frenchman, came from New Orleans to be the museum curator. It was into this hall of culture that Powers wandered one day after paying the twenty-five cents admission fee, and saw his first masterpiece of sculpture, the plaster cast of Houdon's bust of Washington. In later years he recalled, "It woke up in me an emotion which was to become the absorbing passion of my life. . . . I gazed upon it a long time and felt a strong desire to know the process by which it had been made. I returned the next day to see it. . . . It would be difficult to describe the intensity of desire I felt for a long time to know all about this mysterious art."[22]

After three years money and public interest petered out, and public sponsorship of the museum was abandoned. The specimens were bestowed upon Dorfeuille, presumably for lack of other means of disposal. He maintained the sober, "scientific" format of the museum intact but didn't fare any better as its private entrepreneur. Threatened with bankruptcy, he turned commercial.

The first profit-motivated exhibit had for its stage designer and general production manager the young Hiram Powers, whose reputation with the beeswax figure of Kitty Foote had resounded. Dorfeuille hired him to repair some old imported wax figures broken to bits in transit. The show had only moderate success; Dorfeuille's prosperity had to wait for the arrival of Mrs. Frances Trollope, whose creative ideas made the difference. Mrs. Trollope and her two sons had emigrated to America from England to attempt to retrieve her family fortune that her barrister husband had all but dissipated. She traveled with Fanny Wright who led her first to the New Harmony utopian farm in Indiana, where the primitive living arrangements blunted her initial enthusiasm. Turning to the likeliest city for her commercial purposes, she went to the burgeoning frontier at Cincinnati. There she constructed an immense bazaar that promptly failed, casting her into bankruptcy. She considered Cincinnati a cultural wasteland and wrote:

> I never saw any people . . . so much without amusements as the Cincinnatians. Billiards are forbidden by law, so are cards. To sell a pack of cards in Ohio subjects the seller to a penalty of fifty dollars. They have no public balls, excepting, I think, six, during the Christmas holidays. They have no concerts. They have no dinner parties. They have a theatre which is, in fact, the only public amusement of this triste little town, but they care little about it, either from economy or distaste, it is very poorly attended. . . . Were it not for the Churches . . . I think there might be a general bonfire of the best bonnets for I never could discover any other use for them. . . . Were it not for public worship, and private tea-drinking parties, all the ladies in Cincinnati would be in danger of becoming perfect recluses.[23]

Mrs. Trollope evidently could not look idly upon the destitute state of local culture. Somewhere early upon her entry into Cincinnati, she had met Powers, and we have it on the testimony of her son, Thomas Adolphus, that she "at once remarked him as a young man of exceptional talent and promise."[24] As Dorfeuille and Powers were then "casting about for some 'new' attractions for the Museum," and as Mrs. Trollope lacked other divertisement for her fertile mind, she sat up nights with Powers in search of an amply lurid idea for a show.[25] Thus was born the Cincinnati version of Dante's *Inferno*, a nineteenth-century Disneyesque accommodation to the public taste. "The nascent sculptor," according to the younger Trollope, "with his imaginative brain, artistic eye, and clever fingers, caught at the idea on the instant. And forthwith, they set to work, my mother explaining the poet's conceptions, suggesting the composition of 'tableaux' and supplying details, while Powers designed and executed the figures and the necessary mise-en-scene."[25] The show was an instantaneous smash hit. It ran over twenty-five years with few changes, attracting not only the city folks, but farmers from the countryside on their periodic shopping sprees in town. It continued long after Dorfeuille had retired and the museum had changed hands several times. The press of the spellbound crowds threatened destruction of the figures and Powers was asked to solve the problem of their protection. In that pre-Edisonian epoch, he ingeniously created his own electrically charged barrier, as startling in its effect as the staged production itself.

During those carefree days, Powers made a full-length statue of an actor named Alec Drake who was a great favorite in Cincinnati. It had such lifelike fidelity that it was set out as a gag for a curtain call. When it failed to bow, the audience would howl until the actor appeared at its side, provoking thunderous applause for the feat.

When he was twenty-seven, Powers married Elizabeth Gibson, with whose family he had been boarding. The papers available give little of her background or personality but indicate that she must have administered their domestic affairs adequately and met their social acquaintances affably. Letters written by friends in later years refer to her agreeably in general terms. Eventually she and Powers had nine children. She brought no dowry with her and the marriage only exacerbated the practical problems for Powers, who was just launching himself as an artist. Although Powers seemed to have habitual complaints about life in the art world or life in general, he is not known to have ever uttered one word against his wife.

There also came to Cincinnati at this time a thirty-three-year-old painter exiled from monarchist France, Auguste Jean Jacques Hervieu. He was part of Mrs. Trollope's ménage, first in the role of drawing master for her children, then simply as protégé. Hervieu hoped to capitalize on his foreign training and Mrs. Trollope's aptitude for promoting people in society. His modest efforts were rewarded with an order to paint the historical scene of Lafayette landing in Cincinnati.[27] For a brief moment, he was the chief breadwinner of the Trollope household. Powers later described how Hervieu undertook to teach him something of his own art, especially the practice of painting from observation of his subject, without the use of measurements. This practice of the contemporary French school, he claimed, was based on that of the Italian Renaissance artists such as Michelangelo. Powers, ever the punctilious mechanic, maintained skeptical aloofness despite trying some experimental models of his own. As measured by his standards of accuracy, he took exception to the inevitable discrepancies that appeared, and he returned, fortified, to his mechanical technique. He observed,

> It has taken me, however, at least five times as long to measure the distances with my eyes, as it would have done to measure them with the calipers and I saw no advantage in the longer and more painful effort. The measurements are mere preparations for the artist's true work, and are, like the surveyor's lines, the preparatory to the architect's labor. . . . I have had no misgivings since about the economy and wisdom of using the calipers freely. To be useful, they must be applied with the greatest precision; so small are the differences upon which all the infinite variety in human countenances depends. With the aid of careful measurements, I can do in one day what it would cost me a week or two's work to accomplish without, and I am then able to give my exclusive attention to modelling.[28]

From this episode forward, Powers became irretrievably wedded to his calipers. The relationship between Hervieu and Powers was understandably only "half friendly and half hostile," and the influence on Powers that has been attributed to Hervieu seems unfounded.[29]

When the abortive Academy of Fine Arts failed, it was clear that Powers would have to leave Cincinnati if he persisted in his ambition to become a sculptor. The obvious world center of training was Italy, but getting there without funds and encumbered by a family was a problem. In 1827, however, Nicholas Longworth, an affluent art patron, offered to pay Powers' travel expenses to Italy.

Longworth was the successful founder of wine culture and manufacture in the Ohio Valley and he had become a millionaire. He did not mean to sustain Powers through his artistic education to a self-sustaining point; he merely offered to advance Powers' travel expenses to Italy. Although Powers believed himself "personally a stranger" to Longworth at this time, he acknowledged the generosity with deep gratitude. In a gracious note to Longworth, he promised to use every means in his power to refund the money. He mentioned that he hoped to start for Italy as early as the next spring, and he promised conscientiously to "inform [himself] of the expenses of living in that country, of the journey, etc."[30]

With Longworth's backing and encouragement, Powers left Cincinnati in the spring of 1828. He sent farewell messages to his friends and got as far as New York. There he obtained permission to go on a public vessel, which he thought was free of expense. He found there were expenses involved, however, and he wrote Longworth, "I was informed that the government afforded only a passage to a foreign port for artistic and professional men, but I must find myself in everything, even to my hammock. The ship was ready to sail. I had no time to write home for further assistance, and in counting my means, I found I should be left in Gibraltar without money enough to take me to Florence."[31] Powers lingered in New York several weeks, but lacking guarantees of arriving at his destination, he abandoned this premature sally and returned to Cincinnati "with the intention of making another attempt as soon as possible."[32] Evidently the poverty he had suffered as a youth scarred him for life, and, given a choice, he would never again risk deprivation.

He now determined to raise money for the trip to Italy through portrait commissions from leading citizens of his city, obtaining the usual half payment in advance. Little came of this independent notion directly, however, for he received only three orders at home.

Powers had few alternatives and since he was always conservative, he returned to his post as "artistic" director at Dorfeuille's museum and bided his time five more years. His job was to create new acts and keep the old ones in mechanical repair. Clearly, it was not a life's work, only a stopgap. It was useful in meeting the added burden accompanying the birth on June 8, 1833, of the Powers' first son, James.

With characteristic but understandable caution, Powers decided to explore opportunities at the national capital at Washington. He left Cincinnati November 28, 1834, the very day that his original benefactor, Luman Watson, died. He would compete for the market in portraiture of the nation's leading statesmen. These political figures were adept at eliciting portraits of themselves at the expense of their wealthier constituents at home. At once several benefits would accrue: the political leader's fame would be enhanced along with the patron's and the artist's, all in the name of encouraging the arts and expressions of patriotism. The artist had to initiate the procedure by snaring his subject and fashioning his physiognomy in clay. He would then transfer the image to a plaster cast that would be packed with care for shipment to Italy.

Powers' approach to Washington was judicious. Armed with letters of introduction to several distinguished national leaders, he timed his arrival early in 1835 just before Congress convened, so as to find the legislators relatively free from their duties. He forebore making too many contacts before he had a major accomplishment to boast. He first persuaded the susceptible Chief Justice John Marshall to sit. The timing was fortunate, for Marshall died only three or four months later, and Powers' portrait was the last of the dozens which had been made of the justice. Powers naturally hoped that a government commission for the marble would ensue. The model was highly favored and a Congressional subscription was talked of for years by his friends, but Powers spurned the first offer of $500. Just then Persico's two colossal marble statues of *War* and *Peace* arrived from Italy for placement, and conversation at the capital revolved about them and their price. If Persico could command $10,000 for each of his figures, why not a native son of Powers' egregious talent? After a year's wait, Powers accepted the original offer without a murmur at its niggardly size. This was to be his sole government commission for a long time. The reason was always the same, the government was not disposed to meet his prices.

Judge William Cranch, Chief Justice of the United States District Court in Washington, reporter for the United States Supreme Court, and a close friend of Marshall, attested to the likeness of Powers' model and recommended it to President Andrew Jackson. Powers then presented a plaster cast of the bust to the president who was duly impressed. Not long afterwards, through a letter of introduction to the president's housekeeper, Mrs. Forsythe, Powers was invited to the White House to model President Jackson's bust. The affair was cleverly managed. After a president, who would refuse to sit? Besides gaining an admirer for the realism of his rendition, Powers won the oportunity to create his most satisfactory bust. He became glamor-struck with the president's personality and fascinated with his face. Years later, he recalled, "I have never had a more striking subject for a bust."[33] In time, upon recollecting the experience long after he had absorbed Italian art, he claimed that Jackson evoked comparison with Michelangelo's gigantic statues, "natural, but one of nature's exaggerations out of her common working, but still her own work."[34]

During that trip, which extended to the end of July (1836), and a subsequent one early the following spring, Powers succeeded in patterning busts of several notables, including Daniel Webster, John Quincy Adams, John C. Calhoun, Calhoun's daughter Anna Maria, Colonel John S. Preston, Preston's wife, Senator Thomas Benton, Colonel Richard M. Johnson, Vice-President Martin Van Buren, General MacComb, General Memucan Hunt, General Edmund Pendleton Gaines, Judge William Cranch, William J. Stone, Levi Woodbury (secretary of the treasury), Mrs. George Hughes, the daughter of the solicitor of the treasury, Virgil Maxcy, and Senator Robert J. Walker of Mississippi.

Powers set up a workshop in the basement of the Capitol as was often done then so as to be conveniently located and to attract the daily attention of the legislators. This workroom soon became "quite a show shop," chiefly for the foreign set of diplomats, who,

as Europeans, carried weight as arbiters of taste.[35] Powers won the active support of Senator John C. Calhoun as well as that of Senator William C. Preston of Columbia, South Carolina, who introduced him to his wealthy brother, Col. John S. Preston. The latter, after amassing an enormous fortune from his Louisiana plantation, had resumed his law practice and become active with his brother in South Carolina politics. He was to be the most significant connection in Powers' career, for he promptly offered to stake the sculptor to the vital trip to Italy, thereby directing the course of his life. After this, Powers determined that no amount of parochial acclaim over his portrait busts and no lures of a fast dollar could deflect him from his long-cherished plan.

Still Powers tarried, even flirting fleetingly with the notion of selling plaster casts of his models for ten dollars each. The production cost would have been only two dollars but he soon realized that this would lead nowhere. In July of 1836, he learned of a fabulous marble quarry located near Harrisburg, Pennsylvania. Toward the end of the month he prospected the site personally to satisfy himself with the beauty of the product and the extent of its supply. For years he nourished the idea of raising the capital from Nicholas Longworth and forming a company to work the quarry. He also conceived the notion to have Longworth purchase a building in Cincinnati for a museum to house works that he would create or find in Italy. Upon his return home, he would assume its directorship.

Meanwhile, Col. John S. Preston, encouraged by the beauty of his and his wife's busts, undertook to raise a subscription among his southern friends for a marble statue of Calhoun. Powers was flattered on two counts: Calhoun was man of signal importance on the national scene, and the sum of $3,000 mentioned was in a class with the fees of Thorwaldsen, which ranged around $5,000 at the height of his fame. Not a bad beginning for one who had not yet arrived at the Italian proving ground. Powers declared himself satisfied that the offer would be profitable after he had thoroughly investigated all the items of cost. He determined that for both the marble and the workmen, the costs would not exceed seven or eight hundred dollars. He declared privately that he would have accepted $1,500 rather than lose this first major commission. Powers, how-

John C. Calhoun 1839, plaster bust, 22″
Yale University Art Gallery, gift to Calhoun College of the Fellows and Associate Fellows in memory of Stanley T. Williams

ever, was not destined to arrive at that level of success quite that fast. It took several years for this proposal to mature. With the full statue in mind, Powers reserved special treatment for the bust of Calhoun that he had begun. Instead of sending the clay model abroad as he was now doing with the others to save the time of casting them in plaster, he took a plaster cast of this one as insurance against loss or damage in transit and left the original for safekeeping with Boyd Reilly of Washington.

Another small item of possible trade caught his attention. He noticed a lithograph of Senator Thomas Benton made by a Mr. Fenwick for the Capitol. The idea dawned that this cheap reproductive process would lend itself to a brisk sale of facsimiles of his own prized busts, such as those of Jackson and Van Buren. It didn't occur to Powers then to hire some able person to perform this extra task, and since his time was thoroughly preempted in modeling busts of famous personages for shipment to Italy, he let the scheme drop by default.

Toward the end of March 1837, ex-President John Quincy Adams, fiery representative in Congress from Massachusetts, requested a portrait bust of himself. Adams spent two or three hours daily for a week sitting for it. Fashioned of local Washington soil that Powers thought the most superior clay in the world, the model was completed on April 2 and consigned for shipment with the others for Italy. There, Horatio Greenough thought so well of it that he commissioned a copy in marble for $300. Adams was so struck by the work that he composed the following poem in appreciation and commemoration of the sculptor.

John Quincy Adams, 1837 to Hiram Powers

Sculptor! Thy hand has moulded into form
   The haggard features of a toil-worn face,
   And whosoever views thy work shall trace
An age of sorrows, and a life of storm.
And canst thou mould the heart? for that is warm,
   Glowing with tenderness for all its race,
   Instinct with all the sympathies that grace
The pure and artless bosoms where they swarm.

Artist! may fortune smile upon thy hand!

Go forth and rival Greece's art sublime.
Return, and bid the statesmen of thy Land
   live in thy marble through all after time.
Oh, catch the fire from heaven Prometheus stole
And give the lifeless block a breathing soul.[36]

After refusing to sit in response to Powers' first request in 1835, Daniel Webster finally acceded to the pressures of the sculptor's friends. He liked Powers instantly, admired his work, and set about to take advantage of the unfavorable popular reaction to Luigi Persico's statues by promoting an ambitious undertaking for a native son. Webster was not alone in thinking it was a propitious moment to boost an American. His notion was for Powers to execute a series of busts for the Capitol of all the presidents from Washington to Jackson. It was a grand speculation, but Webster never proposed it to Congress.

Webster was notably more successful in Powers' behalf in his own personal and political circle at home. Early in August 1836, Powers went to Boston to take Webster's likeness and found waiting for him the promise of six other portrait commissions. There was even talk of an Athenaeum commission for a marble copy of the Webster bust, but no one took the sugestion seriously enough to promote it. Powers soon modeled other leading Bostonians, the most famous of whom were the very aged Governor John Winthrop, former Governor John Davis of Worcester, and Mr. and Mrs. William Lawrence. William was the brother of Amos and Abbott Lawrence of the New England textile fortune and founders of the Lawrence Academy at Groton. There were others who were willing to scramble for their turn to sit, deflecting Powers awhile from his rush to be off. It was clear that he could have work of this sort in Washington, Boston, New York, and elsewhere to keep him "incessantly occupied" as long as he chose to stay.[37]

In Boston he renewed his acquaintance with Horatio Greenough, whom he had met in Washington, and Greenough assured him that he would not lack for orders in Italy. There foreign tourists were commissioning liberally of talented artists, regardless of their origin. The crux of Powers' situation was that in America he, like Greenough, could hardly hope to develop artistically beyond portraiture without the blessing of a government commission. This boon was unlikely without greater proof of his artistic prowess, achievable only by the creation of full statues, the techniques for which had to be learned in Italy. Political contacts were no substitute. Perhaps his chances to attain ultimate success would even be enhanced from afar. He ruminated. If he were to remain at home longer, his artistic progress would surely be stunted.

Steadied by the offer of a subsidy by Col. John S. Preston, he hoped to get off with Greenough in October 1836. But he was delayed another year by the lure of mounting opportunities to model ever more important public figures.

Further enriching his Boston experience was his meeting with the painter Francis Alexander, with whom he formed a fast friendship that was later cemented when Alexander joined the American expatriates in Florence. Powers also befriended Chester Harding, another painter of note in Boston, and at a dinner at Judge William Baldwin's he met the dean of them all, Washington Allston.

During the winter and spring of 1836–1837, Powers made numerous trips between Boston and Washington, the last one to Boston on May 14 to model the busts of Governor John Winthrop and Abbott Lawrence and his wife. On these trips he paused along the way when there was a portrait order. A Mr. LeRoy of New York and Gen. Samuel Smith of the wealthy merchant family of Baltimore had promised to sit when they had met Powers in Washington. Before leaving the capital for the last time in the spring of 1837, he made several more busts. Among these were portraits of Mrs. William H. Wharton and George Tiffany, the Baltimore patron of art.[38] In addition, he made a bust of Representative Francis Granger (son of Gideon Granger, United States Postmaster General under Presidents Jefferson and Madison), that undoubtedly led to one of the prominent New York socialite Mrs. C. Van Rensselaer, a relative of Francis' wife, Cornelia.

Altogether, Powers' itinerant existence between 1835 and 1837 marked an auspicious opening for his professional career. He more than paid his own way during the last two years in the States, but Nicholas Longworth from time to time sent a hundred or two to his wife for household expenses. With commissions for thirteen busts that he had modeled and packed for shipment to Italy for cutting, Powers earned enough to keep him and his family fed while he was building his reputation abroad. He gained sufficient recognition in New York among his fellow artists to be elected, like Greenough, an honorary member in the National Academy of Design in 1827.

He returned from Boston to Cincinnati to fetch his family, now including a second son (named Longworth, but called Nicky) who had been born on June 5, 1835. Powers lingered only long enough for the sake of the hometown to model one more bust locally, that of the renowned Judge Jacob Burnett. Leaving his casts behind to be dispatched from New York to Leghorn by Octavius Longworth, the family left Cincinnati at the end of August and sailed on the American packet *Charlemagne* early in October 1837.

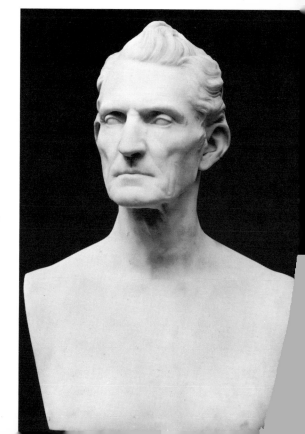

Judge Jacob Burnet
1837, marble, 26¹⁹⁄₃₂″
Courtesy of the Cincinnati Art Museum

Proserpine 1839, marble, $25^{15}/_{16}''$
Courtesy of the Cincinnati Art Museum

11

The World's Greatest
Sculptor of Busts

THE RANGE OF ATTRACTIONS OVERSEAS WAS AS BEGUILING TO POWERS as to the others who settled there to pursue their artistic careers. He never elaborated on his preference for Florence over Rome. Being of a pragmatic turn, romantic considerations favoring Rome would not naturally arise to plague him. Perhaps he never considered the choice, but it is more likely that he was influenced by what he had heard of the cheapness of living in Tuscany. Then again, he may simply have gravitated to Florence because Horatio Greenough stood ready to extend a cordial welcome and helping hand. In any case, Powers had Greenough's word, along with that of others, to hurry over to capitalize on the European and American tourist trade. It was widely conceded that Powers, with his native genius for portraiture, stood an excellent chance in the competition for commissions. Certainly the naturalism of the Tuscan tradition would pose no contradiction to his own set ways. Greenough may have suspected the affinity when he encouraged Powers' migration.

Accompanied by his wife and two small sons, Powers arrived in Florence early in December 1837 after an eventful passage of twenty-four days during which they barely escaped both shipwreck and conflagration. His wife fared even worse, having contracted a light case of varioloid on shipboard. They stopped in Paris for a week to give her some rest. Taking barely enough time to skip through the Louvre, Notre Dame, and sundry tourist spots, they went by carriage down the Rhone Valley by way of Lyons and Marseilles to Leghorn and Florence, assisted on the second lap by a French-speaking fellow countryman that Powers picked up.

Powers' courage was impressive. Almost entirely self-educated, innocent of foreign ways and languages, and lacking training in the technical rudiments of his craft, he was undaunted in his determination to blazon a career abroad. His Yankee ingenuity carried him to the world's top position in sculptural portraiture.

He was better sustained than most of the aspiring émigrés for this adventurous endeavor. In addition to his thirteen bust commissions, which at $300 each totaled an expectance of $3,900 (half of which had been paid and was readily available), he was underwritten by two patrons. His longtime benefactor in Cincinnati, Nicholas Longworth, paid for his transportation from home to Florence and guaranteed him an income of $1,000 a year for three years. Col. John S. Preston promised an additional $1,000 for five years, besides the initial $1,000 he had already advanced for domestic travel. These sums were repaid in time.

Powers was delighted to find living costs in Florence as low as Greenough had described. His family's first abode was heavily balanced on the modest side at the cost of comfort. It consisted of two rooms in the basement of an abandoned convent, one room was for family living, the other was to be used as a studio. His year's rent was a hundred dollars, with twenty-five dollars extra for furniture. It's a wonder he allowed his wife a general servant to perform the domestic tasks at the wage of four dollars a month. Clothes he found very cheap, too: a summer suit of good material costing eleven dollars and a fine hat, two dollars.

With no plans for formal study to deter him, he could plunge directly into his work. The plaster casts arrived without delay or mishap and he lost no time getting on with their execution. He had work enough to keep him busy for nearly two years. His ignorance of Italian, however, presented his first salient problem, that "to live cheaply one must understand the language and bargain."[1] Powers proceeded assiduously to study Italian, but he never attained greater fluency than that needed to direct his workmen. This hampered his social ease, resulting in his aloofness from his Florentine colleagues and other intellectuals whose society Greenough enjoyed. He rationalized his handicap by asserting that nothing was to be gained by his cultivating Italian artists. Only occasionally did he lament his necessity to live within the confines of the English speaking circle. His acclimatization to foreign customs was also constrained.

He was consequently ill-equipped to compete in the marketplace for good workmen. "Greenough had told me how cheap labor in marble was," he explained. "When I got here, I found labor cheap enough, but laborers used to, or capable of reproducing my kind of modelling absolutely unattainable. After trying many, I had to go to work and cast four of the busts myself."[2] These were those of President Andrew Jackson, Daniel Webster, John Q. Adams, and Professor John Farrar of Boston, who commissioned his portrait locally that season within a month of Powers' arrival.[3] Whether he was rationalizing parsimony is open to speculation.

Powers quickly wearied and complained of this labor. Six months sufficed for his adjustment to the local scene on this score. He hired three assistants who worked when needed. The first roughed out the marble block at seventy-five cents a day, and the other two assisted in finishing hair and drapery, each earning a dollar a day. At this intermediate stage, Powers still reserved to himself the job of cutting the facial features. It was not until eighteen months from his arrival in Florence that he found a marble finisher, Romigo Peschi, who met his fastidious requirements. Powers described Peschi, who came from Bartolini's studio, as "the best Italian sculptor in Tuscany."[4] Peschi stayed with Powers thirty-three years, enjoying the excellent wage of $1.50 per day and the unwavering loyalty and admiration of his employer. Years afterward, Powers claimed Peschi as a friend who understood his manner and style perfectly.

Powers learned at once that busts cost $100 to carve, sometimes less, but he soon declared that his $300 fee for heads was inadequate and by the spring of 1839 he raised his price to $400, with Greenough following suit. Bartolini, who was after all Florence's first sculptor at the time, was still getting only $250. Powers felt certain he rated the increase because of his painstaking rendition of the minutiae in his busts in contrast with generalized gloss produced by the Italian workmen in native studios. He got his price too.

Powers had been working unremittingly not quite a year before he reported he had seven busts far advanced in the marble and one finished. In hopes of making a striking entry into the lush British market at the forthcoming London exhibition, his next major effort was concentrated on completing the heads of his most conspicuous subjects, who were also remarkable for their expression, Marshall, Webster, and Jackson.

He soon understood the necessity to display his full artistic capacity in ideal works. He was encouraged to this end by his new friend, Richard Henry Wilde, who, while he sat for his portrait, prodded Powers to proceed with less precision and greater speed with his first ideal bust. This was *Proserpine*, "a female head with a wreath of wheat in bloom crowing her hair, with acanthus leaves, emblem of immortality, around her waist."[5] After a year's labor, it was completed to the instantaneous pleasure of an Englishman who promised to have it shown in London. Powers had a marble copy cut for this purpose along with two others that were to be presented as gifts to each of his American patrons as an example of his accomplishment abroad. After three years, another copy was commissioned for $500, a price that included transportation costs to New York. The Cincinnati historian and publisher Henry C. Lea ordered it as a gift for the art collection of his editorial associate, E. L. Cary. It took Cary two years to make up his mind to accept it and another two years for Powers to complete it. "The bust is done," he proclaimed in a letter home. It is "to be sent on the next sailing vessel April 10th [1845]."[6] The marble cutting alone took nearly a year. Powers could have sold it a dozen times over to foreigners as it was voguish and the English were buying. Three of them purchased other copies. Among the countless additional replicas that Powers subsequently made of *Proserpine*, another was consigned in May 1859 to the Hildeburne shipping firm in Philadelphia.

It was said at this time that the finish that Powers achieved on his busts was higher than any others. This feat was the more remarkable because he had never before wrought in marble. Delighted with his results, he pointed out modestly that, after all, the entire merit of busts derived from accuracy in the modeling. The rest, he averred, just followed mechanically.

Throughout his first season in Florence, Powers suffered continual depression over the prolonged illness and death of his firstborn son, Jimmy, in the spring of 1838. His sole distraction from the tragedy came from concentrated work in the studio. Greenough reported him visibly cheerful again by the end of April. The doleful state was definitely dissipated by the birth of the Powers' first daughter on September 10, 1838. They named the girl Louisa after Horatio's sister. They had grown to love Louisa Greenough during her six weeks' stay in their house, preceding and through the confinement, while Horatio had gone to England to fetch his wife. Powers, again joyful, modeled a statue in celebration, that of a child with a vase of flowers. He used his ten-month old crawler for his model, apologizing for his indulgence with the excuse that "statues of little children are very popular."[7]

By this time Powers and his family had moved into a commodious house at 1372 Via dei Fornaci, on the Siena Road. This house provided a first floor studio opening onto a garden and living quarters upstairs. Powers' reputation as a fine portraitist was growing, particularly since carving the bust of Andrew Jackson with wrinkles and without teeth. This bust of Jackson became a prototype in Florence for depicting age, as the Venus di Medici continued to be the prototype for female beauty. Powers fully appreciated his achievement and refused to sell the original, which he retained in his studio long after Jackson's death. While the marble facsimile was nearing completion, he speculated modestly with Greenough that it should fetch $1,000. Writing home in a sobered mood, he confessed to Nicholas Longworth that he would let it go for $500 if the active Jacksonian democrats of Cincinnati would raise a subscription for it. The political leaders at home were slow to take the hint but the idea of a political outlet was generated. In 1846, the Jackson bust was sold to a Democratic club in New York for $2,500. It was loaned to the Metropolitan Museum of Art for its first exhibition of modern sculpture in 1874 and is still there. It is unquestionably the best of Powers' works for its combination of dignity and fidelity to Jackson's features and personality.

New commissions were slowly coming in. He made two copies of his bust of Louisa Greenough, one of the Reverend Dr. Lowell of Boston, and one of Senator George McDuffie of South Carolina, whom he met through Wilde. McDuffie challenged Powers to complete his likeness in eight days. Since McDuffie was socially prominent it seemed worth the effort, and Powers met the challenge easily. He was then called to take the death mask of Dr. George Brimmer of Boston, who had died suddenly in Florence. He made busts also of Cornelius Low of New York, and David Urquart and John Slidell of New Orleans.

Horatio Greenough praised the bust that Powers made of him as "admirable."[8] In the spring of 1839, Powers finished the Congressionally commissioned bust of *John Calhoun* and worked away at the *Webster* with meticulous care. His great decision of the season was that he would not send these busts to London on speculation at this time. He would wait until that market gravitated toward him naturally. He saw no need to risk their safety and the expense of transport when Florence was turning out to be the equal of Paris or London as a selling place. The carriage trade could come to his door and appreciate his superiority over his lower-priced Italian competitors.

In the midst of all this activity over portrait busts, pressures began to mount for him to venture the next step forward artistically. It was repeatedly brought to his attention that he, too, was "forced to the creation of ideal works of beauty."[9] The Professor of Drawing at the Royal Academy visited his studio and observed the brilliant accuracy of his busts. If this accuracy were carried through an entire figure, he remarked, Powers would achieve an artistic feat of note.

Powers was further prodded along this line by his old friend, Mrs. Trollope, who breezed through Florence in a few days on her first Italian visit and called on Powers immediately. After viewing the numerous busts which lined his studio shelves, she inquired after some ideal work of his. "In marble?" he inquired incredulously. "Yes," she replied, "Some group not merely consisting of a portrait, but something imaginative." He shook his head. "I am married and have two children," he argued. "For busts I have as many orders as I can execute—I must not risk the loss of this lucrative business in order to indulge myself in works of imagination. . . . If my success continues, I may, perhaps, in time, venture to attempt something of the kind.

. . But I cannot afford it yet."[10] Powers felt caught in a vicious circle and complained continually to sympathetic Longworth of his shortage of working capital; with more cash he could employ more workmen and produce more work. He was hesitant to increase the indebtedness necessary to break out of portraiture.

Powers now became gloomy over his chances of success as an artist. He wrung his hands in a letter to Longworth, "The occasion was strong, the circumstances urgent, and I had no alternative but to give up all and return home."[11] He was overwrought from over-work and social isolation. His attentions were concentrated on his studio and on his family, where he worried incessantly over one ailing child after another.

He clearly never meant to relinquish his career, however, and that spring he announced modestly that he was "preparing to begin a statue . . . something in the feminine way."[12] With appropriate self-consciousness, he approached his task, stating that he was fully aware how "dangerous a subject it was to begin upon, for one who had never modelled a statue."[13] The selection of a female nude subject seemed natural to Powers here at the center of the Venus cult, where the very first statue that had caught his imagination was the Venus di Medici. He had thought this Venus unrivaled in this early period and had extolled her virtues to Longworth in superlatives. "It is my opinion," he wrote, "that no entirely original statue of a female can ever equal the Venus de' Medici. . . . No other attitude embodies so much grace. There is not an angle in it. From head to foot, all the movements are curves and in strict accordance with Ho-garth's line of grace."[14]

Powers thought much about his subject and settled first on an illustration of Gesner's Eve "at the moment when she is looking at a dove which lies dead at her feet, and which calls up disagreeable reflections in her mind, in the consequence of her transgression."[15] In short, this would be Eve reflecting on Death. He soon rejected this plan for a study of the temptation of Eve. This interpretation placed Eve "just before eating the forbidden fruit. . . . [She] is standing with the fruit in her right hand raised to a level with the shoulder. . . . The face is inclined . . . in an expression of sorrow, reflection, and desire. . . . After circling her feet, the serpent appears with his head brought in front just below the right thigh . . . his means of seduction. . . . The left hand is hanging . . . [holding] more fruit for 'she gave Adam also.' "[16]

The legend, Powers felt, would justify his statue's nudity. "In the case of my Eve," he said, "clothing would be preposterous for she was conscious she was naked only *after* she had fallen. History and nature both require entire nudity."[17]

Powers lingered interminably over the statue, using as many as thirty models to attain perfection of detail. Much depended on its success. He declared his early determination "not to allow a work to leave my studio till it was as perfect as I could make it," even if the penalty it exacted was three to four times the normal time requirement.[18] At first he thought to make the *Eve* "larger than ordinary life . . . nearly 5'8" high."[19] Then for practical considerations, he pared it down. "To meet expenses and realize a fair profit," he explained, "a copy full size of this statue in Seravezza marble ought to realize $5,000 as it will require a year and a half to conclude it in marble—a copy of ⅔ size, $3,000, and half size—$1,500."[20] The marble block on which he settled came from a newly discovered quarry yielding marble far more beautiful in Powers' judgment than Carrara. It proved entirely free of blemishes and he considered it a huge bargain at a cost of $210. Not until two and a half years later did he announce that his statue of *Eve*, except for the accessories and the serpent, was finished.

Eve attracted numerous admirers to his studio in fulfillment of his hopes and plans. On her return to Florence Mrs. Trollope praised the clay statue in generous terms, stating, "the blended dignity and simplicity of this beautiful figure . . . is nature in its very full perfection . . . the model of woman, as she came from the hand of the Creator, before any accident of earth had tarnished her perfection. . . . The heavenly composure of her fair face . . . trace a slight shade of anxiety just sufficient to make one feel that she is not divine, but human."[21]

Another self-styled critic from America, Joel T. Headley, judged that "Powers' *Eve* is a woman with a soul as well as heart. . . . Her countenance indicated the great, yet silent struggle within. . . . She is a noble woman." He went on, "There is full scope for the imagination in it" giving it the advantage over fiction.[22] Like Nathaniel Hawthorne later, Headley went on to compare it favorably with the Venus di Medici, judging *Eve* her superior in the head and face, the antique being too small and inexpressive. On reflection, however, he found his memory more faithful to the Venus not only for her Goddess figure but for the "atmosphere of beauty beyond and around it."[23]

Bertel Thorwaldsen visited Powers' studio when passing through Florence in the late summer of 1841 on his return to Rome from Copenhagen. Horatio Greenough, whom he respected, insisted that he take a look, having rated Powers two years earlier "at the very top" in portraiture.[24] Pressed for time, Thorwaldsen was gracious enough to cancel another appointment to see the acclaimed piece by the newly arrived American just before the clay model was finished. He is alleged to have remarked, "You say, sir, it is your first statue, any man might be proud of it as his last."[25] His eye also lit upon the unfinished Webster bust with comparable approval and he is reported to have said on leaving, "I can't make such busts and never saw a man that could—nor do I believe he ever had an equal in that department of the art. I esteem Mr. Powers not only as the first sculptor of his age, but as the greatest since Michel Angelo. He will form a school of his own which will be a new era in art."[26] The extravagant account reported the Dane as saying of the *Webster* bust that "the expression surpasses every bust I ever saw, Greek or Roman. I doubt he ever had an equal."[27] Lorenzo Bartolini added his authoritative voice in praise, pronouncing Powers "the greatest portrait sculptor living."[28] The news of Powers' reputation was generously relayed home to a wide public by the American peregrinates who visited his studio.

These lavish reports come to us chiefly through the interviews of a fellow countryman with Powers years later, when Powers recalled the episode. They seemed so excessive in retrospect, that the sculptor felt impelled to discount them as somewhat apocryphal. There is surprisingly no mention of Powers in the papers of Thorwaldsen, as determined by his latest biographer.[29] Powers did allude in his letters to Thorwaldsen's invitation (in response to Powers' suggestion) to come to Rome to model his portrait. Unfortunately, when Powers eventually went to Rome in the fall of 1846, it was too late. Thorwaldsen had left in 1844 to return to his native city of Copenhagen, where he died shortly afterward.

For the Europeans, there was no doubt that this statue of *Eve* proved the making of Powers' artistic career. Two years after her commencement, not only did the Professor of Drawing at the Academy of Fine Arts come to the studio, but also the other leading members of the sculptural faculty, Emilio Santarelli, Luigi Pampaloni, Francesco Pozzi, and Emilio Demi, who were the foremost sculptors of the period in Florence. They were unanimous in support of the verdict already attributed to Thorwaldsen that the statue represented the creation of a serious artist of genius, and they proposed Powers as academic professor in the Academy.

This nomination was formalized in September 1841, when Powers was voted his "diploma of Professorship in the Royal Academy of Fine Arts in Florence."[30] Of the long list of foreign artists at work in Florence since the Renaissance, only Powers and Greenough were singled out for this award of high honor and distinction. No other foreigners are similarly recorded. It is not clear from the archive or the present director of the academy whether this position involved any teaching responsibilities. In any event, the academy listed Powers' name with the faculty of sculpture thenceforward, and Powers participated from time to time in judging the shows of the students.

There had been numerous interruptions in the course of *Eve's* rendition, which seem as natural to the objective observer as they appeared obnoxious to Powers. One of these was occasioned by Powers moving his studio half a mile. He protected the statue from the threat of damage in transit by suspending the plaster cast in "gimbals, which left it swinging gently in all directions" enabling four men to carry it safely.[31] *Eve* received her first American public exhibition in the famous Crystal Palace show of 1853–1854, on loan from Col. John S. Preston, who had purchased a marble copy.

The making of *Eve* over two years was, of course, not dry as dust portraiture, but was often interrupted for it. The number of busts that Powers felt obliged to carve for Americans seemed unlimited and to him it seemed they were "his principal occupation."[32]

He made two busts of Englishwomen, Mrs. Bennett and Mrs. Harrison, both destined for London. The husband of the latter, a clergyman, piously promised to place his wife's bust, "draped in a new and elaborate manner," in the annual exhibit of the Royal Academy, but failed to keep his word. However, Powers exhibited there on his own in 1841 and several following years. At one point Powers reported to Longworth that ten to twelve busts modeled before he came to Florence, as well as the number modeled there, still awaited carving in marble.

Powers also tried his hand at another ideal female bust, *Genevra*, which was an immediate success and superceded the *Proserpine* in his affections. She proliferated in marble copies and filtered into diverse cities of America and England to people whose esteem he had already won. One went almost immediately to Mrs. Van Rensselaer of New York, who pledged to exhibit it there for his benefit, another to George Tiffany of Baltimore, a third to Mrs. John S. Preston, and another to Nicholas Longworth. Powers worried over the transportation of the latter bust as he feared the risks of rough handling over the railroads and canals on a direct route. He settled on sending it all the way by sea, via New York and New Orleans, thence by riverboat on the Ohio to Cincinnati, which meant only one transfer or two in the handling.

It was a hard and tense time for Powers, who found himself in the typical bind of the struggling artist. In December 1840, three years after his arrival, he was irked, as Greenough had been, not to have finished modeling his first ideal statue in clay, which would gain him the recognition he craved and considered his due. Providing three square meals a day for his family required his making and selling portrait busts unendingly. At one point, he vowed to accept no more until the *Eve* was completed. To accomplish this, however, he needed more money to pay the marble cutters than he had been able to accumulate.

Whatever money he had earned and not consumed was tied up in numerous works that languished in his studio for justifiable reasons. Col. John S. Preston was expected to arrive in Florence momentarily, and the sculptor wanted to show off all he had wrought to bedazzle his patron. He wanted to display both his progress and

Genevra 1838, marble, 29^{15}⁄$_{16}$"
Courtesy of the Cincinnati Art Museum, gift of the heirs of Catherine Anderson

his prowess. The second consideration was his consciousness of his own growing reputation, his awareness that the longer he could parlay these holdings, the higher the price would be in time.

Greenough had tried to help all along. He had advanced some money early in the game. He then promised more during the summer of 1839 but failed to follow through, reneging unaccountably. At the moment Powers owed his friend $150, but he expected to square that against the $300 Greenough had agreed to pay for the commissioned bust of John Quincy Adams. For Powers, it was a hand-to-mouth proposition for several years. He weathered the present pinch by turning once again to Nicholas Longworth to borrow an additional $1,000 that was unaccountably delayed in transit.

The loan was clearly no solution. The only secure remedy seemed to lie in work. Portraits had a point of diminishing returns intrinsically, both financially and artistically. Short of a government commission, the way to artistic success and financial security seemed to point to the creation of more significant works for sale and exhibition.

Another immediate alternative was proposed by Edward Everett when he stopped in Florence in 1841 to take up his new post as United States Minister to the Court of Saint James. While sitting to Powers for his own portrait, which he commissioned, he suggested that the sculptor's consummate skill in busts was undoubtedly adequate to bestir patronage in London. If Powers were to make a personal visit there under Everett's tutelage, they might attract consequential public attention with the four portraits already there. This new one of Everett would make a fifth. Powers hesitated. He really had too much going in the studio to risk a protracted absence. Besides, he was coming to the firm conclusion that his career depended on his creating full-sized statues of high artistic merit. He decided he would lose nothing substantial by staying fixedly in Florence, for more business of the ordinary variety was rolling in than he could handle without a radical expansion of his operations.

His worries were strictly confidential. As far as the public could make out, he had arrived in both skill and reputation. His style was widely admired and even plagiarized and he had scaled the heights of official recognition in Florence.

12

The *Greek Slave*

ENCOURAGED BY HIS MANY ORDERS FOR PORTRAIT BUSTS, POWERS FELT assured of his future despite the persistence of nagging problems. He must now muster his confidence and venture to produce full statues of artistic merit. Ever since he finished the *Eve* in 1841, and while it was being cut in the marble, Powers pondered the subject for his next large work. Having a more literal turn of mind than Greenough, Powers avoided, for the most part, symbolic classical generalizations in favor of more easily manageable biblical, historical, or contemporary subjects.

Slavery had high priority at the time in the minds of Americans. The issue was the root of political controversy that threatened the unity and the very survival of the country. Although Powers was as conservative in his politics (for a dedicated republican) as in his personal behavior, he was a Victorian moralist to the core. He selected the subject of slavery but removed it from the contentious American context to the classical Greek islands at the time of the Greek War of Independence against the barbaric Turks, an episode that retained popular romantic overtones.

Powers second ideal figure, his most famous, represented "the embodiment of enslaved Greek womanhood."[1] In explanation of his selection years later to Henry P. Grey, the president of the National Academy of Design, Powers wrote, "I remembered reading of an

The Greek Slave 1843, marble, 66"
Courtesy of the Brooklyn Museum

account of the atrocities committed by the Turks on the Greeks during the Greek revolution. . . . During the struggle, the Turks took many prisoners, male and female, and among the latter were beautiful girls who were sold in the slave markets of Turkey and Egypt. . . . These were Christian women, and it is not difficult to imagine the distress and even despair of the sufferers while exposed to be sold to the highest bidders. But as there should be a moral in every work of art, I have given to the expression of the Greek slave what trust there could be still in a Divine Providence for a future state of existence."[2]

In the statue, Powers envisaged the slave's "bitter despair for the present, mingled somewhat with scorn for all around." Defensive about the figure's nudity, Powers intention was to purge any lascivious overtone so as to render his subject pure. He constructed the legend that "She is too deeply concerned [over her plight] to be aware of her nakedness." He would eschew any vestige of self-consciousness and convey in her stance and expression that "It is not her person but her spirit than stands exposed."[3]

Although he worked rapidly and with greater assurance on this second female nude statue, the composition took eight months to realize. In October 1842, Powers announced to Longworth that he had half composed the model of a new subject, a *Captive Girl*. He hoped to finish her in clay by the close of winter but feared that he might have to neglect her for busts. In March, six months later, she was cast in plaster. She emerged uncommonly well, and Powers thought that his work on the statue was nearly over. He would return to it merely to administer the finishing touches in its marmoreal state.

He took great care to select a choice bloc of Seravezza marble, whose texture was reputed to be "finer and harder than that of Carrara, and more free from blemishes."[4] The figure stood five feet five inches high and was to evoke raptures for its beauty and compassion for the defenseless plight of the victim.

The original marble replica was sold at the turn of the year, while still partially blocked out to the waist, to Captain John Grant of London, a retired British Army officer whom Mrs. Trollope had brought to the studio. Grant desired to have his statue by August first and promised to exhibit it in London at his own expense to launch the sculptor in England. Grant kept his word and had it shown at Graves in Pall Mall. The purchase price was six hundred pounds, half presumably paid in advance. Captain Grant later sat for his own portrait.

With enough money in pocket to carry him for a year and "as many orders as I can execute for a considerable time to come," Powers felt independent and optimistic.[5] He heralded the arrival of "better times" and shed his usual restraint when he related the gleeful tidings to Longworth. For all of his private calculations of fees from anticipated exhibitions of his major statues in Boston and New York, he did not have to await the public showings for solvency. It weighed on his mind to get clear of his last remaining debt to Longworth that now included a down payment that Longworth had advanced for the purchase of some choice Cincinnati property to give Powers a toehold at home.

During the eight months of the *Slave's* cutting in marble, Powers completed the model for Hamilton Fish of New York of a third statue, one that he had been mulling over for three years. "It represents," he wrote, "a lad of thirteen years holding a conch shell to his ear with one hand, while in the other is held a fishing net and boat tiller. He is listening to the sound of the sea, believing that the shell has the power to warn him of the weather."[6] The accessories of net and tiller would lie at his feet, half buried in the sand, "to denote the sea beach on which he stands."[7] Powers called this statue the *Fisher Boy*. When first conceived, the lad was to have been eight or nine, but Powers evidently changed this when he located a perfect model for age thirteen.

As the *Slave* was his paradigm for female beauty, Powers sought a legend to rationalize his depiction of youthful male nudity. He elaborated on the problem to a sympathetic friend.

> It is a difficult thing to find a subject of modern times whose history and peculiarities will justify entire nudity. . . . This figure is a kind of Apollino, but the character is modern, for I hold that artists should do honor to their own times and their own religion instead of going back to mythology to illustrate, for the thousandth time, the incongruous absurdities and inconsistencies

of idolatrous times, especially as our times and our religion are full of subjects equal in beauty and have all the qualities necessary to the full development of art.[8]

Powers was confronted with the same conundrum that bedeviled Greenough. Nudity was the stylistic idiom of Italy and the entire continent, but its public acceptance was doubtful in puritanical America. Powers sought to resolve the dilemma by imbuing his nude subjects with moral respectability by illustrating a realistic story that would vindicate the nude state. He failed to reconcile the disparate elements in his creative works because he was trapped in stylistic classicism that defeated an appropriate rendition of realistic subjects. The *Fisher Boy* was a classical figure whose only realism lay in the accessories that were so diminutive in size as to be adumbrated in the total effect. Some fellow artists rejected Powers explanation and charged Powers with plagiarism of the Apollino that stands in the Tribune of the Uffizi.

In 1841 Powers would have been pleased to have received $2,000 for such a statue, but now he refused to sell it to Prince Anatoli Demidov who offered more than the going market price for it. Powers decided to retain his copy not only for exhibition with the other two but also as an investment in anticipation of the rise of his prices. He accepted at face value the plaudits of the experts, who now included John Gibson and Tenerani, two leading sculptors at Rome, in addition to Thorwaldsen and Bartolini and "other foreigners of real excellence."[9]

Powers expected that *Eve* would be ready any day and hoped to get her shipped to the States by June 1 for exhibit in New York, Boston, Philadelphia, and other cities. He refused purchasers for her too. He hoped that Colonel Preston would want to acquire her at the conclusion of the tour. He placed such high stock in the outcome of this enterprise that even his interest in a governmental commission began to wane. In July he decided to defer the completion and shipment of *Eve* until the other two statues would be ready for the joint show. While the deadline of August 1 for the first *Slave* was fast approaching, he commenced a second copy in a block of spotless marble, scheduled to be finished with the *Fisher Boy* by the next summer or autumn.

The Fisher Boy   1846, marble, 57″
The Metropolitan Museum of Art, bequest of the Honorable Hamilton Fish, 1894

THE GIFT OF HA...

At this time Powers was jolted by the sudden onslaught of tuberculosis on his friend Shobal Vail Clevenger, who had arrived in Florence with his wife and three children in December 1840. The Clevengers had settled into a plush studio nearby with models of twenty-one busts to carve in marble. Plans went topsy-turvy when he was ordered home peremptorily by the local physician. The attack was potentially fatal. There was an urgent S.O.S. call dispatched to Edward Everett, who as American minister in London had a purse for stranded countrymen. Money was needed immediately to pay the passage home for the family. Although Everett responded quickly, Clevenger's departure could not await the complicated process of transmitting money in those days, even from just across the Channel.

Powers solicited a purse among the Americans at hand and dispatched the family. Then he received the news that Clevenger had died eight days out at sea. All of his models had been left in Powers' charge, including his new statue of the *Indian Warrior*. The model for this statue had been commenced by Clevenger in Florence when a subscription of $3,000 was being raised for it in New York for the Mercantile Association. Now it seemed to be expected that Powers would supervise the completion of these works for the benefit of the widow and children. He agreed to do that, but he drew the line at advancing the money to pay the laborers. He would wait until the sum due from Everett was deposited in advance. Powers fussed considerably over the disorder he found in Clevenger's affairs. With marked resentment at the irresponsibility of his dead colleague, he gave top priority to clearing up the debts. Then he supervised the completion of all his works.

That March the Trollopes settled for several years' stay into a house almost adjacent to the Powers. It was a stroke of luck. As Mrs. Trollope loyally talked Powers up among her English friends, she expanded his business prospects considerably. Henry Kirke-Brown was also there for a spell and Powers interested himself in his younger colleague's progress. In addition to Greenough, Francis Alexander, Chauncey B. Ives, and the English sculptor Charles E. Fuller rounded out the English-speaking artists in residence that season. The regular influx of artists to Florence and the progressive magnitude of England as a field for potential sales balanced Powers' constant aching for home. His letters to Longworth and Everett were amply sprinkled with such nostalgic phrases as "I am thinking seriously of leaving Florence within two years," but like Chekov's three sisters he remained rooted to the spot.[10] He "was daily becoming more known and the prospect of success [was] rapidly widening before [him]."[11] In sharp contrast with his auspicious situation in Florence, his dreams of home kindled the specter of struggle and obscurity, and being "obliged to follow some other calling for [his] daily bread."[12]

There were also family exigencies to concern him, for between 1840 and 1843 two more children arrived. The second daughter was named Ann Barker and the second son, Preston, for Powers' South Carolina patron. The eldest child, Longworth, who was nicknamed Nicholas or Nicky, was attending school in Florence at a cost of $5.50 a month. Powers took special pride in his son's mastery of three languages, Italian, English, and French, with a smattering of German for good measure. The Austrian origin of the reigning duke made knowledge and use of that language logical as well as useful. Nicky functioned also as family tutor to the younger members, whose number was increased by another during the winter of 1845–1846.

Powers' commissions kept pace. In the spring of 1845 he was engaged by the city of Charleston, South Carolina, to execute a statue of their revered statesman, John C. Calhoun. The face was to duplicate Powers' portrait bust of 1837. The enlargement would be only a matter of proportional transfer. Although Colonel Preston was skittish about taking up Powers' offer of the *Eve*, his hand was surely behind this new commission, which proved far more lucrative.

At this time an order arrived from Lord Ward in England for a duplicate of the *Greek Slave*. This commission was not arranged by a friend, so it must be attributed to the critical acclaim given the work at its London exhibit. The commission dwarfed Powers' disappointment over being denied the benefit of the show's proceeds at Pall Mall which Captain Grant had promised. His reputation as a creator of statues was growing. "If I could afford to give up portrait works altogether, I would do so," he ventured in confidence to Longworth, "for there is more honour and in the end more gain in ideal works than in busts and statues of real life."[13]

Maria Antoinetta, Grand Duchess of Tuscany
1846, marble, 22¾″
Courtesy of the Worcester Art Museum, bequest of
Dwight F. Dunn in memory of Benjamin T. Hammond

Powers' secret ambition favoring ideal works of merit was set aside for the glamour of executing a bust of Maria Antoinetta, the grand duchess of Tuscany. It was commissioned by Prince Demidov. This wealthy diplomat's royal contacts were cemented by his marriage to the daughter of Jerome Bonaparte, whose bust Powers had made some time earlier. For ten days early in February 1846, Powers went daily to the Pitti Palace on this mission. It was completed in May and everyone agreed that the likeness was the best ever made of the ruler's consort. Powers planned to make two marble copies for a beginning. Eventually ten or twelve were cut and sold at good prices. The bust was so pleasing to the grand duchess that she gave Powers the privilege of borrowing from the Grand Ducal Cabinet a splendid shell which he could copy for his *Fisher Boy*. Even more useful was her assent to take a plaster cast of the original Venus di Medici which later formed the basis for his female nudes. Powers hoped to capture the grand duke also as a subject, but he reported that he could detect "no symptoms of his sitting for his own portrait as yet, at this time."[14] Powers could afford to be patient. He had so much work that he was refusing numerous requests for busts in favor of concentrating on his statutes. He had eight work-men now in his studio, all working steadily.

While nurturing his other private hope to obtain a govern-mental commission for an equestrian Washington, he was delighted with the sale in the late spring of 1846 of his *Fisher Boy* to Mr. Stephenson, the son of the English inventor and railroad tycoon, who promised to exhibit it, as the *Slave* had been, at Graves in Pall Mall. The hope of a governmental commission now receded in view of preoccupation at Washington with the Oregon controversy. Powers concentrated on completing his personal copies of this three major statues for a road tour at home within the year.

Taking stock of his situation early in the summer of 1846, Powers found he had a second *Eve* commencing in a splendid block of marble and a second *Slave* almost finished for Lord Ward. For the first time since his arrival in Italy, he felt that he could relent his driving pace. He took advantage of the advent in Florence in June of the reputable Dr. Mussey to have a small tumor removed from the back of his head.

After numerous postponements, Colonel Preston finally arrived, and in the fall Powers accompanied him to Rome for his first visit. With little beyond his homespun inclinations for guidance, the se-ductive city failed to charm him. Powers defied convention in re-fusing to swoon at its sights, posing in contrast "the superior taste and refinement of our nabobs in America."[15] He found no mitigating wonders to excite his envy. He did not admire the gilt ornamenta-tion of the baroque churches, thinking that it deflected the eye from more solid architectural features and sculptural adornments. In short, he regarded the Eternal City as "an obscure but curious old town in the South of Italy."[16] He returned to Florence and to his work, as Greenough had from Paris, with a feeling of his own superiority.

Powers' studio and residence at one end of the new Piazza Maria Antonia, today known as Piazza Indipendenza, was a step from Greenough's and next door to Mrs. Trollope's. He employed from eight to ten workmen, and his annual budget was in the neighbor-hood of $6,000, against which his minimum costs, including food for his workmen and family, came to "three or four thousand an-nually."[17] His fifth child arrived on January 20, 1847, and he became more than ever conscious of money. He began to complain like a native that "Florence is not as cheap a place to live in as many suppose—that is—for a *family* to live in. . . . Provisions are quite as dear as in Boston. Clothing is much cheaper and so is house rent, but service is especially dear—that is—house service."[18] He must have had lots of it to grumble at the going price of four dollars a month per servant, plus room and board.

The works in his studio had been advancing during his absence in Rome. This was luckier than one would suppose because the roads to the Seravezza quarries had become impassable for nearly a year and Powers would not use Carrara marble because of the frequency of its flaws. When this new difficulty had arisen, he had on hand a plentiful stock, worth in the vicinity of $1,000. In January of 1847, the statue of Calhoun was cast in plaster, soon to be ready for the cutters. Two years later the original portrait bust was finally commissioned in marble. The marble portrait of the grand duchess was moving toward completion that spring, destined to adorn the grand duke's study sitting on a columnar pedestal. The *Fisher Boy* had been finished and sent to England as Powers put it, "to catch fish for me."[19] It was now exhibiting in London as promised and although not as popular as the *Slave*, it nevertheless pleased the connoisseurs. The second copy for his own use was progressing satisfactorily. He now undertook to design a pair of angels for the altar of the cathedral at Cincinnati. Bishop Purcell made the request and three gentlemen from his hometown raised the purse among themselves and awarded Powers the commission.

The significant accomplishment of the season, however, was the completion in January of the second copy of the *Slave* for Lord Ward, who allowed Powers to use it for an exhibition tour while awaiting the cutting of a third that would contain some slight changes that he now preferred. For these advantages, Powers was willing to forfeit an extra £100. The new arrangement left him temporarily short of £200, because Ward's final payment of £300 was now deferred until delivery. Powers wasn't pressed for money, however, and much preferred having the use of the statue.

Another order for the *Slave* came from an art collecting banker of New Orleans named James Robb. It was blocked out in January and promised for completion in marble in about eight months. There were orders for three more *Slaves*, making six in all, one for Sir Charles Coote of England, one for Prince Anatoli Demidov, and one for Mr. Corcoran of Washington, D.C.

At this time the flare-up of the Mexican War caused Powers to abandon all hope of a major governmental commission for the duration and beyond. "Economy will be the cry until the war debt shall be paid," he prophesied.[20] "The people's money must be saved" would be the motto uppermost in the legislative mind in Washington. Consequently, all Powers' efforts were now directed on a successful American tour of his statues. It was already decided that his trusted friend, Miner Kilburne Kellogg, a painter from Cincinnati who was now living in Florence, would recross the Atlantic to manage the arrangements. Only the *Slave* would be featured initially, while the other two were to be held in reserve as reinforcements if business were slow.

Early in July 1847, the *Slave* was shipped from Leghorn to New York, where Kellogg was on hand to receive her. The auspicious outlook for the venture vaulted Powers' expectation beyond reality, dooming them to frustration. A vexing complication arose early in the Robb transaction, causing a web of misunderstanding that gen-

Bust of the Greek Slave
1843, marble, 20$\frac{1}{16}$"
Courtesy of the Cincinnati Art Museum

erated hostility on both sides. Powers fulminated over the matter in self-justification for years after the issue had been adjusted. The facts are not so complicated as to have warranted the wrangling and recriminations they engendered.

Robb had applied for a copy of the *Slave* in August 1845, through his Florentine agent, Richard Henry Wilde. Actually his confirming letter, which arrived April 24, 1846, had substituted the name *Eve* for *Slave*, delaying Powers' commencement of the work until the correction arrived. The contract, entered into June 7, 1846, called for the *Slave*'s purchase for £600, half to be paid in advance and the balance when the statue was delivered in Florence two years hence. In December 1846, Powers wrote Wilde assuring him of progress on Robb's order and since it was the only copy destined for America, requesting the purchaser's consent to exhibit it in the principal cities between Boston and New Orleans, the route which it had to traverse anyway. Wilde's reply, three months later (March 21, 1847), extended Robb's permission on the sole condition that his name be withheld from any publicity attendant on the exhibitions. Powers supposed the odd request was motivated by a desire to avoid misconstrual "lest the Editor should say it was a joint speculation."[21] Powers deemed the proposal fair, as he was, indeed, the singular entrepreneur.

Before Robb's reply arrived in Florence, Powers had received a letter from Lord Ward offering to relinquish his copy in preference for another containing negligible changes in the accessories. By this gambit his copy was freed for the tour. It could conceivably end up in the possession of Robb afterwards, as it would seem pointless to transship it from the far side of the Atlantic. The availability of this second copy should have reassured Powers throughout the controversy.

On August 6, 1847, Wilde informed Robb of the arrangements in process for the exhibition of the *Slave* in the principal American cities, to be followed by its delivery to him in New Orleans, with the pledge that no publicity would attach to his name. Robb, in turn, replied gallantly, "I am pleased to hear of the near prospect of receiving the *Greek Slave* and hope its exhibit will make a small fortune for Mr. Powers."[22] It would appear from this exchange that Robb

Miner Kilbourne Kellogg at age fourteen 1828, wax, 10⅝"
Courtesy of the Cincinnati Art Museum

had acquiesced in all of Powers' plans for the tour. The show in New York ran smoothly and profitably.

At this point, Sir Charles Coote in England encountered financial reverses and, to Powers' embarrassment, canceled his order and requested a refund of his £300 deposit. The resourceful Yankee wrote Robb in October 1847, offering him the statue made for Sir Charles, with assurances of its spotless perfection, thus speeding delivery of his order before the end of the tour. The choice rested with Robb, the conditions were that this copy be shown by Robb only in New Orleans and that Robb should send his final payment promptly to Sir Charles in England. Powers' would thus be relieved at once of the time pressures from this quarter, and the financial demands from England. He felt confident of selling the second copy in the States at the conclusion of the tour. To his astonishment, Robb replied from New Orleans on December 20 with a flat refusal. He had already written a month earlier to Kellogg to say that he felt abused, and now peremptorily, without volunteering any explanation, he demanded his statue by March first, curtailing its tour disastrously for Powers. He even threatened to close the exhibition then in progress in Washington in order to collect his statue.

Robb's reply was a blow to Powers and instead of fathoming the reason for Robb's perversity, Powers vented his spleen neurotically against his colleagues, with all of whom he had quarreled periodically. He now turned them into scapegoats, charging them with hatching a plot to undo him. He wrote Kellogg, "Has he [Robb] been misled in regard to me by some of my artistic enemies? I think this last by far the most probable for I can hardly suppose a man of his character and respectability would stoop so low as to take away from me this only opportunity I ever had during a life of hardship to provide for my family."[23] Powers' resort to self-pity was not warranted on any count. It probably derived from the depths of his depression over the bad break in the midst of a protracted period of recurring family illness.

He allowed himself a month to cool his temper and replied blandly to Robb on January 27. Informing him that the Coote copy was being shipped, he reiterated that the marble was totally free of blemishes. Robb could choose either copy available, provided he would take no coercive steps. Despite the measured tone of Powers' reply, legal papers initiating injunction proceedings by Robb were served in March 1848 to effectuate his demand, although the contract clearly called for delivery in Florence no earlier than June.

Kellogg adjusted the impasse adroitly. Employing the tactic of delay, he avoided legal impediment until the arrival of the Coote statue in New York in May. Following the close of the exhibition in Washington, Kellogg delivered the statue originally intended for Robb on June 7, earlier than required by the contract, to Robb's agent in Philadelphia. He then substituted its replacement for the remaining scheduled showings in Boston, Baltimore, and Cincinnati.

Neither party to the dispute suffered any tangible loss, but Powers was unrelenting in his fulminations against Robb. Robb's subsequent petty behavior does suggest that his motives were not above question. He delayed interminably in sending his remittance of £300 to Charles Coote, who kept pressing Powers for it. Powers had to request an advance from his English banker so that he might pay Coote. Robb, of course, was not absolved of his debt and eventually he paid. Then he precluded any possibility for Powers to show the statue profitably in Philadelphia by lending his copy briefly to the Pennsylvania Academy of Fine Arts. For this Powers brought an unsuccessful suit against Robb in January 1850 for $1,000. Finally, when Robb's copy of the *Slave* arrived in New Orleans, he promptly arranged for its exhibition for his own profit. On his part, Powers expended an inordinate amount of paper, ink, and energy throughout the controversy and afterwards to vindicate himself and to expose Robb's perfidy. Perhaps he might be viewed as culpable to the extent of having grossly exaggerated the lucrative potential of his "masterpiece," instead of contenting himself with his professional accomplishment.

Powers kept meticulous track of the financial accounts, exacting detailed reports from Kellogg, who had volunteered to manage the tour unsalaried. Judging from their prolific correspondence on the subject, finances constituted the major element of interest for Powers. At long distance, he advised Kellogg on the hiring of galleries, supervised all the attendant publicity and advertising, and even participated in fixing the price of admission.

The anticipated profit from the enterprise was Powers' favorite subject of speculation. When the balance sheet of the exhibition tour was drawn by Kellogg from its commencement on August 26, 1847, to its close on December 12, 1849, the receipts were registered at $22,582.21, chiefly from entrance fees, which ranged from twenty-five cents to a dollar, the former being the more usual. Expenditures were $15,482.99, thus the listed profit was $7,099.99. The full gross income gained by the *Slave* must include the sums obtained from the sale of the copies. At £600 each for five of them and £700 for one, the income from this source was somewhere between $18,500 and $22,000. Out-of-pocket production costs for the marble blocks and their cutting for the full-sized statues came to approximately $1,500 each, or around $9,000 for six of them. Powers' profit from the copies clearly represented a fine percentage for the time invested and a tidy overall earning for that day.

The *Greek Slave* brought more than fortune to Hiram Powers; it secured his fame, beyond portraiture, at the top rung of American sculptors. His letters of the year and a half interval of the tour reflected the change of his station. In October 1847, at the outset of the venture, he wrote Kellogg, "Strangers are beginning to come now . . . and as usual a goodly number come daily to my studio, inquiring after the model for the SLAVE. . . . It is the universal custom in Italy to admit them."[24] Instead of instituting a fixed visitor's schedule as Greenough did, Powers adopted a less straightforward tactic. "I keep out of the way as much as possible," he wrote, "but my workmen are somewhat retarded by visitors. . . . I have taken all chairs away . . . to prevent people from lingering."[25]

Barely two months following his exhibition's opening in the States, Powers informed Kellogg, "There is no end of orders now. If I could but accept them, I might employ as many hands as I have fingers and toes."[26] Henry T. Tuckerman, the New York art critic, confirmed the accuracy of Powers' private report. "No modern statue ever awakened more interest or gained for its author such instant fame. . . . Orders flowed upon him from the English and Italians, as well as Americans. When not engaged upon marble portraits," he continued, "he worked on an ideal female figure."[27] No other American artist sold his work, as Powers did, both to English and Italian collectors in addition to the steady American stream of customers, either in his day or subsequently.

With the abrupt arrival of prosperity, Powers did not automatically shed his old habits of caution or his flights into self-pity. A year later the brisk pace in his studio had not relented. "I have had more offers of commissions than I could undertake to execute in years," he disclosed to Kellogg. Then he added plaintively, "How hard that this was not the case years ago when I stood so much in need of them."[28] He confessed to Kellogg that, "It seems odd to me to talk about investing my money."[29] The investment proposals were one-sided, coming consistently from Kellogg. "Do not let it go into any business transactions without ample security," was Powers' characteristically apprehensive response.[30] Fearful of the element of risk that invariably accompanies business enterprise, Powers refrained from venturing, in spite of his yearning for financial security. The only latitude that he allowed himself now was to give his family a respite from the summer's heat of Florence to join the rest of the foreign set in Bagni di Lucca or Siena.

The *Greek Slave's* American tour was triumphant. In addition to praise for its "everlasting beauty," it was romantically coupled with the struggle of the Greek War of Independence. Poets paid their tribute in verse. Elizabeth Barrett Browning's "Hiram Powers' *Greek Slave*—1850" is typical of the literary outpouring the statue evoked.

They say ideal beauty cannot enter
The house of anguish. On the threshold stands
An alien image with enshackled hands
Called the Greek Slave! as if the artist meant her
(That passionless perfection which he lent her,
Shadowed not darkened where the sill expands)
To so confront man's crimes in different lands
With man's ideal sense. Pierce to the centre,
Art's fiery finger, and break up ere long
The serfdom of this world, Appeal fair stone,
From God's pure heights of beauty against man's wrong!
Catch up in thy divine face, not alone
East grief but west, and strike and shame the strong,
By thunders of white silence, overthrown.[31]

Even before the *Slave* was completed Edward Everett was writing his praises. He especially admired the finish that Powers attained with instruments of his own design, and he wrote that these instruments gave "to the surface of the marble a delicate roughness . . . which absolutely counterfeits flesh and produces an illusion not merely beyond anything we have seen in the works of Donatello, Mino di Fiesole, or Gambarelli . . . but beyond anything we have witnessed from the chisel of any other artist."[32]

Henry T. Tuckerman was more restrained in his enthusiasm, noting the absence of particularized expression in the face of the *Slave*, "every detail of which was drawn from nature, and finished to the highest point of plastic truth." He added, "Not for emphasis of expression in feature, but for harmonious expression in form—the legitimate ideal of sculpture—did the *Greek Slave* win admiration."[33] This observation hit precisely on the mark of Powers' objective.

The rapturous praise of the *Slave* aside, the statue also inevitably touched off controversy respecting its nudity that was not greatly at variance with Greenough's experience. The mid-Victorian Americans still debated the question heatedly. In some American cities, public prudery was appeased by admitting separate groups of each sex alternately into the small special gallery selected for the exhibition. This occurred several times during the tour of the *Slave*.

Like many of his contemporaries, Powers inveighed in defense of nudity with the same passionate rationale that Greenough employed. The female nude was at the aesthetic pinnacle of beauty in Florence. An artist might hesitate to attempt the creation of a Venus only for fear of falling short of the standard technically. The nude form was basic to the sculptor's craft. Powers echoed the American Transcendentalists and the doctrines of the Italian humanists in viewing "man as the embodiment of God and, indeed, His divine creation," consequently, the epitome of beauty; "the beautiful form or *images of God*" that harmonized with nature. It followed that man, his handiwork, was intrinsically innocent of sin. "The body of man is always innocent," wrote Powers, "for it only operates the command of His will."[34] Powers remarked that he did not believe that it was "the design of our Creator when he made us naked, that his most beautiful creation of all, and his most precious gift to Adam should be forever veiled in her personal charms from his sight." He added. "The fact that they were presented to each other in a state of nudity proves that it *is* right to look upon the entire human form." He insisted that "a pure heart can do this without defilement."[35]

The argument was Christian rather than pagan, presupposing a hierarchical world order wherein man was the cynosure, outranked only by God. Powers saw "order and a complex system in Creation . . . with God presiding at the apex and man standing nearest to God, "his highest work."[36] Nature was relegated to the rung below. In this Dantesque arrangement, the image of man in his natural state was the highest order of art.

When pressed by reproving Cincinnatians who found his statue "indecent" as it was exposed there on exhibition, Powers cried out, "Surely there is no indecency in the attitude and expression of my *Slave*, and if this be admitted, why then the Lord is reproved by members of the Arts Union. I mean those officers for shaping us poor mortals in so vulgar and indecent a form." He added, "Perhaps those officers might suggest some improvement to the All Mighty."[37]

Neither the *Slave* nor the *Eve* was designed as a lascivious woman set forth in the nude to evoke the baser passions. "I have left out any expression on either *Eve* or the *Slave* of a consciousness of their nudity," explained Powers.[38]

As with the *Fisher Boy*, the insistence upon purity necessitated the construction of a story that would impart an inherent condition of nudity to the subject. If the conception were sufficiently uplifting, the purity would be guaranteed to remain unsullied. Powers adopted this device with all of his nude figures, as did his colleagues. "The Slave is compelled to stand naked to be judged of in the slave market," he narrated. "This is an historical fact." He continued, "It was not my object for interest's sake to set before my countrymen demoralizing subjects, and thus get even my bread at the expense of public chastity. It was calculated to awaken the highest emotions of the soul for the pure and the beautiful . . . and to excite his sympathies for the Ideal being." He concluded his discourse with satisfaction, "Beauty and innocence can bear to be seen from head to foot as God made it . . . his most perfect and wonderful work."[39]

The Reverend Orville Dewey of New York wrote a principled

defense of the *Slave* that was much appreciated by Powers. "There ought to be some reason," wrote the minister, "for exposing besides beauty, life, fidelity to history, as in the *Eve*, or helpless constraint, as in the Greek girl. . . . The *Greek Slave* is clothed all over with sentiment, sheltered, protected by it from every profane eye. Brocade, cloth of gold, could not be a more complete protection than the vesture of holiness in which she stands. . . . The highest point in all art: to make the spiritual reign over the corporeal, to sink form in ideality. . . ."[40]

Nathaniel Hawthorne epitomized the unmitigated New England reaction in a casual reference to Powers in this connection, writing, "He seems especially fond of nudity . . . none of his ideal statues having so much as a rag of clothes."[41]

Other intellectual leaders came to the defense of what they considered an elevated concept of art and an excellent example of it from the hands of our foremost "genius." To the *New York Herald Tribune*, Margaret Fuller wrote, "As to the *Eve* and the *Greek Slave*, I could only join with the rest of the world in admiration of their beauty and the fine feelings of nature which they exhibit."[42] The *Knickerbocker Magazine's* art critic summarized, "Naked, yet clothed with chastity, she stands,"[43] and the *Democratic Review* reported, "In the chastened and beautiful resignation of the face and figure, the artist had embodied the highest idea of a Christian slave. . . . The *Greek Slave* is entirely out of reach of criticism."[44]

This last verdict apparently stood. The *Slave* was received without critical objection to the nudity when it was displayed with the *Eve*, the *Fisher Boy*, and *Proserpine* at the famed Crystal Palace exhibition in New York during the season of 1853–1854. The *Fisher Boy*, however, did not escape disparagement by the art critics who wrote that "it falls far short of the admirable truth and beauty of the busts in which our great sculptor is confessedly unrivalled."[45]

13

Major Statues

HAVING CLIMBED THAT "LONG AND WEARY HILL" TO THE PLATEAU of success, Powers felt he had earned his right to produce more statues in preference to mundane busts.[1] "Perhaps you will wonder at my wasting so much time upon a single statue," he wrote Longworth in reply to a query about progress on the *Eve*. "My motto is that it is far better for an artist to concentrate all his powers in a single statue or picture regardless of the time and labor it requires than to produce many works full of defects for want of proper care and attention."[2]

The decades of the forties and fifties were Powers' most prolific years, witnessing the creation of all his major works. To his catalog of idealized, neoclassical, derivative female nudes, notably the *Eve*, the *Greek Slave*, *America*, and *California*, and busts like *Genevra* and *Proserpine*, he added monumental statues of notable statesmen, statues that were diametrically different from the stylistic nude females.

Early in 1848, while the *Slave* was still on tour, Powers returned to his first nude female statue, *Eve*, with a thought to send her in her sister's wake. He decided to revise her drastically to the extent of "cutting her in two at the waist" to gain the effect of "throwing the upper half of the body a little more back." He described the alteration glowingly to Kellogg. "I have not changed the general features of the figure. . . . But I have refined all the forms, the face, the arms, legs, and the undulations of the body. I have given a good deal of time to the hands and feet."[3]

A month later Powers reported to Kellogg his satisfaction with his progress. At the cost of "an immense deal of study and labor . . . I have gone all over it again and the improvement is manifest . . . particularly the face, arms, and hands. . . . The face is what attracts most attention. It is broader and more dignified and yet younger by two or three years than before. It is somewhat more in the style of *Proserpine* than before, but of a higher order."[4]

Despite Powers' reluctance to commit his capital into stone, he decided it would be advantageous to have a marble copy of *Eve* for exhibition even if a sale failed to materialize. By December he found a rarely beautiful block of marble, of a quality to be uncovered but once every year or two. It more than met his fastidious standards and he could not let it pass, although it cost the exorbitant sum of $400. Although he declared the purchase left him quite out of money," it was still a far cry from the day of his first talk with Mrs. Trollope about making idealized statues on speculation, when such expenditures were unthinkable.[5]

The first marble copy of *Eve* was completed in 1850 and shipped to Colonel John S. Preston, who was then living on his plantation at New Orleans. Like the *Slave* it was to be exhibited in the principal cities at home. Soon there came a report that the ship was wrecked off the coast of Spain. Insured for $3,000 against such loss, Powers had little cause for worry as *Eve* could easily be duplicated from his plaster cast. But the statue was salvaged and continued on her voyage apparently undamaged. There were several copies made of *Eve* altered further, for Powers remained displeased with some detail of each one and fussed over her for years.

During this work, all of Western Europe was caught up in revolutionary republican upheaval. In the spring of 1848, when the grand duke granted the popular request for a national guard to be staffed by citizens instead of hired mercenaries, there was a gigantic demonstration to celebrate the concession. Greenough and several other resident Americans participated. Powers joined without enthusiasm, explaining, "because I felt disposed to show my sentiments to such of the people as I happen to know . . . not to have done so would have been an impolitic thing." He reported to Kellog that "A million Italians were out," making it "a most imposing affair."[6] Although he held decided opinions favoring republicanism, his career had first priority, and he would make whatever political accommodation that was required to stay on. "For my part, I avoid taking any part in politics here," he assured Longworth, "although I sometimes feel much interest in what is going on."[7]

In those parlous days, when liberty hung in the balance for the multitudes in Europe, America seemed "blessed" to the entire Anglo-American set. For Powers, she was more than ever before "the beacon light to all the world . . . distinguished as the only country where good and safe government exists and where there is a general diffusion of all the blessings of life."[8] The lesson was emphasized by the arrival of the Austrian army to abort the republic and reinstate the grand duke. Americans should "cling to our Government and our institutions," asserted Powers, "as a wrecked sailor clings to a floating spar."[9]

Reacting to these events, Powers decided to symbolize "Liberty" in a classical "statue to suit the times." With America reprieved as a positive ideal, Powers could seriously "devote [his] time and humble abilities to [his] own glorious country. . . . Why should artists go to the ancients for subjects, while she affords so many touching themes?" he argued.[10] He meant to illustrate in his latest creation, "the mind and beauty of our Republic," as well as its youth—a symbol of peace rather than the militant stance depicted by Crawford.[11] He explained.

> It is a statute of Liberty, but not in strict accordance with the Liberty of Mythology. She has no rod in her hand nor cap at her feet. She is to be the republican Liberty and I have given her three symbols, which she displays as follows.
>
> She stands as if addressing a multitude and she holds the symbol cap upon her fingers ends high above her head. *This is the prize.* Beneath her foot, and directly under the cap, she is crushing a crown. This is the *danger.* The support for her statue is a bundle of sticks, which she touches significantly with her right hand. This symbol represents *unity or the means.*
>
> She will be draped lightly to just above the knees, and her

arms will be exposed. Her expression will be that of triumph.
The model is upwards of 6 feet high. . . . You will think this
a very *radical Liberty*, and so I mean to have her. I wish her to
say that 'Where crowns are exalted I cannot abide, and if you
would have me live with you, and you would enjoy the blessings which I can give, you must be united, and you must trample
in the dust every semblance of despotism.'[12]

As the figure evolved over the ensuing decade, her setting
shifted visably across the Atlantic. She was rechristened *America*.
To point up his message he incorporated the Union's slogan, "United
We Stand, Divided We Fall." He heatedly opposed nullification,
stating "The calamity would be far worse than breaking down the
dykes would be to the Hollanders. . . . Once inundated by nullification, our heads would never again rise above the civil deluge."[13]
He described *America* as breaking "the chains of tyranny" with one
foot, her hand pointing to Heaven gratefully, and the other foot
upon "the fasces emblem of union and strength."[14] The statue was
given a diadem of thirteen stars and the upraised left hand was interpreted as a sign of national allegiance. Notwithstanding Powers'
ardor for his subject and his desire to depict the contemporary scene,
he was incapable of transcending his stylistic limitations and once
again produced a tepid, generalized female nude representation.

In his search for meticulous execution, Powers hit upon a sound
technical innovation that has been adopted as standard procedure
now but was not followed with any discernible frequency by the
neoclassicists. In order to insure perfect balance in posture and proportion, he first modeled the statue nude and then superimposed
the drapery.

Nathaniel Hawthorne, the usually mordant commentator, found
in *America* "great merit and . . . the ideal of youth, freedom, progress, and whatever we consider as distinctive in our country's character and destiny." He saw "the female figure, vigorous, beautiful, planting its foot lightly on a broken chain and pointing upward." For him, the face had "a high look of intelligence and lofty
feelings; the form, nude to the middle, . . . all the charms of womanhood." She was thus "redeemed out of the cold, allegoric sisterhood
who have generally no merit in chastity, being really without sex."[15]

As the statue gained in national reputation, Powers grew increasingly ambitious for her destiny. He really wanted her lodged in a position of prominence at the national Capitol at Washington, and he would accept no lesser station that a statehouse. He planned his first marble copy to be "9 feet high to the elevated hand on which rests the cap—and 7½ feet to the crown of the head."[16] He hoped to realize $10,000 at the least. At times, encouraged by local praise, his hopes rose to $25,000 to be squeezed out of Congress. He dallied at the expense of the marble cutting. There was a momentary flurry of interest in her purchase by Colonel John Preston, but it petered out quickly.

It was the fault of no one in particular that *America* failed to be commissioned in Washington. Actually she barely missed. Early in 1851, the Congressional Committee on Public Buildings and Grounds, headed by R. H. Stanton, was petitioned by Edward Everett and others "to employ Hiram Powers to execute an emblematic statue of America."[17] The committee reported on the proposal favorably, extolling the statue's virtues in the current literary idiom of flattering phrases (probably composed by Everett himself). "*America* is represented as a youthful female of perfect beauty . . . of a most noble and dignified" expression, embodying "grace and harmony of limb and feature," and "draped in the chaste and graceful style of the ancient divinities, such as Diana and Minerva."[18] The rhetoric overlooked Powers' intention to produce a contemporary representation. In projecting an oversized statue fourteen feet high, Everett evidently sought a commensurately increased price. The report echoed Everett's theme, lamenting the public use of foreign artists to the neglect and humiliation of our prolific native talent, "from either a want of national taste or a niggard regard for cost."[19]

The committee recommended that "authorization be granted Powers, who was acknowledged throughout Europe and America as at the head of his profession," to execute this major statue for the adornment of the Capitol for a sum of $20,000 (the equivalent of Greenough's fee for his *Washington*).[20] The report died aborning but was not entirely forgotten. Powers' name was placed before Congress intermittently, eventually resulting in a different commission that fulfilled his lifelong ambition. Meanwhile, Powers' frustration on this score mounted. Styling himself as the sculptor laureate of America, he irately viewed his rejection by Congress as unjust, illogical, and the outcome of nefarious behavior of "enemies" intent upon denying him his rightful position.

He found consolation in an award on March 16, 1848, by the Louisiana state legislature, which authorized the governor to procure from Hiram Powers a statue of Washington for the statehouse at Baton Rouge. The sum of $5,000 was appropriated in December 1848 for this purpose. Powers received the news in a communication from Governor Johnson of Louisiana in October. Although he disdained the sum mentioned, he behaved discreetly for once. "I have accepted it," he wrote, "believing that the Legislature will increase the sum on being informed that it is less than I can earn by the same labour required to execute it. . . . I have requested the Governor to make my hopes in this respect known to the Legislature. I have heard that the bill passed almost unanimously and this encourages me. I think that a larger amount, say eight or ten thousand, and all in dollars will be given me. But for this hope, I ought not to have accepted the commission."[21] The final contract met his request. On the statue's arrival in New Orleans, he would receive $10,000, a sum appropriated by the state legislature in 1850.

The style of this statue confronted Powers with a crucial decision. Until then, all his statues had been strictly neoclassical. His female nudes were chaste allegorical reproductions of beguiling antique Venuses; his Calhoun was swathed in a toga. Nathaniel Hawthorne reported that Powers "expressed . . . great contempt for the coat and breeches and masonic emblems, in which he had been required to drape the figure."[22] But Powers could find no alternative. He approved neither of nudity nor of the Roman toga for modern statues of statesmen; and, continued Hawthorne, "neither does he find it right to shirk the difficulty [as Chantry did in the case of *Washington*] by enveloping him in a cloak; but acknowledges the propriety of taking the actual costume of the age and doing his best with it."[23] That was how Powers concluded to treat both this statue of *Washington* and the later one of Daniel Webster.

Sculptural tailoring may have been in disfavor in Italy, but it was rigorously prescribed at home, and there his *Washington* would lodge in some public building. Powers was sensitive to the popular derision accorded Greenough's statue. Thomas Crawford in Rome, similarly discouraged, was also veering toward a contemporary representation of Washington. Powers chose to comply with popular taste rather than risk his reputation for the sake of aesthetical principles. Here was his dramatic opportunity to attract the attention of Congress. Instead of repeating a poetical abstraction, Powers selected a specific moment in Washington's life for depiction. "His retirement from public life to domestic pursuits was the crowning glory of Washington, and I have preferred to represent him as a citizen, but still representing the welfare of his country. In the citizen's dress of his time, standing 6'5" high . . . he seems as if meditating, holding the Farewell Address in one hand, while he leans with his right arm upon a column composed of rods bound together, at the foot of which I have placed two emblems of husbandry, the sickle and the pruning hook. . . . I suppose Washington to have been greatest when, by his own voluntary act, he did all he could to make himself least."[24]

Hawthorne applauded Powers' decision, joking about it wittily some years later:

> What would he do with Washington, the most decorous and respectable personage that ever went ceremoniously through the realities of life? Did anybody ever see Washington nude? It is inconceivable. He had no nakedness. . . . His costume, at all events, was a part of his character and must be dealt with by whatever sculptor undertakes to represent him. I wonder that so very sensible a man as Powers should see the necessity of accepting drapery, and the very drapery of the day, if he will keep his art alive. It is his business to idealize the tailor's actual work.[25]

Much earlier, in 1834, Powers had modeled a portrait bust of George Washington from his death mask, which had been preserved in the capital at the State Department. Powers had made several busts from it in Florence, one of which he had presented to Nicholas Longworth. He still had the original to work from. He also sent for a duplicate of the suit that Washington had worn when resigning as commander-in-chief of the army. Powers was getting set for the most accurate rendition possible.

He took his time executing this statue, as if fearing its release for public judgment. Four years later, in 1852, he informed Governor Walker that the model for the *Washington* statue would be ready shortly and the marble block was already purchased and waiting in his studio. He anticipated completing it within the year, but it was late in 1854 when the marble statue arrived in New Orleans. During the Civil War, the statue was carried off to Washington by General Benjamin Butler, who was in command of the Union's occupying army. It was afterwards restored to Louisiana. Its delivery after the war was delayed because of the destruction of the statehouse in Baton Rouge. Finally, in the possession of the Louisiana Agricultural State Fair Association, it was included among its exhibits of livestock and vegetables. The statue enjoyed brief popularity at the city of its destination where, not long after its restitution, it was destroyed by fire.

Accompanying the official state commission for the *Washington* was one from a committee of citizens of New Orleans for a statue of Franklin to adorn a public square. The movement for the subscription was initiated in 1844 by Richard Henry Wilde, who was still living in retirement in Florence. He had located for Powers in Paris a cast of Houdon's head of Franklin to serve as a model. Rapid progress was thwarted when Wilde died in 1847, having raised only a small fraction of the required sum. The effort bogged down and dragged on for years. Powers set the work aside until some payment could be advanced. This period of gestation for conceptions of Franklin and his accomplishments proved useful for a later commission for the national Capitol. In 1873, just before Powers' death, the original statue of Franklin, completed according to the earlier design, was unveiled at New Orleans.

In 1850, inspired by glittering stories of the California gold rush, Powers conceived of an Indian figure to symbolize the West. There were few artists in that epoch who omitted a portrayal of the aboriginal American. It was a focal point in the artistic effort to break from neoclassical subjects and treat the environment either historically or contemporarily. Greenough was completing his *Rescue Group* and Crawford was featuring the Redskin "menace" in his new pediment for the Senate. Clevenger's outstanding work was his

Indian Warrior. Albert Bierstedt was in his prime and George Catlin was painting prolifically, just to mention a few of the Americans. Powers would ride the wave too.

His fatal decision, which he later repeated, was to make this Indian girl another female nude. He sought to differentiate from his other characteristic figures with the numerous accessories he lavished about her. He employed a variety of Indian appurtenances, such as a kirtle, distinctive embroidery, and a cornucopia, and liberally strewed native lumps of gold on the ground. This representation of California, which Powers named *La Dorada,* was about as native an Indian as the Venus was native to New York. The emblematic paraphernalia was powerless to rescue the work aesthetically. The statue lacked animation, although Powers insisted that the eyes were singularly Indian, making the statue "true to the present facts and history of California."[26] Powers counted heavily on the banal accessories to transmit his literal message. He used as many as twenty models for the one idealized nude, each contributing her own particular particle of perfection. It was no wonder that the representation ended, as Hawthorne observed, "Not an actual woman, capable of exciting passion, but evidently a little out of the category of human nature."[27] Although such precise reproduction of the minutiae of detail contained the secret of the best Greek practice of Pericles' time, it failed to remove the curse in this case.

Yet Powers understood the necessity to transcend the generalized neoclassical idiom in which he was imprisoned when dealing with the human figure. If he could have broken into the realm of emotional expression, he might have accomplished his purpose. The change, however, would have required precisely the distortion of features struck by Michelangelo that Powers heartily disapproved. Hawthorne reported that Powers "passed a condemnatory sentence on classic busts in general" because they were "conventional and not to be depended upon as true representations of the persons."[28] Powers hovered on the brink of overcoming the limitations of his classical style, but was handicapped by remaining in Italy.

Hawthorne commended Powers' representation of California glowingly to the American public. This statue, "lately finished and as naked as Venus," seemed to him "a very good work." Resorting to descriptive narrative, he continued, "In one hand she holds a divining rod. 'She says to the emigrants,' observed Powers, 'Here is the gold, if you choose to take it.' But in her face and . . . eyes, very finely expressed, there is a look of latent mischief, rather grave than playful, yet somewhat impish or spritelike; and in the other hand, behind her back, she holds a bunch of thorns."[29]

To Powers' keen disappointment, neither the state of California nor any of the newly settled, mud-ridden boom towns therein displayed interest in any culture to be found an inch above a gold mine; nor did the statue evoke enthusiasm in Washington. In order to inflate the statue's importance as symbolic of the state of California, he rechristened her the *Goddess of Gold*, a somewhat more pretentious name than the original *La Dorada*. The statue languished in his studio for several years until William Backhouse Astor of New York purchased it in 1858 for the rumored price of $7,500, almost twice the ransom of the *Slave*. It brought the artist little publicity because Astor entertained infrequently. A notable exception constituted "one brillant party" that was attended by the art critic, Henry T. Tuckerman. Tuckerman perceived the duality imbedded in the statue, wherein the beauty of its form failed to fuse with its facial expression.

> At a brilliant party given by its owner, this work was the nucleus of a gay crowd. . . . Evidently, the sculptor's idea is to contrast the fascination of form with the sinister expression of face,— the thorn concealed in the left hand with the divining rod displayed in the right,—and thus illustrate the deceitfulness of riches. It is a singular coincidence that such an allegorical statue should adorn the dwelling of our wealthiest citizen. . . . The contours of the figure are very beautiful, and the manipulation exquisite; while the expression of the face is repulsive.[30]

Powers' next female portrayal was another idealized bust, *Diana*, which he executed in 1853. It was unabashedly neoclassical and had the virtue of being an innately classical subject as well. Simpler in conception and pagan in spirit, the subject did not war with its form. Early the following year, the artist reported that he was "engaged on a statue of La Penserosa [melancholy] for Mr. James Lenox of New York."[31] This "female figure with uplifted face and rapt

California   1858, marble, larger than life-size
The Metropolitan Museum of Art, gift of William B. Astor, 1872

look, communing with the skies," was the only female ideal figure that Powers draped.[32] The drapery was necessary as the statue illustrated the character of a pensive nun from a section of John Milton's *Il Penseroso*.

Nathaniel Hawthorne thought the statue "very fine," and said that it probed "deeply into Milton's thought."[33] He then proceeded to demolish it for its plagiarism. "As far as the outward form and action are concerned," he wrote, "I remember seeing a rude engraving in my childhood that probably suggested the idea . . . and was probably as familiar to Powers as to myself."[34] Then he perceptively struck at the heart of the matter by concluding, "It is very remarkable how difficult it seems to be to strike out a new attitude in sculpture; a new group, or a new single figure."[35] A bust of the pensive nun was made in the same year for Edward Everett. The full statue was shipped to the Lenox mansion in New York in August 1857.

On one sunny afternoon in Powers' studio, Hawthorne was shown one of Powers' prized personal possessions. From a hidden recess of his desk, Powers removed a package wrapped in cotton wool. Power stripped off the covering, revealing a gleaming white, spotless marble of an exquisite, pudgy, dimpled child's hand with every infantile wrinkle of the soft skin lovingly recorded. Powers defended his minute rendition of his daughter Louisa's hand, which he called fondly *Loulie's Hand,* as retaining the loveliness he intended, despite its miniature size usually disapproved by the critics. It was withal his most sentimental work and he eventually made several replicas in marble.

The *Eve Disconsolate*, which Powers created in 1859 and completed two years later, was another trite version of the original *Eve*, already overworked through the years. In this study, he aspired to make his "best ideal statue."[36] With other statues competing for his attention, she developed slowly. Powers' "strong partiality to this last 'Eve'" derived from his great need for "relaxation from [the] buttons, coats, and breeches" that were foisted upon him for his public figures.[37] This second attempt, reminiscent of *La Penserosa*, recalled Eve after the Fall, out of Milton's *Paradise Lost*. In rueful sorrow over her sinful deed, she seems to implore forgiveness while fixing the blame upon the serpent. Powers conceived of her "standing in the act of advancing, . . . her face raised to Heaven with an expression of deep contrition; one hand upon her breast, and the other pointing down at the serpent, as if sensible of the accusation."[38] Unfortunately, the expression that Powers meant to convey was not transmitted in the stone. The face imparts no sentiment whatever. Powers hoped she would be purchased by A. T. Stewart of New York as a companion piece to the first *Eve* that he had acquired.

In his last major figure, the *Indian Girl*, all of Powers' efforts at originality succeeded in producing only another neoclassical creation clad in Indian garb. Tuckerman thought the statue graceful, calling it *The Last of the Tribe*. The dress doesn't make the woman,

Eve Tempted
1842, marble, 68″
Courtesy of the National Collection
of Fine Arts, Smithsonian Institution

Eve
1842, marble, 27⁹⁄₁₆″
Courtesy of
the Brooklyn Museum

Indian Girl (*The Last of the Tribe*)   1859–1873, marble, 65½″
Courtesy of the National Collection of Fine Arts, Smithsonian Institution

however, and this case was no exception. It seems strange that Powers lost sight of the fact that he had never seen an American Indian girl or even studied a representation of one. His search for native expression is commendable, and he might have had a chance for a successful rendition if he had gone home.

Powers had far greater success with his idealized female busts which harmonized with traditional techniques. They were simple to execute and commerically viable and were altogether his favorites. Copious copies made their way home and are now diffused throughout the museums of the country. In 1849 the *Proserpine* and *Genevra* were joined by another, *Psyche*, which was made for William Haywood of Charleston, South Carolina. Powers thought that the *Psyche* measured up in every way to his *Proserpine*, as in both the execution conformed with "strict truth to nature."[39] To Hawthorne he declared, "I freely acknowledge the fact; there is no sort of comparison to be made between the beauty, intelligence, feeling, and accuracy of representation of these two faces, and in that of the Venus de' Medici."[40]

These statues soon were followed by busts of *Ceres, Eve, Eve Repentant, Evangeline,* and the *Greek Slave.* The latter was reproduced in innumerable copies, many of which are still unlocated. In his declining years Powers created several more ideal female busts, as they continued to be in vogue.

Psyche
1849, marble, 25 $\frac{3}{16}$″
Courtesy of the Cincinnati Art Museum

In 1865 Powers created for Ignatius Scott of Boston a second *Genevra*. This *Genevra* was entirely different from the first but still adhered to the spirit of Samuel Rogers' poem, *Italy*, and was reproduced in a crop of eight replicas that were equally popular in England and America. She was followed by two of the three ideological virtues, *Faith* and *Hope*, whose main distinctions were that the former gazed upward, while the latter stared ahead, presumably into the future. *Charity* followed inevitably, looking downward conventionally. The last female ideal bust that he modeled was *Clytie*, a classical maid who was transformed into a sunflower for love of Apollo. Tuckerman thought her face lovely and her figure beautiful. He suggested that the sunflower in her forehead was emblematic of her fate in consequence of her jealousy. The chief difference between *Clytie* and her predecessors was her youth; she was represented as being only eighteen.

In contrast with the idealized female creations, Powers faced no insurmountable problems in the monumental portrait statues of the great statesmen he memorialized. Once he decided to dress them contemporarily, he was on his way. He was fully cognizant of their essential deficiency in artistic quality, but he was undeterred. They paid well and escalated his reputation.

Hope
1869, marble, 28¾"
Courtesy of the Brooklyn Museum

He faltered in his choice of dress only at the beginning when he dressed his *Calhoun* in a toga, standing next to a palmetto trunk, holding a scroll on which was carved, "Truth, Justice, and the Constitution." The face was a replica of his portrait bust. Despite its simplicity of conception and execution, Powers averred it "cost him a world of time and labor."[41] It was dispatched in the spring of 1850 in the ship *Elizabeth*, which sank off Fire Island on July eighteenth, carrying Margaret Fuller Ossoli and her family to the bottom with the statue. Money was raised in New York to pay for three months of salvage work, and the *Calhoun* was exhumed relatively undamaged. Tuckerman remarked that "it had been so adroitly packed . . . that when rescued . . . the slight injury . . . was easily corrected."[42] The statue was sent on to Charleston, where it arrived in November to a fanfare of acclaim. During the Civil War, it was transferred to Columbia, South Carolina, where like the *Washington*, it was destroyed in the fire that charred the city in the final months of the war.

In 1853 the administrator in charge of the extension of the Capitol at Washington finally responded to the unremitting prodding of Powers' friends (principally Edward Everett although he was ably assisted by the Preston brothers and Nicholas Longworth). At the specific instigation of Everett, M. C. Meigs, captain of engineers, addressed duplicate letters to Powers and Crawford request-

John Caldwell Calhoun
1847–1849, Parian porcelain copy, 16¾"
Courtesy of the Carolina Art Association,
Gibbes Art Gallery, Charleston, South Carolina

ing them to submit designs for the "Pediment over the Eastern Portico" and to adorn the eastern doorway to the extension. He requested their adherence to the general plan of the building, in an effort to "rival the Parthenon in the front of [the country's] first public edifice."[43]

Powers felt offended on several counts and replied petulantly. First, he was peeved at not being offered the commission exclusively but only in competition with Crawford. How did that novice rate such flattery? What had he done to prove his worth? Why should Powers, viewing himself as the world's foremost portrait sculptor, be equated with an unknown quantity? Why should he expend time and labor on designs without assurance of compensation? He was also annoyed that his statue of *America* was being overlooked. To the astonishment of everyone concerned, he flatly refused to respond to Meigs' proposal, leaving the field to Crawford by default, not, however, without strident private outbursts of regret, envy, and anger. He was irascible on the subject for years. Five years later he was still justifying himself and excoriating the government officials for the "fatal error" of adorning the Capitol sculpturally at "cheap rates." "I have no idea of putting my reputation into the hands of hirelings and do *job* for the government," he railed. "The government must pay for my time and my own work or I can have nothing to do with it."[44]

Again, Powers alleged the existence of a conspiracy that "cheated" him out of his commission. He attributed this, as in the case of the *Slave*, "to the opposition of selfish motives of some of my fellow artists."[45] Powers went so far as to accuse Crawford of having plagiarized his *America* in his rendition of *Liberty*, not only in conception but also in name. He concluded his diatribe with the threat that he would "never go to Washington to make straight what they have made crooked."[46]

Fortunately he did not voice his resentment publicly but confined its expression to reams of pages written to discreet friends at home. Captain Meigs was his chief target. Powers said that "the dispenser of commissions in Washington" did not have a favorable opinion of him as an artist.[47] Powers was guilty of faulty judgment. His anger beclouded such practical facts as his indirect request of

$25,000 for his *America* against Crawford's modest price of $3,000 for his model. Powers priced himself out of the competition and in time he recognized his mistake. "They have a taste for moderate prices," he wrote, "and a precedent has been established at the Capital."[48] More immediately, Powers' price level discouraged action in his behalf both from the administrators in Washington and his promoters.

Captain Meigs stated his case with equal candor. "Congress will vote large sums to fill the niches of the Capitol if they get the statues at such prices as other nations and private persons may, but if each statue is to cost $25,000, there will be but about one ordered in a generation of 30 years and there is room for 100 statues. This is one way in which I think it will injure art."[49] It took several years for Powers to overcome the impediment he erected for himself.

Chiefly on Everett's insistence, on March 3, 1855, Congress voted a resolution "to enable the President of the United States to contract with Hiram Powers for some work of art executed or to be executed by him, and suitable for the ornamentation of the Capitol." For this work $25,000 was appropriated. Powers heard of this act by the Florentine grapevine and immediately requested Everett to continue representing him in this matter, asking him to employ his "singular" discretion.[50]

Powers was tied to his home and studio and could not return home to deal with the politicians personally. Besides, his patience would have run out too soon. Actually, he and his wife were glued to the bedside of a daughter who was a "constant anxiety" for several years, a victim of rheumatic fever.[51] She had suffered three attacks and they feared she might not survive a fourth, which they hoped could be forestalled by meticulous supervision. The vigil wore his wife's health to the edge. She also pined for home after twenty years of exile, even more than he, whose life was filled with work. He felt unable to leave his family, which had by then grown to six children. Whatever the cost, Powers felt forced by these circumstances to implore the intercession of Everett.

It was evidently the *America* that Everett was advancing, but Meigs did not bite. The matter was brought directly to the attention of President Franklin Pierce who readily admitted "there are many positions in the wings of the Capitol, now under construction, which would be appropriate to Mr. Powers' statue of *America*." He was reluctant to place a price upon the statue himself, especially since he had not seen it. He wrote Everett and requested a description, photographs, price, and testimonials. The matter lay dormant for a year when President Pierce wrote a second letter to Everett stating "If offered at satisfactory rates, and found suitable for the ornament of the Capitol, the work will be accepted." He then offered his willingness to submit "any difference . . . [on] the question of fitness and value . . . to the decision of a Committee" (which would include Everett).[52]

To keep the matter alive, Everett made certain two years later that Congress renewed the appropriation, securing it until June 20, 1859. Fearing default again, he strongly urged Powers to come to Washington personally. More unaccountable delay ensued before the contract was finally drawn on January 28, 1859, between President James Buchanan and Hiram Powers. The contract did not mention the *America*. It called for the creation of statues of Benjamin Franklin and Thomas Jefferson for $10,000 each. Powers had offered two pairs of choices: Washington and Franklin at $20,000 or Webster, Clay, and Calhoun for $25,000. With the exception of Henry Clay, he had already conceptualized these personalities and had their plaster casts and accessories in his studio. Powers' suggestion of Clay was a sop to the Kentuckian's popularity at home. Actually, he would have been reluctant to make this one because he still smarted from Clay's rebuff in having "unkindly" refused to sit for him years earlier in Washington.[53]

Happily Everett was a dependably clever negotiator, knowledgeable in the ways of administrators. He obtained for Powers full liberty to select the subjects. Powers made the simplest choice, fixing on those already familiar to him. Not only did he have the Franklin sketched out from the New Orleans commission, but he had also contemplated the Jefferson rendition for the state of Virginia. The sculptor's gratitude to his intermediary was unbounded. He acknowledged to his friend Thomas Buchanan Read that "no human being could have done more to bring about [the] favorable decision."[54] However sincere his sentiments, the only other evidence of Powers' gratitude was his naming his youngest son for the statesman. Everett succeeded egregiously in view of the difficulties, enabling Powers to make a total of three works for the national government, including the marble bust he had made long ago of John Marshall.

Powers worked first on the *Franklin*, having resumed the study as soon as the subject had been broached, retaining in mind the alternative of exhibiting it on tour with the *Slave*. Powers pondered at length over the thematic line for the elder statesman-scientist, explaining, "Franklin was distinguished for so many excellences, and it is difficult to illustrate more than one or two in a single statue."[55]

In September Powers wrote Longworth that he intended "to represent Dr. Franklin in a standing posture with his left hand resting upon a pillar, with a book or two and perhaps some papers upon and against it—his right hand holding on high a chain and a lightning rod, and with a thunderbolt under his right foot."[56] In this statue, as in his others, he placed paramount reliance upon the correct accouterments to symbolize his subject. The books and papers were to symbolize the philosopher; the chains, the liberating statesman; and the thunderbolt and lightning rod spoke their meaning literally. Their arrangement constituted his artistic contribution beyond the portrait. For his rendition of the face and figure, he could depend on his accuracy in copying from the cast and costume. On the base he inscribed: "He snatched the lightning from Heaven and the Sceptre from tyrants."[57]

This highly realistic portrayal of Franklin, including the wrinkles and wart on the face, was completed in marble with Powers' typically splendid finish in two years, a triumph of speed considering the size. The statue arrived in Washington in November 1862 and was placed directly on a temporary pedestal on the principal floor of the Capitol. It was most favorably received by the public. A duplicate, made for the city of New Orleans, was stationed in the central public library where it was unveiled in 1875. Several marble busts of Franklin were executed by Powers from the statue.

The statue of Thomas Jefferson, which was settled upon definitely within a couple of months of the Franklin, is similarly realistic in style and dress. Powers inserted into the portrayal his favorite symbol for unity, the fasces, to represent Jefferson's role in forging the nation and keeping it intact. The device failed to animate the rendition that, on the whole, was deemed praiseworthy for its exquisite finish. The practical details of the statue were wrought with infinite precision. A contemporary observer singled out for admiration "the very texture of the cloth of his garments seems impressed on the delicate marble, and the separate stitches of the worked button-holes of his coat may easily be discerned by the curious eye. The hands, too, are marvels of artistic beauty."[58]

The same critic further remarked that "it is all toned down to such a degree that the creation lacks power. There is nothing here of the strong rugged man Jefferson really was. The impression is very different from what his portrait makes in Trumbull's picture of the Declaration of Independence in the Rotunda."[59]

Unfortunately the minutely detailed tailoring failed to qualify as an artistic creation. Powers was aware of the limitation and disclosed his comprehension of the problem to Everett. "I'm not sure that the time and labour required would not be better spent upon ideal works, for on coats, breeches, and boots, no sculptor can ever expect to do a high work of art. All he can expect is credit for fidelity to the likeness and as much expression as the natural form may give pampered up in the crude coverings of a Tailor's Genius."[60]

The *Jefferson* was a pleasant enough representation withal and was commended in its time. It was delivered to Washington in 1863 and Powers was duly paid. It now stands in the east corridor of the main floor of the House wing of Congress.

Powers' majestic *Daniel Webster* stood eight feet high, looked "even more colossal than that," and was more successful from every standpoint.[61] Edward Everett led a group of local art patrons, all friends of Webster's to commission the statue for their favored Boston cultural club, the Athenaeum, for $7,000. The group desired to memorialize the revered elder statesman and selected Powers because of the stunning bust that he had wrought of Webster in 1841. It took five years to raise the subscription in prosperous Boston even for such a combination of stellar names as Webster and Powers. The order was placed October 25, 1858. Powers reproduced the face with unique fidelity from his own bust aided by the death mask. To Hawthorne, "the likeness seemed perfect."[62] Powers said that it had been

Thomas Jefferson
1859–1863, marble, life-size
Courtesy of the United States Capitol

Benjamin Franklin
1862, marble, life-size
Courtesy of the United States Capitol

a strain "to give an animated likeness of Mr. Webster." During the thirty-seven sittings at Marshfield, soothed by "the cool breezes from the Pilgrim Seas," Powers found that Webster bored easily and drowsed readily. At these moments, all expression drained from his face, his mouth sagged and his chin dropped, creating a frustrating handicap.[63]

Powers recaptured the stance from a daguerreotype. Everett sent Webster's last suit of clothes to serve as model for the body and Hawthorne found the selection of Webster's natural costume most sensible. Webster was exceedingly well portrayed, aided by the decision to depart from the customary marble material in favor of having the statue cast in bronze, a method that seemed superior in preserving the distinctive hallmarks of the artist. For the casting, Powers chose Professor Papi, whose reputation ranked high in Europe as director of the royal foundry outside Florence. Powers, intrigued by the mechanics, wanted to stand close by and assist in the supervision. He also was keen to apply an improvement in the method that he himself had devised. Casting in bronze was a laborious process in several stages involving the use of artificial heat to dry the mold and other special techniques to assure an exact reproduction of the plaster cast.

When complimented on his excellent result, Powers graciously deferred to Papi for his contribution. He took the occasion to rap Clark Mills, the pioneer American, who with no training whatever had gone into this business at Washington and was by all accounts turning out atrociously sloppy work. "The casting," wrote Powers, "is not a very simple process, when well done, but it is simple enough when done—as Mr. Clark Mills does it."[64] Disparaging darts were generally hurled at Mills for the quality of his casting, but these critics overlooked the fact that he was the first one in America to attempt the craft at that time. Hawthorne also derided Mills as "certainly the greatest bungler that ever botched a block of marble."[65]

Nothing seemed to go smoothly for Powers. There was a rival movement afoot in Boston that conspired to have the sculptor Thomas Ball, then on the scene between his two long Florentine residences, execute the Webster since he also had made a model of the statesman. Thomas Crawford had been considered too because of his powerful relatives in Boston. Since Webster had never sat personally for either of these others, the choice of Powers was vindicated. Powers reported that he heard rumors of vicious attacks against him and attributed them to "a concrete plan of a few individuals."[66]

There was more incipient trouble in store before Powers was quit of this commitment. The *Webster* was thought lost at sea on the *Lucy Francis* during the passage from Leghorn to Boston that took 105 days. Although the statue was fully insured, its threatened disappearance was justifiably worrisome to Powers. After its safe arrival early in 1859, there ensued much discussion at the Athenaeum over its placement and lighting. To complicate the affair, Thomas Ball's statuette of Webster had been introduced into the vestibule where the light for so small a figure was flattering. The same confined spot produced a claustrophobic effect for a colossal statue, however, and the lighting was impossible. Powers, like Greenough, placed great emphasis on proper light, insisting that all statues look "tame and insipid" in poor light.[67] It became both desirable and difficult to have the statue moved. In May of 1859 Everett secured the permission of Governor Banks to place the statue in front of the statehouse. In September the *Webster* was moved outdoors, to the gratification of both Everett and Powers. It was fortunate that Powers had cast the statue in bronze, for now it could withstand the ravages of the New England winters.

The statue was assailed by the cabal for various and sundry petty shortcomings which were alleged in the press; such as the pantaloons being too loose, the color of the bronze too gray, the lankness of the figure, the want of erectness in the posture, and finally, the fasces and the inadequacy of the bronze foundry. Powers championed his own defense on each count as well as he could across the ocean. He was especially assertive in justifying the use of the fasces to illustrate his major theme because he thought Webster had preserved the Union in effecting the Great Compromise in 1850. He had underlined the lesson "United We Stand, Divided We Fall" to accord with his own obsession that all American liberty would be lost through scission. He inferred that the difficulty lay in the drastic difference between the American significance ascribed to the emblem and the Roman in which the fasces represented "rods to scourge the backs of State offenders."[68] Powers argued that if Houdon could use the axe in his statue of Washington to symbolize executioners, he should not be criticized for using the fasces, which in this statue was even functional in support of the figure.

Once more Powers detected a conspiracy; this time naming Thomas Ball as its organizer. He believed its purpose was to destroy his reputation in Boston so that Ball could prevail free of his competition. Powers complained of feeling particularly aggrieved because he had befriended Ball in the past and had given him many dinners. He went so far as to suggest that the editor of the *Boston Transcript*, the chief hostile medium, was a relative of his erstwhile friend.

In an address delivered at a meeting of the Committee of a Hundred on the Webster Memorial, Edward Everett defended the statue loyally with his usual rhetorical skill. He stated, "It is a faithful representation of Mr. Webster in middle life. . . . a first rate work; true to nature and to life, in countenance and expression, form and action; worthy of the great artist and of the great man whom it faithfully portrays. . . . The costume . . . has been severely criticized . . . [but] it is modelled from nature."[69]

Everett was seconded by Joseph Ames, who wrote from Baltimore agreeing that the statue is a "most powerful and characteristic representation of the great man."[70] Rufus Choate added his voice, attesting to the statue's being "an exceedingly pleasant likeness" comparable to Houdon's head of Washington. This was the acme of praise in that day.[71] Powers himself thought Webster "the grandest living man in appearance." He posited that he had done his best "to produce a resurrection of that appearance," which accorded with Sidney Brooks' characterization of Webster as "a walking Cathedral . . . a steam engine with breeches."[72]

This fulsome praise was like some distantly echoing accompaniment as compared to the major theme that Hawthorne voiced about this statue. In one of his most positive statements on art, he wrote:

> Like a sensible man, Powers has dressed him in his actual costume, such as I have seen Webster have on while making a speech in the open air . . . dress-coat buttoned pretty closely across the

breast, pantaloons, and boots, everything finished even to a seam and a stitch. Not an inch of the statue but is Webster; even his coat-tails are imbued with the man, and this true artist has succeeded in showing him through the broadcloth; as nature showed him. He has felt that a man's actual clothes are as much a part of his flesh, and I respect him . . . for recognizing the folly of masquerading our Yankee statesmen in a Roman toga, and the indecorousness of presenting him as a brassy nudity. . . .

Webster is represented as holding in his right hand the written roll of the Constitution, with which he points to a bundle of fasces, which he keeps from falling by the grasp of his left—thus symbolizing him as the preserver of the Union. There is an expression of quiet, solid, massive strength in the whole figure. . . . He looks really like a pillar of the state. The face is very grand, very Webster; stern and awful. . . .

Powers made me observe how the surface of the statue was wrought to a sort of roughness, instead of being smoothed, as is the practice of other artists. He said that this cost him great pains, and certainly it has an excellent effect.[73]

In his later years, when he was resting on his reputation and passing his time toying with facile ideal busts, Powers made some of his notable portrait busts. These were now fetching the fancy price of $1,000. A bust of Henry Wadsworth Longfellow, whom Powers admired as a "grand-looking model, his fine beard setting off his face," was commissioned by the family when they visited Florence in 1869.[74] The Reverend Henry W. Bellows of New York sat that same year in order to obtain a prolonged interview on which he based a series of articles about the sculptor. Other notables who sat for portraits in these years included the Honorable Robert C. Winthrop, whose bust was presented as a gift to the Boston Athenaeum by Endicott Peabody of Salem whose portrait Powers also made. Powers made one also of Alexander Hamilton. Professor Jared Sparks, famed historian of Harvard, enjoyed sitting for his portrait as he had for numerous others, and Powers made another of Salmon P. Chase, chief justice of the United States Supreme Court, with whom he maintained a correspondence.

In 1865, Powers tried his hand at one idealized male bust. It was an ideal Christ that was commissioned by William H. Aspinwall of New York. The statue was to represent the Savior as the embodiment of human perfection with all temptation resisted and all evil eschewed. This would appear an odd choice of subject for a self-conscious Protestant like Powers, but in the Tuscan ambience it seemed as natural to Powers as it had to Greenough. Powers defended his theme as representing a modern subject in preference to an antique one, a Christian one that was still operative rather than a pagan one that was extinct.

Just three years before his death, Powers fashioned a full length marble statue of Edward Everett after the bust, for which he received $6,000 (equaling the price of his second *Eve*). Late in 1870 the statue was shipped to Everett's son, who rightly presented it to Harvard University instead of allowing it to go to its intended destination at Mount Vernon, Virginia.

14

Love of Machines

INSPIRATION FOR MECHANICAL INVENTIONS CAME MORE NATURALLY to this mid-western Yankee stonecutter than celestial concepts for idealizations. Neither cultivated nor theoretical, Powers could discourse with didactic certainty over a broad range of mundane subjects tenuously related to art, morals, or politics. His interests were rarely literary. Through the several hundred of his letters which are available in this country, there does not seem to be a single literary reference beyond the Bible, some books of poetry, a volume written by Charles Edwards Lester about Powers, and something by the Swedish theosophist Emmanuel Swedenborg, whose occult religious doctrines converted him.

It seems odd that someone as pragmatic as Powers should have believed in Swedenborg's mysticism. Hawthorne reported, "Powers seems to put entire faith in the verity of spiritual communications, while acknowledging the difficulty of identifying spirits as being what they pretend to be."[1] Powers and his wife had the regular company of Elizabeth Barrett Browning and several other English-speaking colonists in attending the seances of the spiritualist D. D. Home, who had been expelled from Rome for sorcery. Robert Browning scoffed at them all in his lengthy satirical dramatic poem, *Mr. Sludge, the Medium,* and was incredulous that Powers stayed with the believers.

The sculptor recounted the story of his conversion to Sweden-borgian beliefs to Reverend Henry Bellows of New York during their seven interviews preparatory to the publication of Bellows' articles about Powers for *Appleton's Journal of Literature, Science, and Art*.

Confessing freely to having had "no religious education [as] a boy," Powers further discounted his family's role in shaping any religious predisposition. "My father was an upright and honest man, and taught us to do right. My mother was a Universalist . . . [who] did not inculcate any special religious opinions or duties upon me." His early exposure to the "current preaching . . . seemed almost an insult to intelligence. I resented it," he affirmed, "as an offense to reason and conscience. . . . Although always morally alive, I thought I had no religion."[2]

Across the Atlantic, the Catholic Church held no attraction for him either. It rather repelled him for its hypocrisy and its accommodation to oppression. He mocked the practices in a letter to Longworth, stating, "Those two-faced Church goers may lie and cheat you without your knowing it and then gain absolution in the confessional." He later said, "They regard money as the root of all evil and then they take it away from the innocent lest it should corrupt them."[3] He was revolted altogether by Italian profligacy. "A little silver in Europe has wonderful chemical qualities. . . . [it] thaws the icicle and makes the warmest friend of the bitterest enemy."[4] Fortified by his sanctimonious Protestant objections to Italian mores and morality, he blamed the general corruption of the atmosphere upon the Church. In the spirit of human brotherhood which it preached, he was further disquieted by the Church's betrayal of its consecrated function to the extent of permitting beggars to ply their trade within its confines.

Circumscribed as Powers' life was socially because of his inability to communicate fluently in the language, he was further alienated from his Italian environment by his rigid ethical code as well as his republican politics and artistic proclivities. He lived for the most part in the privacy of his workshop, studio, and family circle. Except for the Brownings and Mrs. Trollope, his intimate friends were Americans.

Paradoxically, it was in Catholic Italy and anticlerical Florence that he succumbed to the American transcendental revelation of "God condescending to us in a human form and nature. . . . The universe seems full of illustrations of spiritual truth," he explained. "It was not until I came across Swedenborg's writings, that my mind opened to the truth and claims of Christianity," he asserted. "There I found the Trinity set forth in a reasonable and credible way, as the several manifestations of the divine Wisdom, Goodness, and Power."[5]

Powers carried his renewed faith in Christianity into his world of art. He had already rejected the pagan deities and mythology as fit subjects of his works. Besides objecting to the anti-Christianity of the prevailing classical creations, he looked askance at the possible "danger [to an American artist] of going abroad to study in foreign parts that we might lose our native originality and fall into the impurities of the Greeks and the Romans."[6] Greenough had confronted the same dilemma without any greater success except in his later realistic portrait statues. The similitude is striking.

Powers had a way of hammering away unremittingly at a point. Embroidering his growing squeamishness toward Italy, he went to lengths to lament the lack of natural beauty in its people, as if he were impelled to rationalize his lack of adjustment to his foreign environment. "Among the thousands whom I have seen," he wrote, "I cannot say that I have met one that I could call truly handsome. I speak of natives. . . . You will meet with more pretty faces and forms in one hour's walk of a sunshiny day in Cincinnati or Baltimore, or indeed, in any American city than you will in a week in Paris or Florence."[7]

In all fairness, Powers was forced to acknowledge one saving grace among the Italians—their temperance—which was amusing to him in view of the fuss being stirred up in his moralistic homeland by the Temperance League. "There is no drunkenness," he observed, "where good wine is made in abundance. Tell this to your temperance people who slander the beverage converted from water to wine by our Saviour himself."[8]

Powers cultivated a distinct distaste also for European politics. He railed perpetually against oppression, the effects of which he witnessed daily with disgust. He talked repeatedly of the "chains of despotism," flaying it as a contradiction to republicanism, or even to humanity.[9] Powers detected a relationship between autocracy and war, rejecting both as twin evils. During the monarchist restoration following the abortive Florentine republic in 1849, he commented, "There never before was so black a cloud hanging over Europe. . . . [It] will cause much distress with Europeans, who, for the most part, have not enough in the best of times. [War would] double the price of bread here and thousands would perish."[10] He saw Europe poised on the brink of catastrophe.

The "danger of European contamination" was complex for him, operative on several levels beyond the political and religious, encompassing also the world of art. He unleased a "millstream of talk" against classical works for their lack of accuracy and their excessive generalization.[11] He entertained Hawthorne with his art criticism, which Hawthorne reported half credulously, half skeptically—especially regarding Powers' views of the Venus di Medici.

> The figure . . . was admirable, though I think he hardly classes it so high as his own *Greek Slave* or *Eve;* but the face . . . was that of an idiot. Then . . . it is rather a bold thing to say, isn't it, that the sculptor of the Venus de' Medici did not know what he was about? . . . Powers went on remorselessly and showed . . . that the eye was not like any eye that Nature ever made . . . less like a human eye than a half-worn button-hole!
>
> He attacked the ear . . . as placed a good deal too low on the head, thereby giving an artificial and monstrous height to the portion of the head above it. The forehead met with no better treatment in his hands, and as to the mouth, it was altogether wrong. . . .In a word the poor face was battered all to pieces and utterly demolished.[12]

Hawthorne retired to the tranquility of his private quarters to reflect upon the destructive tirade, and the following day, returned to view the Venus in the Uffizi gallery. Whereupon he protested vigorously,

> This very face had affected me only the day before with a sense of higher beauty and intelligence than I had ever received from sculpture, and . . . its expression seemed to accord with that of

the whole figure, as if it were the sweetest note of the same music. There must be something in this. The sculptor disregarded technicalities, and the imitation of actual nature, the better to produce the effect which he really does produce. . . . But Powers considers it certain that the antique sculptor has bestowed all his care on the study of the human figure and really did not know how to make a face.[13]

Powers' brief for technical precision led him with procrustean rigidity into rejecting as faulty art any work that failed to meet his calipered tests. It seemed to him "a kind of blasphemy to talk or think of improving upon nature."[14] He condemned in one broad sweep also the venerable *Moses* of Michelangelo. Writing in all seriousness of the works of Michelangelo, he pronounced the judgment that they have done more to retard the advancement of art than they have to promote it." Conceding that Michelangelo "exhibited a great display of anatomical development . . . representing the human body," Powers objected to his "overlooking the fact that a human frame without a soul in it is dead."[15] While acknowledging that "perhaps no man ever lived who had a more profound knowledge of anatomy," he still disliked the distortions in the head of the *Moses* that left little room for a brain and the articulation of the lower jaw that was so disjointed as to deprive it of mobility. He criticized Michelangelo's rendering of his massive figures in "the most difficult and uneasy attitudes possible."[16] In the *Moses* he did not see the wisdom of the "meek lawgiver" portrayed; on the contrary, the *Moses* looked fearsome, "as if he had just eaten half an ox."[17] On the whole, Powers took delight to observe that "Admiration for Michelangelo's works appears to be rapidly diminishing. . . . for the same reason that Canova's works are daily losing ground," both being succeeded by a "pure and thoughtful art [that] is rapidly progressing."[18]

He criticized Michelangelo for his departures from nature and failed to appreciate the immense power that Michelangelo achieved through his exaggerations and extreme anatomical articulation. He also missed the humanist essence of the Classical and Renaissance sculptural masterpieces. It eluded Powers that in order to express the galaxy of human emotions that were portrayed in these works the masters, with Michelangelo at the fore, had broken progressively with the static medieval conventions. As the secular quality grew, the works gained proportionally in animation and humanist feeling. The means employed in the transformation were often precisely the very distortions, the departures from punctillious realism, that Powers opposed.

Powers' emphasis on external forms became almost obsessive. To him, "Form was the very essence of expression . . . independent of color . . . express[ing] with exactness the precise signification of the thing."[19] Although he agreed that "color has the power to communicate any voluntary or characterizing expression," he denigrated the validity of color in sculpture as practiced by the ancient Greeks and contemporarily by John Gibson, a British sculptor in Rome.[20] Powers decreed, "Everything in intellect or feeling can be expressed . . . by the sculptor in colorless marble," even unto a blush. For him, the cynosure of expression rested in "the form and actions of the muscles surrounding the human eye."[21] It was here that one could give expression to the soul. Using as many as a dozen models to render one perfect idealized face, he produced in his creative classical statues superficially glossy and sterile human frames, devoid of expression. By deploying his calipers with devastating precision, he attained the severest brand of realism in his portraits.

In the middle years of his career, Powers' personal isolation and alienation took a melancholy toll on his outlook. His artistic production was not so creative as to uplift his spirit, or so preoccupying as to dispel his despondency. Neither his intimate friends, his religious faith, or the medium's mysticism could yield the comfort to perform the wanted cure. His greatest solace was his hobby. He divided his waking hours between his studio by day and his workshop at home, where he spent most evenings alone, immersed in his mechanical inventions and prolix correspondence.

Powers was in this state when Hawthorne arrived in Florence early in June of 1858 on his first visit. Powers was instrumental in securing lodgings for the Hawthorne family at fifty dollars a month on the lower floor of Casa Bello, directly across the street from Powers. Hawthorne thought the commodious apartment and garden "containing arbors, a willow tree, and a wilderness of shrubbery and roses with a fountain in the center" something akin to the "paradise of cheapness" he'd heard of but had not found in Rome.[22] The acquaintance quickly turned into friendship. They called on each other frequently. Powers would often appear "in his dressing gown and slippers and sculptor's cap, smoking a cigar," which, by the way, was one of the best. "He was very cordial and pleasant."[23] Hawthorne reported that he was often "entertained and instructed in his conversation," and that Powers was freely "communicative about his own works or any other subject that came up."[24] Hawthorne very much enjoyed "the man and his talk" for being "fresh, original and full of bone and muscle."[25] Although he thought well of Powers' work, his records of their conversations were not unqualified eulogies. They were peppered with spicy skepticism. He pierced through the veneer of the artist to his essence as a man, noting that the "artistic is only one side of his character, and I think, not the principal side. He might have achieved valuable success as an engineer and mechanician."[26]

Hawthorne understood Powers' ideas to be "square, solid, and tangible, and therefore, readily grasped and retained," rarely encumbered by abstractions beyond his artistic medium. He rated him as "a very instructive man [who] sweeps one's empty and dead notions out of the way with exceeding vigor, but when you have his ultimate thought and perception you feel inclined to think and see a little further for yourself. He sees too clearly what is within his range to be aware of any region of mystery beyond."[27]

Powers turned his practical aptitude to positive advantage. He was truly ingenious in improvising mechanical devices that would assist his craft. Over the years he was engrossed in mechanical hobbies that he never relinquished. "You know my love of machines," he wrote Longworth. He found "the movements of the most complicated machine . . . as easy and as simple a process to comprehend as . . . the eddies and the dashings of flowing and falling water. It's all natural, mysterious force applied to her purposes, but in a storm, with its flashings of lightning and bursts of thunder, may be rendered all the secrets of the steam engine and the lightning rod."[28]

This lifelong preference "was one of my earliest affections before I knew anything of sculpture," he continued to Longworth. He recalled nostalgically "some of my happiest days . . . spent in

Watson's clock Factory and in [the] little workshop in Dorfeuille's Museum." After selecting his artistic profession, "during the twenty years I have been abroad," he said, "I have devoted many an evening, when I could do nothing else, to mechanical contrivances—and I have invented several improvements which I think would pay well if exploited."[29]

Powers devised three significant inventions during his long and active career. His primary goal was economy of time, but he was also intrigued with efficiency. Only a couple of years after his arrival in Florence, Powers had already resumed his experimentation with gadgets. Persuaded of the paramount importance of accuracy combined with speed, Powers had "invented a machine to use instead of compasses in transferring measurements from a cast to the marble."[30] Powers shared his invention with Greenough who was so impressed with the enormous saving of labor, "particularly in bas-relief," that he told Charles Sumner that "his men were only 12 days on one piece, when they would have been engaged 30 without Powers' 'Scorpion.' "[31] Sumner had met both sculptors during his Florentine visit in 1839 and had come away persuaded of Powers' inventive talents which he related to his friends.

A primary technical impediment for sculptors in those days before the advent of central heating was the constant threat of freezing of the clay and its subsequent fragmenting, especially during a protracted work. In severe winter climates, the clay had to be moistened throughout the modeling period to counteract the hazard. Powers began experimenting with his process of modeling directly in plaster in the mid-forties and achieved a great saving of time simultaneously with a highly polished surface on the plaster.

In 1850 he wrote Longworth that he had "a method of working in plaster which is very advantageous, so much so that I use clay no longer for modeling. I have got rid of many inconveniences and difficulties connected with the old process of working in clay. . . . The advantage," he elaborated, "arises out of the *tools*, which I have invented by which plaster can be wrought with great rapidity and ease—and finished in the most exquisite manner."[32] Feeling certain that soon plaster would entirely displace clay in general practice, he advocated his improvement publicly in an article published in *Putnam's Monthly* magazine of August 1853.[33]

His process involved the use of a special open file and a punching machine of his own manufacture. The file evolved over more than a decade, and in 1855, Powers at last declared that he had completed a model that satisfied him. He anticipated that this file would answer a variety of purposes. It would cut copper, tin, zinc, and lead, as well as plaster of paris. It was an open, hollow file "so as to allow the dust to pass quite through (the blades)—thus avoiding shaking and clogging."[34] It was at first thought by friends that this device was a joint invention with Greenough because they were often heard discussing it together. The innovation was Powers' alone, however, and he offered it to his friend. Greenough adopted it readily for its obvious advantages and also relinquished the use of clay in most of his large works.

The file required for its manufacture a new "very powerful and extremely simple . . . compact and strong" punching machine that Powers fabricated himself on the lever principle. With the help of an English toolmaker, he subjected it to severe tests to ascertain its strength and durability. Built to weigh only sixty-two pounds, the machine was so sound that it "punched holes through $\frac{1}{4}''$ iron—$\frac{1}{2}''$ diameter with rapidity and care," and seemed "capable of punching boiler iron." Moreover, it could be worked by a single man. "The punch and socket can be changed in less than one minute without screwing a screw or a pin and no adjustment of the socket required," wrote Powers. Powers thought it could be manufactured for ten dollars and marketed at a profit for less than fifteen.[35]

Powers loved his mechanical implements as a scientist cherishes the laboratory equipment that allows him a breakthrough in his investigations. Whenever Powers felt the need of some technical improvement, he would contrive an appropriate device. In the spring of 1850, he converted one room of his studio into a workshop where he could experiment. He felt inordinately self-sufficient in mechanically retrograde Italy, where for a simple turning lathe it was necessary to order from England. "It is a nice thing to make these tools well," he told Longworth. "In these respects my old mechanical acquirements are often of the highest service to me, for having a turning lathe and a small forge in my studio, I have only to think of some improvement in order to enjoy it, for I can immediately execute it myself. . . . If I had to depend upon the Florentine mustiness for such facilities, I should depend on the merest coblers in their way."[36]

He began to consider how he could turn these inventions to extracurricular profit. He yearned to go into the business of manufacturing them in partnership with someone who would organize the enterprise and supply the capital. With this in mind, he sought to patent his open file. He was put off initially by the legal complications and expense. Finding costs gradually diminishing however, he finally registered the open file in England, with the assistance of Edward Everett, at a cost of forty pounds. He succeeded subsequently also in France for twenty pounds. His friends encouraged this diversion, being impressed with the general utility of his inventions and the inexpensive methods that he devised for their production.

In 1858 Powers seriously attempted to interest an old acquaintance in Cincinnati, Mr. Greenwood, in the manufacture and distribution of his items. Greenwood had a machine shop with facilities to make a variety of iron works. Powers averred that his file would be particularly marketable because it could be made by machine at great savings over those in current use that were wrought by hand. He recommended his file as "just the thing for copper smiths, plumbers, hardwood workers, and fur workers, quarry, etc."[37] He wrote Greenwood that his punching machine was "the very thing for coppersmiths and sheet iron workers."[38] Powers' enthusiasm was to no avail. Greenwood did not even respond to the proposition and Powers never entered into commercial production.

His steady search for labor- and timesaving devices continued. In 1858 he informed Longworth that he had "nearly finished . . . a little contrivance for working marbles with drills and cheaper."[39] His device harnessed air and steam power to mechanize the laborious process of cutting marble and thus minimizing the tedium and fatigue of chipping away at the unyielding stone. He contrived an air pump that was manipulated by foot, which he explained could produce "a constant motion and a power which can be applied to any part of a statue or bust with a strong and rapid effort."[40]

Powers' mind was able to penetrate the mysteries of mechanics to the extent of stating to Hawthorne that "flying will be the future mode of locomotion."[41] He realized the advance depended upon the discovery or manufacture of a new form of power. Although gasoline had been invented in 1842, Powers was unaware of the breakthrough during his discourse with Hawthorne in the summer of 1858. Powers detected an intrinsic limitation in the technological leap that he forecast. He thought that it would not occur in general usage "till the moral condition of mankind is so improved as to obviate the bad uses to which the power might be applied."[42]

His prodigious talent for machines might have brought him a fortune if he had stayed at home during the midcentury industrialization in the midwest. Conscious of his capabilities along these lines, but not visualizing the possible rewards to be accumulated from such enterprise, he wrote repeatedly to Longworth that, if it were necessary, he would divert half of his time from sculpture to mechanics on his homecoming to supplement his income. Instead of risking his certain advantages in Italy for the pleasure of living at home, he continued over the years to bemoan his unfortunate exile. He did not venture seriously to explore the possibilities. "I must stay here, instead of going home with my family," he wailed to Longworth in 1858, "until the good time comes at which I can afford to go home."[43]

His willingness to experiment in practical matters led him in 1843 to the early use of the newly discovered marble at Seravezza, which he found freer from blemishes and spots, streaks, and flaws than the Carrara stone, and of finer grain and of more beautiful color than its rival. He proclaimed the virtues of the new marble and from then on preferred it for his statues. In 1847 he took notice of a new quarry in the Maremma, not too distant from Carrara about thirty-five miles south of Leghorn and only a quarter of a mile above sea-level, hence the marble was easily transportable. Powers claimed that the quarry had been in use in ancient days. He described the marble as having a rich warm color with a coarse grain like Parian. "It works smoothly and easily, taking a high polish," he reported.[44] This marble's ultimate attraction for Powers was its price, less than half that of the Carrara stone. He found the marble satisfactory when he experimented with it in a bust of Washington, and it began to complement the Seravezza in his works, although it did not supplant it for the finer statues.

One day while focusing on inventions and in a rather nostalgic mood, he recalled to Hawthorne his youthful days at Luman's watch factory, when he had invented a "Jew's harp with two tongues" that "was very neatly and elaborately constructed with screws to tighten it, and a silver contrapiece between the two tongues."[45] "Evidently," commented Hawthorne, "a great deal of thought had been bestowed on this harp, but the inventor told me it was an utter failure, because the tongues were apt to interfere and jar with one another; although the strain of music was very sweet and melodious, as he proved by playing on it a little."[46] Powers confessed this failure had been a keen disappointment to him at the time.

He obviously took pleasure in his mechanical accomplishments. The pastime suited his outlook as well as his talent. He prated to Longworth of living by the motto "to be happy is to be useful— to be miserable is to be idle, and they who do not enjoy the gaining will never really enjoy the gains."[47] It was a puritanical attitude un-cluttered by cultural diversions. It also enabled him to rationalize his unrelieved application to work. He embroidered the theme, often using Longworth as his sounding board, enjoying the self-justifica-tion. "Prudent people when young devote themselves to business, in order to lay up something for an imaginary period when they expect to enjoy life." he wrote. "But, alas, that time never comes."[48]

If happiness hinged on work, he did not reckon the toll of his self-imposed isolation on his personality. He turned ever more inward toward the tasks in his various studios. Paying increasingly little heed to those around him, he depended emotionally ever more ex-clusively on his family and his few steadfast American friends at home. Relieved of obligations of friendship, his perfectionist stand-ards fortified him in his untempered criticism of his colleagues. Haw-thorne remarked on this tendency in Powers, mocking "his own evident idea that nobody else is worthy to touch marble."[49] Protest-ing that he "would not do Powers the injustice to imply that there is the slightest professional jealousy in his estimation of . . . others . . . in his own art," Hawthorne independently went about among the artists and gleaned the gossip.[50] "Mr. B. told me," he reported, "that Powers had had many difficulties on professional grounds . . . with his brother artists. No wonder. He has said enough in my hearing to put him at sword's point with sculptors of every epoch and every degree between the two inclusive extremities of Phidias and Clark Mills."[51]

Already ten years before Hawthorne's Florentine sojourn, Powers had conjured a variety of conspiracies against him, culminating in a break even with Greenough. During the period of confidence and collaboration with Kellogg on the tour of the *Greek Slave*, before Powers turned on Kellogg, Powers wrote him unreservedly of his peeves and rights, as if he were the sole injured party. "Greenough is more off than ever. Willis is thick with him and he no longer visits my studio. Even Greenough's brother stays away."[52] As for Thomas Crawford, the old competition for governmental commissions forestalled any possibility of a blossoming friendship. "I have long suspected the Crawfords of being no warm friends," he wrote Kellogg in confidence. "They were sparing enough in their attentions to my wife while she was in Rome and ill there. They called only once upon her—whew! . . . As for the artists here, if I except Cameron [a Scottish artist], I hold no communications with them."[53] His American colleagues, absorbed in their own lives and careers, might have been entirely unaware of Powers' intense feeling of neglect. Powers did not examine their motives for abstaining from his society.

Crawford's prevailing with the government at Washington represented to Powers some sort of betrayal, as he deemed his own work indubitably superior. Powers went to the length of accusing Crawford of having underhandedly obtained the contract to adorn the dome's summit in preference to his statue of *America*. He recounted that after having offered to put forward Powers' statue "when he went to Washington, Crawford had not given it a mention, advancing only his own."[54] Crawford's culpability was aggravated by his low prices, which set cheap precedents. Powers considered this a selfish practice that would hurt all the artists who would work for the government. Captain M. C. Meigs, chief engineer of the Capitol, became the center of the "conspiracy" in the government to consider the price of artistic works before the quality.

The estrangement from Greenough turned out to be only a temporary misunderstanding, with Powers blaming it all on that troublemaker Willis, the United States Consul, who had early befriended Greenough. It was Greenough who took the initiative to patch the rift. Late in February 1848 they met in a friend's studio, and Powers wrote Kellogg that Greenough "in a very frank and cordial manner . . . greeted me as of old." Powers continued, "Greenough called upon me this evening, and he appeared most friendly. So you see things have taken the right turn at last with him.[55] It evidently continued so, for a short while later Powers wrote, "Greenough behaves very well to me; so does Ives."[56] On the other hand, Greenough in his correspondence never expressed any dissatisfaction with Powers. His few references to Powers were always friendly, relating the exchange of favors.

Powers' break with Kellogg occurred after the completion of the exhibition tour in a dispute over the accounting. Powers privately charged Kellogg with dishonesty in withholding some of the proceeds. Kellogg had just published a pamphlet in defense of Powers and his *Greek Slave*. The pamphlet included the financial statements of the exhibitions. The correspondence between Kellogg and Powers during the close of the *Slave's* tour is replete with references to monetary transactions and calculations, all conducted in good faith and apparent mutual confidence. Powers must have harbored a secret grudge over the years, based perhaps on some dissatisfaction with Kellogg's management. This feeling surfaced almost a decade later when an anonymous attack on Powers appeared in Paris. In a letter to Edward Everett, Powers expressed great anger against Kellogg and charged him with dishonesty, asserting without evidence that the attack was the work of Kellogg's spite. Powers never had his books audited, but ranted continually about the personal betrayal, recalling how many Sunday dinners he had fed his betrayer. He became testy on the subject but decided against "engaging in another newspaper controversy."[57] Powers sulked visibly during this period of neglect by the government administrators in Washington who did not offer him a commission. His deep-seated anger on this subject seems to have exacerbated his irritation over other circumstances.

Powers' financial position at this juncture was fairly substantial. Counting the proceeds from his monumental statues and the *Greek Slave* alone, his earnings for the decade from 1848 to 1858 came to approximately $72,000. This does not include the income from his other female nudes and the innumerable idealized and portrait busts. The overhead in his studio could not have risen to much over $6,000 a year, as he never paid even his favorite assistant, Romigo Peschi, more than the usual wage of $1.50 weekly, and he restricted his staff to the customary eight to ten assistants. He preferred to limit his operations through selectivity in his commissions, rather than expand his overhead.

In his final analysis of conditions at home, Powers asked Justice Salmon P. Chase, "What could a sculptor do at home without his 'hands,' . . . the experienced marble cutters [who] do the main part of our work?"[58] Powers probed the subject ceaselessly, manifestly in constant vindication of his decision to remain abroad despite the homesickness that plagued him and his wife. "It is probable that there are not 20 good statuary carvers in all America," he vouchsafed. "These undoubtedly were employed overtime already." Even if this shortcoming were overcome, Powers would still face the "enormous expense of removing a studio with all its models . . . to America—to say nothing of a colony of workmen with their families."[59] Three of the ten workmen he then employed consented to Powers' proposition to migrate to America if he would double their wage and guarantee their return with their families should things go wrong.

Upon exhaustive consideration, the decision was heavily weighted in favor of remaining in Florence. Powers cannot be blamed for choosing against uprooting himself and abdicating his stellar position in exchange for professional uncertainties in America. On the other hand, it does seem like matchless parsimony that he would not spend the money for a single trip across the Atlantic to assuage his longings and do a little self-promotion on the side. Indeed, after twenty-one years' residence abroad and the solid education he gave his children in Italian and other foreign languages, he justified himself with the transparent excuse that he could not desert his family "to take their chance among strangers in a foreign country."[60] He did dispatch his wife home after the recovery of a child from a protracted illness. Mrs. Powers spent her two-year holiday visiting her family and friends in Cincinnati.

In the 1860s Powers began to prospect real estate in Florence with a view to purchasing a site for a home. The search bolstered his decision to remain. He reported, "Real estate here is cheap. A house built like a palace and all the rooms beautifully decorated . . . in short, a house that could not be built in Cincinnati for $10,000 and well-furnished at that," cost a fraction of the price at home. "Rents are amazingly cheap as the House [and] studios, for which I pay about $400 a year, would cost me in New York, I am told, at least $2,000 a year. It is a large saving."[61] Another uncertainty in his considerations about moving home was where to settle. "Cincinnati is the place of all others I desire to live in or near, but can I live there! That is the question!"[62] It became manifest that the answer was no. In America, the brisk portrait trade still lay on the East coast.

A few years before his death, Powers confronted the reality that his yearnings for an American residence were empty dreams. In 1869 when he was sixty-four, he had built for himself a sumptuous villa on Viale Michelangelo near the Poggia Imperiale, the country palace of the Grand Duke. Soon other Americans came to the new neighborhood and purchased lots nearby. Powers' sons, Longworth and Preston, who became sculptors too, built adjacent villas of their own. His daughter Louisa married the English Sheffield steel millionaire, Alfred Ibbotson, and joined the development. Thomas Ball had already settled there. In a few years, the area became a small foreign enclave. Powers took seriously his elevated position as property owner. After the unification of the country had been accomplished under the House of Savoy, he carped over the lack of an American treaty with the new kingdom of Italy for the better protection of his national property rights abroad. Powers died while on holiday with his family at Vallambrosa in 1873 and was buried there. The house in Florence is still maintained and inhabited by his great grandchildren. It is rumored that Powers left a fortune of half a million dollars and that it was augmented greatly by the estate of his daughter Louisa Ibbotson.

Although Powers lived physically thirty-six years on Italian soil, his heart and mind were focused on America. He followed the course of events there with minute interest and prided himself on remaining unswervingly "Republican Powers."[63] He shared with other Americans concern over the slavery controversy at home which threatened to sunder the links of the Union that he thought vital to the survival of treasured republican liberties. He was opposed to the institution of slavery, but he laid the threat to the Union at the door of the extremist abolitionists for the dangers of polarization and confrontation that they stirred. He condemned them harshly. "Do our abolitionists know what they are about?" he wrote Longworth. "Do they know what would be the result of that disunion, which they are labouring so hard to effect?" He answered his own rhetorical question. "Why, instead of greatness, the blacks would be doubly slaves—for they would become the slaves of slaves. We should all be slaves and have kings for our masters."[64]

His views on these matters following the Kansas-Nebraska bloodletting hardened and echoed the conservative Whig opinion at home. He declared fervently to Longworth, "I am not an abolitionist, but go tooth and nail against slavery extension. We have had enough of it. It has been the cause of nearly all [our] troubles as a people, and it is time it was bound down to its present limits."[65]

Although his opposition to abolitionists was strong, Powers did manage to go beyond the chauvinistic attitudes of most middle-roaders respecting black people. He wanted them accorded the human rights of any other people. He took issue with Justice Roger Taney's inflammatory Dred Scot decision in caustic and sardonic tones.

> Englishmen and Italians cannot understand Southern reasoning and I have given it up. . . . They speak about Negroes being men and women. But I tell them they are wrong and I read to them the laws as promulgated by the highest authority in our country (Supreme Court) where it is proved past argument or doubt that they are nothing but cattle!
>
> The last is your idea of equality and liberty, too refined and exalted to be understood by these simple foreigners. I wish that some of your smart writers would write it all out in a form suited to the subtle intellects of strangers. It might encourage them to persevere in their efforts to free themselves from the chains of depotism. As it is . . . they appear to be discouraged at your example of a moral Republic.[66]

Powers' moral fervor was puritanical; his egalitarianism, although steeped in humanism, was qualified by a degree of identification with upper class snobbery. When discoursing with Hawthorne about the grand duchess of Tuscany, Powers had remarked that "royal personnages have a certain look that distinguishes them from other people and is seen in individuals of no other rank. They all have it."[67] Powers' character could have derived from his origins on the American frontier or from the tolerance of his Italian environment. He was essentially "honest Jack," as Greenough had found him. Although often filled with rancor, he discreetly held his counsel, confining its expression to the privacy of his correspondence. A hardworking man of some religious faith but little zeal, he was also a loyal husband and a devoted father. Frances Trollope appreciated his mechanical inventiveness. The Brownings found him delightful and he became Elizabeth's "chief and favorite" friend. To Elizabeth, he was "a most charming, simple, straightforward genial American, as simple as the man of genius . . . needs be." She liked his "eyes like a wild Indian, so black and full of light."[68] Hawthorne agreed that Powers' "own Titanic orb [was] the biggest by far that I saw in a mortal head."[69] They appreciated this startling feature of Powers as symbolic of his animation and perception.

Like Greenough, Powers lived in a period of aesthetic transition. The American artistic atmosphere was too barren to provide optimum productive stimulus. On the other hand, while training in Europe was essential, the studios were "crowded with copies of Greek and Roman works."[70] One contemporary American observer remarked:

> The American student, though he arrives there from a fresh, new country, he will not be able to withstand the tendency of all about him; he will do as the rest do; and devote his time and genius to Apollos, Dianas, Venuses, to the exclusion of those living themes from actual life, and incidents of our own history, which might kindle a new enthusiasm and inspire to more original works. . . .
> The constant presence of the Antique and a daily worship at her shrine, must, as the rule, tend to generate a dull and slavish turn of the mind—all within the limits of the most refined taste, but emasculated by the absence of everything like a vigorous originality.[71]

Greenough had gone to Florence instead of Rome to evade the trap; Powers stayed in Florence for the same reason: to imbibe its flourishing naturalistic tradition and escape the pervasive influence of the antique at Rome. In all his years of residence in Italy, he went to Rome only twice. Although he pleaded a lack of time, he also argued that he would rather not clutter his mind with viewing the plethora of antique works gathered there, but rather retain his own freshness for more contemporary creations.

Hiram Powers dared to break through the mannerism of fashionable bust manufacture and counter the principle of generalization that had infected the Italian school since the time of Bernini. His peculiar style evolved from a "truthful adherence to nature combined with artistic skill and elaborate execution."[72]

According to a contemporary, Powers' genius and particular eminence were "shown in the extreme delicacy and fineness of his finish."[73] The introductory paragraph of a pamphlet advertising a Powers exhibit boasted the legend, "Powers' portrait busts are smoothly but strongly modelled. In spite of their restraint and dignity, however, they convey a feeling of truthful portraiture."[74]

Powers must be credited for his valiant but sterile attempt at revolt against the vapid neoclassical idealizations of the grand style. "His figure pieces, such as Eve, California, and the Greek Slave," observed a contemporary, "bear the trademarks of the neoclassic ideals which dominated Europe in the early decades of the nineteenth century. He must have known the work of Canova and Thorwaldsen, for like them, he reproduced a passive, idealized beauty reminiscent of the classical style."[75]

Powers remained first and always a banal naturalist and literalist in a neoclassical age, unable to counter the dominant conventions although he saw the need to do so. One must admire his fortitude for staying in his alienated exile throughout his adult life, while dogged persistently by nostalgia for home. Although he was unaware of his real alternative at home in a career of mechanics with a pot of gold as a sure recompense, he stayed with his art in Florence. His choice gave him a good measure of rewards in any case, including the art life in a plush Italian setting, his mechanical inventions, financial success, and above all, world recognition.

Part III

THOMAS CRAWFORD
Sculptor Laureate

15

The Roman Lure

WHEN THOMAS G. CRAWFORD CROSSED THE ATLANTIC IN THE SPRING
of 1835 to fulfill his artistic ambitions, he was immediately attracted
to the city of Rome, the world center of sculpture. "The incredulous
may laugh," wrote George Washington Greene, a contemporary observer, "but Cicero, Virgil, Horace, and Livy no where seem so eloquent and so touching as amid scenes which they have hallowed."
According to Greene, the very streets of Rome were "a daily
illustration of classic literature."[1] The classical feeling permeated the
atmosphere. Revived by Johann Joachim Winckelman and Francesco
Milizia a century before, the cultural brilliance of ancient Rome had
been nurtured more recently in the plastic art by Antonio Canova
and Bertel Thorwaldsen. The poetry of Goethe, Schiller, Shelley,
Keats, Byron, and countless others enhanced the background. The
sculptural school of Rome with its majestic neoclassical generalizations dominated the western world in that post-Napoleonic epoch.
How paradoxical it was that Rome, the world center of Christianity,
should share its seat of eminence with the renovated pagan deities
and witness their unlimited illustration.

In 1835 Rome, reduced from its grandeur of ancient times, had
a population of approximately one hundred and fifty thousand inhabitants. The city had not yet expanded beyond its original hills.
It was still confined to what now represents the hub, extending
roughly from Piazza del Popolo along the Corso, past the Fora to

Portrait of Thomas Crawford by Thomas Hicks

the Coliseum, the Aventine, and the Palatine. It was considered dangerous to venture in the other direction at night beyond Santa Maria Maggiore on the Esquiline and Piazza dei Termini, for fear of a chance encounter with a little wild fox of the Campagna.

The art world centered then, as now, around the cosmopolitan focus in the famous "English ghetto" as Piazza di Spagna was sometimes jokingly called. It spilled into adjacent Via del Babuino and Via Margutta and along the Corso. It stretched up the broad flight of 132 Spanish steps to Trinita dei Monti and down Via Sistina through its surrounding maze of winding streets to Piazza Barberini. The Pincian hill was crowned by the great park of the Villa Medici which was already open to the public and especially favored by the fashionable tide that swept its numerous shaded walks on sunny afternoons. It was dominated by the imposing Villa Medici, purchased by Napoleon at no personal cost to house the French Academy, which had been established in 1666 by the opulent King Louis. Here came the winners of the Grand Prix in Paris, recipients of 600 francs plus expenses for their year of study in Rome. They lived as pensionaires in the villa, whose Michelangelesque facade facing the manicured gardens commanded a bird's eye view of the entire city as far as Saint Peter's familiar dome.

Nearby in Via Gregoriana was the house where Salvator Rosa had lived. A few paces down the fork of Via Gregoriana at number 48 on one side or 51 Via Sistina on the other, stood Casa Buti, the house of Claude Lorrain and Nicolas Poussin, where now Bertel Thorwaldsen lived in a modest apartment. Following in the footsteps of John Flaxman and Angelica Kauffman, Thorwaldsen had for over two decades perpetuated the ancient Greek tradition, rivaling the renowned Antonio Canova for the world's first position in neoclassical sculpture. A bust of Thorwaldsen executed by his Prussian pupil, Emilus Wolff, still adorns the garden of Palazzo Barberini. A replica of Thorwaldsen's statue of Byron was only recently unveiled in Villa Borghese. Thorwaldsen, the sculptor for kings, maintained sumptuous studios in Via delle Colonette and in the Scuderia di Barberini. He insisted on dating his birth from the day he had entered Rome; "I was born on March 8, 1797," was his famous remark.[2] The mass of antique casts that littered his numerous crowded rooms furnished the basis of his instruction. He forbade copying his own works, believing that only nature and the antique works could reveal the secrets of successful reproduction.

John Gibson had come from Liverpool to study with Thorwaldsen, who had generously tutored him with his compatriots, Richard James Wyatt and Mary Thornycroft. Although Gibson contended with relative success for the patronage of art lovers on the Grand Tour, his studios in Via Babuino and Via della Fontanella (Borghese) did not extend the traditional welcome to pupils generally, the notable exception being Harriet Hosmer of Massachusetts. Lawrence McDonald inherited space in the Stalle di Barberini from Thorwaldsen. William Theed. Benjamin Edward Spence, and Shakespear Wood completed the English group of sculptors. It was rumored that the Franco-Italian Luigi Bienaimé was the favorite among Thorwaldsen's pupils. The Italians on the whole remained loyal to their own beloved Canova, whose disciples Tenerani, Finelli, and Rinaldi managed to acquire Canova's former studio at 27 Via delle Colonette.

If the international group thronged the French Academy, they could also not afford to ignore the official Accademia di San Luca, firmly held in Italian control. This center specialized in dispensing the mysteries of painting, under the direction of the renowned Baron Vincenzo Cammuccini. He was assisted by the equally distinguished Federigo Overbeck and Cavaliero Pietro Cornelius. Although painting was the chief interest here, the Italians were not so parochial as to leave sculptural training solely in French hands. The faculty of San Luca consisted predominantly of native artists including Adam Tadolini, Pietro Tenerani, Antonio Sola, Antonio D'Este, Filippo Albacino, Carlo Finelli, and Cavaliero Giuseppe Fabris. The trustees also enticed Thorwaldsen to give some of his time for instruction there too, so they could list him in the catalog with the regular faculty. The Royal Academy of Naples (Reale Accademia di Napoli), sponsored by the Bourbon king and queen in the Fornesina across the Tiber in Trastevere, could do little more in the face of such keen competition than to patronize their own promising native talents.

Art was all over Rome; its productions filled the galleries, palaces, and churches. The sculptures in the Vatican galleries were unrivaled. Here the Apollo Belvedere and the Cnidian Venus were the cynosure, flanked by the Laocoon group and Myron's muscular *Discus Thrower*. Michelangelo's allegory of the Creation, which adorns the ceiling of the Sistine Chapel, was a focal point of interest to visitors, as were the Raphael Stanze of the Vatican galleries.

The Campidoglio Museum, which specializes in sculpture, featured the *Dying Gaul*, the *Capitoline Venus*, *Il Spino*, and the *Romulus and Remus* figures. Villa Borghese already housed splendid sculptural masterpieces of Bernini and the brilliantly finished sensuous recumbent figure of *Paolina Bonaparte Borghese* by Antonio Canova. The painting collection, catered especially to nineteenth century taste, showed a decided preference for the warmth and color of such masters gathered there as Raphael, Perugino, Filippo Lippi, Andrea del Sarto, Annibale Caracci, Guido Reni, Giovanni Guercino, Salvator Rosa, Paolo Veronese, Giorgione, Peter Paul Rubens and David Teniers.

Palazzo Barberini vied for attention. It had the glamor of having been designed by Borromini and finished by Bernini under the patronage of the Barberini Pope Urban VIII, who encouraged the arts and letters generously. During his reign, the ceiling of the palazzo's ballroom was commissioned of Pietro da Cortona and the *Fornarina* of Raphael was borrowed from the Vatican collection. The *Fornarina* has stayed there as a prime attraction, joined by the *Beatrice Cenci* of Guido Reni, a *Christ* of Durer, and an exquisite small *Marina* of Claude Lorrain, along with many other pieces. Had the once mighty Barberinis charged admission, they might have fallen from aristocratic grace but have replenished the fortune spent accumulating their treasures.

Each palazzo boasted its own masterpiece along with its royal or papal lineage. The Rospigliosi had Guido Reni's famed baroque *Aurora* on its Casino ceiling, the Ludovisi competed for attention with Guercino's *Aurora* in fresco on its larger Casino ceiling, and the Farnese palazzo featured a perfectly proportioned high Renaissance facade designed by Michelangelo and frescoes by Raphael. The Farnese palazzo is now the residence of the French embassy and is open to the public on Sunday mornings, a goodwill gesture to the

Italians to compensate for their loss to the French of the irremovable art treasures which embellish the rooms. The Doria Pamphili palazzo on the Corso contained works by Pietro da Cortona, Domenchino, Salvator Rosa, Raphael, Veronese, and Guercino as well as a copy of Thorwaldsen's bas relief frieze the *Triumph of Alexander*. Palazzo Odescalchi, formerly belonging to the papal branch of the Chigi family, was designed by Bernini. It was later to house Thomas Crawford's widow and children.

Palazzo Venezia, built in 1468 by the wealthy Doges for the Venetian republic's diplomatic emissaries to the papal state, still attracts crowds to its museum. Palazzo Madama, where today the Roman Senate convenes, was constructed by the less democratic Caterina de' Medici in 1642. The palaces of the Colonna, Ruspoli, Torlonia, Corsini, Rospigliosi, Massimo, Orsini, and Braschi families are still objects of informed tourist interest; the original Ludovsi and Negroni villas were razed to make way for "modern improvements." These palaces were all richly adorned from the old days with tapestries, paintings, and baroque or rococo ceilings. By the nineteenth century, it had become customary for the princely families to subdivide the family palazzos into modern housekeeping units for rental to sustain the expense of upkeep. The family would generally retain the state apartments as a dwelling quarter that would be occasionally open for public view of the art treasures it contained.

The principal squares of Barberini, di Spagna, Navona, and Saint Peter's advertised Bernini's artistic predominance in Rome. Two churches harbored sculptural masterpieces of Michelangelo, his *Pietà* in Saint Peter's and the *Moses* in San Pietro in Vincoli, a simple church near the Coliseum. "Of the 360 churches in Rome, there is not one which does not contain some picture, statue, mosaic, or monumental structure either of positive excellence or historic interest," observed one American traveler.[3]

Although this plethora of scattered masterpieces constituted a focus for the culture seekers on the Grand Tour, they provided the heart of the student's artistic edification in Rome. The paintings typified nineteenth century taste but the vogue in sculpture reverted conspiculously from the baroque to the preeminent classical works. Knowledge of the great ancient culture of Rome and Greece was revived during the Renaissance and spurred through the writings of Winckelmann and others following the excavations at Herculaneum and Pompeii in 1740. During the midcentury Risorgimento, or movement toward national unification, the romantic search of a glorious past rekindled a worship of the classics.

Into this world, twenty-two year old Thomas G. Crawford arrived from New York, armed with letters of introduction from his friend, teacher, and patron, Robert E. Launitz. Crawford had suffered a tempestuous twenty day crossing in a small brig and was detained in quarantine at Leghorn before being allowed to continue to Civita Vecchia, the seaport of entry for Rome. His embarkation in May 1835 climaxed his two year apprenticeship in the firm of Frazee and Launitz, makers of tombstones and carved mantelpieces. His specialty had been carving flowers and wreaths, but he had also learned to impart flesh tones with elegant finish, to mold drapery, and generally to work in marble.

Crawford had learned his three R's in the common schools of New York, where his Protestant parents had arrived from North Ireland a year and a half prior to his birth on March 22, 1813. His father, Aaron, came from the landed gentry and attended Dublin University. Throughout Thomas' childhood, his sister Jane (Jenny), seven years his senior, inspired him with her love of poetry and music. Jenny's influence unwittingly encouraged his early wandering from formal study. Lessons were neglected in favor of a year at drawing school. He wandered off frequently on searches through littered shops in search of old prints, which he bought even as a child. "When very small, he attached himself to an itinerant band, and marched in their company for two or three days. . . ."[4] Another time, he disappeared for several days and was located as an apprentice to a stonecutter. His father ransomed him and led him home. Jenny shielded him from parental ire on these occasions. When Thomas was sixteen and it was time for him to go to work, he refused conventional employment in a store or office but attached himself to a wood carver. He became practiced in decorative designs and proficient in the use of the chisel. He read intensively in the history of architecture, concentrating on the lives and works of the great architects and sculptors of Greece and Rome.

After three years of this undisciplined but instructive regime, he apparently qualified for the next step in his career, that of learning to cut marble, and the studio of Frazee and Launitz on lower Broadway was the best of its sort in New York. Robert E. Launitz, a Russian by birth, had studied seven years in his uncle's atelier in Rome before settling into the marble cutting business in New York. John Frazee, a native, had won some degree of recognition as a portraitist of busts and had received worthy commissions. While in this employ, Crawford very likely worked on parts of the busts of Thomas H. Perkins, the famous mercantile art patron of Boston, and of Judges Prescott and Story of the same city.[5] Chief Justice John Marshall also sat for Frazee, and Crawford may have helped to cut this bust also. There were tombstones and mantelpieces for him to decorate with carefully worked floral designs, which became his trademark. Coincidentally he worked on the firm's commission to design an elaborate mantlepiece for the drawing room of a residence at 8 Bond Street in which he was later to live. Then it was the new home of Samuel Ward and his family. The family attributed the classical carytids supporting the shelf to Crawford's ingenuity, and considering his lack of experience, the figures were highly commendable.

Crawford devoted his spare time during his two years with Frazee and Launitz studying at the drawing school of the National Academy of Design. Fortunately for him, only a short while earlier the academy had acquired over a dozen plaster casts from Rome. While most of them were antique, the collection included the *Mercury* and *Venus* of Thorwaldsen and the *Amorino* and *Columbus* of Trentanova. Although a good beginning could be attained here at the academy, it was clear to Crawford that he must move on to Italy to complete his training. The painters who showed their works at the exhibitions of the academy, such as Henry Inman, William Dunlap, William Page, Thomas Cole, Charles C. Ingham, Robert Weir, Thomas Doyle, and Samuel F. B. Morse, had all been trained in Rome. One of them, William Page, befriended Crawford and painted a "fine portrait" of him during this time in New York.[6] Page and Crawford were later to become better acquainted in Rome.

Biding his time for the transatlantic shift, Crawford worked diligently day and night. When he chose not to go to the academy in the evening, he secured permission from his employers to return to the marble cutting studios after hours to labor on his own studies. He could practice by copying the casts assembled there, which included as in the academy, a copy of Thorwaldsen's famed bas relief, the *Triumph of Alexander*.

Crawford became restive in due course, prodded by the natural desire to progress in his career. When his employers refused a raise that he demanded, he returned briefly to the wood carver for whom he had worked earlier. Fortunately though, Robert Launitz was a generous man, and he sought Crawford out and brought him back at higher pay. But not for long. There was no keeping Crawford in New York when Rome promised artistic fulfillment. Launitz shared faith in Crawford's future and advanced the money for a two year fellowship in Rome and supplied two letters of introduction, one to Dr. Paul Ruga and the other to Bertel Thorwaldsen.

Seventy days after leaving New York, Crawford arrived in Rome with his letters. He presented himself by appointment to Thorwaldsen and lost no time in accepting an invitation to use a corner of Thorwaldsen's rambling studio. There he was directed in copying the antique casts and he learned the principles of perspective, studying "the nature of masses and the law of proportions."[7] In Thorwaldsen's studio, correct mass arrangement and balance took priority over details. Crawford also began to study aesthetics and like most artists of that day attempted to define "true beauty."

Among the components of classical taste in Italy was an appreciation of beautiful landscapes, colorful sunsets, costumed peasants, and vari-toned skies. Literature supplemented the background with mood and metaphor. George Washington Greene wrote of Crawford that he "read Homer early and [familiarized himself] with Greek tragedy in its English dress; and few . . . were more at home in the language of mythology. Of Milton his appreciation was less perfect. Byron, and more particularly Shelley were his favorites among the moderns."[8] If poetic practitioners in sculpture failed to attain adequate illustration of their imagery, it was not for want of aspiration. The best artists of the school of Rome could not, at this time of transition, transcend smooth idealizations. Crawford heeded the master's caution not to lose sight of the particulars for optimum results.

"Impressed with the necessity of forming his taste by a careful study of principles," wrote Greene, who was a close friend of Crawford, "he read Alison and Burke, but soon turned from them with a deep sense of disappointment. His mind had already been agitated by creative imaginings, and he felt the want of wise counsel to help him [to express] them. In Flaxman, he found more, but nowhere what he really needed. He soon found it in the studio of Thorwaldsen, who had kindly received him as a pupil."[9] It was asserted later by another close friend that in Thorwaldsen's studio Crawford "formed that correct and classical taste with the freedom of Canova, but without his meretricious style."[10] Many years later Crawford's daughter wrote that he also studied with the famed Italian master Baron Camuccini, probably at the Accademia di San Luca.

Despite widespread loose practices, a prerequisite of the neoclassical school was a severe adherence to nature. Since this was impossible without a knowledge of anatomy, Crawford soon began regular visits to the hospital mortuary in Rome, where he dissected and drew from life, or death. Many years afterward his daughter found among his numerous portfolios, "a mass of sheets containing drawings, half life-size, of every bone and muscle and sinew in the human body. . . ."[11] This rigorous exercise was supplemented by attendance, in company with the other foreign students, at the French Academy's daily evening sessions of drawing and modeling from live models, both nude and costumed.

Mornings were reserved for working in the studio under the daily scrutiny of Thorwaldsen. Afternoons were devoted to visiting the churches, galleries, and private collections, those great "storehouses of all that is pure in taste."[12] He spent his evenings with his artistic colleagues in the Villa Medici, which housed the French Academy. There was time out for breakfast at Caffè Greco on Via dei Condotti, a step from Piazza di Spagna, and conversational suppers at Lepre's a few doors away.

In spite of these pleasant diversions, the artist's regime was arduous and marked by a constant shortage of cash. There was an occasional exception, but Crawford's experience was typical. He was driven by ambition to fame and recognition. Crawford had taken his first step over the river Styx when he rejected the easy money of a commercial career and crossed the Atlantic. There was no turning back. He must now justify his course. With a slim backlog of financial support and a few friends at home to keep his name alive, Crawford sweated it out with only occasional diversions. From time to time, he slipped into the mire of self-pity, but that was also a fairly general trap. James E. Freeman, the painter, who joined Crawford in Rome in 1837, described the regime as a participant.

> The daily life of an artist in Rome, particularly at the commencement of his career, is hardly worth recording; it is one of toil and perpetual anxiety, where the work of today must provide for the wants of tomorrow, and laboring incessantly for daily support, he has but little time to devote to pleasures; yet however limited his means, he can find that society most congenial to his tastes and feelings at some of the restaurants of Rome, particularly at the Caffe Greco. Here, day after day and year after year, he meets his brother artists and persons of culture and refinement. . . .
>
> It was here, in years gone by, that Reynolds, Flaxman, West, Thorwaldsen, Vernet, Gibson, Turner, Cornelius, Overbeck, Morse, Vanderlyn, Crawford, Keats, Washington Irving and others of artistic and literary fame, rich and poor, gathered. . . . This place was resorted to, not because of its superior appointments and fare, for it was decidedly one of the smallest, darkest, and untidiest of restaurants; its central position and superior coffee were its chief attractions, added to which a greater freedom of speech was permitted, without a strict surveillance of the police, whose spies found their way into all reunions of society; but this brotherhood of artists and students under the pontifical reign of Pius VII and Gregory XVI seems to have enjoyed a license quite exceptional to any other rendezvous. . . .
>
> One day Vanderlyn met me at the Greco and said, "Thirty years ago I was on this very spot," and pointing to different seats, observed, "there sat Allston opposite me; that was Turner's corner, here on my left sat Fenimore Cooper; and there, I was told, Sir Joshua Reynolds and West. . . . Weir, Chapman, and Crawford have, in their turn, made part of the gathering around this table . . . Ward, Collins, O'Neil, Elmore, Phillips, Pine, Leighton, Goodhall and among American artists—Cole, Leutze, Baker, Page, Rogers, Story, Ives, and Rinehart.[13]

Although Crawford was the first American sculptor to settle in Rome, there had been American painters there before. Crawford's special friends now were a Scottish fellow student, Robert Scott Lauder, who painted his portrait in 1837; the English sculptor Lawrence McDonald, who made a marble bust of him, and an American friend of some means, Allen Fraser, who bought the bust. In Thorwaldsen's atelier, Crawford befriended Ludwig von Schwanthaler, a German who would persuade Crawford eventually to desert marble for bronze, as the most suitable material for large public monuments.[14]

Under the aegis of the Danish master, Crawford completed his first idealized figure. Thomas Hicks said it was a representation of "Autumn," but George Washington Greene, reporting on the spot, declared it was a *Bacchante*, a Roman mythical female figure of life-size.

> A Bacchante in the wild festivities of the Bacchanalian rites. . . .
> She had thrown herself upon the ground in a posture between
> reclining and sitting. One hand supports her body, and with the
> other, she holds a bunch of grapes. The head is thrown back and
> the eyes cast upwards. There is an expression of rapture in the
> countenance, to which the movement of the figure corresponds
> in a striking degree. There is a peculiar delicacy, too, in the form
> and in the face, which please the more, inasmuch as they are
> evidently derived from the artist's mind rather than the subject.[15]

Only one year later Greene reported, "Mr. Crawford now condemns the drapery, complains of a sort of hardness and dryness in the general execution and seems to think that the only thing in the figure worth preserving is the action."[16]

After a year's apprenticeship, Crawford established himself independently. His first move was to take a corner in the studio of the famous animal painter, Velatti. This served for a time, while he eked out an existence doing the usual portrait busts. Soon he had accumulated enough savings to set up his own studio in Via del Orto di Napoli. This studio sufficed until he attained recognition with his first major work. One American visitor described Crawford's studio as consisting of "three obscure, small and sunless apartments, so cold and damp that they strike a chill through you."[17] It was undoubtedly cold, being December, and tourists are unprepared for the cold of winter in Mediterranean Italy. Sculptor's studios in Rome are generally located on the ground floor, and these are invariably sunless and damp in winter, even today with a modicum of central heating. In any case, the climate seemed of little concern to Crawford.

Dr. Ruga wrote to Launitz in New York, "Your friend, Crawford works incessantly. He takes no relaxation . . . his health will suffer."[18] Thomas Hicks reported that in ten weeks, Crawford modeled seventeen busts to be put into marble. Among these was a marble portrait of Mary Hone Schermerhorn, the recently married daughter of Philip Hone, a former mayor of New York. It was a fine likeness and probably the first female portrait executed by Crawford.

A notable figure in Rome in those years was the commander of the United States Mediterranean Squadron based in Rome, Commodore Isaac Hull. This former commander of the *Constitution* cut a ludicrous sight with his preposterous bulk, strolling daily through the streets of Rome, arm-in-arm with his old English antagonist of more belligerent times, the commander of the *Guerrière*. Hull commissioned his bust from Crawford, one of the earliest of the sculptor's professional career.

More interesting from the artist's standpoint was the figure of *Paris* executed for a Mr. Calhoun of New Orleans. On reflection, Crawford counted this attempt as a failure and discarded the cast. Crawford also made a copy of the *Demosthenes* of the Vatican galleries but as there is no known record that it was ever ordered, it may be assumed that Crawford eventually relegated it to the scrap heap with the other.

Crawford's prodigious rate of activity would have dispelled his poverty, if it had not been for his punctillious standards. He was dismayed to discover that the sums he earned from his concentrated application just about equalled the wage of an ordinary day laborer. His career, like those of his struggling colleagues in Florence, required the dramatic impetus of a significant public commission. He did not dare to enter those lists yet. It would be two years before he would venture in this direction and many more before he would attain success.

The summer of 1837 was a critical one in Rome, for cholera struck. Crawford stayed through the worst of it and lent assistance where he could. A friend reported that he nursed one victim twenty hours at a stretch. Crawford wrote home "the deaths are over 100 a day."[19] He worked incessantly, fortunately escaping contamination. A secondary scourge of the season overtook him, however. Visitors became scarce and the artists' business ground to a halt. What tourist would risk possible death for a view of the Eternal City under those conditions? To make matters worse, there was financial panic at home. The number of Americans abroad dwindled to a handful. Crawford was beset. He wrote, as they all did, of money being "all humbug,"[20] and to one friend he stated, "I think it is a base nuisance got up as it would seem for the purpose of creating in us a disgust for the world and a feeling of envy for those who are happily situated in this valley of the shadow of death. . . . It is as much as I can do to get along here. I allude to pecuniary matters."[21] Immersed in his endless work in the studio, the invitations of friends to partake of the cooling breeze at Albano over a hot Sunday held no temptations for him. He had no mind "to incur any additional expenses" or to slacken his pace.[22]

Later that winter Crawford, Freeman, and Luther Terry (the painter who had preceded both Crawford and Freeman to Rome) were joined by Frederick W. Phillips, a young and promising student of painting who had been a pupil of Robert Weir.[23] The reciprocity of encouragement among these artists comforted them during the depressed season.

Crawford's time was unscheduled but filled with learning. "My life here is so smooth and quiet," he wrote Longfellow. "I have every convenience for study."[24] He began to change his approach. Less and less did he copy from the antique or draw from life, but he began to spend whole days among the monuments and galleries of the city to enrich his mind with materials. In justification, he cited the example of Thorwaldsen and even Michelangelo, who was said to have refreshed his studies in the Forum at the age of eighty. When he could shake his mind free of financial worries, he was content.

Spring brought more than renewed hope. In May 1838 George Washington Greene came to Rome for a prolonged residence. He had discovered the city experimentally a decade earlier. He had wandered over the continent from Switzerland to Paris and then to

Florence, where he stayed for several years. Now he lodged his Italian wife, Maria, two servants, and a dog into an ample five-room suite that was comfortable for his small income. The apartment overlooked the gardens behind the Palazzo Barberini, 100 yards from the piazza. Greene intended to indulge his penchant for scholarship and literary dabbling. He was within hailing distance of Crawford in this choice location, and the pair became as close as brothers.

In December Greene obtained an appointment as his country's consul general in Rome, a focal position for all visiting Americans. When tourists called upon him on arrival, he ushered them to Crawford's studios at the beginning of their tourist rounds. He wrote eulogistically about Crawford for publication at home and spurred his Boston friends to participate in this activity. When Greene took his holiday late that summer and fall in the hills at Albano, Crawford attended to his sporadic consular matters, processing passports and arranging details with the local police in behalf of the visiting Americans.

Because the consular office abroad did not then receive a regular salary, Greene was obliged to charge fees for his services, a practice that gave rise to vicious gossip, particularly within his own Brahmin intellectual circle in Boston. Crawford and Charles Sumner, armed with facts, sprang to the defense of their friend's reputation. Greene complained of his embarrassing situation to Sumner.

> I am much indebted to you for your efforts about the Consulate. After so many fake expectations I too have come to the conclusion that nothing will be done. It is hard, very hard. I have twice the labor, twice the expense of the Chargé at Naples and Turin and am three thousand dollars out of pocket for my reward. . . . I must continue to hold the office for another winter. But I shall neither receive nor make visits, make no presentations at Court or at the Ambassadors. I confine myself to the signing of passports and permits.[25]

The furor culminated in the firing of Greene in the mid-forties, on the insinuation of misappropriation of funds. Eventually, this resulted in Congress' acceding to Sumner's pressures and voting a regular appropriation for this office. Despite the annoyance, Greene enjoyed his Roman residence thoroughly and served Crawford in sundry ways.

It was altogether an incubating period for Crawford; his attention centered on the search of technique while ideas for artistic works were gestating. With the hope for a public commission in a major city at home, Crawford made his first design for a statue of Benjamin Franklin. George Washington Greene described the design to the American public, stating that Crawford had chosen to "avail himself of the calm, quiet dignity of Franklin's aspect as philosopher." The statue was to have an attitude of "dignified repose" that would infuse "an intellectual grandeur" into the composition. Greene wrote that the work was conceived to "speak not to the eye only, but to the conscience and to the heart. . . . It is a form to stand in some square of our populous cities . . . or to occupy a niche in the hall of some public library." He continued:

> As a philosopher, [Franklin] wears the robe of the sages of antiquity, which falling in simple but graceful lines, covers the limbs without impeding or concealing the action of the figure. The left arm falls by the side, preserving the simplicity of the general movement, which is intended to approach almost to severity. The right rests upon a tablet, on which you see traced an electrical machine. The head is slightly raised, with a grave, natural elevation, and the eye, fixed in close observation, seems to follow the passage of the electric fluid through the clouds.[26]

This attempt to catch the public eye was ill-timed, however, and for years nothing came of the project.

Along with the study of Franklin, Crawford created another design in the mode of the day—George Washington represented as a Greek general—in the hope of a commission from "some civic committee" either at Boston, Newport, or Philadelphia.[27] The latter city held the highest hope since rival prospects were being promoted in the others, but neither Crawford's reputation nor his connections in that city were equal to capturing the prize.

While occupied with these designs for public commissions, Crawford's mind was absorbed with formulating his ideas and principles about art and in selecting guideposts for his technique. For the public monuments that would adorn the expanding cities and multiplying edifices at home, the patriotic motif was sustaining. Crawford stated that art ought to be "an instrument of national and individual culture."[28]

For private subjects, however, he sought in art "the natural expression of beautiful thoughts, tender feelings, and noble aspirations."[29] He saw the creative process as one intimately tied to emotional expression. While this artistic goal was reflective of romanticism, he was doing his utmost to imbibe the techniques of classicism. Although rooted in nature, the latter style was bound to the aesthetical ideals of passivity, sublimity, and majesty—all quite contrary to emotional expression. At this stage, even though he gained insight into the magic of imagination that inspired artistic works, it was uncertain that he would overcome the intrinsic limitations of the classical mold he was learning in Rome that conflicted with his maturing purposes.

16

Auspicious Debut

CRAWFORD'S SCULPTURAL APPRENTICESHIP IN ROME CAME TO A HEAD in the spring of 1838 when he declared his readiness to venture upon his first full statue. For his subject, he selected the romantic Orpheus legend. According to George Washington Greene, the theme derived from "one of the most touching passages of the tenderest poet of antiquity," the tenth book of Ovid's *Metamorphosis*.[1] The legend also inspired the fourth Georgic of Virgil. Oddly enough, neither the Hellenes nor the pagan Romans produced a sculptural prototype of Orpheus. Canova had made two small figures of *Orpheus* and *Eurydice,* but contemporary writers assure us they were scarcely known, even in Rome. It is doubtful that Crawford was acquainted with them. In any case, he could not legitimately be charged with plagiarism for wanting to produce his version of the legendary character.

Greene wrote that "Mr. Crawford saw how grossly the school of Bernini had failed in giving motion to drapery yet he felt convinced that there was enough in the works of the ancients to show that drapery might be made to flow and wave, even in marble."[2] In his effort "to give an air of antique beauty to the whole composition by keeping clear of all extravagance in the movement and working as nearly as possible in the spirit of the ancient Greek masters,"[3] he sought "simplicity and unity of effect."[4] Greene said that Crawford had scrapped one design for fear that it seemed "too ornamental" and "might divide and distract the attention from his central figure, and thus weaken the feelings that he wishes to excite."[5] Crawford desired to reconcile these difficulties so "that ornament might be preserved, without a sacrifice of simplicity, that the action of the figure might be strengthened by drapery properly thrown, and yet the proportion brought out clearly and well defined."[6]

Thomas Hicks spoke of Crawford's statue as "an expression of heroic manhood inspired by Genius."[7] Orpheus was a mortal being of heroic proportions, which, according to classical convention, placed him midway in both size and proportion between the gods and man. This interpretation would render him "still the slave of human passions, and acting by human means," while "imbued . . . with [a] large . . . portion of the divine spirit."[8] Greene found in the statue a perfect harmony of elements. "Strong as the action is, there is nothing forced or extravagant about it," he asserted.[9]

The story that Crawford chose to illustrate in his work appealed to Greene as "certainly the most interesting" moment in the legend.[10] Greene described it graphically.

> It is the first moment of the triumph of Orpheus, and that too in which his courage and his love are put to the hardest test. Before him, you fancy the black jaws of hell; you see him rushing onward through the opening, his face beaming with the passion that steels him to their terrors, and his whole frame glowing with the beauty of his divine origin. Cerberus at his side, has yielded to the powers of his lyre, and the three heads of the monster, dropping in sleep, leave the passages free. He has caught his lyre in his left hand; his right is raised to protect his eyes from what remains of the light of day; the wind as it rushed through the mouth of the cavern, has thrown back his robe, and the rapidity of his movements is strikingly displayed in the action of the limbs, of the body, and the swelling folds of the drapery.[11]

If adherence to nature was the acid test of good sculpture in the classical idiom, Catherine Maria Sedgwick felt that the figure could withstand careful scrutiny of its anatomical rendition. She decided:

The figure will, I believe, bear anatomical criticism; it has the effect, at any rate, to an unscientific eye, of anatomical success. It is light, graceful, and spirited; a most expressive embodying of poetic thought. There is the beauty of perfect symmetry in the face with a shade of earnestness which, though unusual in classical models, does not at all impair its classical serenity.[12]

Greene found that Crawford handled the technical difficulties with "a degree of practical skill and a judicious management, which are seldom attained by so young a man." He described the statue as "full of grace," and elaborated:

The body, the limbs, the head are in perfect keeping; there is a harmony about them. . . . The frame is neither powerful, nor slight, but that well balanced medium, which belongs to health, and a perfect command of all the physical powers. His strength is not that of the arena, nor the bone and sinew of daily toil,

Orpheus and Cerberus (front and side views)
   1838–1843, marble, life-size
Courtesy of the Museum of Fine Arts, Boston

but such as one must gain by healthful exercise in the sunlight and open air; . . .

The attitude is calculated to give full scope to all the vigor of which he is possessed. The rapidity of his motion requires that play of muscles, which is the severest test of an artist's science. The right leg is drawn out to its fullest extent, and touching the ground with the extremity of the foot; the weight of the body thrown upon the left, which bends at the knee with the movement forward; the inclination of the body itself, which is thrown forward to correspond with the general action, and the double movement of the arms. . . . The development of the muscles is carried just far enough. . . ."[13]

While engaged in putting up the *Orpheus*, Crawford found time to produce several smaller works; a bust of a Mr. Ingraham, who was described as "an English gentlemen, well known for his taste in the arts," and a medallion of the historian Carlo Botta.[14]

Crawford produced at this time two other significant compositions in bas relief, a style much in vogue then in Rome. Both were of mythological subjects and were commissioned by Prince Anatoli Demidov. The larger one was oblong and illustrated the legend of the third labor of Hercules. The scene selected by Crawford depicted Hercules leading the golden horned stag to Eurytheus, when he is stopped by Diana, who claims the stag. The location of this piece is unknown but George Washington Greene described it in detail.

The ground is a plain, unbroken surface. Hercules stands at one of the extremities. He leans with his right arm upon his massive club. The left, raised toward the goddess, enforces his words, by a calm yet dignified gesticulation. The skin of the Nemean lion falls from the left shoulder, in a line with the body, and crossing it behind, drops with the motion of the right arm. The space between him and the goddess is filled by one of her usual emblems, a grey-hound. In the centre of the piece, tall, majestic, arrayed in a light robe, that descends to the knee, stands the goddess herself, Her face is turned to the hero, her right arm is extended toward him: the left holds the stag with the firm, easy grasp of a divine being. These two figures are in repose, or rather, the action is calm. In that of the nymph, who fills the opposite extremity of the piece, there is much more of excitement. She is draped to her feet in a loose robe, that flows backward with the wind, and the movement of her body. The band that she has fastened around the neck of the animal, is drawn tight by her effort to restrain his leaping, and in her whole frame, full of grace and vigor as it is, you see the difference between her power and that of her mistress.[15]

Greene wrote that there was a striking balance in the composition regarding the distribution of the figures, their relationship to each other and to the accessories. He said that Hercules was portrayed in colossal, godlike form, but somewhat diminished in stature to convey appropriate rank, as was the wood nymph accompanying the goddess. The wood nymph was given mortal proportions and attributes in contrast with Diana. Green wrote: "Diana is the vigorous, graceful goddess of the bow: the sister of Apollo, and partaking of the same immortal beauty. There is quiet power, a severe grace about her, that marks her at once as the chaste sovereign of the woods."[16]

The second circular relief portrayed a scene from the battle of the Centaurs, an age-old Roman theme. Greene described this one also:

> One of the monsters has seized upon a young bride, whose indignant countenance and uplifted arm, the struggling frame and the mixed expression of terror and anger, that fills her lovely features, reveal at once all the horrors of her situation. But a protector is at hand. His undaunted aspect and vigorous limbs show that he is equal to fearful struggle. Unarmed as he is, he has leaped boldly upon the back of the Centaur; his left hand is set fast in his matted locks; he has drawn the head backward; the monster rears with the motion and seems struggling to shake off the incumbent weight; but the hero, firm in his grasp, retains his hazardous position, and with his right arm extended to its utmost range, is preparing to deal him a blow that will require no repetition. The vigor of the figure is beyond all description. I can give you no idea of it in words; and yet there is nothing strained, nothing theatrical about it. It is a being of great strength; well used to put it forth; and now employing it all in a cause that he feels to be worthy of himself.[17]

These reliefs were admired by Tenerani, who ranked only after Thorwaldsen among Crawford's Roman colleagues.

News of these significant works in progress created a stir, not only in Rome but also in the artistic community at home. Even their incipient promise of distinction caused Crawford to be selected in 1838 as an honorary member of the National Academy of Design in New York. Perversely, the sculptor received the honor with caustic wit. Honorary membership could not feed him, nor could it supply his other primary need of the moment, to receive higher payments for his work. He jokingly referred to the honoring institution as "The American Academy of Coarse Art."[18] He felt keenly the pincer effect of the prevailing system of commissioning works of art, which gave the sculptor half the price as a down payment, but since he was forced to pay cash for the marble block and the cutters' wages, placed the wealthy purchaser in debt to the impecunious sculptor. Inevitably, this indebtedness of the sculptor would continue until cash deposits for his commissions would pile up sufficiently to put him ahead of the game. The customary delay in payment implied a doubled or trebled struggle for the fledgling until the moment of his public acclimation, which generally accompanied the appearance of his first truly artistic creation.

In the late fall of 1838, while Crawford was concentrating on his work and suffering his usual anxiety over financial pressures, news arrived of the death of his father. The combination of stresses proved too much even for Crawford's sturdy constitution. He broke down before Christmas; succumbing to a raging brain fever. He survived but the fever wrecked havoc with his natural vitality. His convalescence took several months and for most of the spring, he was at George Washington Greene's country house at Albano. Greene supervised not only Crawford's nursing care as prescribed by Dr. Ruga, but also the operations of his studio. During this interval, Crawford kept his hand in the clay by modeling a bust of Greene. The bust was intended to repay in some measure Greene's hospitality. He prized the gift but characteristically turned the favor around by offering it to Longfellow if the latter would advance the cost of freight. The idea was to demonstrate Crawford's skill to the Boston set. The offer was accepted, and before long, the bust was reported by Charles Sumner to be "a capital likeness and a beautiful work of art . . . admired by all . . . in a conspicuous place in Longfellow's room."[19]

It was not until late spring that Crawford mustered the energy to resume his normal work. He returned to a busy studio. Greene's propaganda was taking effect and it was bolstered by the artistic recognition Crawford was gaining locally and at home through the reports of the tourists who saw the works in his studio. Commissions for busts now mounted to a steady stream. Solid popular success, however, still hinged on the exhibition of a major work.

The season of 1839 was climaxed with the arrival in late May of Charles Sumner. He came to Europe for his health but filled his waking hours zealously probing the mysteries of art and studying foreign languages. Although he paid a hurried visit to Naples, Rome was the real beginning of his Grand Tour. His three months there were the happiest of his life he wrote Crawford years later. Steeped in the classics, Sumner rediscovered them in Rome in revitalized form. He spent ten hours a day perfecting his Italian and reveling in the glories of Italian literary masterpieces. Already familiar with Dante, he plunged into Tasso, Alfieri, Manzoni, Pellico, Lanzi, and Vasari.[20] There seemed to be nothing Italian he would disapprove, except perhaps the priesthood and its morals. The art and literature of Italy were to him above reproach.

Sumner's law partner, George S. Hilliard, in his book *Six Months in Italy*, recorded local attitudes of the time toward artists in Rome. He stated, "to visit the studio of young artists is one of the approved methods of disposing of an idle afternoon in Rome."[21] For Sumner, such visits would not be viewed as idling away time, but rather as a venture in artistic research. He therefore acceded readily to Greene's offer to escort him to Crawford's studio for presentation to the artist. With his Italophilic disposition, he was a likely subject to be led by Greene to personalize an acquaintance already begun through reputation. Sumner was impressed with the models strewn about, particularly the *Orpheus*, which was already quite far advanced. He also praised the early study for an equestrian Washington monument. Above all, he was attracted by Crawford's personality, his earnest application, his spirited enthusiasm, and his charm. Crawford's character impressed him, and in a later magazine article, he wrote of Crawford's "utter absence of conceit—the independence, but mature formation of his views of art—his just, without idol estimation of Michael Angelo—his boldness of opinion and withal, his real diffidence and desire still further to advance his intellect and powers."[22] Of Crawford's work, Sumner reported that he respected the "fidelity" of his portrait busts and "the classic elegance and simplicity" of their compositions.[23] Sumner felt that he had found a serious aspirant to answer the national need for artistic embellishment of the expanding capital and the burgeoning cities. Here was an American to rank with the best among Europe's artists. All that remained was to make Crawford known at home. Sumner joined Greene in a campaign to promote Crawford as one of America's most promising sculptors. He pursued the task with relish, fully aware that "the moneyed Americans who visit Rome follow names."[24]

Following Greene's example, Sumner sat for Crawford for his bust. Pending the completion of his European tour, he left the bust with Greene temporarily. Sumner's posing provided an opportunity to give direct help to the needy artist and to deepen their acquaintance. Sumner swelled with pride when this first representation of himself was warmly admired by his friend and colleague at home, William Hinckling Prescott, as a "very good likeness and a beautiful piece of work."[25] Sumner eventually bequeathed this bust to the Boston Athenaeum.

The late summer's lull gave Crawford the opportunity to visit Florence, something he had desired since his arrival in Italy. In

Charles Sumner
1839–1842, marble, life-size
Courtesy of the Museum of Fine Arts, Boston

Florence, he would see the splendid collections of Renaissance art that surpassed even the fabulous examples in Rome. An added impetus to the trip was the opportunity of meeting his artistic compatriots who had settled there. Greenough's reputation was already acknowledged and Powers was not entirely unknown. Crawford called on both of them. Thus commenced a comradely relationship among the artists. Greenough especially became a good friend, later visiting Crawford in Rome and then having his visit returned. The friendship with Powers was marred years later by Powers' resentment over the government commissions awarded to Crawford.

Crawford sprang back to work fervidly on his return in the fall, straining himself beyond his curtailed capacity and inducing a brief relapse of his illness. He worked throughout his setback, however, modeling the *Genius of Autumn*, which Greene later called an "exquisite little figure, full of grace and childlike beauty."[26] Crawford struggled with several changes in the statue, and finally produced a statue that Greene described as a "sunny-faced little boy, with his keen sickle and swelling sheaf."[27] This first statue of Crawford's to go from clay to marble was an appealing work, inspiring Crawford to other representations of children. It was purchased promptly by John Paine of New York, who requested another statue based on the *Centurion* bas-relief he had seen in Crawford's studio, presumably for balance in his drawing room. Another New York family became interested in Crawford's work and ordered a commemorative bust of Judge Edmund K. Pendleton. Crawford copied the features from a likeness provided by the family and turned the bust into a marble Roman senator in slavish neoclassical style.

With authentic New England loyalty, Sumner did not forsake his new friend after parting from him in September. On the contrary, he wrote frequent encouraging letters to both Greene and Crawford and assiduously pursued his resolve to promote the artist. Upon arriving in Milan, he wrote Greene, "I have begun to write early to send friends to you. . . . Within a week or fortnight from now Sir Charles Vaughan will be in Rome. For twelve years, he was much respected, I may say, loved Minister of England at Washington; all Americans owe him kindness and attention for the way in which he speaks about our country . . . a little dear, plain, frank.

. . . I do not know if he would care about seeing the *Orpheus.*"[28]
There was no question about Sumner's avowed intentions.

Still attuned to the world of art and the cause of Crawford,
Sumner reported that he found "whole acres of fresco" by the German painter Cornelius.[29] One fresco depicted the subject of Orpheus
and Sumner described it amply to Crawford with the rest of his art
news. In Vienna Sumner made the acquaintance of the Muhlenberg
family who shared his ardor for his favorite sculptor. He wrote
Greene in confidence:

> Miss M thinks Crawford the first artist of Italy and hopes some-
> body will soon order the Orpheus which was the finest thing
> she saw. By the way, she asked me if Crawford had not taken
> my bust, she said that she was struck by my resemblance to that
> plaster face on top of the books in your study. I have spoken
> to Schwartz, our Consul here, who seems to be wealthy and
> liberal about Crawford, and he has given me reason to hope that
> he would send him an order. . . . Tell Crawford that he should
> come here and marry Miss M. He can have her easily if he will
> make her a present of the Orpheus.[30]

Sumner also wrote in this letter that Sir Charles Vaughan was delayed in reaching Rome due to the death of his brother. He said that
he was sending another distinguished English friend "in hopes that
he will order something from Crawford."[31] This was John Kenyon,
whom Sumner described as "the ancient friend of Coleridge, and
now the bosom friend of Southey, Wordsworth, and Landor."[32]
Sumner theorized that glamorous clients would lend the aura of their
fame to the artist. Moreover, Sumner was persuaded that this English
patronage would redound to Crawford's advantage because the
Americans, lacking experience and confidence in judging artistic
merit, would follow the lead of Englishmen. Sumner seemed single-
minded in advancing Crawford with all of his acquaintances. When
in Vienna, he met a wealthy retired merchant from New York,
Mr. Miller, who was traveling with a Mr. Bissell, a multilingual
mining potentate from the Carolinas. Sumner urged both these men
to patronize Crawford by sitting for portraits.

These promotional efforts paid off handsomely. Both Englishmen sat for Crawford for their portraits. Apparently Sir Charles Vaughan enjoyed the acquaintance, for on his return to London he spoke glowingly of the sculptor and of Rome generally. Kenyon liked his bust well enough to order a duplicate to be sent to Ticknor in Boston as a token of their friendship.

Sumner did more. He wrote his law partner and closest friend in Boston, George Stillman Hillard, to do what he could to spark interest at home for the sculptor. Hillard was not encouraging, although his reply did not constitute a rebuff either. He wrote, "I fear it will not be possible to do anything for your sculptor friend. There is great distress in the mercantile community at present; however, I will not abandon the cause of Crawford."[33] Other friends were mobilized by Sumner, who wrote of Crawford to William H. Prescott, Henry Wadsworth Longfellow, Cornelius C. Felton, Edward Everett, and George Ticknor. Eventually Sumner introduced Crawford to his entire acquaintance in the States.

Sumner left Europe in a state of ambivalence. Having spent $5,000, his "glorious privilege" of travel had to end.[34] He wrote nostalgically, "I rely much for my future happiness upon my friends in Europe."[35] He tore himself away in the fall of 1840 to embark upon his own notable career at home. Yet he never forgot his vision of Rome and the splendor of the art he saw there.

Upon arriving home Sumner proceeded to raise a subscription among his Boston friends for the purchase of the *Orpheus*. In a few short months he raised $2,000 in pledges. Everyone realized this was inadequate compensation for such a work, particularly in view of the cost of the marble. Sumner stated that the marble alone was "worth more than $5,000."[36] In March 1841 the treasurer of the Athenaeum was directed to contribute $500 to the subscription fund for the *Orpheus*. The final amount was left open, even in the contract that Crawford signed in Rome on March 31, 1841. The terms provided that Crawford execute the work in twenty months in Seravezza marble. The size and proportion of the statue was to be that of the original model, which was already known to the subscribers through Grüner's engraving.[37] Although Sumner tried to improve the price, the total stood at $2,500.

The money came in slowly in Boston and was transmitted even

more slowly to Rome. Crawford's daughter dramatized the event
years later in an amusing manner:

> At last, one evening, the artist found that he had only . . . two
> pauls left in the world. He was very hungry, but it seemed to
> him a base thing to devote his last pennies to mere food. Since
> he was now convinced that he was destined to die of starvation
> he would at least have one more hour of real happiness. So he
> spent the two pauls on a seat at the Opera, where he forgot all
> his own troubles and heartbreaks in listening to the divine strains
> of the Trovotore. . . . The morrow . . . brought a letter to the
> studio door. . . . Out fell a check. The letter contained an order for
> the Orpheus. . . .[38]

The facts contrast sharply with Mary Crawford Fraser's apocryphal account. The spotless Seravezza marble block from which the
statue was to be carved arrived in Crawford's studio on October 1,
1841. It cost $700, $300 of which Crawford was obliged to borrow
from Greene. No payment of any sort had yet crossed the Atlantic.
Crawford accepted $200 more from Greene for operating expenses.
It was estimated that the roughing out alone would cost $300 more,
thus committing over a thousand dollars in advance of any receipts.
The sculptor waited three months and then wrote Sumner. He requested an advance of half the total sum, in this case asking for a
thousand dollars with an additional $500 in three months. Sumner
had not collected the money from those who had subscribed it but
had simply filed their names. Before Crawford's letter could have
arrived though, the treasurer of the Athenaeum was mysteriously
requested to collect the sums subscribed to Sumner that were still
unpaid. In April Sumner advanced $300 to Crawford, probably out
of his own pocket. Crawford did not hear anything more, and in
July he simply drew the equivalent of $1,308 on Sumner person-
ally. Sumner must have arranged for this ultimate contingency with
some banker. Delays were inevitable in the transfer of money in
those days of slow steamer transport.

Sensitive to any criticism, Greene went to the trouble of de-
fending Crawford's timetable, explaining to the uninitiated at home
some of the complicated operations of a sculptor's studio in Rome.
He wrote: "A young sculptor has not the means to finish piece after

piece like the master of a well organized studio; and Crawford in his anxiety to please, has thrown away block upon block of marble even after some progress has been made in roughing them out, and this merely to secure as spotless a piece as he could."[39]

The duplicate *Orpheus* was completed in the marble and ready for shipment to Boston in the summer of 1843. It was dispatched at Leghorn on a vessel bound for New York and then transshipped by sea to Boston where it arrived September 13, 1843. In the course of shipping and handling, serious injury had been done to the lower portions of the statue. Late in October the Athenaeum's trustees engaged the Boston sculptor Henry Dexter to repair the damage.[40] The repairs were done so adroitly that the principals concerned were relieved to have retrieved the "precious" work of art for a mere $200 more.[41] There was some talk of deducting this expense from the sum due Crawford, but Sumner stopped it short.

A special building for the exhibition of the *Orpheus* was erected next door to the Athenaeum on Pearl Street, costing another $300. The regular rooms in the antiquated building were too badly lighted for the occasion. Sumner personally selected the colors of the walls and draperies and supervised the arrangement of the furniture. He even called on Greene for assistance in these elements of management. Greene rushed from New York to Boston to comply. Sumner proposed that the proceeds of the exhibition should be sent to Crawford and that these expenses should be viewed as permanent improvements of the new building, but he was fought to a draw by the trustees who stuck to the terms of the contract.

Sumner and Greene had been laying the groundwork over some years for a favorable Boston reception of the *Orpheus* and its companion works from Italy. They were assisted by the classical orientation of New England's social and intellectual arbiters of taste, as acutely summarized by Greene, a member of the elite group.

> I can see no difference between the composition of a great poem, and that of a great painting. The same natural powers, the same order of mind, is required . . . in the same region of intellect! It is only the language that is changed. . . . Nature is the foundation of both. . . . The language of poetry changes with age, with climate, with social institutions; that of the artist is always the

same. . . . It is in the ancients then, that the language of sculpture must be studied; a language flowing from the pure fountains of natural feeling, unchanged by the long lapse of ages, fresh now as at its birth. . . .

[The sculptor must] bring poetry to the illustration of art, and penetrating the most recondite symbols of mythology, make their language as familiar as the accents of his native tongue! There is an appropriate term for every idea, a form of expression for every shade of thought, an ideal beauty for all the varieties of intellectual and of physical power. . . .

How different the beauty of the Apollo [is] from that of the Gladiator! . . . There is the beauty of age, too—grave and solemn dignity; there is the voluptuous beauty of the goddess of love, and the severer grace of the goddess of wisdom; and all of these must be studied again and again, till the mind becomes imbued with their spirit, and each rising thought clothes itself as it were intuitively, in the language with which they speak.[42]

Greene had taken the lead over Sumner with an appealing pitch that he wrote for the June issue of the *Knickerbocker*, a prominent New York monthly magazine read by the elite set. In preparation for the article, he had elicited Thorwaldsen's usual encomium. His "Letters from Modern Rome" continued at length and in February 1841 he pursued the subject of a commission for the *Orpheus* by "several opulent and public spirited private citizens . . . so that it will no longer be said that the native city of our artist is tardy in doing justice to his extraordinary genius."[43]

Sumner took up the cudgels too. In an especially ardent article, entitled, "Crawford's Orpheus," which appeared in May 1843 in the *United States Magazine and Democratic Review*, he issued a stinging rebuke to New Yorkers for having ignored their impressive native son. After citing the panegyrics of the reputable experts at Rome, Bertel Thorwaldsen and John Gibson, he stated the facts about Crawford straightforwardly. He said that Crawford "has bespoken the marble for the statue. He has no order for the work! New York will disgrace itself if fifty gentlemen do not club ten pounds each together, and send it to your Consul at Rome to contract for such a *first* work, and *first* encourage such a self-taught man of genius."[44] The article was accompanied by a steel engraving made from Crawford's drawing in Rome in 1840 and previously published in the *Roman Bee,* a publication devoted to engravings and to describing important works of art.

Crawford's sister Jenny did not stand aloof from the promotional efforts of his friends. Apparently they were in contact with her and recruited her willingly in the cause. She wrote a long poem entitled "Orpheus: The Sculptor in his Studio," which was published a month after Sumner's article in the same magazine.[45]

Against this background, the *Orpheus* was launched in May 1844 with its own particular fanfare. Crawford's affairs in Rome and lack of money prevented him from crossing the ocean to attend the opening. The statue was generally acclaimed, as was to be anticipated from the management of its proficient public relators. His public reputation was firmly established in Boston. Although no public commissions resulted directly in New York, Crawford's name became known and private orders did ensue. Crawford was sufficiently encouraged to dream of success through his first "masterpiece." He confided an optimistic vision to his sister, who hoped to advance his reputation by publishing it along with her poem. In his fantasy, he was seated in his studio, in full view of the *Orpheus* during a frightful thunderstorm. This recalled to his impressionable mind the legend of Phidias and his "wonderful statue of Jove." Crawford confided to his sister:

> You know that upon finishing it, he requested some sign from the god, to know if he were pleased with the representation; it seems the nod was given for at that moment, the statue was circled by lightning, which came and passed off with such a noise as could only be produced by heaven's artillery. Were we living in that age, as were ours the religion of the ancient Greeks, I too might interpret the sign in my favor."[46]

17

The Fruitful Years
(1840-1849)

THE ARTISTIC COLONY IN ROME CONTINUED TO SWELL THROUGHOUT the nineteenth century, and the season of 1839–1840 witnessed its share of influx distributed equally from America, England, and Germany. A contemporary American editor, who had the news on excellent authority, reported, "Our young painters, too, are doing themselves great credit in Rome."[1]

In the imperial eyes of the British, however, the Americans were still untutored colonials undeserving of notice in the listings of artists' studios published in their guidebooks. When Frances Trollope came through Rome in December of 1841 she visited the American painter George Peter Alexander Healy, who was already established in his studio for a three year stay before his removal to Paris. She also saw Crawford and admired his work. Yet her travel account omitted any reference to them, she merely declared that "both Gibson and Wyatt are decidedly in the van."[2]

It took the editor of the *Knickerbocker* monthly magazine in New York to inform his readers of the contents of letters he received regularly from Americans in Rome. In a brief article entitled "Our Young Artists," published in September 1840, the editor paraphrased a letter from Healy, stating that Daniel E. Huntington, "whose productions were so justly commended in the National Academy last season . . . has sent home two or three pictures worthy of his reputation, and [is] evincing a ripening of his fine talents. Huntington's companion, Mr. Gray," the report continued, "but recently a mere amateur . . . bids fair to emulate his success with no faltering hand. His *Roman Girl* . . . reflects honor upon the artist."[3]

It was a busy season for transients too. Most of the stellar Americans hailed from Boston, with a sprinkling from the other seaboard cities where leisured wealth was now manifest. Catherine Maria Sedgwick, the well-known writer, returned in May from her more southerly travels. George Sumner, following exactly the course of his brother, Charles, arrived in Rome in September. William Minot, Jr., spent the season with several hometown friends, all clustered around Piazza di Spagna.

Before quitting Europe, Charles Sumner had apparently talked up Crawford's stock considerably among the Americans he met after he left Rome. His first letter to Greene from Milan in October 1839 contained such phrases as "Preston will probably order something of Crawford to the tune of $1,000, and I think will also order the Orpheus on account of his brother. Lewis will probably do something, but on a smaller scale. I feel particularly anxious, therefore, that you should do what you conveniently can to promote their views."[4]

The propaganda bore fruit quickly, for on January 15, 1840, a letter was dispatched from George R. Lewis in Rome to the secretary of the Boston Athenaeum stating:

> A few American gentlemen, now in Rome, having made the acquaintance of Mr. Thomas Crawford, . . . a young artist of great promise—and being desirous that he should be extensively and favorably known at home, have ordered of him, . . . four small bas reliefs, representing the Winds . . . and ask permission to deposit them in the Athenaeum . . . the course best calculated to promote the end . . . make the artist generally known. . . . We would esteem it a favor if you would cause them to be favorably noticed in the Journals, for the benefit of the artist—making no mention . . . of our names. . . . We would refer you to Mr. Charles Sumner . . . who knows and esteems him highly. . . . The names of the contributors to the bas reliefs are Mr. Thomas Preston of Virginia,

Mr. DeHone of South Carolina, Mr. William Minot of Boston and myself from Connecticut.[5]

The subscribers gave assurances that the pieces would be completed in six months and duly forwarded by Consul George Washington Greene.

These figures were never executed and probably not even designed. Crawford may have become disenchanted with the over-worked allegory and sought a fresh idea. In any case, he offered no explanation to the Athenaeum trustees. He informed his patrons curtly through Sumner. "If you should see Mr. Minot, Jr., he wrote Sumner, "please tell him that I have changed from the *Winds* [to an] apotheosis of Washington [and from that to] an illustration of the *72nd Ode of Anacreon*."[6] The metamorphosis of this subject hints at some hidden motive. The Anacreon theme had been repeated since the days of ancient Greece. Thorwaldsen had revived it recently in several bas-reliefs. Crawford probably decided to try his hand at a work in private competition with the master's. If he came out favorably, the comparison would surely be noticed by the perceptive critics in Boston.

Crawford's bas-relief *Anacreon* is a simple representation of a dancer accompanied by an old man playing the lyre. It was thinly conceived and superficially wrought as if the simplicity of the classical Greek style were its singular objective. It suited the taste of the day and earned some money for the artist. Crawford completed the marble rendition in Rome in 1842 while he was finishing the *Orpheus*. Contemporaries deemed it a work of "rare beauty" when it arrived in Boston in June 1843 ahead of the *Orpheus*, just in time to be included in the Athenaeum's exhibition on June 20.[7]

Crawford's star was on the rise that season. It had already been heralded at home by Sumner as early as 1840 when he had begun to raise the purse to commission the *Orpheus*. Crawford moved his studio to larger quarters in Via Purificazione 29, at the foot of Via Sistina, just off Piazza Barberini. The new studio was one block from Thorwaldsen's atelier and a stone's throw below the convent of Trinità dei Monti which stands on the crest of the hill where Via Sistina and Via Gregoriana converge. The building is no longer

Anacreon 1842, marble bas-relief
Courtesy of the Boston Athenaeum

there, but the street still harbors studios and shops, although the
center for these studios has now shifted to Via Margutta.

Complementing the patronage that Crawford was receiving
from Bostonians, New Yorkers, and Russians, George Tiffany arrived
from Baltimore and requested a monumental marble bas-relief for
the tombstone of his wife. Crawford selected the subject *Lead Us
Into Life Everlasting*. It was nearing completion in the marble in
January 1842 but waited two more years to be finished. Tiffany also
ordered marble copies of Thorwaldsen's *Day* and *Night*. A small
copy of *Cupid in Contemplation* was commissioned by Jonathan
Phillips of Boston. These orders yielded Crawford nearly $1,000,
temporarily relieving the financial distress that was a constant condition prior to the exhibition of his *Orpheus*. It had been reported
by Greene to Sumner that Crawford had been "managing on $300
a year."[8]

A new rumor was abroad that Philadelphia was now casting about for a Washington equestrian statue. Out came Crawford's earlier design for revision to conform to the equestrian requirement. Greene thought the new design had grander proportions than the first and admired the allegorical figures at the corners of the pedestal and the bas-reliefs at the sides. Unluckily, Philadelphia was too distant for Crawford to make headway without personal connections. When he learned that Dr. Rush's influence respecting the project was "now great," Crawford wrote Sumner to inquire whether he knew the man and could help.[9] Sumner did not know Dr. Rush and nothing came of this desultory attempt by Crawford to capture the commission at long distance. Crawford took small comfort from the news that the proceedings of the Philadelphia committee were confused.

There was an immediate positive result, however, of Crawford's revived interest in an equestrian Washington. On the anniversary of Washington's birthday the following February, Greene displayed the design with his usual social fanfare for his numerous guests who responded generously. Thorwaldsen's approval was elicited too. Greene's party in honor of the work advanced Crawford's reputation markedly in Rome that season, but it failed to evoke pressures at home sufficient to gain a commission so soon. When Professor Jared Sparks' biography of George Washington was published that year, Crawford's design was selected for lithographing and printing. Taste has since reverted to the portraits of Gilbert Stuart and Rembrandt Peale.

The Bostonians were still at the center of Crawford's social and artistic life. The American group in Rome eagerly awaited the visit of their eminent friend Edward Everett, who was touring Europe before assuming his ministerial post in London at the end of 1841. Crawford angled to capture Everett's interest in his work, so as to have an influential agent at the British capital. Everett arrived late in October and Greene took him on the rounds, first to Thorwaldsen's studio and then to Crawford's. Impressed with what he saw, Everett readily consented to take notes of the works in progress on which he would base an article for an English journal that would serve to supplement those that Sumner and Greene wrote for home consumption.

The plans for a public commission did not impede Crawford's daily work routine. He was especially pleased when a Mr. Homans of Boston ordered a marble head of the *Orpheus*, as it cost him no additional personal effort and yielded a welcome dividend. This genre of work was as popular as idealized female busts. The patron could be assured of rapid delivery and could boast of owning an essential portion of a "masterpiece."

At the same time, Crawford made a sketch for a rather intricate bas-relief. He stated that he was "better pleased with it than with any bas-relief . . . [he had] yet made," and described it as showing "the wise men and shepherds bringing their offerings to Mary and the Infant Savior, who is surrounded by Angels, humming His praise."[10] The composition showed a mature sense of perspective, especially in comparison with his previous illustrations which frequently depicted as few as two figures.

Encouraged by the positive reaction, Crawford projected a series of seven more bas-reliefs. In a letter to Sumner he stated, "[These] will contain compositions representing the great poets of ancient and modern times . . . Homer, Virgil, Dante, Petrarch, Tasso, and Milton, and an ideal arrangement of Apollo with the horse Pegasus." Crawford mentioned Shakespeare too but then explained to Sumner, "I am thinking of reserving him to a place in another series intended for the Tragic Poets. . . . The most important of these will be, perhaps, illustrations of the whole of Ovid."[11] Crawford was concentrating on fitting subjects for bas-relief as they could be executed far more quickly than sculpture in the round.

The plans for these seven bas-reliefs were soon set aside in favor of the still speedier medium of pen and ink sketches for engraving. Crawford explained, "To model them would require too much time, unless they were ordered."[12] The first set of three of these designs was actually completed in 1842 and published in Rome early in the summer of 1843. The remainder of the series did not materialize. Greene, during his trip home, prospected with Sumner the distribution of the engravings in the States. "I have brought a few copies of the first number, one for you, and one to be placed wherever you think it will assist most in getting subscribers," he wrote. "The Apollo Association has accepted the Agency and the prospectus is by this time out in New York. The moment I get a copy I will send it to you and you will do what you think best in Boston," continued Greene. He then added, "The newspapers and magazines must be set at work. I did something towards this while I was in New York, but Willis was out of town, and I do not know the Editor of the Democratic. I shall send a few lines to the Knickerbocker. . . . What can you do?"[13] Immediately nothing could be done.

These diversionary notions got nowhere, and the illustrations were relegated to their folder for almost 100 years. The subject was transformed in the course of time from the classic poets to religious themes. They were eventually published in the *Boston Evening Transcript's* religious section on December 21, 1935. The first one was entitled *Glory to God in the Highest and on Earth, Peace and Good Will Toward Men*. The second depicted *The Wise Men* and was based on a verse from the Bible, Matthew 11:9, "when they had heard the King, they departed, and lo, the star which they saw in the east, went before them, till it came and stood over where the young child was." The third subject was *The Shepherds* and was based on Luke 11:15, "The shepherds said to one another, 'Let us now go unto Bethlehem and see this thing.'"[14]

Crawford was perturbed over the failure of his engravings, but he cleaved tenaciously to his experiments with new outlets for his creative energy. His next attempt to quicken the pace of business had a good deal of merit. Why not sow the notion that sculptural works could be just as decorative in plaster of paris as in the most expensive materials? "The great work of modern times," as Crawford judged Thorwaldsen's *Triumph of Alexander*, suffered the fate of remaining forever in plaster and it still augmented its author's fame.[15] The advantages of working in plaster of paris were manifest. Delivery would be speedier and prices brought into a popular range. The sculptor would be paid for his design and greater profit would accrue from reduced expenditures. Copies in plaster could be cast by the score. These speculations remained unrealized. Alone, Crawford lacked the authority to overturn the system. He sighed, "I regret I have not a hundred hands to keep pace with the working of the mind."[16] George Hillard noted Crawford's impatience to speed production of creative ideas beyond the pace of chipping away at refractory marble and wrote, "It was particularly characteristic of Crawford who suffered something of the impatience of genius: before an image of beauty has been turned to form, another takes possession of his mind, and the new impulse will not let him linger over the task in hand."[17]

While in search of greater facility in form and material, Crawford received another important commission. This from a Mr. Hicks, a New Yorker. The commission was for a figure of a young boy, patterned after the successful *Genius of Autumn* executed for John Paine. Crawford may have had another series in mind or may have just been following the fad in Rome for creating "genii." He decided on a smiling bacchanalian figure of a boy seven to eight years old, which he described to Sumner as his *Genius of Mirth*. The figure, he wrote, "is dancing in great glee and tinkling a pair of cymbals, the music of which seems to amuse him exceedingly. The sentiment is joyousness throughout. It is evident no thought of the future troubles his young mind, and he may consider himself very fortunate

Genius of Mirth
1844, marble, 46″
The Metropolitan Museum of Art, gift of Mrs. Annette W. W. Hicks-Lord, 1897

in being made of marble, for thus his youth remains without change."[18] There are garlands around the figure's head, and a tambourine lying near the feet. The base is strewn with Crawford's typical floral patterns, reminiscent of his marble cutting days in New York. The feeling is entirely classical. The three-foot high model was completed in 1842 and cut in marble the following year. When the statue was presented to the Metropolitan Museum of Art in 1897 by Mr. Hicks' daughter, she entitled it *Dancing Girl*, and for many years it was exhibited with this erroneous title.

There were other figures of children that Crawford created intermittently. In 1851 he designed his most famous children's composition, the *Babes in the Wood*, for Hamilton Fish of New York. This group illustrates a morbid theme taken from an old English ballad, "The Norfolk Gentleman's Last Will and Testament," also known as "The Children in the Wood" or "Babes in the Wood." It reads in part:

> Thus wandered these two pretty babes,
> Till death did end their grief,
> In one another's armes they dyed,
> As babes wanting relief:
> No burial these prettye babes
> Of any man received
> 'Til Robin-Red-Breast painfully
> Did cover them with leaves.[19]

Babes in the Wood 1851, marble, 52″ by 36″
The Metropolitan Museum of Art, gift of the Honorable Hamilton Fish, 1894

It is likely that Crawford's inspiration for this rendition came from an engraving of the same subject that appeared in the London Art Journal in 1847. It was a popular subject in Victorian England as Charles Dickens' novels about poor, benighted children attest. The queen had two illustrations of the ballad in her private collection at Osborne House in the 1850s. One was a painting by Peele and the other was a marble group by the Belgian sculptor Greefs. In Crawford's version the children's costumes appear to be a Victorian approximation of the style of dress worn in France in the sixteenth century. To better illustrate the story the children are surrounded by shoes, little birds, flowers, and laces. Admiring contemporaries reported "touching pathos" in the sleeping children and described the group as "consistent and exquisite" in the classical genre.[20]

The *Babes* were followed shortly by a marble statue of a *Boy Playing Marbles* that was ordered by Stephen Salisbury of Worcester, Massachusetts, and another of *Children Holding a Bird's Nest Tenanted by a Bird* that decorates the entrance hall of a lovely house on Beacon Street in Boston.

Second in magnitude among Crawford's classical productions was his life size group of *Hebe* and *Ganymede*, which he modeled while awaiting the completion of the *Orpheus*. Although this was another banal Roman subject wrought in the neoclassical mode, it did provide Crawford with the opportunity to develop technical skill in the interweaving of two figures. Crawford explained the concept of this latest group carefully to Sumner:

> Hebe and Ganymede [are represented] at the moment Hebe is leaving the service of the gods and in sorrow giving her cup to the Shepherd boy, who offers his consolation to the virgin. She stands in a pensive attitude which is also expressive of deep grief. Ganymede is leaning carelessly upon her shoulder and hesitates to take the vase she offers. He already holds the cup which signifies the office he is about to undertake.[21]

The clay model of *Hebe and Ganymede* was very far advanced in 1842. It had been praised by Thorwaldsen and others in Rome and it soon found a purchaser, Charles C. Perkins of Boston. Crawford sped its execution in a few months despite his shortage of cash for

Boy Playing Marbles 1853, marble, 27¾" high, 30¹⁵⁄₁₆" wide
Courtesy of the Worcester Art Museum

outlay on the marble block and the cutters. It was eventually bequeathed by Perkins to the Boston Athenaeum.

Work was literally pouring into his studio now. A fellow artist, Thomas Hicks, reported, "In 1843, his studio was crowded with original works and had become one of the centers of attraction of strangers visiting the studios of Rome."[22] There was a marble bust of Charles Brooks dispatched to Boston in May of 1843 and Crawford was completing designs for statues of Jefferson and the late Dr. William Ellery Channing, as well as of Washington.

His principal creation that year was an ideal head of *Vesta*, which Hicks reported was replete with "lovely innocence and beauty."[23] *Vesta* was extolled for its "purity of expression." It also received the other trite phrases of the day used in praising a classical figure. Thomas Hicks insisted that the *Vesta* was instrumental in Crawford's marriage. At any rate, the *Vesta* was by all accounts the sensation of that artistic season in Rome and focused public attention on Crawford.

This was the season of Louisa Cutler Ward's arrival on the scene. She had been born in New York on February 25, 1823, the sixth child but second of the "Three Graces of Bond Street," as the daughters of Samuel Ward were called. Ward, a grandson of the colonial governor of Rhode Island and son of the Revolutionary colonel of the same name, was the partner of Nathaniel Prime in the banking firm of Ward and Prime. Louisa was named after one of her mother's sisters. (The elder Louisa had married Matthew Hall McAllister of Savannah.) The young Louisa took after her aunt in both physical beauty and obliging temperament. When she was two her mother died and she was raised by her father until his death in 1839 when she was sixteen. Her uncle John took charge, assisted by her older sister Julia and her brother Sam. Louisa grew into an exceedingly attractive young lady of cultivation and charm.

On April 26, 1843, Louisa's sister Julia married the educator and reformer Dr. Samuel Gridley Howe, a handsome and brilliant friend of Sumner and Greene and a part of their Boston circle. Howe took his bride on a wedding trip to Europe in company with Horace Mann and his bride, Mary Peabody of Salem. Annie, the youngest sister of Julia and Louisa, was taken along to sooth her drooping spirits on account of losing her favorite older sister in marriage. The party traveled not quite "en grand Seigneur" as Julia described it to Louisa, but their grand tour included a multitude of interesting sights and culminated in a season's residence in Rome.[24] Meanwhile at home, Louisa, left in brother Sam's charge, was abandoned by his sudden marriage. It was decided that she should follow her sisters to Rome accompanied by George Washington Greene, her cousin from Rhode Island, who was returning from New York to his diplomatic post in November. Howe had arrived with a letter of introduction to Crawford from Sumner, but it was rendered unnecessary by Greene's arrival. It was inevitable that Crawford and Louisa should meet in the expatriate clique's confined society. They were mutually attracted immediately.

The city of Rome was receptive to artists in spite of what George Hillard described as their "eccentricities and fantasticalities of dress . . . jaunty caps . . . quaint shapes . . . bearded and mustachioed."[25] It was reportedly a city where "the name artist is the best passport to favor and kindness."[26] Crawford was dashingly handsome and tall. He was later described as having "blazing eyes" and chestnut hair.[27] He had a naturally expansive personality and reacted to enjoyment with a ringing boyish laugh. He loved mimicry and gave the impression of fluency in many languages. Although basically abstemious, his cultivated taste led him, when he had the money, to select the finest batiste for his handkerchiefs and to smoke only particular brands of Havana cigars. Moreover, he had always enjoyed the society of women.

Louisa, for her part, was pretty, good natured to compliancy, and the daughter of New York's leading banker, who was said to have "distributed not less than $15,000 to the poor every year."[28] Ward and Prime were reputed to have been two of the richest men in New York. If Crawford was the artist of the season, Louisa was indeed the belle. At seventeen, she had already made her mark socially as "the beautiful Miss Ward."[29] Henry Wadsworth Longfellow, a friend of her brother Sam, readily confessed after a family dinner party, that "the lovely Louisa made an impression on my heart."[30] He was not unique in his reaction to Louisa. During her visit to Mary Ward in Boston in 1842, George Hillard had written Longfellow to say, "The lovely Louisa is here. . . . I have seen her only once at Mrs. Ticknor's and was charmed by her sunny smiles, her dazzling teeth, her gentle voice and thoroughbred manner."[31] Louisa attracted many suitors, most notably John Ward, son of Thomas Ward, the Boston banker, and brother of Mary, who just missed marrying Louisa's twenty-two year old brother Henry because of his untimely death in October of 1840 of typhoid fever.

The brief courtship of Louisa and Thomas coincided with the unsurpassed artistic event of the year, the debut at Boston of the *Orpheus*. The combination of attractions in this comely couple, against the romantic Roman setting, was irresistible. The engagement was announced in the spring, before the family's departure from Rome to return home.

Here was incentive to spur a spirited man. He must now get home as rapidly as possible to claim his bride, overcoming somehow his insufficiency of money to pay the passage. There were also works to complete and new plans for possible commissions. John Parker of Boston ordered a figure and a bas-relief. For the figure Crawford created the *Bride of Abydos*. The bas-relief turned out to be another religious illustration, *Christ Blessing the Little Children*.[32]

The mating mood surely inspired his clay model of *Adam and Eve*. This group was smaller than life size and was not finished in marble for another decade. It was yet another decade before it was exhibited at the Athenaeum. Howe and Perkins admired this group in Crawford's studio early that winter and sent an enthusiastic report of it home to Sumner. Sumner, however, was spending all of his spare time on arrangements for the imminent exhibition of the *Orpheus*.

In June Crawford received the news that some Boston merchants had formed a committee to purchase a statue to adorn a square in their city. If Crawford did not arrive soon, this plum might fall to some lesser artist to the detriment of all concerned. Thomas Ball was competing conspiciously at home and Samuel Howe reported that "Powers is the artist of the day."[33] Howe prodded, "You must do else to open the eyes of the public here."[34]

Crawford was willing, but it was not simple. The various commissions had been a good career opener but had not brought him a cash reserve. His operations were still hand-to-mouth. The *Hebe and Ganymede* stood in the studio unpaid. Charles Perkins had left Rome and Crawford's investment of labor and wages remained tied up in the marble for two years. Other debts were also pressing. Howe had generously advanced him a small sum before he had departed. Crawford had already missed the opening in Boston of the *Orpheus* exhibition, but Sumner had things in hand there. Now there was more than money at stake. Crawford was in love with Louisa, and for the moment, Boston held greater promise of a major public commission than Rome.

He took the bull by the horns. With barely train fare to

Adam and Eve After Their Expulsion
C. 1853, marble, smaller than life-size
Courtesy of the Boston Athenaeum

Paris in hand, Crawford left his affairs in Rome in Greene's charge and started the journey homeward, stopping in Paris and London to make connections and to see the works of art. His constrained circumstances, however, were a constant source of irritation. He buttonholed Charles Perkins on the street in Paris and demanded the $500 owed him on the *Hebe and Ganymede* figures. He considered it an unjustified imposition for him to suffer financial embarrassment while his patron and erstwhile friend pursued the delights of art treasures, broad boulevards, and colorful companions. With "about 10 sous" in his pocket and "any quantity of curses," pride had to be shelved.[35] He needed the money. There were bills left behind in Rome to be paid, and he was determined to get home. He underwent the "excessively disagreeable" experience of extracting the $500 balance from Perkins in $200 installments, then protested bitterly that "some . . . devil seems to be hovering along between me and money. . . . Blasted! It has caused me more inconvenience and trouble of spirit than can ever be relieved."[36]

The incident with Perkins put a pall on Paris. For all the balm of the constant companionship of George Sumner, the society of Francis Lieber, the friendship of Ned Perkins and Mrs. Cleveland, and the optimistic reports from Charles Sumner that "the exhibit at Boston . . . seems to give universal satisfaction." Crawford was "disgusted" with Paris. "It is but a great shop and chest tempered by such confounded noise," he wrote.[37] He would be glad to leave. His real peeve was his slim purse, which exacerbated his apprehension about Louisa and his general reception at home following his protracted absence. He could muse privately, but hardly seriously, upon the alternative of "settling down in America to make money" and forget the fine arts "if for nothing else but to heap disgrace upon our national taste."[38]

New York had been his home, but it was not home any longer when he arrived late that summer of 1844. He had been gone too long. He naturally welcomed his reunion with his mother and sister, but Louisa had changed. Her faith in their love had waned during their separation. According to Julia, she was constitutionally incapable of combating opposition and her Uncle John was definitely opposed to her proposed marriage to Crawford. Uncle John's con-

servatism led him to the conclusion that his precious ward was
headed for disastrous exploitation by an irresponsible adventurer
who smelled fortune and social preferment. Tall and forbidding in
presence, a bachelor himself and one-time president of the New
York Stock Exchange, Uncle John's natural disposition was not
favorable to marriage, especially to a plebian, and his intermittent
attacks of gout did not sweeten his temperament. The official family
recorder, Mary Crawford Fraser, wrote: "The word 'artist' suggested
everything impecunious, unstable, suspicious. . . . [He] entirely
refused his consent to the marriage."[39] Worse luck, Louisa's other
uncles, Richard and William, shared John's view, as did her brothers,
Sam and Francis Morton. They all plumped for Arthur Mills, an
attractive young Englishman who had succumbed to Louisa's charms
during the voyage home. Julia, Howe, and Charles Sumner were
Crawford's only staunch allies. They had witnessed his social and
artistic acceptance in Rome and felt assured of his "genius" and
integrity. Even better, Julia was fond of Crodie, as she called him
affectionately. She wrote Louisa comfortingly, in Crawford's defense:

> My poor Lou, my heart aches for you, and for Uncle too. . . .
> When he learns, as he must one day learn, Crawford's worth, he
> will cease to regret so bitterly that one so precious was committed
> to his care. Crawford should not be irritated at this overweening
> affection. It should make him feel the more responsibility he in-
> curs in taking you from those who love you so much. . . . His love
> for you is too deep for words. God help him [Uncle John]. His life
> of devotion and kindness will express it. . . . I cannot but think
> that you will spare him, as well as yourself, much suffering by a
> speedy termination of the affair. We shall be with you and for
> you, coute qui coute. You tell me to tell you that people like
> Crawford—upon this subject, there is but one voice.—Every one
> likes him.—Every one speaks favorably of him and his *Orpheus*
> more than warmly.[40]

While Louisa was bordering on despair, beset with doubts and a
psychosomatic cough, Crawford sought solace from Julia in Boston.
She gave him a dinner, following which William Felton, George
Ticknor, Samuel Eliot, and others renewed their praises of him publicly. This refurbished acquaintance with Boston society from the
inside would be no detriment to his career.

Encouraged by his acceptance generally, Crawford returned to New York late in October to press his suit with an ardent, even urgent declaration of his love and honorable intentions. Once more Louisa succumbed. She had come of age literally. The family assembled for the wedding. To Julia's discerning eye, Louisa looked wracked by indecision. Worried, she wrote her sister, "Crawford and you both looked so suffering yesterday. [You] looked as if you have been through many troubles. Oh, Wevie, best beloved, do you love him?"[41]

To Crawford she wrote the same day:

> I was much touched by Louisa's sadness yesterday. She seemed quite subdued. She has suffered much. She told me you have been very gentle and patient with her. You will always be so, will you not? Of course, you are assured of her love for you; otherwise, you would not think of marrying her. To me, she seems strangely mournful for a young girl on the eve of a happy marriage. Have you made sure of her heart, Crawford?[42]

Apparently the answer was yes, for the wedding took place soon after, on November 4, 1844. Proudly, Crawford refused to have anything to do with his wife's finances and "never touched a penny of it."[43] Louisa's Uncle John became reconciled to the marriage and continued to manage her money until her brother Sam took over. Her income was forwarded regularly to her at Rome, affording many luxuries for the family. From all accounts, the marriage was "singularly happy."[44]

The Crawfords settled for a while in Sam's country house, Hamilton Grange. This was the former residence of Alexander Hamilton and was located at the upper reaches of New York on Convent Avenue south of 141 Street.

On December 28, Philip Hone presided over a meeting in the Astor House that included in its agenda a discussion of the possibilities of advancing Crawford as a sculptor. There was general agreement regarding his "undoubted talent," coupled with expressions of guilt for having forfeited to the Bostonians the honor of patronizing this native genius. Several suggestions for his employment were offered, the most promising of which was "to raise $10,000 to send Mr. Crawford the sculptor to Kentucky to take a cast of Mr. Clay and to execute a statue in marble of that noble but ill-used patriot" to be erected in the rotunda of the Merchants Exchange or some other suitable place.[45] This project came to naught, but the fact that art had been introduced as a subject of concern of a committee of community-minded businessmen did register a degree of cultural progress in the city. If only the wives had been invited to attend such public meetings in those days, artistic advances might have abounded. Some of the women sought him out anyway. Mary Hone Schermerhorn was one, and another schoolmate of Louisa's led her grandfather, Mathias Bruen, the wealthy China trader, to the studio.

Before their return to Rome and settled family life, the newly-weds visited around a good deal in the States, renewing acquaintances and seeking commissions. There were two extensive visits to Boston as guests of Julia and Samuel Howe, for two weeks before Christmas and again the following May. These visits were festive occasions. Julia had enticed her sister with promises of diversion, writing, "I will give you a dinner party and a grand ball."[46] Encouraged by past acclaim for Crawford's works and fortified by the "delight and pride" of seeing the *Mercury* in Boston, Charles Sumner welcomed Crawford cordially and renewed his promotional efforts.[47] Something ambitious was needed to catch national attention. He caused the sculptor to explore his chances for a possible commission for an equestrian Washington at the nation's capital, where he put him in the hands of Justice Joseph Story.

His small-scale plaster model in hand, Crawford made a quick trip to Washington in late January of 1845 and in mid-February went back several times to Boston, where Louisa was staying with Julia. Sumner coralled Charles Brooks as an ally. Matters proceeded as far as the passage of a resolution in the Joint Committee of the Library "to employ Thomas Crawford to construct an equestrian statue of General Washington in bronze, to be placed on a pedestal of the naval monument at the western front of the Capitol, and appropriating for these the sum of $20,000."[48] The resolution was never reported out of committee. Sumner's interest persisted. The following year, when Robert Winthrop assumed the chairmanship of the Joint Committee on the Library, Sumner approached him promptly on behalf of Crawford's design. These direct attempts failed, but Crawford consoled himself optimistically that "what had been done will pave the way for further advancement."[49]

Other ideas were proposed too. Crawford reported: "Slidell thinks of introducing a bill or resolution to employ both Powers and myself to adorn the remaining bases in front of the Capitol. These . . . are already occupied by the group of Persico [and] Greenough. Yet, I would prefer the Equestrian work . . . facing Pennsylvania Avenue. The situation is such as to enable the statue to be seen from the avenue itself."[50] With Choate, Marsh, and General Dix seconding Slidell's and Sumner's efforts to advance him, Crawford could write reassuringly to Louisa, "All will go well, my precious one." The hotel in Washington, costing three dollars a day for his room, was not to his liking, and he would not linger except in the hopes of attaining success.

Meanwhile, Crawford's *Mercury and Psyche* which had been described as "most exquisite" and a "perfect vision of beauty and delight," were being discriminatingly displayed in Boston at the Parkers'.[51] Julia was discomfited by the rumor that the work cost $5,000. She feared the impression of inflated prices might damage Crawford's potential business. "These foolish, purse proud Parkers," she railed.[52] She was hard put to restore the price to its actual $800 to $1,000 level in the minds of her dollar respecting Boston acquaintances.

Heartening, too, was the admiring reception for his "Little David in marble," which Julia and Howe coveted and aspired to own as soon as they could "save six hundred dollars."[53] This must have been an early study of the subject which inspired elaboration later. The Pickmans asked for a David, which turned into *David Triumphant* when Crawford worked it out the following year in Rome.

Another member of the Boston set, Mrs. Cleveland, was initiated into the Crawford cult and soon owned a work that Julia described as Crawford's "lovely drawing of Ganymede, aside Psyche."[54] Mrs. Cleveland later commissioned a statue, which turned out to be the marble *Christian Pilgrim* of 1847. It was described as a lovely female carrying a bronze cross with an "escallop shell on her shoulder, emblematic of her pilgrimage."[55]

Christian Pilgrim
1847, marble figure
with bronze cross
Courtesy of the
Boston Athenaeum

The reappearance of the Crawfords in Boston gave rise to a general desire within their circle of friends to patronize him. Several busts were commissioned, most notable of which was that of the Honorable Josiah Quincy, who was to retire at seventy-four as president of Harvard after sixteen years' service. A group of under-graduates requested the honor of presenting his bust to their alma mater. President Quincy consented and Crawford commenced the model late in May. He worked daily in a room under the president's study in Cambridge while Louisa and Annie joined Julia at Make-peace, her home in South Boston. Charles Sumner urged the committee of students to commission a full statue but their funds were limited.

The bust was later executed in Rome in gown and cassock, the presidential dress on public occasions. The likeness was sufficient to please. The only reservation deemed significant at the time was "the dingy looking vein on the forehead, which is in the marble."[56] After some mismanagement in its handling permitted it to gather dust in the New York customhouse for a year, it arrived at Harvard on September 28, 1847.

After a pleasant holiday side trip to Niagara, which replaced a southern tour during which they had planned to visit Louisa's aunt, Mrs. Matthew Hall McAllister of Savannah, and a farewell visit with the Howes, the Crawfords set to packing for the long ocean voyage. By the end of July, they had eight enormous cases ready for shipment, three containing clay models for execution in Rome and the others carrying household equipment. The burden of transit was considerably eased by Uncle John's farewell present to Louisa of $500. Joseph Cogswell, family tutor and long-standing friend of the Wards, undertook with Robert Launitz, to superintend and promote Crawford's interests in New York, as Sumner was doing elsewhere.

Louisa was pregnant but well able to withstand the fatigue of moving. They embarked for France August 8, 1845, on the *Argo*. Annie reported that Louisa was surrounded with every conceivable comfort, "fruit, flowers, the nicely arranged stateroom and all the little comforts which friends have had the pleasure to provide."[57] After the sadness of parting from her family, Louisa looked forward to her European experience.

The pair arrived in Paris in mid-September and took an apartment for a month, ostensibly to rest, at No. 10 Rue de la Paix, overlooking Place Vendôme. There was George Sumner "looking smarter than ever" to give them a thorough tour of Paris, commencing with the Louvre; quite a departure for Crawford from his previous benighted state.[58] He enjoyed his improved status and newfound security unself-consciously. The Crawford's journey to Rome continued by private carriage to Chalons, boat to Avignon, public carriage to Marseilles, and steamer to Civita Vecchia. They engaged a private carriage to take them to Rome, where they arrived with maid, dog, and bird early in December. Henceforth, Crawford was liberated from the pressures of financial threats and could concentrate on his creative work.

Louisa's very nature helped too. "Young and painfully shy," she could not cope advantageously with Roman society.[59] Unable to accept the socially inferior position Rome's snobbish aristocrats would relegate to her, she simply withdrew into the snug preserve of home. At the turn of the year the birth of their first child, Annie, after fifty-two hours of labor attended only by a midwife, reinforced her domestic proclivity. She read avidly, studied languages, played the piano, sewed a good deal, and made few friends outside their artistic circle. Consequently, few diversions arose in their family life to interrupt Crawford's serene routine of work. He was not dragged about endlessly in society. Besides, their drawing room was sumptuous, hung with choice works of art, lit and warmed by a wood fire that was flanked by cats and a large black dog named Cato. Their hearth became the center for the "kind and agreeable society," that characterized their steadily growing group of intimates.[60]

Thomas Hicks was conspicuously prominent among their friends. Crawford was among the first to call on him in welcome upon arriving in October 1845. His friendship did not entirely compensate for their loss of Greene, who fled to Paris in December to evade impertinent but insistent creditors. The James Freemans remained and John Kensett, Christopher Pearse Cranch, George Loring Brown, Henry Kirke-Brown, Thomas Buchanan Read, Jaspar Francis Cropsey, and William Wetmore Story swelled the ranks of the American artists in Rome in the mid-forties. George W. Curtis, the poet, friend and traveling companion of the Cranches, was a constant evening visitor, as were Thomas Hicks, Luther Terry, George Stillman Hillard, Franklin Dexter, Charles C. Perkins, and William Wetmore Story. Hillard proclaimed his gratitude to the Crawfords for their cordial hospitality by dedicating his travel account of Italy to them. He remarked that "toward his brother artists, [Crawford] always turned a countenance of friendliness and sympathy."[61]

Charles C. Perkins, according to Christopher Cranch, "turned his wealth to good account" when he opened his house to five of his artist friends so they could draw from the nude as at an academy.[62] Perkins assisted these friends more substantively by commissions. Despite his cavalier treatment of Crawford in paying for the *Hebe* and *Ganymede* figures he had ordered, he eventually met his obligation and maintained the friendship. They shared a reverence for art and love of music. Perkins went daily to his studio to work at musical composition. Both of them gave occasional musical soirées, presenting choice programs of German music. There were frequent less formal gatherings at Thomas Hicks'. Thanksgiving dinner of 1846 was held at Luther Terry's, and the New Year was celebrated with a notable full dress party at the Crawfords, featuring a fine supper and "Mr. Solyman play[ing] the piano."[63] The Story's entered the group heartily, entertaining constantly. Besides enjoying the warmth exuding from the married set, they all resorted to the conversational coffee meetings at Caffè Greco or Caffè Nuovo; while, for those without menage, there remained the Lepre for dinners at five.

Only a year after her installation in Roman residence, Louisa was observed to call on Mrs. Cranch. "In her carriage, attended by baby, nurse, and all the accessories of a grand lady, [Louisa] invited [her] to ride with her to St. Peter's."[64] Louisa adjusted to her family's requirements and Crawford's needs and gave a warm reception to their acquaintances and friends. Crawford easily overreached her. His work and intellectual curiosity externalized his outlook. Having learned to speak Italian perfectly, he could communicate with ease. He directed the workmen in his studio and soon acquired a large group of Italian acquaintances too. He had learned German early also, while still in Thorwaldsen's studio, and kept up with the German artists, eventually gaining membership in the Deutscher Kunstler Verein, the German artists club in Rome.

After quickly expediting the bust commissions undertaken upon leaving the States for Mrs. Charles Perkins, Leverett Saltonstall, and the one of President Quincy, Crawford set to creating a bust of his wife in her bridal dress. Launitz provided the pedestal for this, as for the others, when it was placed in New York. It was said by contemporaries to epitomize "intellectuality, dignity, and womanly

sweetness," with the effect on the whole, being "classical, preserving
. . . in almost faultless symmetry the minutest individuality of
character."[65] The laces and flowers "in their ornate and delicate
tracery," were reported to enhance "the imposing perfection of the
work."[66] The bust was highly prized in the family for its faithful
likeness and satin-like finish. In 1848, it was shown, with a railing
around for protection, as *Portrait of a Lady* in the spring exhibition
of the National Academy of Design. For a long while, it belonged
to Louisa's uncle, John Ward, but it is now owned by a descendant
of Louisa who has loaned it permanently to the Museum of the City
of New York.

During this early period of domestic life, Crawford started
several of his major works, outstanding among which was his

Louisa Ward Crawford
1846, marble, larger than life-size
Courtesy of Lawrence Terry;
photograph courtesy of the
Museum of the City of New York

Beethoven. It was not surprising that he should select this giant among German romantic composers as a subject for study during that time of his abundant exposure to live music. Crawford didn't get beyond initial sketches that season of 1847. The statue was eventually completed for the Bavarian ruler of Munich in whose brass foundry it was cast and for the Boston Music Hall. Crawford's *Adam and Eve,* modeled prior to his visit home, came in for adulatory attention in his studio at this time, even if it found no ready purchasers. It was almost acquired by Franklin Dexter, but was given up on reflection. Dexter had considered separating the figures as complete drawing room pieces, but rejected the notion that Adam standing alone could be decorative. The idea for Crawford's later representation of *Peri* was born then as was the concept of the *Babes in the Wood.* Crawford executed some bas-reliefs for Launitz and struggled despairingly over a design for a statue of Washington Allston. Much earlier Allston had hailed Crawford as a potential genius. He repeated this to Sumner during the last two visits Sumner had with the aging painter. Sumner readily assented and wrote of these conversations to Crawford by way of encouragement. Upon learning of Allston's death, Crawford wanted to express his esteem of his preceptor and to memorialize him, but an appropriate composition eluded him. He discarded one sketch after another, and lamented the effort in a letter to his brother-in-law Samuel Gridley Howe. "I am doing nothing here but unnecessarily bothering myself with a design of a statute of Allston. I say unnecesarily because I am sure it will sink into the river of forgetfulness, where so many of my sketches have gone already."[67]

Alongside the *Christian Pilgrim,* which was processed in marble for Mrs. Cleveland, Crawford completed the models for two other life-sized female figures. One was the daughter of Herodias, holding the head of Saint John under her arm. Friends thought it was "very beautiful."[68] For this work in marble, Crawford was now asking $2,000, as a "very low price,"[69] a one hundred percent increase over the usual price he had commanded before his marriage.

The other figure was a typical Victorian piece entitled *Dying Mexican Princess.* The subject probably derives from an incident in Prescott's *History of the Conquest of Mexico* that fascinated the

Dying Mexican Princess 1848, marble, 58½″
The Metropolitan Museum of Art, gift of Mrs. Annette W. W. Hicks-Lord, 1897

sculptor, although he changed the story in his representation. His statue was probably a portrait of Marianne, the Mexican friend of Cortez. Prescott described Marianne as a Mexican slave who died of old age in Mexico City, but Crawford rendered her more romantically —as a recumbent young beauty dressed in Indian skirt and headdress with her head thrown back as if she were dying. The New World subject did not deflect the sculptor from his Old World style, which in this case resembles the Greco-Roman dead Amazon in the Royal Bourbon Museum in Naples.

Having his material selected for illustration apparently flattered Prescott and he explored the possibility of owning a work of Crawford's himself. His bid was advanced too late though. In 1852, Crawford's prices had climbed beyond his reach.[70] The *Dying Mexican Princess* was purchased by Hicks of New York, who had previously acquired the *Genius of Mirth*.[71] Julia had seen the *Dying Mexican Princess* in progress and had admired it. In the summer of 1847 she wrote Louisa to suggest that Crawford make a bust of the statue for separate sale as Powers was doing with his *Eve* and *Slave*.

In the midst of this steady stream of production, the second Crawford child, Jenny, was born on November 20, 1847. The growing family spent the hot months of 1846 at Frascati, within hailing distance of Rome and the studio. Afterwards they moved into larger

and more lavish apartments on the Corso near the Piazza del Popolo. Crawford reported that they were charmingly situated. In July of the following year, Julia wrote with delight to Louisa that "the papers [report] Crodie . . . in Venice."[72] He probably stopped there for an exploratory visit on his way to Munich, where he went to inspect the brass foundry to determine the quality of casting for the large public statues he was planning.

The spring of 1848 brought Republican upheaval to Rome as to the rest of western Europe. The surge of republican revolution swept forward more dramatically in Rome than in Florence. Crawford had too active a personality to remain a passive witness. With characteristic zest, he participated. Years later, his daughter vividly recalled the episode.

> I am sorry to say that my dear parents . . . had distinctly republican tendencies, and I was brought up to think it quite an heroic act in my father to join the Civic Guard a little later, when Europe had undertaken to reinstate the Pontiff on his throne, and General Oudinot was beseiging Rome with that object. . . . A big sword, a brass helmet and a beautiful crimson sash, the souvenirs of my father's short service, had a cherished place among our playthings; and when our mother used to tell us of her terrible anxiety when "Papa" was helping to defend the city walls, my heart beat fiercely in unison with all things free and republican.[73]

Crawford took his Guard duties seriously, serving twenty-four hour shifts when necessary. The entire American group favored the short-lived republic that was organized by Mazzini. The United States minister, Lewis Cass, Jr., had difficulty retaining the official stance of neutrality imposed by his directives from Washington. His own liberalism and his friendships among his engaged compatriots embroiled him in a variety of helpful acts.

Crawford's Guard duty brought him into sympathetic rapport with Margaret Fuller and Princess Christina di Belgioioso, both of whom had to flee before the victorious French "liberators" under General Oudinot. They had already been introduced by Julia, who subsequently wrote a biography of Margaret Fuller. Pio Nono's liberalism had been toasted by Samuel Howe and his dinner guests as far afield as Boston only a year before. In the interim, Pope Pius

IX betrayed the liberal cause. Lewis Cass, Jr., reported to Margaret Fuller "that [the Pope] has seen enough of the consequences of liberal concessions. . . . It is evident from all the acts of the agents of the French Government that it will neither recognize a Roman republic, nor tolerate the presence of any other foreigners who have crowded to Rome . . . who have fled hither from other revolutionary conflicts."[74] Nor was the Pope favorably disposed in any way to the adoption of a constitution. As he retrieved his throne of the Papal States, it was said within the American circle that the calendar of liberty was set back. Rome continued in a "frightful state" all that winter, with "no commerce, no credit, no confidence owing to the posture of public affairs," Cass reported to Margaret Fuller, who had taken refuge at Rieti in the Abruzzi hills.[75] By February 1850, however, Cass wrote, "Rome [had] subsided into its usual tranquility . . . interrupted by collisions between the people and the French soldiers, and by the proscriptive course of the Government, which [was] hunting out with fiendish ferocity, every individual who [was] tainted with republicanism." The American minister concluded his account grimly. "They might as well undertake to exhaust the ocean by draining as to eradicate this spirit," he wrote. "Rome is no longer the Rome it was and the condition of things at times has made me inexpressibly sad and melancholy."[76]

Here was a disheartening state of affairs for a militant republican who had risked fire on the city walls. For all the protection that his foreign passport could offer, life in Rome would inevitably be uncomfortable under these circumstances. Nor was it likely that Rome would be overrun with art-hungry tourists that season. It was a propitious time for another visit home. The Crawfords made the decision swiftly. Number 8 Bond Street was large and empty, ready to receive them. They were ensconced in New York by May 1849.

18

Equestrian Washington

CRAWFORD FOUND A WARMHEARTED WELCOME AWAITING HIM AT home from Charles Sumner and his Boston set. Promising, too, was the public notice of a unique bequest in Philadelphia. A man named Burd had commissioned a monument of Crawford in memory of his two daughters who had died. Not having specified the exact place of the monument in the confirming letter that Burd had sent Crawford in care of his sister-in-law, Annie Ward Maillard, at her home in Bordentown, New Jersey, Crawford now surmised, in writing to Captain Meigs, that "it was probably the one presently under discussion for erection in Saint Stephens Church, Philadelphia."[1] Meanwhile Mr. Burd had also died, leaving $10,000 to be dispensed by his widow for the monument. The account in the bulletin of the Art Union mentioned Crawford as having been selected for the design. As he had not yet received the letter that Burd had sent to Bordentown for him, Crawford thought it strange that he had received "no communication whatever" in the matter.[2] He hurried to Philadelphia directly after Christmas 1849 to see Mrs. Burd and discover the cause of her silence.

On the scene, he detected what he reported to Captain Meigs as "very slippery proceedings."[3] From what he could make out with the help of Mr. Burd's executors, these "slippery proceedings" were in essence a plot hatched by two bon vivants, Ducachet and Hagerstown, abetted by a fellow vestryman of the church named Price, all three proceeding apparently with the complicity of Mrs. Burd. As Crawford narrated the tale to Louisa, "A learned meeting of the vestry of St. Stephens, giving only 24 hours' notice, had Mr. Burd's proposal to place the monument in the church submitted for their approval—Price made an effort to stop this proceeding by a request that the entire number of designs should be seen by them before coming to a conclusion. He has met with the answer that they were only called upon by Mr. Burd to examine the one paid by him and they considered their duty finished and approved of it. Now who did all this?"[4]

It's no small wonder that Crawford concluded that he had "small faith in the coming events."[5] As he saw it, Mr. Burd had committed himself to Crawford in writing for $10,000 in payment of the work he had ordered. The obligation was recognized in the bequest. Now, Mrs. Burd was obviously countermanding the terms of her husband's will. She took this matter out of the hands of the executors with whom Crawford had been dealing. Before Crawford could explore the avenues of recourse and weigh the consequences of possible legal proceedings, his attention was diverted by the imminent promise of a far grander project that had long simmered, that of an equestrian Washington.

Only a few months after he arrived in the States, Crawford read in the newspapers the advertisement of a competition for such a monument for the state capitol at Richmond, Virginia, offering a $500 prize for the best design. Pressed by a petition submitted by the Virginia Historical Society, the legislature on February 22, 1849, had passed a bill providing for the creation of a Washington monument on Capitol Square. It was accompanied by a proviso stating that when the $40,000 already available was expended, additional funds up to $100,000 should be appropriated. They had come by the initial sum interestingly.

The project was originally broached in 1784 but didn't get beyond the passage of a resolution at that time. A few years later, a statue representing Washington in the dual roles of warrior and peaceful farmer was executed by Jean Antoine Houdon in Paris under the guidance of Thomas Jefferson. This statue was subsequently placed in the state capitol. Not long after Washington's death in

1799, John Marshall proposed a resolution to erect a monument to commemorate Washington's life and victories. In 1816, flushed with patriotism from the victory over England, there was a movement in the Virginia legislature to remove the remains of Washington and his wife from Mount Vernon to the site of the capitol, over which would be erected a fitting monument. Though permission to shift the remains was denied by Washington's heir, Bushrod Washington, the legislature pursued its intention to create a monument. Resolutions were passed on Washington's anniversary the following two years in response to which thirteen thousand dollars was donated in sums no larger than ten dollars each. In 1828 the legislature voted to invest the principal and by October of 1848, this yielded over $40,000.

On the nineteenth of October 1847, the cornerstone of a monument to Washington was laid in New York City, and Virginia's vanity was piqued. Petitioners of the historical society cleverly prodded the legislators with the reminder that "state pride is a great friend of state rights" and suggested that a committee of five be appointed to initiate the creation of a surpassing monument before the approaching 22 of February.[6] The committee would further be charged with supervision of its erection. The petitioners requested that money not be spared to realize a monument grander in conception and scale than the various rival projects afoot in other cities. Governor John B. Floyd convened a meeting in his office on October 16, 1849, of the five commissioners he had appointed to chart their course. The result was the competition that Crawford entered.

Of the seventy designs submitted, sixty-four in Crawford's opinion consisted of "an enormous number of Pagodas, Columns, arches, obelisks . . . a mass of absurdity."[7] According to Crawford, the competition called forth "the vasty nothing in the brains of our architects" that demonstrated their artistic regression for not transcending the obsolete fashion initiated by the obelisk of the Bunker Hill Monument.[8] Horatio Greenough, whose design of an obelisk for this monument had been passed over in favor of a larger obelisk, had thought the concept appropriate in that case, as it called attention sharply to the historic spot that sparked the Revolutionary War; it said clearly, "Here it is." Now Crawford wrote Sumner denigrating the profusion of obelisks and columns to memorialize national heroes or events. "I doubt exceedingly," he said, "if overgrown obelisks and ungrown columns are to prevail over intellectuality and good sense much longer in the United States."[9]

The committee began studying the submitted designs on January 8, 1850, and continued at intervals until February first. Crawford settled into the American Hotel in Richmond and politicked his cause. He wrote Louisa that he dined with Conway Robinson, one of the commissioners to whom he had been introduced by Sumner. Present also at the dinner were the governor and "Mr. Giles, one of the Commissioners, a gentleman of the first quality."[10] Discouraged, Crawford returned to his hotel and told Louisa, "My fears are mastering my hopes. The governor has not, I fancy, deep sympathy with artists."[11]

In this despondent mood, he attended a meeting of the Virginia Historical Society at the capitol to hear an address by Mr. Houghton, recounting his European experience in terms that Crawford branded as "banal" and valued as "nonsense." "In his view," reported Crawford, "Brunelleschi's Dome, Michelangelo's Medicean Chapel, the Tribune were as nothing compared to the studio of Powers whose divine fancy has created the *Eve*, the *Slave*. . ."[12] Crawford marveled at this "impudent attempt to force the *divine fancy* of Mr. Powers upon the American public."[13] He derided the "blind patriotism of the American population" that could accept "the insipidity of the *Eve, Slave, Fisher Boy* as works of art and foist on their creator the reputation of a 'modern Phidias.' "[14] Crawford disposed of Powers privately as "lamentably deficient."[15]

Marking time in the vicinity of the commissioners, Crawford became restive. He sincerely thought his "designs look very beautiful upon paper . . . and the model looks very beautiful and gives them a clear idea of what the work will be [when] executed. . . . I do not think the Angel of Light would make the matter clearer," he said.[16] Of a sudden, it seemed "dark, dreary, and lonely in Richmond," he wrote Louisa. "There is a good time coming," he added ruefully, reaching for the patience to sustain his waiting for the verdict of the commissioners. He conjured a nostalgic vision of the lovelier life he and Louisa had known in Rome. "Roma, Roma with the blossoms and the rose in the sunshine and the fountains and the ruins and the solitude, there is to be found the true balm of Gilead for the crushed hope."[17]

Not wishing "to appear in the character of a hanger-on," and leaving his address with Giles, Crawford chose to employ his time more usefully in a side trip to Washington. There he would petition the congressional Joint Committee on the Library for a commission. He traversed the hundred twenty-one miles in nine hours, a fast run in those days. His connections in Washington, based on his coterie of Boston friends, were excellent. For added power, George Ticknor sent him "the kindest note in the world . . . enclosing an introduction to Webster."[18] He dined promptly with "other gentlemen digs."[19] He got around swiftly among his social acquaintances; seeing General Totten and his wife and daughter, family friends who would visit in Bordentown that spring, General John Dix, Colonel Halsey, and Dudley D. Field (counsel in New York for Jay Gould and James Fisk) and Mrs. Field. James King of New York, an acquaintance from Newport, was also there, as were Professor Joseph Henry, a physicist from Princeton presently engaged in architecture and director of the Smithsonian Institution, and others. On the nineteenth, Crawford went to the White House with the mathematician and astronomer stationed at the Naval Observatory, Dr. Joseph Stillman Hubbard. He reported to Louisa that he "had the pleasure of seeing the President and shaking hands with him of course. . . . Mr. King recognized me at this reception and appeared very friendly."[20]

Despite the personal glamor, Washington appeared to him a "contemptible city," a "hot-bed of hypocrisy and double-dealing," filled with "rascally politicians, dirty waiters, abominable tea, and tallow candles at sputtering dinners trying for the eyes."[21] Crawford decided that the Smithsonian Institution looked "precisely like an ambitious railroad station . . . [a] mass of red stones . . . like a gigantic round of overcooked beef that has been well hacked with a dull carving knife." Amid "the same unmeaning jumble of buildings" that they had seen five years before, there still stood the Capitol's dome resembling a "mustard pot."[22] Although he had the active support of a significant congressional contingent including among others Choate, Marsh, Slidell, Cooper, Webster, and Sumner, Crawford still feared that the economy-minded politicians, each believing himself "quite capable of deciding the merits of any design," would behave antipathetically toward continued art patronage.[23] A negative reaction seemed likely after Greenough's failure at the Capitol and Powers' "extraordinary capacity for disquieting men who are seeking to encourage the arts."[24] Powers' controversy with the New Orleans banker, James Robb, and with Captain M. C. Meigs was then raging. Crawford wrote Louisa that Powers' "contest with Mr. Robb . . . has prevented that gentleman from giving any more orders to our sculptors. . . . He had intended to do so but his experience . . . has been of such a disagreeable nature."[25] Crawford kept his opinions private for fear of giving the legislators the impression that he was as contentious as Powers. This would merely strengthen their natural inclination to avoid controversy and reduce the likelihood of their moving ahead with a public commission.

While waiting in the National Hotel to present his petition, he was spending the "mountainous" sum of twenty-three dollars a week for his room, board, and laundry, with an occasional extra item of two dollars for a decanter of sherry when he felt obliged to repay the hospitality that was liberally bestowed on him. He sought a commission for a group, preferably an equestrian Washington, and presented sketches of his work as proof of his capability, feeling assured that "this is more than Greenough and Powers can show united."[26]

He conversed at length with Montgomery Cunningham Meigs, captain of engineers in charge of the Capitol extension at Washington, who was delegated by the secretary of war, acting for the president, to select plans and artists for the construction and adornment of the new wings to be built. Since the extensions had not been built, the time of decision for these embellishments was still distant.

Thinking that his chief handicap might emanate from "the editors in half the papers and people [who] know nothing about my work," Crawford sought publicity avidly.[27] He also hoped publicity would help to counter any rival schemes. Sumner, Hillard, Henry T. Tuckerman, and Cornelius Felton were solicited to instigate some northern press support. The original date of Crawford's presentation of his project to the Library Committee was set for Thursday morning, January 24, but it was postponed by Henry Clay's "resolution to purchase the manuscript of Washington's Farewell Address," which engendered considerable discussion.[28] He made his presentation on the twenty-eighth of January and was followed by an excellent supportive speech by the Whig Senator from Pennsylvania, James Cooper, a member of the Committee. Now Crawford's proposal would be printed in full and gain national distribution.

Two days later Crawford received word from the commissioners in Richmond requesting his immediate presence. "They have reduced the number of plans to six and wish to consult with me regarding my own. They wish to prepare for laying the cornerstone by the twenty-second of February," he disclosed to Louisia.[29] He hastened to Richmond the next morning and went directly before the commissioners, who wanted to know "if it would be possible to construct a room in the Monument to contain the Archives or rather all the papers in relation to the monument . . . then a stair to reach the top . . . entry height should be 60 feet" [instead of the 50 feet originally proposed].[30] To these trivial details, Crawford readily assented. On a motion of Mr. Ritchie, editor of the *Richmond Enquirer*, Crawford's equestrian statue was selected that afternoon. Ritchie lost no time in conveying the news personally to Crawford in his hotel. Crawford wrote Louisa enthusiastically, "The sun shines at last, dear Lou! I have beat them all and the monument is mine! I have at last been permitted to realize all my aesthetic dreams and have received a work that any artist might be proud to have the honour of executing. My position in art is now defined."[31]

Sumner shared his friend's joy and estimate. "This engagement will advertise you to the whole country," he said in his congratulatory note.[32] To his brother George he expanded, "This order definitely fixes Crawford's position in art. He has become uneasy, fretful, discontented, irresolute, and almost Ishmaelitish. He seemed to feel that he had been neglected and was soured. All will be changed now."[33] He took the occasion to write a blurb announcing the award in the *Boston Transcript* of February 11, 1850. Sumner was triumphant. His judgment on art in general and his selection of this particular talent were now vindicated. His prophecy made in Rome at the nadir of Crawford's career, that the sculptor would one day attain national, perhaps international fame, and inhabit a palace, was now fortified.

The *Enquirer* in Richmond broadcast the news in a "highly complimentary manner."[34] The Virginia Legislature endorsed the commission's award on the fifth of February, followed by Governor John B. Floyd's official approval on the eighth. Still Crawford discovered a "contemptible proceeding now got up with a view to thrust [him] out and . . . let in mediocrity . . . from an artist rejected, of course."[35] It was a campaign bearing the "meanest insinuations," against the imposter from the north and more lately, from overseas. The southern legislators were implored to be "chivalrous" and favor a southerner against the alien intruder.[36] The culprit was probably Robert Mills, the state's architect, whose design was rejected. Mills was apparently doubly irked at being forced, by virtue of his official position, to approve Crawford's design on March 4. He harbored reservations towards it and never ceased his efforts to subvert Crawford's work. For his part, Crawford scorned Mills' design, "Column of the Revolution," mercilessly as "the bastard Column, pretentiously entitled."[37]

Crawford was disappointed to be deprived of the $500 prize money that had been offered the winner. The commissioners deftly included the sum in their payment on the commission and Crawford felt too insecure to object. He was forced to ask his wife to send him fifty dollars to carry on through the twenty-second as he felt obliged to attend the ceremony of laying the cornerstone. Even the modest hotel bill of three dollars a day at the American multiplied in time. After the fifty dollars arrived, his tensions eased and he could cheer Louisa once more. "I ought to have $10,000 placed at my disposal when we start for Europe," he wrote.[38]

He asked Louisa also to relay the news of his commission among her acquaintances to stimulate potential business elsewhere. He suggested that their old friend, Joseph Cogswell, well acquainted with the editor of the *Art Journal* of London, "ought to be asked to forward a copy of the article in the Richmond Enquirer . . . as well to Philadelphia, Boston, Washington, and New York."[39] His apprehensions should have been allayed by his wife's reassurances that "many congratulations from every quarter" have been pouring in at home.[40]

Crawford had pondered the conception of a Washington equestrian statue for almost a decade and had received distinct approval in Rome for his second design. That study was an almost exclusively classical interpretation. Although Washington, mounted on his horse atop a plinth, was wrapped in a contemporary cloak, the four subordinate figures to be placed in the corners at his feet, were allegorical Greek goddesses representing Abundance (agricultural), Commerce, Victory, and Peace. Crawford envisaged differentiating them by means of the various conventional classical accouterments he assigned them. He described his design thoroughly to George Washington Greene, writing that he had the statue of Abundance "richly draped in obedience to the best examples given us by the Greek artists." Abundance was to have a "cornucopia and a wheat sheaf." The allegorical female figure was to be draped lightly above, "while the lower half . . . [would be] enveloped in drapery of a heavy and warm texture . . . to signify the two great divisions of the year —summer and winter." The face was to be turned upward as if it were watching the course of "the sun whose influence is of so much importance to the agriculturalist."

Crawford wrote that Commerce was to have a globe to indicate "the four divisions of the earth and the seas." He expounded, "She is studying the point which connects America with Europe [and] . . . explains that the commerce of America is universal and spread over the whole earth . . . her dress . . . 'tis modelled in imitation of the drapery given to sea goddesses. . . ."

The Victory and Peace figures were designed to express contrast. Victory, with a protective shield by her side, was to hold a wreath to be used as a crown for the "triumphant defender and not for the aggressor." Peace was to be seated, with an olive branch beside her and her head "wreathed with olive," while she destroyed with a burning torch symbols of war, "shields, swords, and spears," that lay at her feet.

Bas-reliefs would connect these statues, which would be placed below the raised equestrian Washington. The frontal subject be-

tween those of Abundance and Commerce would depict "the surrender of Lord Cornwallis to General Washington at Yorktown,"
representing the "point in our history, the prosperity of America
must date its commencement." This prosperity was to be represented as deriving from agriculture and commercial navigation. The
second bas-relief to go between the figures of *Victory* and *Peace*
would portray "Washington's appointment as Commander-in-Chief
of the American armies." Both reliefs would have "the Eagle of
America holding in its claws a few broken chains to express the
liberation of the country from bondage."[41]

The Virginia commissioners were historically minded. They
vetoed the classical figures and designated that there be only one
allegorical figure, one that would characterize the state of Virginia.
Six statues were now projected. For the other five subordinate figures they substituted full-sized portraits of the state's historical
heroes. They tentatively selected Thomas Jefferson, Patrick Henry,
John Marshall, General Daniel Morgan, and General Henry Lee.
They specified that the Washington figure atop the plinth be shown
in contemporary dress with the face modeled after Houdon's portrait in the Capitol, in the general belief that it was "the only correct
representation . . . that a true conception of the actual appearance
of the Washington might [thus] be universally gained."[42] The commissioners further stipulated that "the group . . . be enriched by the
proper introduction of Gold on such parts of the costume as may
require it" and the whole be embellished by two shields. The shields
were to show the Great Seal of the Commonwealth with wreaths
of laurel and oak leaves and thirteen stars. The equestrian group was
to measure not less than fifteen English feet in height, and the
pedestrian figures not less than ten, "to be taken from the best likeness[es] to be obtained," while the costumes were to be "in the dress
which was most commonly worn by each in the performance of
his public duties."[43]

Crawford was rooted in Richmond to attend the cornerstone
laying ceremony on February 22. Despite his boredom, he could
hardly rush off to Washington to accept the invitation he received
to go to the Masonic Ball honoring the president. He was featured
as the star of the cornerstone laying ceremony in Richmond. He

wrote Louisa that on the occasion he found himself "shaking hands with little children as the parade stopped at various places on the road" and thinking sentimental "thoughts of my own pretty babes at home." The grand ball that climaxed the ceremonial celebration in the evening was comparable to "icing on a tall wedding cake, elegant and very pleasant."[44]

Crawford appreciated his triumphant role in the lustrous fete, but, as he wrote Louisa, his ebullience waned overnight and he was all set "to proceed with the necessary drawings." He stated, "It will be 8 months before I can commence the models! During the next three months I shall be very laboriously employed in correcting and also perfecting my model [of the horse]."[45] He recapitulated the tasks in store as guidance for Louisa in her schedule for their sailing to Europe. He was further obliged to devise detailed architectural plans for the entire monument and collect materials for the portraiture and costumes of the statues. Information about the lives, interests, and accomplishments of his subjects would serve pertinently too. He wanted to leave a handsome oil painting of the monument with the finished plans as a gift in the governor's office to advertise the work and would ship the model to his studio in Rome. He would have liked also to sell lithographs of the painting to defray running expenses, but time limitations prevented these promotional schemes from materializing.

His first move was to go to Washington to begin collecting his materials. He arrived at the capital in time to catch Daniel Webster's historic "Ides of March" speech in the Senate, urging the Great Compromise. Finding that "the absorbing question of north and south demands the extreme attention of Congress," he reduced his hope for the present "to get a favorable report from the Library Committee and have it before the Senate," postponing further pressures for a commission until his return in May.[46] He did not prolong his stay to learn the committee's verdict on his petition. He lingered only long enough to have one more satisfactory talk with Senator James Cooper, who assured him of having "the subject at heart" to pursue with assurance a favorable outcome of Crawford's petition. Confident that "it could not be in better hands," he packed off for a day in Philadelphia on March 14 before joining his family at the

Maillards in Bordentown.[47] After two months' absence from home, he was impatient to be reunited with his wife and children. He had accomplished quite enough business on this trip to Richmond and Washington.

He did not stay long either at Bordentown, at 8 Bond Street, or at Boston, driven to obtain two essentials that he lacked before he could return to Rome: the background materials for the monument and the contract itself with the $10,000 cash payment that was to accompany the signatures.

Despite a threatening heat wave, Crawford was southward bound early in June. He stopped for several days each in Philadelphia and Baltimore and then proceeded to Washington to see Robert Mills, who promised to join him in Richmond. Crawford wired Governor Floyd requesting a brief audience of some twenty minutes to review some minuscule details that only Crawford could clarify. The commissioners and the governor with whom he negotiated were, after all, ignorant of the elements of production of a bronze monument. On the seventeenth, he submitted his first draft to the governor. He hoped for an immediate decision, but he had to mark time once more until the governor returned from a seaside holiday at Point Beaufort.

The heat in Richmond was oppressive, far beyond anything that Crawford had experienced in Rome. "Everybody carries an umbrella to get a little shade," he noted.[48] He managed to dine with General Henry Lee's son, Richard Carter Lee, who provided him with a likeness of his father for reproduction in one of the pedestrian statues. He ran into an old acquaintance, Thomas Preston, a cousin of the governor, who helped him to acquire additional materials on Jefferson and General Lee. To Louisa, Crawford wrote, "My present plans are to get away from this place as fast as I can and return to New York—stop just long enough in Washington . . . spend a day in Philadelphia . . . New York and then away to Boston."[49] He still meant to sail from New York on the steamer of July twentieth, but could not commit himself positively to the deadline by allowing Louisa to confirm their steamer reservations.

The contract was signed by Governor John B. Floyd and Thomas Crawford in Richmond on June 27. It provided for a payment of $30,000 for the equestrian Washington and itemized $9,000 each for the six pedestrian figures. Only two of these were definitely fixed, those of Thomas Jefferson and Patrick Henry. Because of uncertainty, the others were omitted. Several changes occurred in their selection before the final choice was determined. Crawford would be paid $2,000 for each of the two shields and $975 for the thirteen wreaths and thirteen stars. The total sum amounted to $52,975, aside from the costs of casting, transportation, and insurance for which the state would reimburse the artist. The sums were specified to be paid in installments at various stages of execution, upon certification by the U.S. Consul. Crawford committed himself to the group's completion on or before the twenty-second day of February 1856, and to oversee its shipment to Richmond. In the event of his earlier demise, the models would revert to the Commonwealth of Virginia, whose governor would appoint a successor to carry on. Should the sculptor live on, he would retain the models.

With the signed contract in hand, there was nothing further to detain Crawford in the States. He had work enough on the Washington monument to fill several busy years, and whatever political conditions happened to prevail in Rome, the skilled workmen were still there. In precisely eighteen months' time, he must have ready two of the pedestrian statues and both shields, besides completing the innumerable portraits and other statues he had undertaken.

The family, too, was ready for Rome. Following a long summer's visit at Bordentown with Annie, whose generous hospitality was abetted by her likable husband, Alphonse Maillard, a grandson of Joseph Bonaparte, Louisa and her two little girls had been staying at Green Peace with the Howes. Julia fretted considerably that their social life did not equal her sister's rich Roman experience. On the defensive, she explained that the Boston season rarely got going before January. She determined doggedly that Louisa would yet "see something of Boston society" before she left. In addition to the "pleasant dinner at Ned Perkins'," she promised that "next week, there will be a large party at Mrs. Appleton's."[50] If quantity was lacking, at least the quality of their social connections was maintained. Despite these efforts, Julia was self-conscious about the "gloomy and unsocial atmosphere of her home," which she felt more keenly in the presence of Louisa who was the prototype of sociability.[51] Julia wrote Annie that on one train trip from Boston to New York, Louisa had known seven of the ten passengers aboard. Acquaintances and friends alike readily acknowledged her radiant charm and graciousness.

Exacerbating Julia's discomfort was the development of discord between the sisters over their children's unbringing. Julia found Louisa's girls "very violent" and was relieved to have found a "pleasant little school" in which to deposit them for several hours during the day.[52] Puritanical New England and Samuel Howe had conditioned Julia to a regime of discipline, while the permissive tolerance of Rome reinforced Louisa's natural easy nature. Living under the same roof became impossible. After Christmas Louisa retired with her girls to the family house on Bond Street even though her husband's absence deprived her of entertaining socially. Crawford's success in the Richmond competition cheered them all greatly, and it was welcome news that he would be free in July to return to Rome and their own lax routine of living.

"At last, dear Lou," he wrote on July 2, "there appears a proposal of my leaving this bone of a place. . . . I shall take advantage of it immediately. . . . Tonight I received the Bond (contract), transact all necessary business tomorrow and leave by the 4th. I am really anxious to sail on the 20th." He asked if she could be ready with Annie to accompany him to Boston for a farewell visit while the sculpture was being placed upon its bases. "Set the ball rolling," he urged. "I shall be in New York most certainly on Monday afternoon." If accommodations could be procured for passage on the steamer *Washington*, it would not only be fitting symbolically but would enable them to evade the heat of New York in August. With $10,000 in hand, he was heady with the "triumphant results" of his mission. He continued to Louisa, "I give up Mount Vernon and Arlington because my work is of greater importance . . . besides I have all the material. . . . I have a feverish kind of anxiety to be up and doing."[53]

They sailed on July 20 on the *Washington*, thereby meeting Crawford's optimistic schedule. His program called for spending two weeks in London and at least a full month in Paris to obtain models and other materials relative to the horse. He would have liked a "few months some summer to go to Munich to ascertain whether that city should be preferred to Paris for the bronze casting."[54] But that exploratory trip would have to await a freer time. Clearly it could not be made this summer for he wanted to get back to his studio in Rome by October at the latest.[55]

The family settled into Rome more luxuriously than ever. Being naturally addicted to the "old grandeur," and in need of space for the colossal works just commissioned, Crawford took a lifelong lease on the upper portion of Villa Negroni from Prince Massimo who reserved the first floor for his fleeting family visits in the spring and fall. This villa had been built on the upper outskirts of the city centuries ago by Cardinal Contalto, who had reigned five years as Pope Sixtus the Fifth. It had been built by materials filched from the Baths of Diocletian, which it abutted. Years later Mary Crawford Fraser described it: "Its enormous windows command[ed] a view of the entire city below." Its grounds consisted of "old-time gardens and avenues of lordly cypresses, . . . bitter orange-trees, moss-grown fountains, and long walks fragrant with half-wild roses and sweet flowers," extending from Santa Maria Maggiore past "a wild field and broken land" to Piazza dei Termini and beyond to the perimeter of what was then Rome. On moonlit nights, the children could see "a ring of little Campagna foxes drinking silently out of the low marble basin" of the 300 year old fountain.[56]

The villa afforded them huge living quarters but contained only an average studio built in the gatehouse some decades earlier to house the English painter Joseph Severn, a close friend of John Keats. The studio was quite inadequate for Crawford's purposes. Prince Massimo gave Crawford permission to erect a series of large studios on the eastern side of the house, adjacent to the Baths of Diocletian. When all was ready, Crawford resumed his old routine. One visitor in 1851 reported assuringly to the commissioners at Richmond that "Crawford is again at work with all his ardor and enthusiasm and even carries his labors far into the night."[57] For nocturnal work sessions, Crawford created another studio in the tower of the villa, where he could retreat after dinner to ponder his designs.

The household was Louisa's province, for Crawford "made it a principle to leave the entire management of the children to his wife."[58] The arrangement endeared Crawford to his children; not one of them "could remember a word of reproof or a stern look from him."[59] Louisa held Wednesday afternoon receptions that were well attended. In the mornings from eleven o'clock until lunchtime, she held court, paying particular attention to expatriates in need of assistance. She carefully distributed the family's worn clothes, used candles for impecunious students to read by, and books and jellies for invalids.

On April 8, 1851, Mary ("Mimoli"), the third Crawford daughter, was born.[60] Julia, now reconciled with Louisa, was visiting at the time. Due to the baby's arrival and Crawford's pressures of work, there was no family exodus from Rome that summer.

Crawford gave the monument his undivided attention for two years or so. He was plagued intermittently with the threatened and occasionally active interference at home of Robert Mills, who had been charged by Governor Floyd, in response to his own request, with superintending the erection of Crawford's monument. Despite the rejection of his own plan, Mills insistently pressed on Crawford, Governor Floyd, the legislators, the newspapers, and anyone else of influence whom he could reach, his proposal for a "slight modification" of the accepted design to incorporate his "Column." Crawford was polite but forthright with Mills and was obliged to expend much time and energy to combat Mills' subversive campaign. At one time he lectured Mills, "I would recommend less reliance upon the examples of the Greeks, and a more just hope in American Genius."[61] Taking a cue from his Florentine colleague Powers, Crawford understood even better the pragmatic American mind. He and Meigs at Washington were in accord that "while the naked Washington of Greenough [was] the theme of admiration of a few scholars, it [was] unsparingly denounced by the less refined multitude." They agreed that the American mentality was "not able to appreciate too refined and intricate allegorical representations."[62]

Although Crawford never broke entirely with classical aesthetics and techniques, his *Equestrian Washington* was a significant departure in the direction of realistic historical interpretation. He wrote Captain Meigs that he was persuaded of "the necessity of producing a work intelligible to our entire population. The darkness of allegory must give place to common sense."[63] He stated that he hoped his Washington monument would "serve as a practical exponent of [his] desire to illustrate American history without having recourse to sculpture as practiced in the age of Pericles."[64]

While Greenough was theorizing on the subject, Crawford was working out the new approach in his studio. The innovation was beginning to invade Crawford's thinking in the realm of drawing-room statues as well. He confided his changing view to Franklin Dexter, who wrote to inquire whether Crawford would be willing to create a figure or two for William H. Prescott, the historian. In his response Crawford said, "I have myself no great fancy for allegorical statues as pictures."[65] What he meant was that he now felt that portraits ought to be rendered realistically in contemporary dress.

Crawford's shift from the classical idiom for public works was initially imposed by the Virginia commissioners when they rejected his allegorical female statues in favor of commemorating the state's heroes realistically. Now Crawford was becoming enamoured of bronze as a material, especially for works that would be placed outdoors. After sampling various fragments of Virginia's native stone and attesting to several of its merits, Crawford pronounced his judgment to Conway Robinson, the commissioner with whom he kept in touch. He informed him, "I have selected bronze as being in all respects the most enduring and suitable material for the statuary."[66] His German friends at Munich had weighed heavily in the decision.

Crawford had concluded during his visit to Munich in the summer of 1852 that the royal foundry there was the finest in the world. He had left Rome early in May to fulfill his wish to go to Munich, passing through Vienna, Prague, and Berlin. He stopped in Vienna to examine the various public monuments and he wrote Louisa of his appreciation for the "Gothic architecture and stained glass, and a wonderfully impressive picture" at the cathedral.[67] He felt at home in the city, saying that it "very much resembled Paris with its crowded streets and numerous shops."[68] Rushing through baroque Prague though, Crawford could find nothing to catch his eye except the cathedral.

He arrived in Berlin on the nineteenth, carrying a letter of introduction from Emilus Wolff in Rome to the famous Prussian sculptor Christian Rauch, who had made the large monument of Frederick the Great. Although Rauch's personality recalled Thorwaldsen's hospitality and expansiveness, Crawford considered his work was "wanting in simplicity very much."[69] Among the public monuments, only the statue of Blücher pleased him. Another leading sculptor, Rudolph Lehmann, arranged for Crawford to meet the younger group, who all longed to go to Rome to work. Crawford was dined one day by a Mr. Magnus, a fashionable portrait painter who had been to the States as attaché to the Prussian Embassy and had struck up a friendship with Louisa's brother, Sam Ward, and his wife, Medora. Crawford's outstanding experience in Berlin was his visit to the museum, where he admired "the splendid collection of casts from the antique . . . made out in the most elegant taste."[70] The royal palace turned out to be "a sickly looking affair," but the Berlin visit was rescued for him by the excitement over the reception of the Russian emperor with his court.[71] He attended the opera at every opportunity, being especially fond of German music, but he was disappointed in the unadaptability of the language, concluding that "the Italian language is the only right one for music. . . . Italians only can sing."[72]

In Munich he visited the royal foundry and watched the casting of a statue, later stating that he had witnessed "the most delicate modeling . . . being rendered in bronze, with a purity and precision truly astonishing."[73] This would indeed be the only place for casting his public figures.

Returning home by way of Lake Como and Milan, he found "one of his sketches for the Washington Monument already finished." He promptly applied the completing touches. He had taken Patrick Henry as his first subject and the *Virginia Historical Register* reported it "an exquisitely graceful statue . . . of Virginia's great orator."[74] Crawford was still not satisfied with the statue, however, and he set it aside for further consideration while he proceeded to the statue of Jefferson. That was completed rapidly without problems and dispatched to Munich for casting on August 6, 1852, together with the second shield. He anticipated reworking and finishing the *Henry* to be ready for casting in a few months. Not too long afterwards, his friend Robert Launitz disclosed that Crawford had finished both statues in "splendid style," and was "now all intent to produce the 'father of his country' on horseback more successfully than any artist has done hitherto."[75]

Again Crawford worked through the hot Roman summer. Early in September of 1852, he was still hoping to get out to Albano to join his painter friend George Loring Brown for a week's holiday, either later that month or the following one. But he could not spare the time. Aside from the equestrian statue, which occupied him almost exclusively over the full year, he made an idealized classical bust, *Flora*, for Mr. Haight of New York. This was shown during the second season of 1854 in the permanent exhibition in the Crystal Palace, newly reopened in New York by G. Barman, who undertook to pay all the debts incurred during the opening season of 1853. The show was reported to have been attended by about two thousand persons a day. This work was eventually possessed by Henry Hilton who loaned it to the Metropolitan Museum for exhibition in 1897 but retrieved it for his personal collection.

Crawford also made a full statue of *Flora* that was over seven feet high. It was shown in the Crystal Palace at London in 1855 and many years later was his sole entry in the Columbian Exposition of 1893 in Chicago. In a guidebook of the exposition *Flora* was described by the sculptor and art historian Lorado Taft as "a light, airy personification of *Flora*. She is poised on tip-toe and with outstretched arms holds aloft a flowering branch, to which she turns her smiling face. Around her feet are plants and blossoms profusely decking the earth in response to her glad presence."[76]

Flora 1853, marble, 86″
Collection of the Newark Museum, Newark, New Jersey

19

Capitol Adornment

CRAWFORD'S ESTIMATE OF THE SOLIDITY OF HIS IMAGE AT WASHINGTON proved entirely accurate. His conversations with Captain Meigs and his early acquaintance with Edward Everett were now harvesting practical results. During the summer of 1853, the captain of engineers requested of Everett, just returned from his tour of duty abroad, his recommendation of American artists capable of "designing and executing the works in sculpture contemplated for the enrichment of the pediments to the Capitol extension buildings."[1] Everett unhesitatingly designated Hiram Powers and Thomas Crawford as two candidates who were "at the head of the artists of this country; and perfectly competent."[2] The reputation of Powers, accruing from the acclaim of his *Greek Slave* and his recent commission of the *Daniel Webster* in Boston, and that of Crawford, by virtue of his *Equestrian Washington* in preparation for Richmond's capitol square, formally justified the dual recommendation.

Of course these names were no revelation to Meigs, who was seeking to give an impression of objectivity that might forestall legislative wrangling and avoid any accusations of favoritism. Meigs addressed duplicate letters on August eighteenth to both sculptors in Italy, under his authority from Jefferson Davis, secretary of war, to whom the president had delegated the task. Meigs requested the sculptors "to submit designs for the enrichment" of pediments for the east front of the new north (Senate) and south (House) wings of the Capitol building. With an eye to setting the precedent for prices at a low level, Meigs talked about sculptural works galore, as if they could be had cheaper by the dozen. He hinted shrewdly in these opening letters that the west front might later also have pediments to fill, and there would be innumerable niches for statues and areas for bas-reliefs. High reliefs were specifically requested now to surmount the doorways. A copy of a group designed by the German sculptor Shinkel for some European building was enclosed as an example, with tracings of the eastern doorway, the south wing, and the pediment over the eastern portico. At the moment, the entablature of the portico was crowned with a horizontal balustrade for which Meigs sought to substitute a pediment "as more beautiful, and affording in its tympanum space for sculpture."[3]

The sculptures were designated to be in white marble to match the material of the extensions, which Meigs described as of "very fine grain and texture . . . and nearly equal to statuary in beauty." The stone, he posited, was plentiful in America and could be cut there, but no objections were posed to the execution of the models abroad. Meigs desired "the pediments and doorways . . . [to be] a part of the original construction of the building," and he concluded his request with a characteristic patriotic flourish of the times. "I do not see why a republic so much richer than the Athenian, should not rival the Parthenon in the front of its first public edifice."[4] He dangled the promise of a sculptor's paradise.

Five days later, Meigs rushed a private note to Crawford in Rome. In part it read: "I think it would be advisable to forward sketches as soon as possible . . . not to give too much publicity to the matter until your designs are adopted. If it gets abroad too soon, we may have jarring interests and claims urged by personal influence to make members of Congress interfere."[5] In retrospect, this private note of Meigs to Crawford may be construed as collusion, but no one raised the question.

Meigs' two letters to Crawford were unaccountably delayed an extra month beyond the usual one for trans-Atlantic correspondence, not arriving until late in October. Meanwhile, Crawford worked incessantly through the summer with few diversions, "entirely occupied with the equestrian statue."[6] He was also contriving a group statue called *The Hunter's Horn* for James Lenox of New York. The colossal *Beethoven* was definitely commissioned in mid-June by Charles Perkins for the Boston Music Hall to be executed entirely according to the sculptor's taste.

He saw occasionally only his intimate circle of American artist friends like the John Gadsby Chapmans, "with whom [he] dined every Sunday," the Richard Saltonstall Greenoughs, Edward Freemans, Joseph Moziers, and especially the William Wetmore Storys.[7] When Emelyn Story was preparing her seasonal exit from Rome with her children on June twelfth, headed for Bagni di Lucca, her husband talked at dinner one evening of taking a small room for himself in the Palazzo Barberini until he should be free to join his family. Crawford insisted on extending the hospitality of Villa Negroni, as much to relieve his own loneliness during Louisa's absence with the children at Interlaken as to repair a breach in their friendship deriving from a misunderstanding. Story accepted the invitation with alacrity and Crawford wrote Louisa that he was very pleased, as he "did not wish to see the friendly relations between the families broken in any way."[8]

Crawford put up a bed for Story in the Green Room and gave him the range of the house during his month's stay. "He is enabled to get comfortably to his studio without the fatigue of a long walk," he wrote his wife. "We dine at 2 o'clock, of course, very simply and at 7 in the afternoon, we get together at the Trattoria of the Belle Arti . . . for supper," often joined by other artists. "I have great pleasure in thus cementing the friendship between us again," he told Louisa, adding that Story was good company, "never dull."[9]

In July, Crawford was flattered by the visit to his studio of Pietro Cornelius, the famous German painter, who had just arrived for a year's stay in Rome. Crawford reported that Cornelius evinced much interest in his work. It cheered Crawford considerably to have a reliable objective opinion of his sculptures, for he felt himself that "having looked at a work for 8 months, it can readily be imagined that the eye of the artist must be somewhat fatigued."[10] Crawford paid homage to his guest with a little dinner at the villa for which he prepared a magnificent laurel wreath with a card attached inscribed

"North America to Cornelius." "The old German was quite taken aback with all the attention," related Crawford.[11]

Soon the others would be decamping to escape the worst of the summer's heat. The Freemans would go to Subiaco, the Chapmans and Greenoughs to the Castelli, and the Moziers to Sorrento. Of the entire American group, only Crawford stayed behind. Fortunately he could report to Louisa that "this August is cooler by several degrees than last month."[12] After Story's departure in mid-July, he was alone but content with the solitude as conducive to greater concentration on his work. "I cannot leave my statue of *The Hunter* . . . having decided to cast it next Monday" he announced.[13] He did cast it in plaster on the eighth and then proceeded to revise completely his design for the *Beethoven*, which he planned to commence in a few days and "endeavor to make it a 'capo di opera.' "[14] By the sixteenth, he told Louisa that the beginning of its modeling required considerable attention, and within a week he wrote, "The *Beethoven* group is going up rapidly from the sketch. He is represented very great in deep thought instead of the fast action I had."[15]

He also reported that he was "getting on tolerably well with the *Equestrian* group," the success of which "depended entirely upon the balance of the group on the modeling stand. I have made all my calculations with such precision," he recounted, "that the enormous weight mounted on the six brass rollers like clock work.—I shall soon hope to have it as far advanced as the other is—so I confidently look to casting it in three months. Perhaps I shall cast sections of it, such as the head of the horse, long before then and have them complete in plaster of Paris by the time the remainder of the work is ready for casting. I have thus gained considerable time."[16]

Louisa returned to town with the children in October in time to share the joy of receiving Meigs' offer and private letter. Crawford replied to Meigs unreservedly, "I shall give immediate and earnest attention to the composition of a suitable design. . . . You may rely on my sending to you in the course of the next three weeks a photograph from the sketch I shall make."[17]

For his part, Powers was piqued to be placed in a competitive position in view of his own estimate that he possessed the superior reputation and talent. As if detecting collusion intuitively, he refused to submit plans without prior assurances of their acceptance and of his compensation. The excuse he gave for this request was that he lacked the time to comply. After his strenuous effort over the years to elevate his prices, Powers was irritated by Crawford's willingness to depress the market and submit to what he considered exploitive conditions. He determined that he would not design anything without recompense.

Meigs' tactical gambit proved a discreet maneuver when two years later he felt impelled to justify his choice of Crawford to the secretary of war, to whom he was responsible. Meigs wrote, "I wish only to prevent any impression which might lead you to suppose that I had been guided by prejudice or favor in my action in this matter. I knew neither of the artists and I sought designs from both. It is not my fault if unsuccessful with Mr. Powers."[18] This, of course, was manifestly untrue. He had become acquainted with Crawford during Crawford's visit to Washington in the winter of 1850, before he had corresponded with him.

Adhering closely to Meigs' suggestion to look to the "history of the struggle between the civilized man and the savage, between the cultivated and the wild nature,"[19] for themes worthy of the artist and capable of appealing to the feelings of all classes, Crawford proceeded. He shared Meigs' notion "that poetry and grandeur are inseparably connected with the history of our country's past and future, and that the dignity of sculpture may well be devoted to the perpetuation of what the people love and understand."[20] He was wedded to the conviction that our country's representation had greater validity and popularity when conceived historically than through Greek symbolism. These notions reflected the currency at home of evolutionary theories which were insinuating themselves into artistic compositions. Bearing some similarity to Greenough's theme in the *Rescue Group,* Crawford's conception portrayed the superiority of the white man and his developed civilization over the indigenous hunting Redskins. The implicit racism of the concept escaped him as it did Greenough. White chauvinism was generic in their day.

Crawford evolved a composition for the pediment with incredible speed. It embodied fourteen figures and numerous accessories, illustrating the story of America's development from the primitive hunting stage of the Indians to its settlement by the fair Caucasians who imposed their advanced civilization on the virgin continent, components of which were agriculture, commerce, industry, and education. The central figure was a colossal representation of *America,* symbolized by a classically draped female resembling a goddess. Crawford was not freer of the Greek mode in his execution than was Greenough or Powers. He described the design as follows:

> [America is] standing on a rock, against which the waves of the ocean are beating. She is attended by the eagle of the country; while the sun, rising at her feet, indicated the light which accompanies the march of liberty. In one hand, she holds the rewards of civil and military merit—laurel and oak wreaths. Her left hand is extended toward the pioneer for whom she asks protection of the Almighty. The pioneer is the athletic figure of a backwoodsman clearing the forest. The Indian race and its extinction is explained by the adjoining group of the Indian chief and his family.
>
> The son of the chief is returning from the chase with a collection of game slung on a spear over his shoulder. In the statue of the Indian chief . . . [is seen] despair and profound grief resulting from the conviction of the white man's triumph. The wife and infant of the chief complete this group of figures, while the grave, being emblematic of the extinction of the Indian race, fills up this portion. . . .
>
> The opposite half of the pediment is devoted to the effects of liberty and civilization. The first figure on the right of *America* represents its soldier. He is clothed in the costume of the revolution, as being suggestive of the country's struggle for independence; his hand upon his sword indicated the readiness of the army to protect America from insult. By the soldier is placed a merchant sitting on the emblems of trade; his right hand rests upon the globe, by which the extent of American commerce is symbolized. The anchor at his feet connects this figure with those of two boys advancing to devote themselves to the service of their country.
>
> The anchor is easily understood to be the emblem of hope; behind them sits the teacher instructing a youth. The mechanic completes the group. He rests upon the cog-wheel, without which machinery is useless. In his hands are the emblems of trade, and at his feet are sheaves of corn expressive of fertility, activity, and abundance in contradistinction to the grave at the corresponding corner.[21]

Crawford dispatched photographs of the sketches for his design to Washington on October 31. He estimated thirty months would be required to complete the models. He requested $20,000 for the entire group.

Meigs was delighted with all aspects of the proposition. He thought the design "appropriate and intelligible," and he wrote Crawford that the design could not "fail to be a noble ornament to our Capitol and a worthy monument of the youthful and vigorous artistic power of our country."[22] He considered the terms reasonable and strongly urged their adoption to the secretary of war, Jefferson Davis. The following day, November 30, 1853, he announced the secretary's acceptance of the conditions and his authorization to proceed with the execution of the group. Details, such as dimensions, mode of execution, and so forth, were postponed to a more leisurely time ahead.

Crawford soon ran into several amusing, petty difficulties with some of his figures. According to Meigs the figure of the soldier bore a certain resemblance to Washington and would "incur the danger of being misapprehended, the many will say that you have attempted a portrait and failed."[23] Crawford readily acknowledged the error of his treatment agreeing that Washington "should never be placed in a secondary position."[24] The Indian family gave Crawford the most trouble in the execution. "You have not caught the Indian countenance in the boy," Meigs objected. "The figure is very graceful and beautiful, the attitude . . . always reminds me of an antique . . . but in a type of the Indian race it is essential to get the type of the face . . . and that you have not got."[25]

The problem recurred with the Indian chief. "What shall we do to supply you with a model?" inquired Meigs. "Have you not in Rome, McKinney and Hall's *Indian Tribes of North America?* The large folio edition in three volumes contains a great number of chiefs who have figures."[26] Several books on Indian customs and manners did exist in Roman libraries, having been distributed by the Smithsonian Institution. Crawford had no need of the books, however, being well supplied privately with his own authentic Indian portrayals. His friend Philips had brought to Rome the portrait busts of two Indian chiefs. After having shifted to painting, he had given the busts to Crawford. Despite Crawford's remodeling these figures repeatedly, they remained, like Powers' *Indian Girl*, essentially classical, the Indian trappings tacked on like vestigial appendages.

A marble copy of the *Indian Chief*, the sole nude figure in the group, would be presented in 1875 by President Frederick de Peyster to the New-York Historical Society, where it still commands its own room (one, however, that is far too small for proper display). It is a characteristic example of the problem faced by the American sculptors in Italy at that time, the conflict between classical and

The Chief Contemplating the Progress of Civilization   1856, marble 55″
Courtesy of the New-York Historical Society

realistic interpretations of historical subjects. Meigs tried to console Crawford by relating the parallel experience of a promising Italian talent working in Washington, who attempted to show an Indian kneeling at a fountain but created a figure that "promises to be an exact portrait of a dirty Italian boy of no particular beauty."[27]

Another snag now arose. Crawford recommended that the marble statues be cut either at Carrara or Rome for several telling reasons. He preferred the Carrara marble for its superiority and durability and the workmen in Italy were not only the best but were in plentiful supply. Moreover, the advantages gained from his personal supervision were manifest.[28] Meigs countered with surprising force in favor of having the statues executed in America. He argued that "Carrara marble does not last in [Washington's] climate, it cracks. The belt fell from the sword of Greenough's *Washington* the other day." He conceded that "while American stone has not the beautiful transparency of Italian which gives such flesh-like appearance to a statue in a room . . . it is quite as white, and at the height at which this statuary is to be placed, this transparency will not be missed."[29] The estimated trebled cost would be vindicated by the hope that "some of the workmen would become educated so as to become artists in time."[30] The public and the congressmen, by observing the daily routine, would learn something of the labor and cost involved. Lastly, argued Meigs, nothing would be lost artistically if the works were to be supervised by an Italian. Two years later, Crawford sent Tommaso Galiardi over for the job.[31] Lewis Cass, Jr., the U.S. Consul at Rome, seconded the selection, recommending Galiardi "as a most capable artist for basting [roughing] out and finishing."[32] They found another Italian, a man named Vincenti who also had aspirations to be a sculptor, to assist. Crawford was later forced to disown his confidence in Galiardi's capacity to finish and urged Meigs to confine Galardi's efforts to roughing out.

To obviate the problem and reduce the cost of copying into marble, Crawford and Meigs investigated a new "Galvano Plastico process" introduced at Rome. It had the virtue of being cheap but was soon abandoned by Crawford when he realized "the necessity that would always exist for painting the figures at intervals of time with white lead to imitate marble."[33] Crawford proposed casting the statuary in bronze but Meigs questioned the gaudy effect that the statuary would have against the white marble building. Crawford capitulated, partially due to the strength of Meigs' reasons but undoubtedly also for Meigs position of authority. Crawford confessed that he was thoroughly convinced of the "great impossibility of the models being artistically copied in the United States."[34]

Crawford finished his sketches for the pediment and dispatched them to Meigs in Washington before Christmas of 1853. He then took a short breathing spell. He was urgently pressed to enlarge his studio to accommodate the multiplying colossal statues he had undertaken. The equestrian model was still to be finished, his seven-foot model of *Beethoven* was in the works, and fourteen figures were imminently projected for the tympanum. He took advantage of the holiday break to order the necessary alterations in his studio.

In the course of time, Meigs had proposed to Crawford another commission, to design a pair of bronze doors in relief for the Senate entranceway of the new Capitol extension. Crawford was immensely interested. Now, during the interruption of work in his studio, he made a quick visit to Florence to study the world famous bronze doors of the Baptistry wrought by Ghiberti. Crawford wanted also to see Powers to attempt to conciliate their breach. He had feelings of guilt at having displaced Powers in the work on the Capitol extension. He offered Powers the entire commission. Powers declined summarily. Crawford countered by suggesting their working as a team but was again rebuffed. There the matter ended and the breach continued. Crawford studiously made his sketches, took his measurements of the Ghiberti doors, and accepted the commission forthwith. Meigs received the news early in January with equanimity.

Crawford returned to his work in mid-January and set about immediately to compose a design for the doors. He sent photographs of his sketches to Washington for approval before the month was out and then turned to the *Beethoven*, which he finished rapidly preparatory for its casting in the Munich ovens. He was prompted to the speedy production of this statue so as to demonstrate graphically to Meigs his ability to handle the contemporary costume they were discussing for the pediment figures. These he started modeling in February.

It seemed strange to him that Meigs failed to comment on his designs for the bronze doors. Not receiving a reply by March, he posted duplicates. Meanwhile, Meigs had made another offer to Powers of a commission for the second pediment of the Capitol extension and Powers had spurned the offer unhesitatingly. Crawford was left by default in sole possession of the field at Washington. He told Meigs, "I beg to assure you that my utmost efforts are entirely at your command."[35] He repeated soon afterward that he stood "ready at any time to prepare designs for the entire sculptural department of the Capitol Extension."[36]

His habits of work hewed to the methods prevailing in Rome. He took care to keep Meigs abreast of his thinking and reviewed the entire subject from time to time in his prolific correspondence with Washington.

> The secret of being able to complete a great variety of work is to be found in the power of the artists to invent, compose, and direct, thus the hands of others become as it were, his hands, and younger artists who can do nothing alone may be made serviceable in many ways.
> . . . Assistants properly directed have at all times enabled the great artists of the past and present to accomplish innumerable works, each having the distinctive impress of the master mind. Thus, schools have been created, youthful talent has been brought forward, and the country of the master artist has been enriched.[37]

Crawford had perhaps fifty workmen under his supervision at this point in his career. Among these were two Americans who had come to Rome to study architecture and who apprenticed themselves to him as he had done to Thorwaldsen. One was Maria Louise Lander, who arrived in April 1855 and remained until his death. She later made a bust of Hawthorne when he came to Rome but little else is known of her. J. Augustus Beck of Harrisburg, Pennsylvania, was the other American. After Crawford's death, Beck moved to Florence to work with Hiram Powers. He eventually switched to landscape and portrait painting but never became well known.

Meigs parried Crawford's aggressive advances cagily and was always careful not to discourage him. When Crawford tried to pin him down on further, solid orders, he dodged a direct commitment,

being attuned to the political vicissitudes at Washington. His tem-
porizing response to Crawford explains his dilatoriness.

> I shall expect to call on you for many things as they arrive, but
> I do not feel at liberty yet to recommend to the President to give
> you a second commission of this magnitude to the same artist.
> Yourself and Mr. Powers were selected from your known reputa-
> tions, and I think that as he declines, the second should be left
> open for a while. Possibly we may need other pediments, we may
> conclude to put two on the west front. . . .
>
> When you complete or are well-advanced upon the present
> work, it will be time to consider the other, and if no other artist
> by evidence of work accomplished achieves the reputation giving
> him the right to share in the embellishment of the Capitol, the
> commission will not fail to be awarded to you as the worthiest.
> I am not insensible to the advantage of having the unity and har-
> mony of design resulting from one mind directing the whole of
> these works, but I think that if we have the artists, they should
> share in the glory. I think that it is of importance that a part of
> your composition should arrive here as soon as convenient.[38]

It was clear that Crawford would once again be stuck in his
studio through the summer months even if his speed of production
kept pace with his vaulting ambition. "I assure you," he wrote Meigs,
"that no time is being lost."[39] In May he anticipated completing
eight of the statues within the ensuing three months: the mechanic,
schoolmaster and pupil, the group of school boys, the merchant, the
soldier, and the Indian boy. Only one month later the plaster of paris
models of the Indian boy, the mechanic, the schoolmaster and pupil,
and the group of school boys were completed.

The problem of escaping the heat of Rome that season of 1854
was hard upon Crawford now. His wife was expecting momentarily.
She took the children and all the servants but one and went with
the Storys to the warm water spa of Bagni di Lucca in Tuscany.
They rented Villa Betti, which was located at the foot of a picturesque avenue. Louisa was captivated by the stately white Palladian
villas interspersed through the valley of the swiftly flowing Serchio
River enclosed by the green and purple mountains of the Lucchese
Province. The Shelleys had discovered this idyllic scene in 1818. It

epitomized to Heinrich Heine the "oasis of poetry" and was the place where Alphonse Lamartine wrote "sous les ombrages ses plus beaux vers."[40] A corner of British Arcadia, it was made known to the English world in 1845 by Clotilde Elizabeth Sisted's *Letters From the Bye Ways of Italy*, which was edited and published by John Murray in London. The author's husband, Colonel Henry Sisted, chamberlain to the grand duke of Tuscany, had fought at Waterloo and had befriended Horatio Greenough in Florence. The Brownings had come in 1849. This cosmopolitan society was headed by the duchess of Lucca, Maria Luisa di Borbone, who had deposed the sister of Napoleon, Elisa Bonaparte, "Queen of Etruria." The latter had endeared herself to the Italians with her charm and her marriage to the Tuscan Prince Felice Bacciocchi. Prince Anatoli Demidov came from Florence and bequeathed an imposing little pantheon that now serves as a hospital.

Despite the "general clearing out" of the American group early in June, enough of them stayed behind to keep Crawford company during this strenuous period of work. He was in regular touch with the Chapmans and Freemans, and he saw Randolph Rogers and Ives at his twice weekly dinners at Lepre. Perkins had gone to Spain and Philips to Florence. The Moziers were leaving momentarily with Harriet Hosmer for Florence, but this was no great loss to Crawford. He had called on Mozier but once in the past five months, there being "no love lost between them," as Crawford readily explained.[41]

Crawford was detained in Rome until mid-July, working on the statues for the pediment which he had vowed would be completed "within the . . . month of June."[42] He also intended to complete the equestrian group to his satisfaction. On June 20 he was busy casting the soldier but declared himself "delighted to leave Rome and the Fine Arts behind for a couple of months at least. . . ." He wrote Louisa, "The last of the eight statues will be finished next week, so I may give my entire time to the horse."[43] These figures would be cast in plaster while he attended to the equestrian one. He could then leave them to be shipped during his absence while he attended the bronze casting in Munich. He announced, "The end of this portion of work [is] in sight. I feel confident of acomplishing the Herculean task I gave myself on January last."[44]

In the midst of his demanding commitments, he accepted several others. He did not spurn an order for a copy of his bust of Washington from the model for the equestrian. The copy was executed by his assistants, for a quick profit of $100 out of the $200 fee. Crawford forwarded the sum to Louisa to hire a carriage to take her about on afternoon excursions.

He also found time to finish his statue of the *Boy Playing With Marbles* and to create an original sketch for a life-size statue, *Peri*, to be executed in marble for a gentleman from Philadelphia. "The subject," wrote Crawford, "is from *Lalla Rook* and represents a partially draped standing figure of a young woman wearing large folded wings, long hair, wreaths of flowers on her head, and holding her hands down and folded in front of her."[45] Crawford explained that his inspiration for the subject came from a poem in the *Lalla Rook* of Thomas Moore, entitled "Paradise and the Peri." Crawford said the pertinent lines were:

> One morn, Peri, at the gate
> Of Eden stood, disconsolate.[46]

A larger than life-size copy, labeled *Fecit Roma*, 1856, was bequeathed by Mrs. Clarissa Burd, who was probably a descendant of the person who commissioned it, to the Pennsylvania Academy of Fine Arts. The statue is described in the files of the academy as "though just lighted before the celestial portals, one foot being poised on the fore part. The body and limbs are lightly clothed in a loose, classic vesture which relieves the effect admirably, while not impeding the graceful play of the limbs or fettering the skill of the sculptor."[47] Possibly in consequence of this commission, the Academy of Fine Arts in Philadelphia voted to elect Crawford to honorary membership.

While awaiting the transmission from Meigs, through an English bank, of his initial $10,000 fee, the sum due him upon the completion of the plaster models for the pediment, casts were made for the "entire female model," probably the central figure of *America*. A few days later, he anounced the completion of his colossal horse, ready for casting, a vital prelude to his leaving Rome for parts north. The seated figure of Washington "twenty feet in height" received its finishing touches at the same time. Crawford justified its "extraordinary proportion . . . the largest in the world" to Meigs as being "demanded by the size of the monument."[48] The completed colossal models were carefully packed and sent to Munich.

Crawford got away from Rome to his wife's side only two weeks before the birth of their fourth child and first son. The son, whom they named Francis Marion for Louisa's brother, was to eclipse his father's fame and fortune as a local color novelist of Roman society. The town of Bagni di Lucca recently celebrated his centennial anniversary, but no one was aware of his father. Francis Marion subsequently was signally successful with pot boilers that he turned out with a speed similar to that of his father's modeling. He amassed a fortune of over a million dollars, some of which he spent building a luxurious villa hewn into the cliffs at Sorrento, overlooking the Bay of Naples. Some of the largess went to maintain a fast sailing yacht which he moored at the foot of his villa's wall. Sorrento is equally proud of his having resided there and recently posted a sign to guide tourists to his gate.

Three days after Francis Marion's arrival, Crawford went to Florence to restudy and remeasure the Ghiberti doors of the Baptistry. After his return he stayed with his wife and children in Bagni until August 25, when he departed for Munich to check on the finished statues of *Henry* and *Jefferson* and to arrange for their transportation to Richmond. He also had to plan the casting of his colossal horse in sections to allow for their safe shipment and proper assembly at Richmond. These matters had to be engineered precisely to preclude any possibility of error when the horse was assembled by strange hands overseas.

The journey from Rome to Munich was a trip of about three weeks overland in those days, although time could be cut more than half by traveling twenty hours to Paris, overnight by train to Marseilles, boat to Civita Vecchia (not available daily), and by diligence to Rome. Simple prudence demanded the greatest care in overseeing the minutiae of detail before Crawford could feel free to leave the scene of execution.

Crawford arrived at Munich on the evening of September ninth and the next morning Superintendent Ferdinand Von Miller took him to the foundry. Crawford wrote Louisa in detail of his feelings: "You can imagine the anxiety I felt for the statues for the monument; I was to see them for the first time in an entirely different material, light, and arrangement. . . . The result is most triumphant in every respect. My modesty was really tested. . . . I could scarcely keep from praising myself."[49] The figures of *Thomas Jefferson* and *Patrick Henry* were being exhibited in the center of the hall. Crawford reported that they were "charmingly arranged" with a "background of dark green. . . . They are the most important statues in the exhibition [which] contains everything from soap pyramids to steam engines."[50] Attendance was estimated at 3,000 persons daily. Crawford extended his stay in the Blaue Traube Hotel in Munich to attend the successful casting of his *Washington* at seven o'clock on September 17.

An accident caused further delay. The uplifted foreleg of the horse broke off and fell into innumerable pieces, Crawford wrote Louisa that "there was nothing left but to collect the small and large pieces and patiently fit them together, a work that would puzzle a Chinese."[51] After the bits were painstaking assembled, Crawford touched up the limb with plaster and reported "the horse was looking very finely. I think the bronze will be very striking.[52]

At the end of September Crawford was still busy with the horse. He changed the movement of the tail "into something more spirited," and the alteration necessitated a good deal of work.[53] Encouraged by the general acclaim of visitors to the foundry, Crawford now hoped that the loud praise for the "spirited action and novelty of the position of the horse" that was voiced by the director of the Vienna Academy might gain him membership in that prestigious institution. Similar recognition had already been bestowed on him by the Academy of Saint Mark at Florence on the strength of his equestrian group in progress, and in 1851 his family had reportedly "felt real pride and pleasure" to learn of his election to membership in the Royal Academy at Saint Petersberg, where he probably had been sponsored by Prince Anatoli Demidov.[54] He savored the European fame, which meant more to him than his successes at home. These were solid hallmarks of distinction.

Crawford was disappointed with Miller's estimate for casting the equestrian work. "He offers to do it," Crawford reported to Louisa, "and deliver at Amsterdam complete for $20,000."[55] Crawford hoped that Sevastopol would be taken in the course of the Crimean War so the price of cannon needed as raw materials for his statue would decline. "It will be cast in several pieces and put together at Rotterdam," he informed Louisa. "As the packing case would be too large for any ordinary vessel, the State of Virginia would be obliged to ship it on a U.S. war vessel."[56]

Satisfied that Miller was "the very soul of honesty" and that "the Statue has been vastly improved," Crawford left on October 10. He stayed long enough to plan the dispatch of the *Henry* and *Jefferson* for Richmond following the close of the exhibition on the fifteenth. The last steamer of the season from Bremen, the most direct route, had gone and the arrival of the figures was delayed for at least a month.

After the strain of Munich, Crawford eagerly looked forward to his reunion with Louisa and the children at home in Villa Negroni, where they had been since September. He returned to a beehive of activity.

In addition to endless discussion of the commissioned works, Meigs was writing Crawford voluminous letters about artistic speculation on other features of the Capitol's adornment for which he sought free advice. A great problem demanding resolution was the new towering dome, which rose four times as high as the old. The actual demolition of the old triple dome was begun in the fall of 1855. The dimensions of the new cast iron dome were stupendous, 290 feet high, 95 feet in diameter, and 124 feet in the diameter of colonnade. Meigs intended that it be "richly ornamented," inside, to conform with its impressive exterior. He asked Crawford's opinion of a 300-foot frieze, 9 feet high, such as in the Parthenon at Athens, that would illustrate the history of America. He also asked his opinion of having "brackets supporting its beams ornamented by caryatids representing the several states."[57] Since the cost of marble block and the lengthy time of cutting were prohibitive for the number of figures envisaged, he asked Crawford if it would be feasible to have the figures "covered with copper or bronze by the electrotype process?"[58]

Taking a completely different approach, Meigs asked if it

would simplify matters and reduce cost substantially to distribute thirty-six columns 27 feet high around the space. Immediately Meigs realized that these, costing $1,200 each, would consume $43,200 in one swoop. Although he had almost a million and a half to dispense on the decoration, the price still seemed excessive. Meanwhile, he was incessantly irked by the sluggish pace of quarrying marble from Lee, Massachusetts, and the insufficient quantity available to face the building.

The proposed frieze sounded like a sculptor's heaven to Crawford, who eventually responded with an offer to execute it in five years at a cost of $50,000. Meigs could never summon the courage to place a request of this magnitude before Congress. The problem of embellishing the dome was eventually solved when Nicholas Brumidi arrived from Rome. He had some experience in the complicated technique of fresco. There were no rivals in America. Leutze and Weir were satisfactory historical painters but they were not available then. Besides, what did they know of fresco? Daniel Huntington had experimented with it and failed. The paramount problem of Brumidi was cleverly detected and handled by Meigs. "I can use him only in decoration," he informed Crawford, "an American historical picture he would not paint, as his picture would be Italian, a classic."[59] Crawford studied Meigs' complex queries seriously and responded at length, taking much of his valuable time. Meigs was struck by his "great fertility of invention," a factor that solidified Crawford's further employment on the Capitol extension.[60]

Crawford really did not have time to spare as he encountered continued trouble in executing the Indian family, especially the boy and the chief. The latter, being nude, required pronounced anatomical detail. Late in February 1855, he disposed of most of the other pieces, shipping the mechanic, school boys, schoolmaster, merchant, soldier, wheat sheaves, anchor, and columns. This left eight more cases to follow by spring but his hopes ran six months ahead of his performance. Another two seasons would pass before he would feel sure enough of their rendition for release.

The summer of 1855 marked the zenith of Crawford's career. Several of his major colossal works were featured at once in a number of cities. On August 15 the colossal bronze statues of *Thomas*

Jefferson and *Patrick Henry* arrived at the capitol square in Richmond, accompanied by bas-reliefs bearing the state coat of arms. They were placed temporarily by mid-October on each side of the steps of the western front of the Capitol, objects of "general approbation to the delight of the commissioners."[61]

The Boston Athenaeum's annual show featured Crawford's colossal *Beethoven*, his *Hebe and Ganymede*, and William Wetmore Story's statue of his father, Supreme Court Justice *Joseph Story*, which was destined for the chapel of Mount Auburn cemetery in Cambridge. The *Beethoven* had been cast in the Royal Foundry at Munich in February of the previous year to bountiful acclaim and publicity. The inaugural celebration that was held in March was attended by the king and queen in a vast music hall reverberating with the stormy music of the composer's symphonies. Until its shipment overseas, the statue was the cynosure of the foundry's exhibition of works. It arrived in Boston in time to be included in the Athenaeum's annual show.

The city of Washington also had a public display of Crawford's works. The first batch of figures designed for the pediment arrived intact at Washington by mid-April. Meigs had them uncrated and displayed at the Capitol in the order they would eventually occupy in the pediment. Meigs reported to Crawford that the statues were hailed for being "full of life and expression."[62]

Before dispatching the remaining figures, save the Indian family, Crawford made a wooden replica of the tympanum to test their fit. To his distress, he found it too tight for the most favorable exhibition of the sculpture. He had utilized the last inch of height in the figures and now realized that their view would be greatly improved if the heads of the statuary were liberated from the lower members of the cornice. He tried to get Meigs to have the apex raised a foot, but it was too late. A major alteration would have been required, involving structural changes in the wrought iron frames for the roof, which was already in place. The proposed change was altogether too costly to be entertained. There was no external remedy. He would have to adjust the figures proportionately to conform. Before shipping the group to Washington via Leghorn and New York in April 1855, he made a detailed sketch and wrote minute instructions for the reduced proportions of the figures when they would be reproduced in marble, and for their assembly.

The cutting of the figures took years to complete in the Capitol's basement workshops which Meigs had created. When the second shipment arrived, the rooms were cramped for space, requiring enlargement of the carpenter, machine, and smith shops. Delays occurred continually over the location of suitable blocks of stone and the availability of competent workmen. Meigs clearly regretted his decision to have the work done in the States. In October 1856, he requested Crawford to resume supervision of the cutting in Rome for the price of $1,500 each. The shift was not made, chiefly because Meigs was too far committed to the use of domestic talent and materials. He also wanted the legislators to observe the slow progress of the work so as to apprehend the problems of production, thereby justifying his expenditures. In March 1856, Crawford wrote Meigs that the Indian group was nearing completion, and promised, "In the course of a few weeks, I will forward to you the Indian Chief, the Indian Woman, and the hunter boy with the grave, thus terminating the pediment."[63]

In view of the enormity of the project, the cost was most reasonable. Crawford had calculated the budget from his Italian experience, taking into consideration the wage differential between Rome and Washington for marble cutters. For once, the estimate was not exceeded. After $20,000 was paid to him for his models, the statues cost another $25,950 for the cutting and transportation. Two gigantic marble blocks were used that were procured for the bargain price of $1,000 each, bringing the approximate total, including incidentals, to within $50,000.

Simultaneously with his pediment figures, Crawford began creating designs to surmount the Senate doorway. He composed allegorical representations of *Liberty* and *Justice* in the form of two recumbent semidraped colossal females and sent the photographs of these to Washington for approval. Secretary of War Jefferson Davis, whose respect Crawford was gradually earning, posed a minor objection to the rendition. Davis took exception to the cap on the head of the figure of *Liberty*. He suggested that the cap derived from the Roman custom of liberating slaves, thence called freedmen, who were allowed to wear this cap. The cap was universally adopted to symbolize the freedmen, especially in France. Davis objected to its application to America, where, he averred, the condition of liberty is original without any previous condition of servitude for the white man. Davis also did not care for the rods in the hand of *Justice* because of the possible ambiguity of their interpretation.

There was an interval of two years from Crawford's submission of the sketches of *Justice* and *Liberty* early in the summer of 1854 until Meigs felt secure enough to grant his final approval in September 1856. The *Liberty* metamorphosed into a representation of the muse of *History*. In this figure, as in the *Liberty* and the *America*, Crawford dispensed with the disputed cap.

For the figure of *Justice* on the right over the doorway, he tentatively used a sword and scales, but these symbols also met with criticism. They were scrapped temporarily for a book of law, but were later restored and included with the other accouterments. Crawford sedulously defended his last remaining symbol, a palm branch, as "typical of the triumph of the principles of justice in our country."[64] He required this detail to underscore his thematic point. He thought it essential to the unity of his composition and he prevailed. The figures were not completed in marble until after his death.

A gift of Charles Perkins, the *Beethoven* was officially installed on a six-foot pedestal in the Boston Music Hall on the first of March 1856. An observer reported "The program . . . suffered mutilations; choral symphonies were performed without chorus. . . . Yet on the whole . . . the occasion [was] truly noteworthy. . . . [the statue received] enthusiastic welcome by an immense audience and [was] celebrated in fitting strains by an American poet . . . W. W. Story."[65]

The seven-foot high *Beethoven* was wrought in bronze, a novel material in Boston then, generally conceded to "contribute a rich effect of light and shade."[66] Once again, Crawford made a realistic representation, literal rather than poetic, as befitting a statue exposed to public view. *Beethoven* is clad in a flowing stole and holds a musical score in his left hand which is clasped by his right hand. Contrary to previous illustrations of Beethoven as the "dyspeptic

Titan," Crawford's rendition was described as having a face with a "gleam of grace and tenderness." It was reported that "the simple grandeur of the conception" met with uninhibited approval, and that Crawford managed the modern costume "with surprising skill."[67]

This finest single statue from Crawford's hand received its just share of favorable appraisal in its own time. It is now in the New England Conservatory of Music in Boston. Crawford understood that he had wrought a fine work. In appreciation of the opportunity given him by the donor, his friend Charles Perkins, who had shared his gay musical soirées in Rome in 1846, he sent as a gift a plaster bust of the statue, which has remained in the possession of the Perkins family.

20

American Ghiberti

THE PROLIFIC CORRESPONDENCE THAT PASSED BETWEEN MEIGS AND
Crawford since the commencement of their acquaintance in the
winter of 1850 contained endless discussion of a pair of bronze doors
which Meigs wanted to embellish the eastern entrance of the new
wing of the Capitol. Crawford pondered the plan intermittently in
response to Meigs' request, which was formalized in September 1851.
The choice of style as between a classical or an historical treatment
was the focal point at issue. The question was tossed back and forth
considerably, oscillating in proportion to the weight of the contending pressure groups represented by the politicians who plunked for
literal realism and the intellectuals who preferred the grand style.
The lesson of Greenough's *Washington* was still alive and tipped
the balance against poetic generalization.

Although allegory would have given him "greater freedom of
composition," Crawford decided against running the risk.[1] On the
other hand, the example of Ghiberti was persuasive. Crawford determined to illustrate the "principal events in our history by a series
of bas-reliefs."[2] The sole deterrent that he saw immediately was the
limitation inherent in the brief span of the country's history. He
wanted at all cost to avoid duplication of the notable events depicted
by the painters for the Rotunda.

It took him eight months to work out his composition in a

series of rough sketches. He divided each half of the door into eight panels, the upper three pairs would be rectangular in shape as at the Baptistry at Florence; the two lower pairs would be circular. He forwarded photographs of his designs to Meigs on May 8, 1855, accompanied by the following explanation:

> I have selected for illustration a few prominent points in our National History and arranged them as follows:
> The left valve contains those of a civic character, the right valve is devoted to War, the titles of each subject are engraved beneath the bas-relief, but they are not rendered on the photograph.
> The subject of the first bas-relief on the War valve, beginning at the top is Bunker Hill, illustrating the death of Warren. The second one is Monmouth . . . the point of time when Washington orders Lee to re-attack the enemy. The third is Yorktown with the American assault upon the British works . . . The first bas-relief on the Peace valve, also beginning at the top, represents Washington laying the cornerstone of the U.S. Capitol, the second is Washington taking the presidential oath. . . . The third, Washington enters Trenton . . . on his way to New York after the war of independence.
> The two circular bas-reliefs are designed to represent in general way the subject of each valve—Peace and War. The top of the door is perforated for the admission of light. I have endeavored to make a harmonious distribution of the divisions upon the valves and have thought such a result could be obtained by introducing the circles below and repeating them above in the open work.[3]

The circular war medallion in the lower left corner illustrated the conflict of the Hessian soldier and a New Jersey farmer.

Approaching the work with the solemnity of a self-conscious disciple of Ghiberti, Crawford proclaimed to Meigs, "The modelling of this work will require the greatest study united with the highest degree of finish. Costumes and portraiture are of utmost importance." He announced that he would strive for "richness of effect . . . produced by the sculpture and the intellectual triumphs over the merely ornamental."[4] He kept the bas-reliefs as large as possible to avoid heavy paneling and extraneous ornaments, which would detract from the design.

When Crawford went to Florence to restudy the Baptistry doors, he discovered that they had far greater space than the meas-

Bronze Doors of the Senate Entrance 1855–1860, bronze
Courtesy of the United States Capitol

urements of thirteen feet ten inches by six feet six inches which were being alloted by the current architect of the Capitol, Thomas U. Walter. This vital fact had not been specified in the agreement with Meigs and Crawford had assumed that he had the right to determine the dimensions. He protested the dimensions alloted to the doors, but in vain. The smaller size meant that the size of his figures would have to be reduced, they would be less distinct, and the effect of the whole would be blurred.

Spurred by a definite feeling that he was breaking ground at home, as the Renaissance genius had done in Italy, Crawford was anxious to obtain the commission and the others that would ensue. He began to view himself in the guise of his country's sculptor laureate. He believed low prices would encourage the economy-minded legislators at Washington to pursue art patronage for the adornment of public edifices. The fine arts would flourish to the enrichment of the people and the nation. Lastly, he had no need to make a personal fortune out of his work. These considerations were as the yeast of his decision to peg the precedent low for the price of such works. He decided to charge $6,000 for the designs of the bronze doors. Crawford's personal generosity in this gesture was never appreciated and actually went unnoticed. Moreover, he failed to set a precedent. The price rose by fifty percent on the very next project and continued the inflated course.

An amusing turn soon developed. Meigs, the staunch defender of art for the masses, art designed to express national tradition and aspiration, now suddenly did a volte-face. "I regret to see you confined by the nature of the subjects so much to the clothed figure and the modern costume," he told Crawford.[5] He suggested that Crawford return to the "nobler treatment" of an allegorical representation of *War* and *Peace* in the lower circular designs. Crawford was delighted with the opportunity. It was an ironical twist coming from Meigs who had remonstrated in favor of literal historical illustration. The proposed compromise suited Crawford ideally.

As a result of a minor misunderstanding by Crawford, the execution of designs for a second pair of doors to adorn the House entranceway was delayed a month. Crawford retained the general plan of the first pair for the Senate, varying only the historical events to be portrayed. These were ready by July 10, 1855, when Crawford forwarded the photographs to Meigs with the accompanying explanation:

> I have kept the same general arrangements treating, however, the circles below in a more simple manner by leaving out the victories. I have also omitted the stars in the wreath at the top of the valve.
>
> The subjects I have selected are all National in every sense of the word. . . . The first in the left valve is the massacre of Wyoming, Pennsylvania. . . . The second is an illustration of the pursuit of the British at Lexington. . . . The third is the presentation of British colors and a medal to General Green after expelling the British from South Carolina. . . . The fourth . . . the death of Montgomery.
>
> The first subject in the right valve is the public reading of the Declaration of Independence at Philadelphia. The second, the signing of the treaty of peace between Great Britain and the United States at Paris. . . . The third, Washington's farewell to his officers at New York. . . . The fourth . . . represents Franklin in his studio, the subject of his studies being electricity as indicated by the electric machine on his table.[6]

Crawford commended his second series to Meigs as being "no less American for having been made in the city of the Caesars."[7]

Meigs did not present Crawford's first set of designs to the secretary of war, but withheld them until the second set arrived and he could present the pair simultaneously for consideration. Both series of designs were approved by the secretary with slight modifications on October 11, 1855. Jefferson Davis recommended a change in one of the panels, that illustrating Washington's reproof of General Charles Lee after the Battle of Monmouth. Davis felt that the episode did not commemorate a moment of greatness in American history. In his view, it was too ungenerous a subject for perpetuation so prominently in bronze. Indian treaties and Indian pastoral life were vaguely suggested as alternative subjects, but the choice was left to the sculptor. Crawford was not convinced by Davis' arguments and delayed replacing the panel until it became too late. After his death, his widow urged its retention out of respect for his memory. Captain W. B. Franklin, who replaced Captain

Meigs briefly in charge of the Capitol Extension, made this recommendation to Secretary of War John B. Floyd who acceded.

While busily completing the designs for his doors, Crawford also worked on a composition to crown the new dome of the Capitol. He made three designs from June to October 1855. He described his first design as follows:

> Freedom triumphant in Peace and War, the wreath on her head has a double significance in allusion to this one, half of it being composed of wheat sprigs, the other half of laurel. In her left hand, she holds an olive branch, while her right rests on the sword, which sustains the shield of the United States. These emblems are such as the mass of our people will understand. In order to connect the richness of effect in the statue gradually with the architecture of the Dome, I have introduced a base surrounded by wreaths indicative of the rewards Freedom is ready to bestow upon distinction in the Arts and Sciences.[8]

The figure was to be supercolossal due to the height of its location at the summit, 294 feet from the ground. Crawford computed its size from the proportion of the cross atop Saint Peter's which measured 14 feet 3 inches and stood at an elevation of 265 feet. His figure was to be 16 feet high. Crawford guided his estimate of a price for the statue by his previous scale of payment by the government. Taking as his prototype the eight-foot high statue of America that had cost $1,400, and considering the minimal detail required of a figure to be placed so high, Crawford finally estimated the statue to be worth $3,000.

Crawford requested a tracing of "Mr. Walter's Dome." He took exception to its ungraceful termination and was pleased to have the opportunity to rectify it. His first design, however, received objections, for its ponderous effect and for the use of the cap and rods. His second design introduced a globe, which was to show the geographical location of *Liberty Triumphant*. It was Crawford's third design that ultimately satisfied Meigs, who commended it to Jefferson Davis as being lighter, while retaining "more vigor . . . and such boldness and shadows [as] will give it a distinctness when raised."[9] He requested Davis' approval of the design.

Crawford explained to Meigs that his paramount concern in

this figure, which would be seen only at a great distance, was "especial regard to its presenting an agreeable contour in all views." Crawford stated that the statue symbolized *Armed Liberty* in the guise of a flowingly draped woman at "rest upon the shield of our country . . . triumph is made apparent by the wreath held. . . . The sheathed sword . . . shows the fight over for the present but ready for use whenever required." Crawford explained that the "stars upon her brow indicate her heavenly origin . . . her position upon the globe represents her protection of the American world."[10]

Crawford still feared (and with good reason) Jefferson Davis' continued carping at the cap and rods. Davis persisted in interpreting the liberty cap as "the badge of the freed slave," which he held inappropriate in reference to a people born in freedom.[11] A native of Mississippi and soon to preside over the Confederacy, he was particularly sensitive to distinguish between the white and colored races in society. He argued that "the bundle of rods [were] no longer employed to suggest the functions of a Roman lictor," but were

Armed Liberty
1855-1862,
bronzed plaster model
Courtesy of the
National Collection of Fine Arts
Smithsonian Institution

being used allegorically. The symbolism could be stretched or narrowed. "Why should not armed Liberty wear a helmet?" he reasoned. He favored the use of a visor "so as to permit . . . the display of a circle of stars expressive of endless existence, and of a heavenly birth."[12]

Crawford's racial views resembled those of his colleagues' abroad and at home. These, with a few notable exceptions, did not differ from Davis'. During the Congressional debate on the Nebraska Bill of 1854, Crawford had expressed a "wish to see all the Niggers out of the country and the anti-slavery population with them," so great was his apprehension over the threat to the Union implied by the impending conflict.[13] Davis' objections posed no difficulties of conscience or conviction for Crawford.

The cap was discarded in favor of a helmet encircled with stars and surmounted by a crest composed of an "eagle's head and a bold arrangement of feathers, suggested by the costume of our Indian tribes."[14] The country's initials were inscribed on the breast. In this way, *Armed Liberty* was Americanized. Davis was satisfied and behaved with characteristically good southern manners in handling his secondary objections. He forwarded them to Meigs on January 15, 1856, in concert with his authorization for Crawford's execution of the statue. Meigs played the game cautiously, withholding the news from Rome until May when he received the revised design. The model was built up by Crawford's workmen according to his design and finished at the end of 1856.

21

Terminus

THE INTENSE WORK ON THE BRONZE DOORS AND THE MAJESTIC STATUE for the Capitol dome detained Crawford in Rome into the summer of 1855. He had wanted to go to Munich in May to inspect the bronze cast of the *Equestrian Washington* but he had had to relinquish the notion. Following his well-beaten track via Civita Vecchia he traveled instead on the steamer of August third to Marseilles and over the dusty roads northward by carriage to Paris. There he settled for a four week visit in Rue Castiglione "within twenty steps of the Louvre" in one direction and twenty steps from Place Vendôme in the other.[1]

Stopping in the Hotel de Londres, he chanced one day upon Richard Saltonstall Greenough, who handed him a letter he had been requested to deliver to Crawford in Rome from the president of the Mount Auburn cemetery in Cambridge, Massachusetts. It contained a commission for a life size marble statue of *James Otis* for a memorial "to accompany those already ordered of Rogers, Greenough, and Story."[2] The memorial was organized by a committee headed by Jack Bigelow, which served to decorate the old Gothic chapel at the cemetery and to construct the romantic tower and the monumental Egyptian gateway. Crawford informed Louisa of this commission from Paris. Given the "liberty to treat the subject as [he] pleased," he related that he "was offered $5,000 for the statue delivered at Boston."[3] He explained to Jack Bigelow at London that he had "some hesitation in accepting the order." He took exception at "being placed upon the same level with Story and Rogers." He had little quarrel over the price and even conceded "it pays well" although the sum fell short of his top fee.[4] His prices for the public works had ranged between $3,000 for his *Armed Liberty* and $9,000 each for the pedestrian figures of the *Washington* monument at Richmond. Now he quipped derisively to Louisa, "As a regular price [it] might well authorize me to put in a demission as the lawyers say. On the other hand, there is the opportunity of being seen. . . . If I make good use of it, it may be to my advantage."[5] He accepted the commission. It proved to be his last major work. The face was an idealized portrait, very likely after the frontispiece engraving of Otis contained in William Tudor's *The Life of James Otis.*

The arrival in Paris of Queen Victoria on the eighteenth of August created much excitement. Crawford often went around with Luther Terry and Richard S. Greenough to the art repositories. They visited the Madeleine, explored the Beaux Arts, and attended the grand opening of the special exhibition at the Louvre. Several old-time acquaintances turned up, such as the Hookers, the Pickmans, and George Sumner from Boston; the Clarkes; Mr. Ireland; and his artistic colleagues George Peter Alexander Healy, Thomas Rossiter, Randolph Rogers, and the Christopher Pearse Cranches. He renewed the acquaintance he made in Rome with Mrs. Carlotta Constant, a figure in the best literary and social circles in Paris. Her husband, Benjamin Constant, won fame with his novel *Adolphe* and through his amorous attachment to Madame de Staël. Crawford spent his short holiday in Paris zestfully, booked solidly for social events. He was soon surfeited and he alleged that he was "fairly sure [to] leave Paris without a single regret" and glad to leave behind the intense heat.[6]

Feeling impelled also to visit London to inspect the foundry and see how his *Flora* was being shown in the Crystal Palace, he took his leave of Paris on Friday the twenty-fourth. He arrived in London on Saturday and checked into the Trafalgar Hotel. He wrote Louisa that he called immediately on Mrs. Pickman and went again that evening to meet her friends. In the afternoon he visited

Portrait Statue of James Otis 1856, marble, 90″
Courtesy of the Harvard University Portrait Collection

Westminster, reporting to Louisa afterward that the "wretched sculpture" within Westminster was so bad as to be "almost ornamental."[7]

Refreshed by the fine weather—no fog—no rain—and agreeable coolness, he stretched the original four days allotted for London to twelve and found time "to go down to Hampton Court" with Sanders Marshall, twelve miles by rail, to see the collections.[8] "I have been extremely busy here," he wrote to Louisa, "being out most of the time with my friend Marshall who has planned that I shall dine with him in farewell tomorrow after which we are to visit the Foundry. . . . [and] Greenwich Hospital."[9] He reported that the Marshalls and others had rescued him from being "killed in London with their beef chops and potatoes."[10]

Paris seemed "very quiet after London," and he left September 5, sorry to have missed Terry who preceded him to Rome.[11] They were to have traveled southward together. As there was no steamer from Marseilles to Civita Vecchia on the seventh, he booked passage for the thirteenth, giving him almost another full week in Paris. His return to the studio on the seventeenth had protracted his absence two weeks beyond his scheduled month.

In the fall while Louisa took her holiday in Paris, he worked on a "new design for the dome," which he completed at the end of October. He also sketched sundry drawing-room pieces which he never executed, one a revised ideal *Sappho* for Mrs. Wadsworth.

The year 1855 was acknowledged within Crawford's family as marking the zenith of his career. The year was fittingly climaxed for the family at the Christmas holiday. Long afterward his daughter recalled the occasion nostalgically.

> The year 1855 is especially marked for me by its Christmas season, the last my father spent with us. . . . Beauty was everywhere that Christmas Day in Rome. In an ecstasy of admiration, I stood and watched my mother being dressed for the evening's festivity, her lively lips smiling at the reflection of herself in the glass, which certainly never showed a fairer picture. I took it all in—the perfect oval face, the dark sweet eyes, the camellia whiteness of the bare shoulders framed in old Venetian point that lost itself in the folds of her tearose moire gown, just the tint of her cheeks. She had big pearls in her ears, and a silver girdle knotted around her waist and falling to her feet.[12]

Catholic tradition made much of Twelfth Night, which in Rome was dizzily celebrated with Epiphany Fair in Piazza Navona. The family participated in the gay festivities. Mary Frazer captured vividly the excitement of the annual event.

A few weeks later the excitement of the Carnival illuminated life for ten days. To be dressed in a real domino and stand on a balcony in the Corso, flinging bushels of confetti and hundreds of posies at all and sundry, was something to dream of for the rest of the year. Every window in the street was hung with tapestries and garlands; the bands were playing in every square; the towering cars, wreathed with flowers, and filled with men and women in dazzling costumes, passed up and down in endless procession; the crowd below surged, and screamed, and danced a thousand antics, till the great moment struck when a company of mounted Dragoons came pounding along to clear the way. Breathless silence followed their passage. Then far away, from the Piazza del Popolo, sounded a muffled thundering of hoofs and a roar of voices, ever nearer and nearer, more and more deafening, till the "Bárberi," the riderless racehorses, wild with fear at the yells of the populace and the clattering of tinsel hung all over their bodies, swept into sight, flew past, and were lost to view as the crowd broke and closed in behind them—and the day was over!

Only on Shrove Tuesday did the festivities begin again after the race. Then every man, woman and child flourished a "móccolo," a lighted taper, and tried to keep it burning while extinguishing as many as possible of those around. For a couple of hours the street was a river of shifting light, and when it died out, thousands of voices joined in the dirge of the dying Carnival: "Il Carnevale è morto! Chi lo sepillirà?" (The Carnival is dead. Who will bury it?)[13]

Early that spring the family left Rome for a visit at home. Louisa had not returned in three years and longed to see her friends. Crawford's mother, now very old, was ailing and looking forward to meeting her two youngest grandchildren, Crawford himself wanted to see his mother once again, but before they were able to complete their arrangements, word came that she had died. The news was a great blow to Crawford, who had always been a devoted son. Having missed a farewell visit with his mother, he no longer felt pressed to leave his busy studio. He stayed behind to work on final details of the *Washington* monument. Several times ex-President

Millard Fillmore, who was recuperating that season in Rome, honored him by visiting his studio. Each time he praised the pediment figures.

Great news came from Richmond late in April, forwarded by Louisa's Uncle John. "Governor Wise assisted at the ceremonies of the Virginia Monument, determined to make a contract with Mr. Crawford for the completion of the four statues not yet contracted for. He acted under a law of the Legislature just adjourned. . . ."[14] Wise, under the impression that Crawford was bound for New York, wanted him to come as soon as possible to Richmond to conclude the new contract.

In the interim, a new board of commissioners had been appointed in Richmond to supervise the completion of the *Equestrian Washington* and revise the list of Virginia's heroes for the pedestrian statues. General Andrew Lewis, a Revolutionary War hero and a colleague of Washington's in the French and Indian Wars, was substituted for General Daniel Morgan. James Monroe was substituted for General Henry Lee. Monroe was then displaced by George Mason of Gunston Hall, author of the constitution of the revolutionary government of the commonwealth that was instituted in 1776 and of Virginia's Declaration of Rights. Madison was then eliminated in favor of Thomas Nelson, who had signed the Declaration of Independence for Virginia and succeeded Jefferson as governor. When Virginia had been threatened with invasion, he was appointed commander-in-chief of the state's forces and raised the money on his own credit to pay his troops. He was given the honor to be designated to accept the surrender of Lord Cornwallis. The final list comprised Thomas Jefferson, Patrick Henry, John Marshall, Andrew Lewis, George Mason, and Thomas Nelson.

The good news of the proferred contract reached Louisa in Paris just in time. She had been staying with the children in Crawford's favorite hotel, the Hotel de Hollande, before boarding the steamer at Le Havre. They proceeded to the grim establishment on Bond Street, where they were welcomed by Louisa's ascetic bachelor uncles, John and Richard Ward. For the summer they took a house at Newport near Julia's place, Oakglen. Louisa resumed her favorite American pastime, the round of family and social visits, while the children were allowed to romp freely at the seaside.

Meanwhile, Crawford pursued his usual frenetic routine in the studio. Now he felt the need to "rush to Richmond . . . for the contract . . . then to Washington, Boston, and New York and get ready to be off again for Europe in August, if possible.[15] He communicated his sense of urgency to Meigs, explaining that he would have a very limited stay in the States, and he would be "incessantly occupied."[16]

While the statues for Washington were being boxed, he supervised the casting in plaster of one of the bas-reliefs for the bronze doors, *The Evening Star*. He found time in the evenings to see his friends and give an occasional dinner party. Departing from his custom of inviting only male guests in Louisa's absence, one evening a Miss Fridel "woke up the Piano Forte" while the Freemans voiced their appreciation. Luther Terry, John Gadsby Chapman, Cephas G. Thompson, George Loring Brown, and Charles Perkins were frequent visitors.

Crawford finally disposed of the more urgent matters in his studio late in May to go "with lightning speed" to Munich, Parma, and Dresden. Three weeks later, on June nineteenth, he was once again installed in the Blaue Traube Hotel in Munich. It was eight months since the colossal horse, "a reincarnation of old Turkish bronze guns," had emerged from the molds of the Royal Foundry and twenty months after the casting of the equestrian figure of Washington.[17] An American eyewitness to the casting of the horse wrote an ecstatic and informative account of the event for a newspaper of Savannah, Georgia. He informed the public that the excess armament of the Crimean War that was melted down contained ninety percent copper and ten percent tin. Zinc was added to the mixture "to give the composition lustre and malleability, and to prevent the statues from becoming green by years of exposure. . . . These bronze surfaces are so worked up as to resemble flesh, cloth, etc., as, for example, Washington's sash had the fibre and lustre of silk, and the other surfaces, even of his leather boots, are all characteristic."[18]

Now Crawford had at last arrived to witness the results of his labors in their final form. He wrote Louisa exultantly "I have been to the Foundry and seen the Washington and a superb statue it is. My only regret is that you could not see it with me. It is now on exhibition for a week and has created quite a sensation in Munich. I am perfectly satisfied with the bronze work. I am just about writing Richmond for a ship of war to come to Amsterdam and take the statue home."[19] He then announced with pretended modesty to mask his pride that he had "only half an hour to get ready for an audience with the King." He resumed his letter following the royal audience. King Maximillian, who was accompanied by the queen and the empress of Austria, expressed "profound pleasure at seeing the equestrian statue," Crawford recounted. "He congratulated me upon its complete success and desired to know if anything could be done to render my stay in Munich more agreeable."[20] Unable to refrain from crowing just a little, he added, "Crodie is making his mark."[21] As if to bear out his remark, he was soon to learn that the king, on his own initiative, had sponsored him for election to membership in the Royal Academy at Munich.

His Munich business concluded, Crawford rushed back to Paris on the twenty-first of June, bound to sail on July 20 on the steamer *Sultan*. There he found a letter from Meigs informing him of the official approval given his colossal figure for the Capitol dome. Meigs said further that he had refused a design from another sculptor for the second pediment of the Capitol and hinted broadly that he was holding this next commission for Crawford. Unofficially, he requested Crawford to make a design, although he could not yet contract for the work.[22]

There was more good news to relate to Louisa. "I also have a letter from the chairman of the Clay Monument Association at New Orleans," he wrote, "requesting a design for a colossal statue of Henry Clay." Crawford informed Louisa that he had replied "declining any competition for the work and referring him to the major work in the U.S. Capitol for evidence of my ability."[23] He continued to tell of his having "offered to make a statue 12 feet high, delivered at New York for $16,000," his counter offer to the proposal mentioning sums in the range of $15,000 to $20,000.[24] He was doubling the price he had received for the pedestrian statues of the *Washington Monument*.

He revised his sailing schedule and arrived in Boston toward the end of July. He was promptly included in a dinner party at Mrs.

Fields, followed by what Crawford described to Louisa as a "charming dinner Saturday with several gentlemen at Parker's New House. There was Emerson . . . Whipple—Agassiz—Fields. Agassiz presided over the fish literally. We drank . . . and in spite of the heat continued to pass a few hours delicately . . . and we would have passed more had I not been obliged to bolt at 5 for the Dexters."[25] For the remainder of the weekend Crawford stayed with the Dexters at their summer house at Beverly on the North Shore.

He had a good talk about the *Otis* statue with members of the committee, but he told Louisa that he was even more "anxious to see the *Beethoven* in the Music Hall with Charlie Perkins."[26] He recounted, "I have been most enthusiastically praised to my face." This was unusual behavior for New Englanders, and Crawford declared that he was "highly gratified."[27]

Only at the end of the month did he go to Newport to visit Louisa and the children for a couple of days. Revising his original intention to sail on August 2 from Boston to Richmond with Mr. Ritchie, he went directly to Washington from Newport on August 1. He stopped on the way for a surprise visit with Annie and Adolph Maillard at Bordentown and stumbled into a party. He described the scene to Louisa, "The house was lighted with gas in every corner and appeared so brilliant as I approached it . . . like a fashionable hotel."[28] It was just an overnight stay as he left in the morning for Washington.

In addition to discussions about the dome figure, and plans for the second pediment, Meigs had still other projects on his mind. In charge also of constructing the new post office, he wanted the interior keystones to be decorated (provided the costs were reasonable) with nine bronze or zinc masks "symbolizing the Passions, such as Hope, Fear, Anger, Distrust, etc." Meigs wanted these portrayals to be "labelled for the benefit of those not accustomed to read characters and expressions."[29] He soon discovered that he could use fifteen more masks of this sort in plaster, bronzed zinc, or bronze, depending on price, to ornament the keys on the gallery fronts of the House of Representatives. Crawford agreed to make all twenty-four of these in plaster of paris ready for casting at fifty dollars each. He recommended the masks be cast in zinc by the inexpensive electrogalvanic process and then bronzed. In response to Meigs' queries respecting the niches in the Senate and the House of Representatives, Crawford urged the use of full-length statues in marble, not smaller than seven feet in height, as most harmonious with the decor. In this case the proximity of the viewer confined the choice of material to the best. The cost would not be prohibitive, especially when compared to the disastrous waste of money caused by the decision to cut the figures for the first pediment on location.

The main subject still undecided was that of the bas-reliefs for the interior frieze of the dome. Meigs and Crawford found themselves following the precedent of Thorwaldsen, patterning their thoughts after the *Triumph of Alexander*. They had already rejected figures in the round as being "not only heavy, but exceedingly disagreeable and not at all in harmony with the architecture."[30] Relief appeared the only logical form. Should the relief be high or low? What height should the figures be, what thickness? They concluded tentatively that a recess of nine inches in depth would be most desirable. Plaster would do for the material as it had suited well enough for Thorwaldsen's masterpiece. But what about the theme? Historical or allegorical? This would again require cogitation. This work was to involve an expenditure exceeding $70,000 and span the ensuing five years.

All this ground was covered in two days of concentrated talk. "I was so much occupied with Captain Meigs," confessed Crawford to Louisa, "that I could not catch a moment to write you during the two days I was in the city." He sent this apology from Richmond where he did obtain the requisite moments, mostly because the matter in hand, that of settling on the new contract, had been firmly decided beforehand. "Today, I have been with Governor Wise and tomorrow the contract for the remaining statuary will be drawn and signed and cleared, so that the affair will be completed without any more difficulty."[31] The contract was signed on August 9, 1856, for the four additional pedestrian statues for the monument, those of John Marshall, Thomas Nelson, George Mason and Andrew Lewis. Crawford left immediately, reporting to Louisa that he had been "kindly received by gentlemen of all parties."[32]

He spent five additional days in Washington trying to concretize his plans for the second pediment but ran into a second attempt to unseat Captain Meigs from his post of authority respecting public buildings. A bill containing this threat actually passed the House but failed in the Senate. "In the present state of this affair," concluded Crawford, "nothing can be said about the 2nd pediment. I suppose all that has been ordered remains intact."[33] He was getting used to the vagaries of Washington and did not lapse into despair as he might have in his younger days. He could feel sure it would all come to him in time. He was right. Soon after he left Washington he heard that the move against Captain Meigs was "quashed in the Senate. If displaced, no one with taste would have succeeded him," Crawford commented.[34]

He hastened his departure from Washington and stopped for a long weekend in a small town called Florence, which he described to Louisa as "a very beautiful spot only four miles from Bordentown." He wrote, "The gentleman who has invited me here desires to have a small statue of mine and thus business and pleasure go hand in hand."[35] Heading toward New York he went directly to John Ward's office to pick up his mail and settle other business matters before going home to Bond Street to meet Louisa's aunt, Louisa McAllister.

Louisa was now visiting the Dexters at Beverly and Crawford was trying to join her for a few days at least before his departure for Europe. He wanted especially to avoid dragging her about to suit his frantic travel schedule. After their reunion, he spent an evening in Boston with Hillard, Doughty, Whipple, and Woodman. After a literary discussion centering on a work of Goethe, he left to board the overnight train for New York.

Crawford had still another trip to make to Philadelphia early in September. He reported from there, "We are casting up the old subject of the equestrian statue and I fancy something will come out of it."[36] There was talk of $40,000 for this monument, implying a major work such as the monument in Richmond. After devoting a week in pursuit of this commission, he returned to New York to complete his plans to depart. He had also to collect the necessary portraits, costumes, and biographical material for the newly commissioned statues at Richmond. Ritchie, the editor of the *Richmond*

Enquirer, procured the likeness of Lewis and Senator Mason obliged regarding his forebear. The head of Marshall was still lacking but Crawford decided that a plaster copy of the bust in the Boston Athenaeum would do and asked Louisa to attend to this chore through Chickey and Ganer. Crawford gave Louisa exact instructions on how he wished her to proceed. "Edward Perkins will get the permission and thus reciprocate the act of Virginia in allowing the Washington of Houdon to be cast for the Boston Athenaeum. It should be done immediately. Copy this and give it to Edward. The bill will be paid by Uncle John and the head well packed and sent to him. It can be placed in the box with the books."[37]

After Crawford's departure plans were made, he went to Newport for a proper farewell with Louisa and the children. He stayed only five days, departing sadly from Louisa and calling her his "perfect heroine," in order to meet important engagements in New York on the nineteenth with Mr. Ritchie and Charles Sumner before sailing on the steamer *Fulton* the next day.[38] It had been decided between them that Louisa would remain in the States. She was to live with the Maillards at Bordentown for the academic year and enter the children in American schools to enable them to know their own country.

It was fortunate for Crawford that he had decided to invite his sister, Jenny Campbell, along to give her a European whirl and to provide company to alleviate his loneliness at Villa Negroni in his family's absence. Liberated from the care of their ailing mother, she easily obtained her husband's assent as a sort of reward for her devoted efforts.

During the last harried days in the States, Crawford developed pain and marked swelling in his left eye, but he did not take the time to have it treated, assuming that some foreign body had entered causing infection.

When they landed in Liverpool on the third of October, thirteen days from New York, the eye had not improved. Still thinking he had a foreign object in his eye, he wrote Louisa from shipboard on the *Fulton,* "I have not found any way so far of getting it out. I thought by this time, I would get clear of this trouble. . . . I am almost blind, blundering along. . . . I have scarcely read a page of print since I left you."[39] By the time they arrived in Paris, it was clear the eye trouble was not the ordinary variety. He wrote Louisa, "This eye of mine is getting really troublesome and I must find an occulist today and ascertain what can possibly be the matter with it."[40] Crawford did not go through with this plan, writing that he had decided "to let nature have her way for a while instead of doctoring it [which] could perhaps only make it worse. . . . I shall succeed better, I know, in Rome."[41] He stalwartly put his sister through the tourist paces on her first trip to Paris, although he went with a silk handkerchief tied over one eye and the other squinting. They had dinner in the Bois de Boulogne and went to the museums. Jenny even had a new wardrobe fabricated at a fine couturier for her entry into Roman life. Crawford's activities were not enough to bolster his sagging morale over the eye.

On October 23, they reached Villa Negroni via the familiar route of Marseilles and Civita Vecchia, after a miserable forty hour passage in atrocious weather that caused them to be "sick as dogs." Crawford reported that everything was in the most perfect order and "transcendentally clean."[42] Giuseppe had had the carpets cleaned and turned, the books dusted, the piano tuned, and had put flowers everywhere. From the window of the green room, Jenny had her first glimpse of the Campagna.

Crawford's friends turned out promptly to welcome him home and receive Jenny properly. They had just missed a big party for the resident American artists given by the American minister to Rome, Lewis Cass, Jr., who desired to ingratiate himself with the group. Crawford wrote Louisa regularly, relaying the news and the gossip. "The Thompsons have called. . . . Mrs. Freeman and her niece . . . Mrs. Chapman as usual . . . Terry up Sunday, the same good fellow, but I fancy getting older. . . . Brown has got rid of all trouble with his Casa Sposa. . . . The affair was decided by law —he has all the children, they being placed at a pensione paying $70 a year for their support and nothing to Madame!"[43] He reported that Harriet Hosmer had come by "looking more like 'a little pickle' than ever," and accompanied by Mrs. Mozier, "who appears to have taken possession of Mr. Cass' carriage and him too for that matter . . . Of course, Mrs. Mozier will be dropped with the usual style of Resident Ministers. . . . The Storys are expected in a few days. . . . Mrs. S. cannot resist the enchanting society of the snobs here."[44]

Crawford finally consulted a Dr. Smyth, a Philadelphian residing in Rome, about his eye and reported that he felt better quickly. "At least I got some sleep last night for the first time in a week. . . . I am hopeful I shall get better now. At least I can work with much greater freedom than I could."[45]

With the afflicted eye covered by his silk handkerchief, he returned at the end of October to his studio, where he found everything in perfect order. He announced that he had "commenced to work upon the dome statue," the model for which had been built up in clay from his design during his absence in the States.[46]

As his eye condition deteriorated steadily, Crawford reluctantly submitted to a minor operation by another doctor from Philadelphia. All hope was given for his total recovery. "Dr. Gibson says the whole affair will probably with a little time disappear as unaccountably as it came," Crawford wrote reassuringly to Louisa.[47] During the period of convalescence, he was confined to darkened rooms at home, where Jenny read to him from a chair while he lounged, listened, and dozed from another. "He has no company," said Jenny, "no evenings from home except with Mr. and Mrs. Hooker."[48] The friends, however, rallied around and called frequently. The Freemans, Cephas Thompsons, Chapmans, Ticknors, and especially the Storys were attentive and sympathetic.

Crawford was getting some work done intermittently and just before Christmas he was able to report "The colossal statue of the dome is being cast in plaster of Paris. The bas-reliefs for the doors of the Capitol are progressing. Next week goes up one of the Virginia Monument statues. . . . Even though I am not always in the studio, I am not idle."[49]

Christmas this year at Villa Negroni was a far cry from the little girl's recollection of the gay musical soirée of an earlier year. It rained throughout the night on Christmas Eve, and Crawford reported, "Christmas was such an abominable day."[50]

At the turn of the year the eye condition worsened drastically. Jenny felt obliged to inform Louisa. "His eye has been very troublesome. He has told you that there will be a consultation before he goes to Paris."[51] The news had been broken by Hooker on his own authority and Louisa began to demand the truth. Crawford was vexed with Hooker for he had not wanted Louisa to worry. He wrote to reassure her.

> I have made up my mind to start for Paris next week and place myself at once in the hands of the most superior occulist there. I fully believe this is the only way of conquering this inconvenience, as nothing has resulted for the better from the physical treatment I had at the hands of Smyth and Gibson of Philadelphia. Friday, we shall have a consultation on the subject . . . Dr. Pantaleon, Dr. Shattuck of Boston. . . . I want to start for France and accomplish as rapid a cure as possible . . . as I cannot be absent from the studio for any great length of time. I shall take Giuseppe with me . . . to the Hotel de Hollande where I know I shall be very comfortable. Jenny remains at the villa during my absence.[52]

He left the villa on the morning of January 14 for Civita Vecchia, giving himself a day of rest before going aboard. He wrote in further reassurance to his wife, "I go armed with letters from Dr. Pantaleon to the most eminent doctors in Paris and I may expect the most careful treatment and have a hope on its good result."[53] At the last moment Luther Terry decided to accompany his friend. Crawford wrote that Terry was to go with him as far as Civita Vecchia and "maybe to Paris as he says he always gets ill in Rome about February." Crawford added, "I shall be very glad to have his company."[54]

Terry went all the way and stayed close to Crawford, having found a more modestly priced hotel nearby. He lost no time delivering Dr. Pantaleon's letters. Dr. Nelaton, the great surgeon, and Dr. Ichett, the occulist, decided in consultation not to perform any further operation but to let medicines work, given reasonable time. The wait was "something of a bore" to Crawford, boxed up in new rooms he had taken at No. 4, Rue d'Algerie, in sharp contrast to his normally active pace. He reported himself as calm but not quite resigned. "I cannot say how long I will be here . . . 'tis a long and trying case—perhaps one month, perhaps three. I count the days and the months," he confessed.[55]

Crawford had been reluctant to subject Louisa to a trans-

Atlantic crossing during the winter season, but he submitted to Hooker's prompting in January and did not countermand his initiative in sending for her.

Depositing the children with the Maillards, Louisa braved the stormy winter seas, broke through the ice-bound New York harbor, and got over. The Parisian surgeons realized that the tumor was carcogenic, but no one would tell Crawford. He passed the time in pain and darkness, with occasional attempts at modeling for distraction. Charles Sumner found him in this condition one beautiful day in March after some search in various familiar hotels. He understood immediately from Louisa that the disease was fatal and came to pay his farewell call, even if he was only allowed to stay but a few minutes. The mood was sombre and heartrending, particularly because Crawford still anticipated a cure. Sumner recorded that Giuseppe, upon hearing of their eighteen-year friendship, "fell on his knees . . . and poured out his affection and his grief for his master."[56] Then Crawford entered the room. Sumner noted in his journal that Crawford's "diseased eye was covered with a shade," but the other eye and Crawford's face looked well. Sumner held Crawford's hand, expressed "fervent good wishes," and left.

Crawford's last letter from Paris was addressed to Meigs on April 1, six months before he died. It relayed news of the bargain price for casting the *Armed Liberty* that he had exacted from Von Miller at Munich and urgently appealed for consent to expedite the statue there. It was signed by Louisa, yet it concluded: "You will be glad to know that I am suffering somewhat less than a month ago, and have hope of ultimate recovery of health and strength, if not the use of my afflicted eye."[57] Three months later he was blind.

A distinguished eye surgeon, Dr. J. Weldon Fell, was imported from London. He recommended the removal of the tumor and the diseased eye, in an attempt to alleviate the suffering by eliminating the pressure on the brain. With little hope, Crawford was carried to London by Louisa, accompanied by Jenny. At the end of May he executed his last will and testament, leaving his entire estate, except for dower, to his children, under the direction of his wife. The operation did not exceed expectation. He lingered some months and died in London on October 10, 1857, at the height of his career "in full possession of his senses and in great peace of mind."[58]

Crawford's body was conveyed home to New York by Louisa and Jenny for burial in the Greenwood Cemetery following a funeral in Saint John's Episcopal Church. The pallbearers were Charles Sumner, Henry T. Tuckerman, George Washington Greene, James Lenox, John F. Kensett, and Dr. Francis Lieber.

On November 4, 1857, a meeting of artists and other friends was convened in Rome. James E. Freeman presided and Luther Terry acted as secretary. Those present unanimously adopted resolutions of deepest sympathy for the widow and family. These were transmitted and the list of forty-five signatories was impressive. They were:

> Luther Terry, James E. Freeman, John Gibson, John Gadsby Chapman, Henry Williams, Cephas G. Thompson, H. Toormer, Rudolph Lehmann, George Loring Brown, D. W. Dindan, M. Seitz, Edgar Welby, Emilus Wolff, Benjamin E. Spinel, Sol Troschel, P. T. Rothermel, Isaac Jackson, Carl Prundt, E. L. Schremfurt, J. O. Montalant, Paolo Guglielmi, Max Michael, August Riedel, William Page, J. Callen Tilten, Abel Nichols, T. Gerrard Small, M.D., Robert Macpherson, Joseph Ropes, Chauncey B. Ives, L. S. Barridge, J. S. Haseltine, J. Mozier, P. Girometti, William S. Haseltine, William Whitridge, J. G. Haviland, William Ewing, J. C. Hooker, John McDonald, Thomas Desoulavy, Holmes Caldwell, Jeremy Wilson.

John Gibson, dean of the group, delivered a tribute to Crawford's genius and high productivity. Considering the *Indian Chief* to be Crawford's finest production, Gibson proposed that the friends assembled see to it that the model be cast in bronze and placed in a public hall "as a monument to the author, an American sculptor of great original genius."[59] The vote was unanimous that the artists and friends should raise the subscription. It is questionable that the bronze was made, but some years later a handsome replica was presented to the New-York Historical Society by its president, Frederick de Peyster.

Shortly after the funeral in New York George Washington Greene wrote a commemorative piece for the *Evening Post*. On

February 26 Julian C. Verplanck presided over a memorial meeting of artists and friends which was held in the Century Club at New York to hear an eulogy read by Thomas Hicks. The eulogy was printed and it furnished the major source of information about Crawford's life until George Washington Greene's essay appeared in his *Biographical Studies* and Samuel Osgood's laudatory article was published in 1875. Crawford's memory was eclipsed by the great popularity of his son and to this day most people identify him through his son.

Louisa undertook to supervise the completion of Crawford's important unfinished works. She not only gained the confidence of Meigs but that of his successor, Captain W. B. Franklin, who issued his authorization to her on June 9, 1860, to proceed with the works. She had already recovered from her grief at her husband's death and had initiated the proceedings in consultation with Luther Terry, John Gadsby Chapman, William Henry Rinehart, and Randolph Rogers.

The acclaimed equestrian group of horse and seated figure of Washington was dispatched from Munich early in July 1857, accompanied by minute details for its assembly and mounting provided by the foundry director, Ferdinand Von Miller. The brig *Walborg* brought it to the dock in Richmond and it was transported to Capitol Square on November 24, 1857. It was assembled and erected immediately upon arrival along with the statues of *Thomas Jefferson* and *Patrick Henry*. An elaborate inaugural celebration was held on February 22, 1858, and Louisa attended. There was a procession of military and Masonic bodies down Main Street, ending at a grandstand at the capitol square where Governor Henry A. Wise presided and eulogies were read. An oration was delivered by Edward Everett on the character of George Washington.

Crawford had completed the statues of *George Mason* and *John Marshall* in plaster cast, leaving only their casting to be overseen. He had shaped out the figure of *Andrew Lewis* in clay and sketched that of *Thomas Nelson*. At Louisa's request, Randolph Rogers supervised the completion and casting of all the remaining pedestrian figures. He was paid the balance of $4,500 each owing to Crawford for the statues of *Mason* and *Marshall* and signed his

Equestrian Washington   1850–1857, bronze
Courtesy of the Virginia State Library, Richmond

own contract with the state of Virginia on December 18, 1857, for the other two statues of *Lewis* and *Nelson*, at $9,000 each. He contracted further to execute six bronze trophies and bas reliefs for the six lower pedestals and for the six allegorical figures that would stand on them, symbolizations of *Justice, Revolution, Colonial Times,* the *Bill of Rights, Finances,* and *Independence.* All the statutes were added to the monument as they arrived between 1860 and 1869. The cost of the entire monument eventually came to $259,913, two and a half times the anticipated sum.

The *Equestrian Washington* monument at Richmond was undoubtedly Crawford's most successful work. He broke artistic ground with it in several ways. Foremost among these was the shift from rigid marble cut by skilled workmen with calipered mathematical dispassion to bronze molded in a precise replica of the artist's minutest line. He fulfilled his goal to achieve a pleasing contour from all angles of the monument, and he satisfactorily realized in his historical figures the transition from classical idealizations to realistic portrayals in contemporary costume.

The bronze doors were the most complicated and novel of Crawford's works. It is a pity that he did not live to witness their completion. Before he was stricken, he was far advanced on the plaster models for the Senate entranceway and had finished the clay models for the House doors. These were both later completed by William Henry Rinehart, who had come to Rome from Baltimore and was selected by Louisa to continue the work. Considerable technical skill had been exercised from the very beginning by Crawford's able German assistant, Kanpest, who remained under Rinehart and gave some measure of continuity to the execution.

The first pair of doors for the Senate represented Crawford's work exclusively, as Rinehart merely applied finishing touches to the plaster models. For the House pair, Rinehart executed the plaster models after Crawford's clay sketches. The work took Rinehart some four years. Contrary to Crawford's admonition "that experiments were too hazardous in works of this description," the doors were not cast in Munich, the only foundry in the world whose capability Crawford would trust.[60] The artists at Rome and Florence, Louisa, and Captain Franklin all concurred. At the Royal Foundry in Munich the maximum estimated cost of casting in solid bronze with a fire gilt finish outside was $8,000 each. By some mysterious slight of hand, the work was shifted to the Ames foundry at Chicopee, Massachusetts. Five years earlier, the superintendent of the foundry there had seen Crawford's bronze *Beethoven* and confessed to Crawford "that such a work was beyond his power and would be for many a day."[61] Yet the doors were cast there by James Ames and installed in 1868 at the Capitol.

For the task of modeling the plaster casts of the House doors, Rinehart was paid $8,940. These, too, were cast at Chicopee in 1904, under the supervision of Melzer H. Mosman. The cost was $45,000, bringing the total cost to $53,940. These doors were installed in 1905.

Randolph Rogers, who designed the interior pair of doors for the same entranceways, consigned his plaster models for baking under the supervision of Von Miller at the foundry at Munich for $17,000. He took full advantage of Crawford's last lengthy round of bargaining with Von Miller. Rogers was paid $8,000 for his work. Upon learning of this sum, Crawford had protested in view of his remuneration of $6,000 and in recognition of his superior training and standing to Rogers. Meigs' defense of the discrepancy was disingenuous, resting his case on the difference in the size of the doors, those of Rogers being a good deal larger. Trying to placate Crawford, Meigs wrote, "The ratio of size is as 1 43/100ths to 1 and Mr. Rogers agrees to deliver his model in Washington City. . . . It contains a surface of 128⅓', one of yours has a surface of 90'."[63] The total cost of these doors, wrought with far superior workmanship than Crawford's (as completed by Rinehart), was only $25,000 exclusive of transportation. They illustrated the life of Columbus and were considered "a real American home made work of art."[64]

The completion of Crawford's works for the Capitol at Washington was supervised by Captain Meigs, followed by his successor, Captain W. B. Franklin, in the course of fulfilling the tasks of their office. The model of Crawford's gigantic statue for the Capitol dome that had been built up by the workmen in his studio from his design was shipped home on April 19, 1858, on the bark *Emily Taylor*. The ship sprang a leak and put into Gibraltar on May 19 for repairs. During a stormy passage, the leaks recurred. It was rumored that the statue had sunk to the ocean bottom with the ship, but the tale proved apocryphal. Other cargo had been jettisoned to lighten the limping vessel, but the statue was safe. In December it was forwarded to New York on the bark *G. W. Horton*, which had been dispatched from Boston especially for the mission. For no discernible reason, except perhaps to avoid winter storms, it was not transshipped to Washington until the end of March the following year.

The statue was cast in bronze during the Civil War, not at Munich as Crawford had urged but in Washington in response to the political pressures exerted by Clark Mills. His foundry was situated near Bladensburg, Maryland, northeast of the capital. Of greater weight in the decision to cast the figure in America was the adamance of both Meigs and Jefferson Davis to subsidize, if they must, American entrepreneurs "to introduce the art here."[65] Mills was paid $20,796.82 for labor, ironwork, copper, and the casting in bronze. Exclusive of machinery and the statue's placement on the dome, the aggregate cost $25,770, inclusive of the fee paid Crawford for his model. It was estimated broadly that the price was "at least three times as large as any private gentleman in any other city could have got such a work done for."[66] The half would have more accurately approximated the Munich estimate of $14,000, including, after bargaining by Crawford, the expense of transportation to Amsterdam or Bremen. According to an informed source, the casting by Mills "was of a very inferior kind."[67]

The completed figure measured nineteen feet six inches and weighed 14,985 pounds. For a year it decorated the grounds east of the Capitol until it was erected at noon on December 2, 1863, to a national salute of thirty-five guns (one for each state) from a field battery on Capitol Hill, answered by similar salutes from surrounding forts. The work was pronounced a failure by contemporaries. The report of the secretary of the interior stated that "at that great altitude it is placed, it loses shape and outline."[68] Even now it is often mistaken for an Indian figure because of its crest and the illegibility of the other emblems at the distance.

The colossal recumbent figures of *History* and *Justice* that Crawford designed to surmount the Senate entranceway were cut into marble in Rome and arrived at Washington during the winter of 1859. They were stored in the old Hall of Representatives until the portico was ready to receive them. Captain W. B. Franklin reported the receipt of the "beautiful figures."[69] The last remaining figure for the Senate pediment was completed in marble in 1860. It was a colossal allegorical female statue symbolizing *America*. Too large to be brought into the old Hall of Representatives where the others were displayed, it was temporarily set upon a pedestal in the eastern wing of the Capitol. The last stage of raising them to their permanent destination in the Senate pediment occurred in the fall of 1863.

The task of supervising the completion of Crawford's major works forced Louisa's return to Rome. Four years later she married Crawford's devoted friend Luther Terry, with whom she had three more children. In her old age, she once again basked in reflected glamour, this time that of Francis Marion's phenomenal literary success. Terry never really arrived as a painter, but the marriage was by all accounts a happy one.

During his lifetime Thomas Crawford produced a prodigious number of works, more than sixty finished statues and bas reliefs, some of monumental size. He made some fifty sketches in plaster and left scores of incompleted designs. Crawford fancied himself imaginative as well as creative and lamented his inability to give form to all of the works he could conceive. He gained the respect of his colleagues for his talent and won public acclaim for his works.

Progress of American Civilization 1853–1863, marble
Courtesy of the United States Capitol

Governmental administrators gave him the opportunity to create lasting decorations for the United States Capitol and other public places. His *Beethoven* was deemed by George Washington Greene as "a form as grand as the grandest symphonies of the mighty German."[70] His *Equestrian Washington* was judged similarly as "a conception of moral sublimity and intellectual power," and his *Armed Liberty* atop the Capitol dome was said to reflect "a glowing, exultant, almost defiant patriotism . . . looking forth in the pride of her beauty and her strength."[71]

With Horatio Greenough and Hiram Powers, Thomas Crawford set his country's nineteenth-century pattern of portraying American themes in Italian forms. These early professional sculptors went to Italy to learn the rudiments of their craft and to imbibe the arts generally. Their taste accorded with the art that surrounded them during their lengthy foreign residence: classical sculpture and Italian painting, music, literature, and, especially, aesthetics. They retained their native American character and outlook, their puritanical drive and morality, and their industrious habits. They participated in the American intellectual pastime of lamenting the dearth of culture in their homeland, but they remained quintessentially American in their personal attachments and national loyalties.

These first three American sculptors were pioneers in the development of American art. They sought to contribute to their country's artistic expression and embellishment but were unable to transcend the neoclassical Italianate aesthetics in which they were grounded.

Greenough's theories pervaded the entire Transcendentalist circle and his criticism took root, but during the midcentury both public and private American buildings and gardens were embellished in the Italian neoclassical style. The gap between American artistic ideals and their expression in native forms had to wait another half century to be closed.

These three sculptors, however, moved toward the goal of serving their native land artistically: Greenough as the pioneer sculptor and aesthetical critic at Washington; Powers in the excellence of his realistic portraiture; and Crawford in his Capitol adornments and bronze monumental statues.

Notes

Notes to Introduction

1. John Smythe Memes, *Memoirs of Antonio Canova*, p. 14.
2. Frances Boott Greenough, ed., *The Letters of Horatio Greenough to his Brother, Henry Greenough*, p. 46.
3. A prime example was Lord Thomas Bruce Elgin (1766–1841), a diplomat whose memory is maligned for having pilfered some of the choicest classical remains of the Parthenon from the Athenian Acropolis. He transported them home to London at his own expense for which he was never entirely compensated by the government. His collection, known as the Elgin Marbles, was deposited with the British Museum in 1818 and consigned to basement storage for ten years before being accorded appropriate recognition. The marbles might have been lost to posterity, as were numerous similar treasures taken from the Acropolis, if Elgin had not foreseen their historic value.
4. James Fenimore Cooper, *Correspondence*, vol. 1, p. 164.
5. James Fenimore Cooper, *Gleanings in Europe by an American*, vol. 1, p. 34.
6. Horatio Greenough to Cooper, August 22, 1821, Cooper Letters, Yale University Library, New Haven, Connecticut.
7. Horatio Greenough to R. H. Dana, September 21, 1843, Dana Collection, Massachusetts Historical Society, Boston, Massachusetts.
8. Vernon Louis Parrington, *Main Currents in American Thought*, vol. 2, p. v.
9. Charles E. Fairman, *Art and Artists of the Capitol of the United States*, p. 3.
10. Giuseppe Franzoni's father was president of the Academy of Fine Arts at Carrara. Considered by Mazzei to be an excellent sculptor, Giuseppe was brought over by Latrobe in February 1806 along with Giovanni Andrei, who was reputed to excel in decoration. With an eye to the future, Latrobe wrote within a month of their arrival, authorizing them "to hire one or two apprentices to teach them the art of sculpture."

Ibid., Mazzei letter, March 25, 1806. The dependence on these Italians and the difficulty of uprooting them from home complicated the task of our early planners. This was confounded by the initial problem of fusing Italian preconceptions with American requirements. There was trouble, for example, with Franzoni's eagle, which seemed Italian. Latrobe demanded "an American Bald Eagle." (Ibid., letter, March 18, 1806.) An appeal was made to Charles Willson Peale in Philadelphia, whose natural history collection had a specimen of the desired species. Peale supplied an accurate drawing of the head and claws of the bald eagle in proportion, and the eagle was Americanized. The confusions of tradition were further compounded by the barrier of language, but the Italians were conscientious, competent, and precise in their work. Andrei was appointed as superintendent of carving statuary and ornamental work of the U.S. Capitol until his death in 1824, when he was succeeded by another Italian, Iardella, who died in 1830.

11. Their colleague, Valaperta, who executed the eagle on the frieze of the south colonnade in the old House of Representatives, came over the same year.

12. Edward Everett, "American Sculptors in Italy," *Boston Miscellany of Literature and Fashion*, January—June, 1842, pp. 4–9.

13. Giuseppe Ceracchi modeled portrait busts of George Washington, Alexander Hamilton, Benjamin Franklin, and other revolutionary leaders. He left the United States in 1801 for Paris, where he was guillotined for suspicion of plotting against the life of Napoleon.

14. Several of Charles Willson Peale's eleven children were named for famous painters: Raphael, Angelica Kauffman, Titian, Rubens, and Van Dyck.

15. "Extracts from the Correspondence of Charles Willson Peale Relative to the Establishment of the Pennsylvania Academy of Fine Arts," *Pennsylvania Magazine of History and Biography*, no. 1, vol. 9, July, 1855.

16. Ibid.

17. Allan Nevins, ed., *The Diary of Philip Hone*, p. 207. *Death on a Pale Horse* was shown in New York April 12, 1836.

18. After the Peales' withdrawal in 1822, the museum was run by a succession of entrepreneurs until 1856, when it was closed.

19. Samuel Irenaeus Prime, *The Life of Samuel F. B. Morse*, vol. 1, p. 121.

20. Frances Trollope, *Domestic Manners of the Americans*, pp. 65–66. Eckstein and his wife finally opened a private school that offered "an elementary literary and scientific English education" to young ladies, but this effort also failed, and Eckstein later moved his school to Kentucky.

21. Ibid., p. 66. Around this time, an attempt to organize a mechanics institute came to naught in its first and last meeting, failing to attract more than fifteen people.

22. Samuel Morse collected a number of plaster casts in Italy for presentation to the National Academy of Design for exhibition and study. These included Thorwaldsen's *Venus* and *Mercury*, Trentanova's *Cupid* and bust of *Columbus*, Gibson's *Venus* and *Cupid*, the *Farnese Hercules*, the *Isis* and the *Ariadne* of the Capitoline Museum, the Braschi's *Antinous*, a bas-relief by Michelangelo, and from the Vatican, the *Cnidian Venus*, *Minerva Medici*, the colossal *Lys*, and the *Cupid* or *Genius*. (Felix Cicognari [U.S. Consul at Rome] to S. F. B. Morse, March 7, 1832, Morse Papers, Library of Congress, Washington, D.C.). Through the intervention of the American minister at Paris, Chancellor Robert R. Livingston, Emperor Napoleon ordered a dozen plaster casts made of antique nude statues

for shipment to the National Academy of Design.

23. Cooper, *Gleanings in Europe*, vol. 1, p. 37.

24. Henry T. Tuckerman, *A Memorial of Horatio Greenough*, pp. 11–16.

25. Mabel Munson Swan, *The Athenaeum Gallery, 1821–1873, The Boston Athenaeum as an Early Patron of Art*, Introduction, p. 1.

26. Ibid.

Notes to Chapter 1: American Background

1. Frances Boott Greenough, ed., *Letters of Horatio Greenough to his Brother, Henry Greenough*, p. 14.

2. Horatio Greenough file, New York Public Library.

3. William Dunlap, *History of the Rise and Progress of the Arts of Design*, quoted in the *American Magazine of Useful and Entertaining Knowledge*, vol. 2, 1836, p. 367.

4. On leaving Harvard two years ahead of Horatio, John went to London, where he was directed by Washington Allston to the guidance of the already famous Charles Leslie, who had formed a triumvirate with Coleridge and Allston a decade earlier. In the late forties John joined Horatio in Florence, remaining a constant source of worry due to his lack of success. John then went to Paris, where he died in 1852 at the age of forty-nine.

5. Greenough, *Letters*, p. 219. Richard Greenough's group of the *Shepherd Boy and Eagle* is in the Boston Athenaeum and his statue of *Benjamin Franklin* still stands in School Street, Boston.

6. *American Magazine of Useful and Entertaining Knowledge*, vol. 2, 1836, p. 367. William S. Shaw was the director of the Athenaeum at the time.

7. Henry T. Tuckerman, *A Memorial of Horatio Greenough*, p. 46.

8. Ibid., p. 16.

9. *American Magazine of Useful and Entertaining Knowledge*, vol. 2, 1836, p. 368.

10. Tuckerman, *Memorial*, p. 15.

11. Ibid.

12. Horatio Greenough to Richard Henry Dana, September 21, 1843, Dana Collection, Massachusetts Historical Society, Boston, Massachusetts.

13. Horatio Greenough to Richard Henry Dana, June 11, 1844, Dana Collection, Massachusetts Historical Society.

14. Jared Flagg, *Life and Letters of Washington Allston*, vol. 1, p. 99.

15. Ibid.

16. Ibid., p. 64.

17. Ibid.

18. Justin Winsor, *A Memorial History of Boston*, vol. 4, p. 477.

19. Greenough, *Letters*, p. 20.

20. Years after John Trumbull's death, Weir was commissioned by Congress to paint the last unassigned panel in the rotunda of the Capitol, for which he did the *Embarkation of the Pilgrims*.

21. Horatio Greenough to Richard Henry Dana, September 19, 1829, Dana Collection, Massachusetts Historical Society.

22. Flagg, *Life and Letters of Washington Allston*, pp. 215–216. The self-portrait, a marble bust, I have located in Paris in the former residence of the Coopers.

23. Tuckerman, *Memorial*, p. 19.

24. Allston to Morse, January 24, 1828, Historical Society of Pennsylvania.

25. Flagg, *Life and Letters of Washington Allston*, pp. 215–216.

26. Greenough, *Letters*, p. 26.

27. Ibid.

28. Ibid., pp. 21, 32.

29. Ibid., p. 31.
30. Ibid., p. 29.
31. Ibid., p. 30.
32. Quotations in this paragraph are from Greenough, *Letters*, pp. 25, 37, 35. Charles Bird King (1785–1862) was born in Newport, Rhode Island. He studied in New York City with Edward Savage and with Benjamin West in London and settled in Washington, D.C., after some years in Philadelphia and Baltimore. He is known for his still life paintings and his portraits of Indians. (George C. Groce and David H. Wallace, *The New-York Historical Society's Dictionary of Artists in America, 1564–1860*.)
33. Quotations in this paragraph are from Greenough, *Letters*, pp. 33, 35.
34. Quotations in this paragraph are from Greenough, *Letters*, pp. 36, 35.
35. Greenough, *Letters*, p. 41. Causici did well in Baltimore where his commission earned him $30,000.
36. Ibid., p. 38.
37. Ibid., p. 39.
38. Ibid.
39. Horatio Greenough to Robert Gilmor, May 17, 1828, Pennsylvania Historical Society.
40. Ibid.
41. Horatio Greenough to Morse, May 15, 1828, Morse Papers, Library of Congress.
42. Horatio Greenough to R. H. Dana, October 10, 1828, Dana Collection, Massachusetts Historical Society.

Notes to Chapter 2: Florentine Attractions

1. William Ware, *Sketches of European Capitals*, p. 92.
2. Ibid.
3. Ibid., pp. 112–114, 125.
4. Giovanni Dupres, *Thoughts on Art and Autobiographical Memoirs*, p. 157.
5. James Fenimore Cooper, *Gleanings in Europe by an American*, vol. 1, p. 38.
6. The Pergola was opened as the chief theater and opera house of Florence in 1652 and reconstructed in 1738. It could seat 2,500 spectators. The entrance fee was two Florentine lire. See *Notizie e Guida di Firenze e de' suoi Contorni* (Florence: Guglielmo Piatti, 1841).
7. Quotations in this paragraph are from George Stillman Hillard, *Six Months in Italy*, p. 85.
8. Rembrandt Peale, *Notes on Italy*, p. 242.
9. After working in Paris under the benign, appreciative eye of the art-loving Emperor Napoleon, Bartolini had gone for a while to Carrara in Tuscany, where he enjoyed the beneficient protection and largess of Princess Mathilde, patroness of the School of Imperial Works. After the emperor's defeat at Waterloo, Bartolini had to flee a mob from the small town, finding refuge in Florence.
10. Dupres, *Thoughts on Art*, p. 117.
11. Ibid.
12. Ibid., p. 121.
13. Peale, *Notes on Italy*, p. 242.
14. Horatio Greenough to R. H. Dana, November 17, 1829, Dana Collection, Massachusetts Historical Society.
15. Peale, *Notes on Italy*, pp. 242, 243. Although the judgment on Greenough's scientific study of sculpture was rendered in 1831, the statement remained true throughout his career.
16. Horatio Greenough to Cooper, May 28, 1832, Cooper Papers, Yale University Library.
17. Horatio Greenough to R. H. Dana, April 18, 1829, Dana Collection, Massachusetts Historical Society.
18. Horatio Greenough to R. H. Dana, November 17, 1829, Dana Collection, Massachusetts Historical Society.

19. Horatio Greenough to R. H. Dana, September 19, 1829, Dana Collection, Massachusetts Historical Society.
20. Horatio Greenough to R. H. Dana, November 17, 1829, Dana Collection, Massachusetts Historical Society.
21. Ibid.
22. James Fenimore Cooper, *Correspondence*, vol. 1, p. 165.
23. Ibid., pp. 167–168.
24. Ibid.
25. Horatio Greenough to Cooper, April 10, 1830, Cooper Letters, Yale University Library.
26. Horatio Greenough to Cooper, June 21, 1831, Cooper Letters, Yale University Library.
27. "Greenough, the Sculptor," *Putnam's Monthly Magazine*, March, 1853, p. 318.
28. Horatio Greenough to R. H. Dana, November 17, 1829, Dana Collection, Massachusetts Historical Society.
29. James Jackson Jarves, *The Art Idea*, p. 260.
30. Horatio Greenough to Gilmor, February 25, 1829, Maine Historical Society, Portland, Maine.
31. Ibid.
32. Ibid.
33. Cooper, *Correspondence*, vol. 1, pp. 167–168.
34. Horatio Greenough to Gilmor, January 13, 1832, Boston Public Library.
35. Cooper, *Correspondence*, vol. 1, pp. 167–168.
36. Ibid.
37. Ibid.
38. Horatio Greenough to Gilmor, May 16, 1829, Historical Society of Pennsylvania, Philadelphia, Pennsylvania.
39. Horatio Greenough to Cooper, December 20, 1830, Cooper Letters, Yale University Library.
40. Horatio Greenough to Gilmor, May 16, 1829, Historical Society of Pennsylvania.
41. Horatio Greenough to R. H. Dana, September 19, 1829, Dana Collection, Massachusetts Historical Society.
42. Horatio Greenough to Cooper, December 20, 1830, Cooper Letters, Yale University Library.
43. Cooper, *Correspondence*, vol. 1, p. 170.
44. Horatio Greenough to Gilmor, February 25, 1829, Maine Historical Society.
45. Horatio Greenough to Cooper, June 21, 1831, Cooper Letters, Yale University Library.
46. Horatio Greenough to Gilmor, May 16, 1829, Historical Society of Pennsylvania.
47. Cooper to Horatio Greenough, November 25, 1829, Joint Universities Library, Nashville, Tennessee.
48. Horatio Greenough to Cooper, May 16, 1829, Historical Society of Pennsylvania.
49. Ibid.
50. Cooper to Horatio Greenough, November 25, 1829, Joint Universities Library.
51. Horatio Greenough to R. H. Dana, September 19, 1829, Dana Collection, Massachusetts Historical Society.
52. Cooper to Horatio Greenough, November 25, 1829, Joint Universities Library.
53. Horatio Greenough to Cooper, December 20, 1830, Cooper Letters, Yale University Library.
54. Cooper to Horatio Greenough, February 18, 1831, Joint Universities Library.
55. Witness the nude statue of *Wellington* in Trafalgar Square and the equally nude representation of *Emperor Napoleon* in Paris. Canova had been commissioned to execute a statue of Washington for the new statehouse at Raleigh, North Carolina. His first plan depicted Washington as nude as the others, but, upon reflection, he literally "converted Washington into a Roman soldier" in a seated position. (L. Jarvis to Allston, June 6, 1834, Massachusetts Historical Society, and Edward Everett to Horatio Greenough, July 19, 1832, Joint Universities Library.) The finished statue depicted Washington fully dressed in a Roman warrior's decorated breastplate with a toga draped over

his breast and shoulders, sandals tied twice above the ankles, and with weapons of war, the sword and rod, discarded on the ground. According to Allston, this was the pose for posterity of the "gentleman farmer," the man of peace. The figure is looking at the lawgiver's tablet held in his left hand, while gripping a pencil or stylus in his raised right hand, poised to write. There is a plaster model of this statue in the Canovian Museum in Possagno, Italy. The study in plaster was completed in April of 1818. The marble statue was received enthusiastically in 1821 but destroyed by fire in 1822. (Elena Bassi, *La Gipsoteca di Possagno*, [Venice: *Neri Pozza*, 1957], pp. 235, 237.

56. Cooper to Horatio Greenough, March 14, 1831, Joint Universities Library.

57. Cornelius C. Felton, review of "The Chanting Cherubs of Horatio Greenough," *North American Review*, vol. 41, 1835, pp. 167–169.

58. [Stillman, George Hillard.] "Letter on The Chanting Cherubs." *New England Magazine*, vol. 1, July 1831, p. 20.

59. Frances Boott Greenough, *Letters of Horatio Greenough to his Brother, Henry Greenough*, p. 70. Another

eulogistic review of the *Chanting Cherubs*, probably written by George S. Hillard, appeared in an article about Greenough entitled, "Sculpture," in *New England Magazine*, December 1833.

60. Horatio Greenough to Gilmor, February 25, 1829, Maine Historical Society.

61. Greenough, *Letters*, p. 72.

62. James J. Jarves, *The Art Idea*, p. 260.

63. *New York American Reviewer*, April 30, 1831, quoted in the *Dictionary of American Biography* article on Greenough.

64. Cooper to Horatio Greenough, December 24, 1831, Joint Universities Library.

65. Horatio Greenough to Morse, January 5, 1832, Morse Papers, Library of Congress.

66. Cooper to Horatio Greenough, February 18, 1831, Joint Universities Library.

67. Ibid.

68. Cooper to Horatio Greenough, December 24, 1831, Joint Universities Library.

69. Cooper to Horatio Greenough, April 22, 1832, Joint Universities Library.

70. Horatio Greenough to Cooper, December 17, 1831, Cooper Letters, Yale University Library.

Notes to Chapter 3: Bread and Butter Staple

1. Horatio Greenough to Gilmor, February 25, 1829, Maine Historical Society, Portland, Maine.

2. Horatio Greenough to Gilmor, May 16, 1829, Historical Society of Pennsylvania, Philadelphia, Pennsylvania.

3. A francesconi was roughly equivalent to the American dollar.

4. Horatio Greenough to Gilmor, April 12, 1831, Maine Historical Society.

5. Horatio Greenough to Gilmor, March 12, 1829, Pennsylvania Historical Society.

6. Horatio Greenough to Gilmor, May 17, 1828, Pennsylvania Historical Society.

7. Horatio Greenough to Cooper, January 14, 1832, Cooper Letters, Yale University Library.

8. Horatio Greenough to Gilmor, April 25, 1830, Cooper Letters, Yale University Library.

9. Horatio Greenough to Gilmor, April 12, 1831, Maine Historical Society.

10. Ibid.

11. Horatio Greenough to Gilmor, September 7, 1830, Boston Public Library.
12. Ibid.
13. A copy of Thorwaldsen's statue of *Byron* stands in the Villa Borkgese, Rome. The ceremonial unveiling took place in the spring of 1959.
14. George Gordon Noël Byron, *The Poetical Works of Lord Byron* (London: Oxford University Press, 1904), p. 292.
15. Horatio Greenough to Cooper, November 8, 1831, Cooper Letters, Yale University Library.
16. Ralph Waldo Emerson, *The Complete Essays and other Writings of Ralph Waldo Emerson.* (New York: Modern Library, 1940), p. 524.
17. Horatio Greenough to Gilmor, June 10, 1832, Boston Public Library.
18. Ibid.
19. Horatio Greenough to Samuel Cabot, November 12, 1832, Massachusetts Historical Society, Boston.
20. Ibid.
21. Horatio Greenough to Samuel Cabot, November 12, 1832, Massachusetts Historical Society.
22. *North American Review,* vol. 41, 1835, p. 167.
23. Leonard Jarvis to Allston, June 6, 1834, Massachusetts Historical Society.
24. Alfred Greenough to Gilmor, June 28, 1834. New-York Historical Society.
25. James M. Nicholson, Mrs. B. I. Cohen's Fancy Dress Party, *Maryland Historical Magazine,* vol. 14, 1919, p. 354. Nathalia Wright, "Horatio Greenough, Sculptor,–R. Gilmor, Jr., Patron," *Maryland Historical Magazine,* March, 1956, pp. 11–13. Upon the death of Robert Gilmor, his widow returned to her native Charleston, South Carolina, carrying the bust with her. As there were no children, the rest of the collection was sold at auction in 1849. The *Medora* is now in the possession of Mrs. Sumner Parker of Baltimore.
26. Frances Boott Greenough, *Letters of Horatio Greenough to his Brother, Henry Greenough,* p. 46.
27. Horatio Greenough to Cooper, April 10, 1830, Cooper Letters, Yale University Library.
28. Horatio Greenough to Morse, January 5, 1832, Morse Papers, Library of Congress.
29. Horatio Greenough to Cooper, March 3, 1830, Cooper Letters, Yale University Library.
30. Ibid.
31. Greenough, *Letters,* p. 66.
32. John Gadsby Chapman's portrait of *Horatio Greenough* hangs in the Boston Athenaeum.
33. Horatio Greenough to Cooper, December 6, 1830, Cooper Letters, Yale University Library.
34. Ibid.
35. Cooper to Horatio Greenough, December 10, 1830, Joint Universities Library, Nashville, Tennessee.
36. Cooper to Horatio Greenough, February 18, 1831, Joint Universities Library.
37. Horatio Greenough to Allston, October 1831, Massachusetts Historical Society.
38. Horatio Greenough to Rembrandt Peale, November 8, 1831, New-York Historical Society. Greenough lived at 25 rue de Surene, which was located in a fashionable neighborhood near the Madeleine and the artistic faubourg St. Honoré. The house is now the residence of the Belgian ambassador.
39. Greenough, *Letters,* p. 86.
40. Ibid., p. 88.
41. Horatio Greenough to Rembrandt Peale, November 8, 1831, New York Historical Society.
42. Horatio Greenough to Morse, April 23, 1832, Morse Papers, Library of Congress.
43. Greenough, *Letters,* p. 88.
44. Ibid., p. 89.
45. Ibid.
46. The American Committee for the Assistance of the Polish Liberation was organized to aid the revolt of

the Polish landowners against the Czarist Russian occupation.

47. Horatio Greenough to Cooper, November 8, 1831, Cooper Letters, Yale University Library.
48. Ibid.
49. Greenough, *Letters*, p. 99.
50. Horatio Greenough to Allston, October 1831, Massachusetts Historical Society.
51. Horatio Greenough to Rembrandt Peale, November 8, 1831, New-York Historical Society.
52. Ibid.
53. Greenough, *Letters*, p. 99.
54. Horatio Greenough to Cooper, December 17, 1831, Cooper Letters, Yale University Library.
55. Horatio Greenough to Cooper, November 8, 1831, Cooper Letters, Yale University Library.
56. Edward Lind Morse, *Letters and Journals of S. F. B. Morse*. Vol. 1, p. 413.

57. Horatio Greenough letters to Cooper of those dates, Cooper Letters, Yale University Library. Greenough's total debt to Cooper of 1,600 francs was repaid in May of 1833.
58. Horatio Greenough to Cooper, January 14, 1832, Cooper Letters, Yale University Library.
59. Horatio Greenough to Morse, January 5, 1832, Morse Papers, Library of Congress. Greenough had moved to Via San Sebastiano, Florence.
60. Horatio Greenough to R. H. Dana, September 19, 1829, Dana Collection, Massachusetts Historical Society.
61. Horatio Greenough to Cooper, January 14, 1832, Cooper Letters, Yale University Library.
62. Horatio Greenough to Cooper, December 20, 1832, Cooper Letters, Yale University Library.
63. Horatio Greenough to Rembrandt Peale, November 8, 1831, New-York Historical Society.

Notes to Chapter 4: George Jupiter Washington

1. Horatio Greenough to R. H. Dana, April 18, 1829, Dana Collection, Massachusetts Historical Society.
2. Cooper to Horatio Greenough, September 15, 1829, Joint Universities Library.
3. The Indian figure was a plagiarism taken straight out of Persico's *Discovery Group*. It reappeared in Greenough's last major work, the *Rescue Group*.
4. Quotations in this paragraph are from a letter of Horatio Greenough to Cooper, March 7, 1831, Cooper Letters, Yale University Library.
5. This representation of George Washington was already a hackneyed concept.
6. Cooper to Horatio Greenough, May 1, 1830, Joint Universities Library. Also see Cooper to Horatio Greenough, December 24, 1831, Joint Universities Library.

7. Edward Everett to Horatio Greenough, April 12, 1832, Joint Universities Library.
8. Gales and Seaton, *Register of Debates*, Document 45.
9. Thomas Cole to Morse, August 4, 1832, Morse Papers, Library of Congress.
10. Gales and Seaton, *Register of Debates*, Document 45.
11. Horatio Greenough to Cooper, January 29, 1833, Cooper Letters, Yale University Library.
12. Ibid.
13. Allston to Joseph Cogsdell, February 27, 1832, Massachusetts Historical Society.
14. Horatio Greenough to Cooper, April 10, 1833, Cooper Letters, Yale University Library.
15. Horatio Greenough to Morse, May 31, 1832, Morse Papers, Library of Congress.

16. Edward Everett to Horatio Greenough, May 29, 1839, Joint Universities Library.

17. Edward Everett to Horatio Greenough, July 29, 1832, Joint Universities Library. The eminent French writer, Quatremere de Quincy, published a paper at that time in Paris on *Jupiter Olympus*.

18. Edward Everett to Horatio Greenough, January 13, 1834, Joint Universities Library.

19. Edward Everett to Horatio Greenough, December 15, 1834, Joint Universities Library.

20. Ibid.

21. Edward Everett to Horatio Greenough, June 28, 1841, Joint Universities Library.

22. Cooper to Horatio Greenough, January 19, 1833, Joint Universities Library.

23. Horatio Greenough to Lady Bulwer, n.d. Greenough File, Library of Congress.

24. Ibid.

25. Ibid.

26. Ibid.

27. Ibid.

28. Leonard Jarvis to Allston, June 6, 1834, Massachusetts Historical Society.

29. Allston to Leonard Jarvis, June 19, 1834, Massachusetts Historical Society.

30. Ibid.

31. Ibid.

32. Edward L. Pierce, *Charles Sumner, Memoir and Letters*, vol. 2, p. 110.

33. Ibid.

34. Horatio Greenough to Sumner, November 16, 1839, Charles Sumner Autograph File, Harvard University Library.

35. Sumner to Horatio Greenough, February 28, 1841, Lincoln Library, Shippenburg, Pennsylvania.

36. Ibid.

37. Sumner to Horatio Greenough, Nov. 8, 1839, Lincoln Library.

38. Ibid.

39. Ibid.

40. Ibid.

41. Horatio Greenough to Cooper, December 18, 1832, Cooper Letters, Yale University Library.

42. Francis Boott Greenough, *Letters of Horatio Greenough to his Brother, Henry Greenough*, p. 98.

43. Ibid. Greenough also acquired a copy of Stuart's *Washington*, painted by his friend, Francis Alexander, for assistance in obtaining the best likeness. He passed his cost of $200 on to the government when he included it among other expenses for the statue.

44. Horatio Greenough to Morse, August 24, 1834, Morse Papers, Library of Congress.

45. Ibid.

46. Ibid.

47. Ibid.

48. Gales and Seaton, *Register of Debates*, Document 45, p. 7.

49. Ibid.

50. Ibid, p. 10.

51. Ibid, p. 8.

52. Damages costing $6,000 were included in Greenough's bill of expenses submitted to the government. Ibid., Document 45, p. 6.

53. Ibid., Document 45.

54. Ibid., March 12, 1841.

55. Ibid., Document 45, p. 4. Even in those days, wages in the United States were several times those in Italy.

56. Horatio Greenough to Hiram Powers, August 1842, Joint Universities Library.

57. Ralph Leslie Rusk. *The Letters of Ralph Waldo Emerson*, vol. 3, pp. 121–122.

58. Ibid.

59. House Report No. 219, 27th Congress, Third Session. Available in the Office of the Architect of the Capitol.

60. Charles Akers, "Sculpture in the United States," *Atlantic Monthly*, vol. 22, November, 1868, p. 561.

61. Diary of Philip Hone April 29, 1844, New-York Historical Society.
62. Trollope, *A Visit in Italy*, 1, p. 96.
63. Edward Everett, "American Sculptors in Italy," *Boston Miscellany of Literature and Fashion*, January–June 1842, pp. 4–9.
64. Ibid.
65. Ibid.
66. H. T. Tuckerman's "The Statue of Washington" was printed in his *A Memorial of Horatio Greenough*. S. D. Dakin's "Lines on the Statue of Washington," was published in *The Knickerbocker*, vol. 20, 1842.
67. Alexander Everett, "Greenough's Statue of Washington," *United States Magazine and Democratic Review*, vol. 14, June 1844, pp. 618–621.
68. Greenough, *Letters*, pp. 180–181.

Notes to Chapter 5: Prolific Years

1. Frances Boott Greenough, *Letters of Horatio Greenough to his Brother, Henry Greenough*, p. 66.
2. Ibid, p. 102.
3. Horatio Greenough to Morse, April 23, 1832. Morse Papers, Library of Congress.
4. Greenough, *Letters*, p, 101.
5. Ibid., p. 107.
6. Ibid., p. 101.
7. Ibid., p. 93.
8. Horatio Greenough to Morse, April 23, 1832, Morse Papers, Library of Congress.
9. Ibid.
10. The *Angel and Child* is in the Boston Museum of Fine Arts.
11. Horatio Greenough to Cooper, December 18, 1832, Cooper Letters, Yale University Library.
12. Horatio Greenough to Morse, April 23, 1832, Morse Papers, Library of Congress.
13. Horatio Greenough to Cooper, January 29, 1833, Cooper Letters, Yale University Library.
14. Horatio Greenough to Allston, March 7, 1835, Massachusetts Historical Society.
15. "Sculpture," *New England Magazine*, vol. 8, January 1835, pp. 41–44.
16. Greenough, *Letters*, pp. 104–105.
17. Horatio Greenough to Cooper, May 28, 1833, Cooper Letters, Yale University Library.
18. Horatio Greenough to Cooper, May 15, 1833, Cooper Letters, Yale University Library.
19. Horatio Greenough to Cooper, May 28, 1833, Cooper Letters, Yale University Library.
20. Ralph Waldo Emerson, "English Traits," *The Complete Works of Ralph Waldo Emerson*, 12 vols. (Boston: Houghton Mifflin Co., 1883), vol. 5, p. 9.
21. Horatio Greenough to Allston, undated, 1835 or 1836, Massachusetts Historical Society.
22. Greenough, *Letters*, p. 106.
23. Ibid., p. 111.
24. Ibid.
25. Horatio Greenough to Allston, undated, 1835 or 1836, Massachusetts Historical Society.
26. Horatio Greenough to Gilmor, November 28, 1835, Boston Public Library.
27. Horatio Greenough to Allston, undated, 1835 or 1836, Massachusetts Historical Society.
28. Gales and Seaton, *Register of Debates*, pp. 1314–1318.
29. Ibid., p. 1316. James Buchanan of Pennsylvania, later president of the United States, was the protagonist favoring Persico in the House of Representatives. Persico was retained by the government on a regular salary of $1,500 a year for the job.
30. Horatio Greenough to Cooper, May

15, 1835, Cooper Letters, Yale University Library.

31. Greenough, *Letters*, pp. 111, 110.

32. James Fenimore Cooper, *Correspondence*, vol. 1, p. 357. See also p. 355.

33. On the flyleaf of S. F. B. Morse's French-English dictionary, Morse Papers, Library of Congress.

34. Horatio Greenough to Cooper, July 30, 1836, Cooper Letters, Yale University Library.

35. Horatio Greenough to Cooper, September 23, 1836, Joint Universities Library.

36. Greenough, *Letters*, p. 68.

37. Horatio Greenough to Cooper, September 23, 1836, Joint Universities Library.

38. Greenough, *Letters*, p. 114.

39. Ibid., p. 129. There was a typical two year gap between the completion of the model in plaster and its execution in marble.

40. Greenough's statue of *Aristides* is now in the Art Gallery of Yale University, New Haven, Connecticut.

41. Horatio Greenough to Mr. Elton, September 23, 1836, Brown University.

42. Tuckerman. *Memorial*, pp. 33–34.

43. Ibid.

44. Ibid., p. 33.

45. In 1846, Greenough sold two marble copies of the *Head of Christ*, one of which stands at the entrance hallway of the Boston Public Library.

46. Greenough, *Letters*, p. 114.

47. Ibid., pp. 114–115.

48. Horatio Greenough to Morse, May 31, 1832, Morse Papers, Library of Congress.

49. Louisa Gore's given name was Eliza according to a letter attached to the flyleaf of Tuckerman's *Memorial of Horatio Greenough* in the Boston Athenaeum. She went by the name of Louisa, however.

50. Edward Everett to Horatio Greenough, June 26, 1836, Joint Universities Library.

51. Greenough, *Letters*, p. 117.

52. Ibid. p. 119.

53. Ibid., p. 121.

54. There is a room in the Massachusetts General Hospital that is dedicated to Dr. John Collins Warren in recognition of this achievement.

55. Copies of the busts of Dr. John Collins Warren and his father are at Harvard. In 1852, Dr. Warren offered to exchange his bust for an inferior one made by Dexter which was in the Boston Athenaeum. This was done and the Greenough bust was shown in the 1854 exhibition as belonging to the Boston Athenaeum.

56. Greenough, *Letters*, p. 119.

57. Ibid., p. 124.

58. Ibid., p. 116.

59. Ibid., p. 129. A hundred napoleons was the approximate equivalent of $400.

60. Ibid., p. 128.

61. Horatio Greenough to Allston, February 18, 1838, Massachusetts Historical Society.

62. Greenough, *Letters*, p. 124.

63. Ibid., p. 127.

64. Ibid., p. 125.

65. Ibid., p. 127.

66. Ibid., p. 170.

67. Ibid., p. 139.

68. Ibid., p. 227.

69. H. T. Tuckerman, *Memorial*, p. 32.

70. Greenough, *Letters*, p. 135.

71. Tuckerman, *Memorial*, p. 32.

72. Greenough, *Letters*, p. 135.

73. Ibid., p. 125.

74. Henry Greenough to Charles E. Norton, March 31, 1860, Archive, Boston Athenaeum.

75. Cooper to Horatio Greenough, June 2, 1832, Joint Universities Library. The *Venus* was actually commenced before Greenough's marriage.

76. Greenough, *Letters*, p. 119.

77. Horatio Greenough to Allston, February 18, 1838, Massachusetts Historical Society.

78. Ibid.

79. Ibid.
80. Greenough, *Letters*, p. 130.
81. Horatio Greenough to Allston, February 18, 1832, Massachusetts Historical Society.
82. Greenough, *Letters*, p. 121.
83. Edward L. Pierce, *Charles Sumner, Memoir and Letters*, vol. 2, p. 111.
84. Ibid.
85. James Schouler, paper read to the American Historical Society meeting in Boston, Massachusetts, May 23, 1887, Miscellaneous File, New York Public Library.
86. Greenough, *Letters*, p. 153.
87. Along with other treasures, Salisbury bequeathed the *Abdiel* and the *Angel* to Yale University, where they are now in the Yale University Art Gallery.
88. Greenough, *Letters*, p. 122.
89. Ibid., p. 129.
90. Boston Athenaeum *Letterbook*, vol. 17, p. 5, September 1851. Copy for an advertisement in the *Daily Advertiser*.
91. Greenough's letter of acceptance is in the files of the Accademia di Belle Arti, Florence, Italy, July 6, 1840.
92. Greenough, *Letters*, p. 136.
93. Frances Trollope, *A Visit to Italy*, vol. 1, pp. 174–175.

Notes to Chapter 6: Sculptural Hiatus

1. Graefenberg lies in the sector of Austrian Silesia that was incorporated into Czechoslovakia when that state was established independently in 1918.
2. Horatio Greenough to Rev. R. Waterston, March 25, 1845, Massachusetts Historical Society.
3. Ibid.
4. Francis Boott Greenough, *Letters of Horatio Greenough to his Brother, Henry Greenough*, pp. 195–196.
5. Ibid., pp. 196–197.
6. Ibid., p. 199.
7. Greenough, *Letters*, p. 200.
8. Ibid., p. 201.
9. Ibid., p. 202.
10. This monument for the poet Giuseppe Guisti, a leading figure of the Risorgimento, was apparently never completed in the marble, nor were Greenough's companion bas-reliefs for the monument, the *Genius of Italy* and the *Genius of Poesy*. They were probably sketched and modeled in clay, as Greenough claims in his letters. They were both reported by Giuliana Artom Treves in *Gli Anglo-Fiorentini di Cento Anni Fa*, and by Van Wyck Brooks in *Dream of Arcadia* to exist in Pescia, a small town in Tuscany, not far from Florence. On a recent trip I interviewed both Giuliana Artom Treves and Professor Rolando Anzilotti, the former mayor of Pescia who now teaches at the University of Pisa. I am satisfiied that this statue does not exist in Pescia, nor have I been able to locate it anywhere else in centers of Giusti lore. Madame Treves confessed to me that she had never actually seen the work, as did Professor Anzilotti.
11. Greenough, *Letters*, p. 212.
12. Ibid., p. 216.
13. H. T. Tuckerman, *A Memorial of Horatio Greenough* (G. P. Putnam, 1853), p. 36.
14. Greenough, *Letters*, p. 93.
15. George Ticknor, *Life, Letters, and Journals*, 2 vols. (Boston and New York; Houghton Mifflin, 1909), vol. 2, pp. 241–242.
16. Greenough, *Letters*, pp. 220–221.
17. Horatio Greenough to Joseph Cogswell, September 26, 1850, Boston

Public Library, Boston, Massachusetts.

18. Ibid.

19. Ibid.

20. Greenough, *Letters*, p. 225.

21. Ibid., p. 227.

22. Horatio Greenough to Joseph Cogs-Well, September 26, 1850, Boston Public Library.

23. The *Castor and Pollux* bas-relief is located in the Boston Museum of Fine Arts.

24. Greenough, *Letters*, p. 224.

25. Horatio Greenough to Joseph Cogswell, September 26, 2850, Boston Public Library.

26. Horatio Greenough to Belmanno, October 29, 1850, Boston Public Library.

27. Greenough, *Letters*, p. 228.

28. Ibid., p. 224.

29. Horatio Greenough to the Prefect of Florence, January 9, 1851. Greenough protested to the prefect of the city against the poor policing to protect residents against ruffians in the neighborhood, who menaced children as well as adults. Police Record No. 323, File 59, Archivio dello Stato, Florence.

30. Greenough, *Letters*, p. 234.

31. Ibid., p. 235.

Notes to Chapter 7: Untriumphant Return

1. Horatio Greenough to William Cullen Bryant, November 4, 1851, Cooper Letters, Yale University Library.

2. Ibid.

3. Francis Boott Greenough, *Letters of Horatio Greenough to his Brother, Henry Greenough*, p. 239.

4. Ibid., p. 237.

5. Ibid.

6. Edward Everett to Horatio Greenough, March 14, 1845, Joint Universities Library.

7. Horatio Greenough to William Cullen Bryant, February 5, 1852, New York Public Library.

8. Quotations in this paragraph are from a letter of Henry Greenough to Horatio Greenough, April 7, 1852, Griswold Collection, Boston Public Library.

9. Horatio Greenough to Susan Cooper, August 11, 1852. Cooper Letters, Yale University

10. Greenough, *Letters*, pp. 238–239.

11. Horatio Greenough to Morse, August 1852, Morse Papers, Library of Congress.

12. Both quotations are from a letter of Horatio Greenough to William Cullen Bryant, November 4, 1851, Cooper Letters, Yale University Library.

13. Horatio Greenough to Morse, August 1852, Morse Papers, Library of Congress.

14. Horatio Greenough to William Cullen Bryant, November 4, 1851, Cooper Letters, Yale University Library.

15. Horatio Greenough to Morse, August 1852, Morse Papers, Library of Congress.

16. Greenough, *Letters*, p. 240.

17. Samuel Longfellow, *The Life of Henry Wadsworth Longfellow*, p. 230.

18. Ibid.

19. Horatio Greenough to Susan Cooper, August 11, 1852, Cooper Letters, Yale University Library.

20. Greenough, *Letters*, p. 239.

21. Record of MacLeans Hospital, now located at Belmont, Massachusetts. The cause of death is listed as "brain fever." The dates of admission and death are also available. There is no record of his death in the office

of the City Clerk, either at Somerville, Newport, or Boston, Massachusetts. The Cambridge Death Records bear the legend "nervous derangement."

22. R. H. Dana to Charles Sumner, December 20, 1852, Harvard University Library.

23. George Gibbs, *The Gibbs Family of Rhode Island*, p. 107.
24. Nathalia Wright, *Horatio Greenough, The First American Sculptor*, p. 261.
25. Ibid., p. 295.
26. Henry T. Tuckerman, *A Memorial to Horatio Greenough*, p. 235.

Notes to Chapter 8: Summation of Influence

1. A microfilm copy of this contract is in the Joint Universities Library.
2. Francis Boott Greenough, *The Letters of Horatio Greenough to his Brother, Henry Greenough*, p. 116.
3. Ibid.
4. Judge Edward G. Loring (a friend of the Greenough family) to Senator James Pearce, chairman of the Joint Committee on the Library, March 14, 1859, Office of the Architect of the Capitol.
5. Ibid.
6. Greenough, *Letters*, p. 232.
7. Ibid.
8. Edward Everett to Horatio Greenough, February 7, 1842, Joint Universities Library.
9. Edward Everett to Horatio Greenough, February 22, 1842, Joint Universities Library.
10. Greenough, *Letters*, p. 240.
11. *Statutes L*, vol. 10, p. 95, August 21, 1852, for the fiscal year 1853, National Archives, Washington, D.C. One estimate of the cost of the *Rescue Group* (Hazelton's *Washington Guide Book*, p. 89) was $28,201.89 and is obviously in error. There are no figures available relative to Greenough's expenses for materials, workmen, and others, so that no accurate estimate was possible for his reimbursement from the government.
12. Judge Edward G. Loring to Senator James Pearce, chairman of the Joint Committee on the Library, March 14, 1859, Office of the Architect of the Capitol.
13. Ibid.
14. On April 26, 1939, Representative Burdick introduced this joint resolution into the House of Representatives, House Resolution 276, 76th Congress, First Session. Office of the Architect of the Capitol.
15. Horatio Greenough, *Travels, Observations, and Experience of a Yankee Stone-Cutter*, pp. 75–77.
16. Horatio Greenough to Emerson, September 11, 1852, Harvard University Library.
17. Oliver Larkin, *Art and Life in America*, p. 183.
18. Greenough, *Travels*, pp. 53–54.
19. Ibid., p. 55.
20. Ibid., p. 54.
21. Ibid., p. 55.
22. Margaret Fuller Ossoli, *At Home and Abroad*, p. 246.
23. Greenough, *Travels*, p. 55.
24. Ralph Waldo Emerson, *Journals*, vol. 8, p. 390.
25. Larkin, *Art and Life*, p. 183.
26. Ibid.
27. Henry T. Tuckerman, *The Criterion*, or *the Test of Talk about Familiar Things, A series of Essays*, p. 343.

Notes to Chapter 9: Aesthetics

1. Horatio Greenough to R. H. Dana, June 11, 1844, Dana Collection, Massachusetts Historical Society.
2. Ibid.
3. Horatio Greenough, *The Travels, Observations, and Experience of a Yankee Stonecutter*, pp. 197–198.
4. Quoted in John Smythe Memes, *Memoir of Antonio Canova*, p. 213. The quote is from a saying of Lysippus.
5. Johann Joachim Winckelmann, *History of Ancient Art*, vol. 2, p. 301.
6. Ibid., p. 302.
7. Ibid., p. 310.
8. Horatio Greenough, *Form and Function*, p. 92.
9. Ralph Waldo Emerson, *The Complete Works of Ralph Waldo Emerson*, vol. 1, p. 24.
10. Winckelmann, *History of Ancient Art*, vol. 1, p. 214.
11. Greenough, *Travels*, p. 202.
12. Winckelmann, *History of Ancient Art*, vol. 2, p. 310.
13. Ibid., vol. 1, p. 216
14. Horatio Greenough to Ralph Waldo Emerson, December 28, 1851, Harvard University Library.
15. Greenough, *Form and Function*, p. 120.
16. Ibid.
17. Greenough, *Travels*, p. 201.
18. Ralph Waldo Emerson, *Complete Works*, vol. 6, pp. 274–275.
19. Greenough, *Travels*, p. 203.
20. Greenough, *Form and Function*, p. 118.
21. Ibid., p. 107.
22. Plato, *Dialogues*, vol. 3, pp. 66–67.
23. *Aristotle's Treatise on Rhetoric*, Theodore Buckley, ed., pp. 36–37.
24. Greenough, *Travels*, pp. 137.
25. Ibid., p. 202.
26. Ibid., pp. 139–140.
27. Greenough, *Form and Function*, note, p. 61.
28. Greenough, *Form and Function*, p. 104.
29. Ibid.
30. Both quotations in this paragraph are from Greenough, *Travels*, p. 206.
31. Ibid., p. 44.
32. Greenough, *Form and Function*, p. 105.
33. Greenough, *Travels*, p. 44.
34. Ibid.
35. Greenough, *Form and Function*, p. 100.
36. Plato, *Dialogues*, vol. 3, p. 218.
37. John Smythe Memes, *Memoir of Antonio Canova*, p. 339.
38. Francesco Milizia, *The Lives of Celebrated Artists*, vol. 1, preface.
39. Quotations in this paragraph are from the introduction to Milizia's *Lives of Celebrated Artists*, pp. 13, 44–45, 51, 44, and 44.
40. Greenough, *Form and Function*, p. 98.
41. William Hogarth, *The Analysis of Beauty*, p. 39.
42. Milizia, *Lives*, vol. 1, p. xliv.
43. Greenough, *Form and Function*, p. 98.
44. Greenough, *Travels*, pp. 137–138.
45. Milizia, *Lives*, vol. 1, p. xix.
46. Ibid., p. xxxiii.
47. Winckelmann, *History of Ancient Art*, vol. 2, p. 371.
48. Milizia, *Lives*, vol. 1, p. xxxiii.
49. Greenough, *Travels*, p. 31.
50. Milizia, *Lives*, vol. 1, p. liv.
51. Ibid., p. lxiii.
52. Greenough, *Travels*, p. 141.
53. Ibid.
54. Ibid., p. 142.
55. Ibid.
56. Ibid., pp. 132–133.
57. James Fenimore Cooper, *Home as Found*, p. 22.
58. Greenough, *Travels*, pp. 140–141.
59. Ibid., pp. 138–139.
60. Ibid., p. 145.

61. Greenough, *Form and Function*, p. 116.

62. Winckelmann, *History of Ancient Art*, vol. 2, pp. 285–299.

63. Ibid., p. 296.

64. Ibid., p. 287.

65. Greenough, *Form and Function*, p. 111.

66. Greenough, *Travels*, p. 16.

67. Ibid., p. 126.

68. Ibid., p. 20.

69. Ibid., p. 18.

70. Ibid.

71. Greenough, *Form and Function*, p. 103.

72. Horatio Greenough to R. H. Dana, September 19, 1829, Dana Collection, Massachusetts Historical Society.

73. Greenough, *Form and Function*, p. 103.

74. Greenough, *Travels*, p. 132.

75. Samuel Henry Butcher, *Aristotle's Theory of Poetry and Fine Art*, p. 127.

76. Winckelmann, *History of Ancient Art*, vol. 2, p. 371.

77. Ibid., pp. 287–288.

78. William Hogarth, *The Analysis of Beauty*.
Sir Joshua Reynolds, *Discourses*. The Royal Academy at London, where these discourses were delivered, was founded in 1768 and Sir Joshua was president for most of its years until his death.

79. Sir Archibald Alison, *Essays on the Nature and Principles of Taste*.
Sir Charles Eastlake, *Contributions to the Literature of the Fine Arts*. As the late president of the Royal Academy at London and director of the National Gallery, he lived many years in Italy and was an acquaintance of Horatio Greenough and a neoclassicist.
Lady Eastlake, *The Life of John R. Gibson, R.A.*
James Ferguson, *An Historical Inquiry into the True Principles of Beauty in Art, more especially with reference to Architecture*.
Edmund Burke, *A Philosophical Enquiry into the Origin of our Ideas of the Sublime and the Beautiful.*

80. Edward Lacy Garbett, *A Rudimentary Treatise on the Principles of Design in Architecture*. Among the English aestheticians of this period, his position was closest to Greenough's and he was excluded from Greenough's disparaging generalizations. Although he published after Greenough's first essay appeared, Greenough was familiar with his ideas. Garbett admitted of three components of good architecture, fitness, stability, and beauty, which, taken together, assimilated to Greenough's concept of functionalism. He affirmed "the end of art is truth," and "the highest beauty is fitness." (P. 255.)
John Ruskin, *The Seven Lamps of Architecture*, *Lectures on Architecture and Painting* and *The Stones of Venice*.

81. Burke, *A Philosophical Enquiry*, p. 97.

82. Ibid., pp. 99–125.

83. Ibid., p. 121.

84. Ibid., p. 141.

85. Greenough, *Form and Function*, p. 90.

86. Ibid.

87. Ibid., p. 103. These generalizations excepted Garbett and Ruskin whose works appeared after the publication of Greenough's essay on "Aesthetics at Washington" in 1843. Ruskin's first appeared in 1849. Garbett's in 1850.

88. Ibid., p. 105.

89. Greenough, *Travels*, p. 33.

90. Ibid., p. 136.

91. Ibid., p. 47.

92. Robert Dale Owen, *Hints on Public Architecture* (New York: G. P. Putnam, 1849), p. 102. Robert Dale Owen was the son of Robert Owen, the Utopian who launched his experiment in community living at the New Harmony farm in Indiana.

93. Horatio Greenough to Charles Sum-

ner, November 16, 1839, Harvard University Library.

1. Charles Edwards Lester, *The Artist, the Merchant, and the Statesman of the age of the Medici and of our times,* vol. 1, pp. 65–66. Charles Edwards Lester (1815–1900) became American consul at Genoa during Polk's administration. He was greeted and befriended by Powers on arrival in Florence and he spent two months with the sculptor to get his story.
2. Ibid., vol. 1, p. 65.
3. Hiram Powers to Nicholas Longworth, February 19, 1835, Powers Collection, Cincinnati Historical Society.
4. Lester, *The Artist,* 1, p. 37, quoting B. B. Thatcher, "Sketch of a Self-Made Sculptor," *The Knickerbocker,* April 1835.
5. Lester, *The Artist,* vol. 1, pp. 29–36.
6. Ibid., p. 29.
7. Ibid., pp. 37–38, 29, 31.
8. Ibid., p. 26.
9. Ibid., p. 39.
10. Annie Hoge Lockett, "Hiram Powers, Clockmaker's Apprentice," *The Bulletin of the Historical and Philosophical Society of Ohio,* vol. 12, October, 1854.
11. Lester, *The Artist,* vol. 1, p. 40.
12. Reverend Henry W. Bellows, "Seven Sittings with Powers, the Sculptor," *Appleton's Journal,* vol. 1, June 26, 1869, p. 403.
13. Nathaniel Hawthorne, *Passages from the French and Italian Notebooks,* vol. 2, p. 54.
14. Ibid.
15. Lester, *The Artist,* vol. 1, pp. 45–46.
16. Powers to Longworth, January 14, 1858, Cincinnati Historical Society.
17. Lester, *The Artist,* vol. 1, p. 46.
18. Henry Boynton, "Hiram Powers,"

94. Henry T. Tuckerman, *The Criterion,* p. 343.

Notes to Chapter 10: Frontier Beginnings

New England Magazine, vol. 20, no. 5, July 1899, p. 522.
19. Lester, *The Artist,* vol. 1, p. 55.
20. Powers to Longworth, April 21, 1845, Cincinnati Historical Society.
21. Bellows, "Seven Sittings with Powers, the Sculptor," p. 404.
22. Lester, *The Artist,* vol. 1, pp. 46–47.
23. Frances Trollope, *The Domestic Manners of the Americans,* pp. 74–75.
24. Thomas Adolphus Trollope, *What I Remember,* vol. 1, p. 176.
25. Ibid.
26. Ibid.
27. Trollope, *The Domestic Manners of the Americans,* p. 65.
28. Bellows, "Seven Sittings With Powers, the Sculptor," p. 342.
29. Trollope, *Domestic Manners of the Americans,* p. xxx.
30. Powers to Longworth, August 20, 1827, Cincinnati Historical Society.
31. Powers to Longworth, August 6, 1829, Cincinnati Historical Society. The government overlooked this generosity on the part of its sea captains to provide sleeping space and free transportation to artists and their families. There does not seem to have been a statute or a Navy Department directive to this effect at any time. This information has been confirmed by Professor Samuel Eliot Morison.
32. Lester, *The Artist,* vol, 1, p. 61.
33. Ibid., p. 66.
34. Ibid., p. 67.
35. Powers to Longworth, February 15, 1835, Cincinnati Historical Society.
36. Adams, Charles Francis, ed., *Memoir of John Q. Adams, comprising portions of his Diary from 1785 to 1846,* 12 vols. (Philadelphia: J. P. Lippincott, 1876), vol. 8, p. 286. After

Greenough's death, his copy of Powers' bust of John Q. Adams was purchased by the ex-president's son, who transferred it to a church in Quincy, Massachusetts, the site of the Adams family shrine.

Notes to Chapter 11: Sculptor of Busts

1. Powers to Nicholas Longworth, December 7, 1837, Powers Collection, Cincinnati Historical Society.
2. Reverend Henry Bellows, "Seven Sittings with Powers, the Sculptor," *Appleton's Journal*, vol. 1, June 26, 1869, p. 404.
3. The bust of *Daniel Webster* was commissioned for the sum of $500 for the Boston Athenaeum in 1840 by a group led by James S. Amory. The subscribers raised $365 among themselves, and the trustees of the Athenaeum appropriated the balance. It was deposited in the Athenaeum Gallery by June 13, 1842.
4. Lester, *The Artist*, vol. 1, p. 77.
5. Powers to Longworth, November 3, 1838, Cincinnati Historical Society.
6. Powers to Longworth, April 21, 1845, Cincinnati Historical Society.
7. Powers to Longworth, July 11, 1839, Cincinnati Historical Society.
8. Francis Boott Greenough, *The Letters of Horatio Greenough to his Brother, Henry Greenough*, p. 126.
9. Ibid.
10. Frances Trollope, *A Visit to Italy*, vol. 1, p. 143.
11. Powers to Longworth, April 22, 1839, Cincinnati Historical Society.
12. Ibid.
13. Ibid.
14. Powers to Longworth, December 7, 1837, Cincinnati Historical Society.
15. Powers to Longworth, April 22, 1839, Cincinnati Historical Society.
16. Powers to Henry C. Lea, January 10, 1841, Cincinnati Historical Society.
17. Lester, *The Artist*, vol. 1, p. 85.
18. Ibid., p. 78.
19. Powers to Henry C. Lea, January 10, 1841, Cincinnati Historical Society.
20. Powers to Longworth, September 17, 1841, Cincinnati Historical Society.
21. Frances Trollope, *A Visit to Italy*, vol. 1, pp. 144–145.
22. Joel T. Headley, *Letters from Italy*, p. 198.
23. Ibid.
24. Greenough, *Letters*, p. 131.
25. Lester, *The Artist*, vol. 1, p. 84.
26. Ibid., p. 83.
27. Ibid., p. 82.
28. Greenough, *Letters*, p. 133.
29. *Dr. Jorgen Hartmann*, former executive secretary of the Danish Academy at Rome, now retired. Biography in preparation.
30. Hiram Powers to Giovanni Baptiste Niccolini, secretary of the Academy of Fine Arts in Florence, October 2, 1841, Archive of the Royal Academy of Fine Arts, Florence, 1841, no. 89.
31. Lester, *The Artist*, vol. 1, p. 79.
32. Powers to Longworth, September 17, 1841, Cincinnati Historical Society.

Notes to Chapter 12: Greek Slave

1. Charles Edwards Lester, *The Artist, the Merchant, and the Statesman of the age of the Medici and of our Times*, vol. 1, p. 85.
2. Hiram Powers to Henry P. Gray, November 20, 1869, Miscellaneous File, New York Public Library.
3. Statements of Powers quoted in this

37. Powers to William C. Preston, May 15, 1837, Cincinnati Historical Society.
38. Mrs. Wharton, who owned an immense plantation in Louisiana, was the wife of a Texas minister.

paragraph are from the letter to Gray referred to in note 2.

4. Henry F. Adams, ed., *Powers' Statue of the Greek Slave* (Boston: Eastburn Press, 1848) p. 5. Pamphlet published in conjunction with the Boston exhibit of the *Greek Slave*.

5. Powers to Nicholas Longworth, March 5–19, 1844, Powers Collection, Cincinnati Historical Society, Cincinnati, Ohio.

6. Ibid.

7. Powers to Henry Lea, January 10, 1841, Cincinnati Historical Society.

8. Lester, *The Artist*, vol. 1, pp. 85–89.

9. Powers to Longworth, March 5–19, 1844, Cincinnati Historical Society.

10. Powers to Edward Everett, March 7, 1843, Everett Papers, Massachusetts Historical Society, Boston Massachusetts.

11. Powers to Longworth, March 5–19, 1844, Cincinnati Historical Society.

12. Ibid.

13. Powers to Longworth, April 21, 1845, Cincinnati Historical Society.

14. Powers to Longworth, May 12, 1846, Cincinnati Historical Society.

15. Powers to Longworth, January 20, 1847, Cincinnati Historical Society.

16. Ibid.

17. Ibid.

18. Ibid.

19. Ibid.

20. Powers to Longworth, December 7, 1847, Cincinnati Historical Society.

21. Powers to Kellogg, January 27, 1848, Cincinnati Historical Society.

22. Powers to Longworth, August 23, 1847, Cincinnati Historical Society.

23. Powers to Kellogg, January 27, 1848, Cincinnati Historical Society.

24. Powers to Kellogg, October 12, 1848, Cincinnati Historical Society.

25. Ibid.

26. Ibid.

27. Henry T. Tuckerman. *Book of the Artists: American Artists Life*, p. 279.

28. Powers to Kellogg, February 27, 1848, Cincinnati Historical Society.

29. Powers to Kellogg, October 12, 1847, Cincinnati Historical Society.

30. Powers to Kellogg, October 31, 1847, Cincinnati Historical Society.

31. Elizabeth Barrett Browning, *The Complete Poetical Works of Elizabeth B. Browning*, p. 198.

32. Powers to Kellogg, October 12, 1847, Cincinnati Historical Society.

33. Tuckerman, *Book of the Artists*, p. 279.

34. Powers to Kellogg, November 16, 1847, Cincinnati Historical Society.

35. Ibid.

36. Powers to Edward Everett, March 19, 1859, Powers Collection, Cincinnati Historical Society.

37. Powers to Kellogg, December 12, 1848, Cincinnati Historical Society.

38. Powers to Kellogg, November 17, 1847, Cincinnati Historical Society.

39. Lester, *The Artist*, vol. 1, pp. 85–87.

40. Reverend Orville Dewey, "Mr. Powers' Statue," *Union Magazine*, October, 1847.

41. Nathaniel Hawthorne, *Passages from the French and Italian Notebooks*, 2 vols. (Boston: James R. Osgood, 1870), vol. 1, p. 293.

42. Henry F. Adams, ed., *Powers' Statue of the Greek Slave*.

43. Ibid.

44. Ibid.

45. Silliman, Benjamin, and C. R. Goodrich, eds., *The World of Science, Art, and Industry Illustrated from Examples in the New York Exhibition, 1853–54*, p. 91.

Notes to Chapter 13: Major Statues

1. Hiram Powers to Nicholas Longworth, October 8, 1858, Powers Collection, Cincinnati Historical Society.

2. Hiram Powers to Miner Kellogg, January 1848, Cincinnati Historical Society.

3. Ibid.
4. Powers to Kellogg, February 27, 1848, Cincinnati Historical Society.
5. Powers to Kellogg, December 8, 1848, Cincinnati Historical Society.
6. Powers to Kellogg, September 13, 1848, Cincinnati Historical Society.
7. Powers to Longworth, September, 1849, Cincinnati Historical Society.
8. Ibid.
9. Powers to Longworth, September, 1849, Cincinnati Historical Society.
10. Powers to Longworth, October 22, 1848, Cincinnati Historical Society.
11. Powers to Longworth, March 27, 1858, Cincinnati Historical Society.
12. Powers to Edward Everett, May 28, 1858, Everett Papers, Massachusetts Historical Society.
13. Powers to Longworth, September, 1849, Cincinnati Historical Society.
14. Powers to Edward Everett, May 28, 1858, Everett Papers, Massachusetts Historical Society.
15. Nathaniel Hawthorne, *Passages from the French and Italian Notebooks,* vol. 2, p. 161.
16. Powers to Longworth, September 5, 1849, Cincinnati Historical Society.
17. *Report No. 92, 31st Congress, 2nd Session, House of Representatives,* Report of R. H. Stanton, from the Committee on Public Buildings and Grounds, Office of the Architect of the Capitol.
18. Ibid.
19. Ibid.
20. Ibid.
21. Powers to Longworth, October 22, 1848, Cincinnati Historical Society.
22. Hawthorne, *Passages from the French and Italian Notebooks,* vol. 1, p. 293.
23. Ibid., vol. 2, p. 34.
24. Hiram Powers to Honorable Charles Clayarre, secretary of state for the state of Louisiana, June 9, 1850, *Louisiana Historical Quarterly,* 1919, vol. 2, pp. 272–273.
25. Hawthorne, *Passages from the French and Italian Notebooks,* vol. 1, p. 293.
26. Ibid., p. 294.

27. Ibid., p. 293.
28. Ibid., p. 304.
29. Ibid., pp. 293–294.
30. Henry T. Tuckerman, *Book of the Artists, American Artists Life,* pp. 288–289.
31. Powers to Longworth, February 2, 1854, Cincinnati Historical Society.
32. Hawthorne, *Passages from the French and Italian Notebooks,* vol 2, p. 25.
33. Ibid.
34. Ibid.
35. Ibid.
36. Powers to Edward Everett, March 19, 1859, Everett Papers, Massachusetts Historical Society.
37. Ibid.
38. Powers to Edward Everett, May 16, 1869, Everett Papers, Massachusetts Historical Society.
39. Hawthorne, *Passages from the French and Italian Notebooks,* vol. 2, p. 23.
40. Ibid.
41. Powers to Longworth, January 1, 1850, Cincinnati Historical Society.
42. Tuckerman, *Book of the Artists,* p. 289.
43. Captain M. C. Meigs to Hiram Powers, August 18, 1853; Captain M. C. Meigs to Thomas Crawford, August 18, 1853, Office of the Architect of the Capitol.
44. Powers to Longworth, March 27, 1858, Cincinnati Historical Society.
45. Powers to T. B. Read, September 17, 1857, Cincinnati Historical Society.
46. Ibid.
47. Ibid.
48. Powers to T. B. Read, April 1, 1858, Cincinnati Historical Society.
49. Captain M. C. Meigs to Edward Everett, December 8, 1856, Letterbook, Number 4, Files of the Architect of the Capitol, Office of the Architect of the Capitol.
50. Powers to Edward Everett, June 5, 1855, Office of the Architect of the Capitol.
51. Powers to Edward Everett, March

19, 1859, Everett Papers, Massachusetts Historical Society.

52. President Franklin Pierce to Edward Everett, June 5, 1855, Office of the Architect of the Capitol.

53. Powers to Edward Everett, June 20, 1858, Everett Papers, Massachusetts Historical Society.

54. Powers to Read, March 12, 1857, Cincinnati Historical Society.

55. Powers to Kellogg, May 2, 1849, Cincinnati Historical Society.

56. Powers to Longworth, September 22, 1847, Cincinnati Historical Society.

57. Powers to Kellogg, May 2, 1849, Cincinnati Historical Society.

58. Samuel Douglas Wyeth, *The Federal City or Ins and Abouts of Washington*, pp. 81–82.

59. Ibid.

60. Powers to Edward Everett, March 12, 1859, Everett Papers, Massachusetts Historical Society.

61. Hawthorne, *Passages from the French and Italian Notebooks*, vol. 2, p. 157.

62. Ibid.

63. Lester, *The Artist*, vol. 1, pp. 67–68.

64. Powers to Kellogg, May 15, 1850, Cincinnati Historical Society.

65. Hawthorne, *Passages from the French and Italian Notebooks*, vol. 1, p. 292.

66. Powers to Edward Everett, October 14, 1859, Everett Papers, Massachusetts Historical Society.

67. Powers to Longworth, January 12, 1859, Cincinnati Historical Society.

68. Powers to Edward Everett, May 20, 1859, Everett Papers, Massachusetts Historical Society.

69. Edward Everett, *A Defense of Powers' Statue of Webster*.

70. Ibid., Joseph Ames to Edward Everett, June 3, 1859.

71. Ibid., Mr. Horney to Edward Everett, June 8, 1859.

72. Ibid.

73. Hawthorne, *Passages from the French and Italian Notebooks*, vol. 2, pp. 157–158. The second paragraph of the quotation is from the manuscript edition edited by Professor Norman Holmes Pearson, Yale University, pp. 539–540.

74. Powers to Edward Everett, May 10, 1869, Everett Papers, Massachusetts Historical Society.

Notes to Chapter 14: Love of Machines

1. Nathaniel Hawthorne, *Passages from the French and Italian Notebooks*, vol. 2, p. 119.

2. Reverend Henry Bellows, "Seven Sittings with Powers, the Sculptor," *Appleton's Journal of Literature, Science, and Art*, vol. 1, August 7, 1869, p. 595.

3. Hiram Powers to Nicholas Longworth, February 2, 1854, Powers Collection, Cincinnati Historical Society.

4. Powers to Longworth, April 21, 1855, Cincinnati Historical Society.

5. Bellows, "Seven Sittings With Powers, the Sculptor," pp. 595–596.

6. Powers to King, May 30, 1867, Cincinnati Historical Society.

7. Powers to Longworth, February 2, 1854, Cincinnati Historical Society.

8. Powers to Longworth, February 27, 1859, Cincinnati Historical Society.

9. Powers to Longworth, January 24, 1868, Cincinnati Historical Society.

10. Powers to Longworth, February 2, 1852, Cincinnati Historical Society.

11. Hawthorne, *Passages from the French and Italian Notebooks*, vol. 1, p. 304.

12. Ibid., vol. 2, pp. 21–22.

13. Ibid., p. 22.

14. Bellows, "Seven Sittings with Powers, the Sculptor," p. 360.

15. Powers to Longworth, June 7, 1847, Cincinnati Historical Society.
16. Henry T. Tuckerman, *Book of the Artists. American Artists Life*, p. 143.
17. Bellows, "Seven Sittings with Powers, the Sculptor," p. 343.
18. Powers to Longworth, June 7, 1847, Cincinnati Historical Society.
19. Bellows, "Seven Sitting with Powers, the Sculptor," p. 342.
20. Ibid.
21. Hawthorne, *Passages from the French and Italian Notebooks*, vol. 2, pp. 305–306.
22. Ibid., vol. 1, p. 290.
23. Ibid, vol. 2, p. 20.
24. Ibid.
25. Ibid., p. 3.
26. Ibid., p. 55.
27. Ibid.
28. Lester, *The Artist*, vol. 1, pp. 45–46.
29. Powers to Longworth, January 12, 1858, Cincinnati Historical Society.
30. Powers to Longworth, March 4, 1850, Cincinnati Historical Society.
31. Edward L. Pierce, *Charles Sumner, Memoir and Letters*, vol. 2, p. 112.
32. Powers to Longworth, March 24, 1850, Cincinnati Historical Society.
33. Hiram Powers, "The New Method of Modelling in Plaster for Sculpture," *Putnam's Monthly Magazine*, vol. 2, August 1853.
34. Powers to Longworth, April 21, 1855, Cincinnati Historical Society.
35. Powers to Greenwood, May 13, 1858, Cincinnati Historical Society.
36. Powers to Longworth, March 4, 1850, Cincinnati Historical Society.
37. Powers to Greenwood, May 13, 1858, Cincinnati Historical Society.
38. Ibid.
39. Powers to Longworth, May 5, 1858, Cincinnati Historical Society.
40. Ibid.
41. Hawthorne, *Passages from the French and Italian Notebooks*, vol. 2, p. 85.
42. Ibid.
43. Powers to Longworth, February 27, 1859, Cincinnati Historical Society.
44. Powers to Kellogg, October 2, 1847, Cincinnati Historical Society.
45. Hawthorne, *Passages from the French and Italian Notebooks*, vol. 2, p. 100.
46. Ibid.
47. Powers to Longworth, April 21, 1855, Cincinnati Historical Society.
48. Ibid.
49. Hawthorne, *Passages from the French and Italian Notebooks*, vol. 2, p. 23.
50. Ibid., vol. 1, pp. 304–305.
51. Ibid., vol. 2, p. 23.
52. Powers to Kellogg, January 18, 1848, Cincinnati Historical Society.
53. Ibid.
54. Hawthorne, *Passages from the French and Italian Notebooks*, Pearson manuscript edition, p. 537.
55. Powers to Kellogg, February 27, 1848, Cincinnati Historical Society.
56. Powers to Kellogg, March 4, 1848, Cincinnati Historical Society.
57. Powers to Edward Everett, September 19, 1858, Everett Papers, Massachusetts Historical Society.
58. Powers to Salmon P. Chase, October 13, 1866. Cincinnati Historical Society.
59. Ibid.
60. Powers to Robert Hosea, October 19, 1858, Cincinnati Historical Society.
61. Powers to Longworth, January 4, 1868, Cincinnati Historical Society.
62. Ibid.
63. Powers to Longworth, February 1, 1854, Cincinnati Historical Society.
64. Powers to Longworth, September 15, 1847, Cincinnati Historical Society.
65. Powers to Longworth, January 12, 1858, Cincinnati Historical Society.
66. Powers to Longworth, January 4, 1858, Cincinnati Historical Society.
67. Hawthorne, *Passages from the French and Italian Notebooks*, vol. 2, p. 23.
68. Elizabeth Barrett Browning, *The Letters of Elizabeth Barrett Browning*, vol. 1, p. 337.

69. Hawthorne, *Passages from the French and Italian Notebooks*, vol. 2, p. 23.
70. William Ware, *Sketches of European Capitals*, p. 133.
71. Ibid., p. 137.
72. *Genius of the West* (Cincinnati: Historical and Philosophical Society of Ohio), vol. 2, April, 1854, pp. 120–121.
73. Ware, *Sketches of European Capitals*, p. 133.
74. Walter H. Siple, introduction to a pamphlet prepared by the Historical and Philosophical Society of Ohio at an exhibition of Powers' works at the Cincinnati Art Museum, manuscript collection, New York Public Library (Mar. P.V. 1258).
75. Ibid.

Notes to Chapter 15: Roman Lure

1. George Washington Greene, "Letters from Modern Rome." *Knickerbocker*, vol. 15, June 1840, p. 488.
2. Eugene Plon, *Thorwaldsen, Sa Vie et Son Oeuvre*, p. 33.
3. George Stillman Hillard, *Six Months in Italy*, vol. 2, p. 435.
4. Mrs. Hugh Fraser, *A Diplomatist's Wife in Many Lands*, vol. 1, p. 2.
5. Edward L. Pierce, *Memoir and Letters of Charles Sumner*, vol. 2, p. 105.
6. James E. Freeman, *Gatherings from An Artist's Portfolio*, vol. 1, p. 247.
7. George Washington Greene, *Biographical Studies*, p. 131.
8. Ibid., p. 151.
9. Ibid., p. 130.
10. Charles Sumner, "Crawford's Orpheus," *United States Magazine and Democratic Review*, vol. 12, no. 59, May 1843, p. 455.
11. Fraser, *A Diplomatist's Wife in Many Lands*, vol. 1, p. 3.
12. Greene, "Letters from Modern Rome," p. 493.
13. Freeman, *Gatherings from an Artist's Portfolio*, vol. 1, pp. 10–15.
14. Fraser, *A Diplomatist's Wife in Many Lands*, vol. 1, p. 35. Schwanthaler was to create a colossal statue of *Bavaria* for Munich, and pave the way for Crawford's frequent visits there. Munich at that time was the site of the largest and finest brass foundry in Europe. King Louis I of Bavaria encouraged the arts, priding himself on being a poet, sculptor, and virtuoso in all the fine arts. He was especially impressed with Thorwaldsen and commissioned him to restore an ancient Greek pediment in Munich and to execute an impressive statue of his father Maximillian, the Elector, which was duly admired by Charles Sumner, who attended the unveiling ceremony in the fall of 1839. Sumner called the statue "the finest equestrian I ever saw." (Sumner to Greene, October 18, 1839, Greene Papers, Harvard University Library.)
15. Greene, "Letters from Modern Rome," p. 489.
16. Ibid.
17. Catherine Maria Sedgwick, *Letters from Abroad to Kindred at Home*, vol. 2, p. 157. She visited Rome on December 30, 1839.
18. Thomas Hicks, *Thomas Crawford: His Career, Character and Works, A Eulogy*, p. 15.
19. Greene, "Letters from Modern Rome," p. 489–490.
20. Thomas Crawford to George S. Hillard, undated, Massachusetts Historical Society.
21. Thomas Crawford to F. W. Phillips, August 15, 1837, Massachusetts Historical Society.
22. Ibid.

23. Luther Terry had come to Via Margutta in 1833 to study painting with Baron Camuccini but was not yet part of their daily group. He had lost one lung and had been forced to leave Connecticut for a more salubrious climate. Phillips became a fast friend of Crawford but unfortunately in less than two years he returned home to Brooklyn, where he soon died of tuberculosis.

24. George Washington Greene to Henry Wadsworth Longfellow, December 6, 1838, Greene Collection, Harvard University Library.

25. George Washington Greene to Charles Sumner, July 28, 1842, Greene Papers, Harvard University Library.

26. Greene, "Letters from Modern Rome," p. 490.

27. Thomas Crawford to George Washington Greene, 1840, Virginia Historical Society.

28. Greene, *Biographical Studies*, p. 153.

29. Ibid.

Notes to Chapter 16: Auspicious Debut

1. George Washington Greene, "Letters from Modern Rome," *The Knickerbocker*, vol. 15, June 1840, p. 490.

2. Ibid., p. 494.

3. George S. Hillard, "Thomas Crawford, A Eulogy," *Atlantic Monthly*, vol. 24, no. 14, July 1869, p. 46.

4. Greene, "Letters from Modern Rome," p. 494.

5. Ibid.

6. Ibid.

7. Thomas Hicks, *Thomas Crawford, His Career, Character, and Works, A Eulogy*, p. 22.

8. Greene, "Letters from Modern Rome," p. 493.

9. Ibid.

10. Ibid., p. 490.

11. Ibid., pp. 490–491.

12. Catherine Maria Sedgwick, *Letters from Abroad to Kindred at Home*, vol. 2, pp. 158–159.

13. Greene, "Letters from Modern Rome," p. 493.

14. Ibid., p. 494.

15. Ibid., pp. 494–495.

16. Ibid., p. 495.

17. Ibid.

18. Thomas Crawford to George Washington Greene, October 1838, Brumbaugh Collection, Virginia Historical Society.

19. Edward L. Pierce, *Memoir and Letters of Charles Sumner*, vol. 2, p. 176.

20. Ibid. Sumner also asked Greene to secure rooms for him in the vicinity of Piazza di Spagna, near his friends Shattuck and Harrison, also from Boston, who lived at numbers 71 and 171 Piazza di Spagna.

21. George Stillman Hillard, *Six Months in Italy*, vol. 2, p. 256.

22. Charles Sumner, "Crawford's Orpheus," *United States Magazine and Democratic Review*, new series, vol. 12, no. 59, May 1843, p. 454.

23. Ibid., p. 453.

24. Ibid.

25. Pierce, *Memoir and Letters of Charles Sumner*, vol. 2, p. 95, footnote.

26. George Washington Greene, *Biographical Studies*, p. 139.

27. Ibid., p. 140.

28. Sumner to Greene, October 5, 1839, Greene Papers, Harvard University Library.

29. For years, Cornelius was, with Overbeck, at the head of the German group in Rome.

30. Sumner to Greene, November 6, 1839, Greene Papers, Harvard University Library. Muhlenberg was the

Austrian Ambassador to the Papal States in Rome.

31. Ibid.

32. Ibid.

33. Sumner to Greene, October 18, 1839, Greene Papers, Harvard University Library.

34. Pierce, *Memoir and Letters of Charles Sumner*, vol. 2, p. 133.

35. Sumner to Greene, December 30, 1839, Greene Papers, Harvard University Library.

36. Sumner to Boston Athenaeum, May 10, 1845, files, Boston Athenaeum.

37. Greene, *Biographical Studies*, p. 141, Grüner was an eminent German engraver. The original contract is owned by Thomas Brumbaugh; a copy is in the Boston Athenaeum.

38. Mrs. Hugh Fraser, *A Diplomatist's Wife in Many Lands*, vol. 1, pp. 5–6. A paul was worth ten cents.

39. Greene to Sumner, July 28, 1842, Boston Athenaeum notes regarding the *Orpheus,* Boston Athenaeum.

40. Henry Dexter was the brother of the distinguished lawyer and art patron of Boston, Franklin Dexter.

41. Fine Arts Committee Report, January 1, 1844, Boston Athenaeum *Letterbook.*

42. Greene, "Letters from Modern Rome, pp. 490–491.

43. Greene, "Letters from Modern Rome," p. 174.

44. Charles Summer, "Crawford's Orpheus," *United States Magazine and Democratic Review,* new series, vol. 12, no. 59, May 1843, p. 453.

45. Jenny Campbell, "Orpheus: The Sculptor in his studio," *United States Magazine and Democratic Review,* new series, vol. 12, June 1843, pp. 567–568.

46. Ibid., p. 568, footnote.

Notes to Chapter 17: Fruitful Years

1. "Our Young Artists," *The Knickerbocker,* vol. 16, no. 3, September 1840, p. 271.

2. Frances Trollope, *A Visit to Italy,* vol. 2, p. 305.

3. "Our Young Artists," *The Knickerbocker,* vol. 16, no. 3, September 1940, p. 271.

4. Charles Sumner to George Washington Greene, October 5, 1839, Greene Papers, Harvard University Library.

5. George R. Lewis to the secretary of the Boston Athenaeum, January 15, 1840, Boston Athenaeum *Letterbook,* January 15, 1840.

6. Crawford to Sumner, January 4, 1842, Pennsylvania Historical Society.

7. *Boston Daily Evening Transcript,* June 20, 1843, p. 2, on file in the Boston Athenaeum.

8. Greene to Sumner, November 8, 1840, Greene Papers, Harvard University Library.

9. Crawford to Sumner, January 4, 1842, Pennsylvania Historical Society.

10. Ibid.

11. Ibid.

12. Charles Sumner, "Crawford's Orpheus," *United States Magazine and Democratic Review,* new series, vol. 12, no. 59, May 1843, p. 455.

13. Greene to Sumner, August 12, 1843, Greene Papers, Harvard University Library.

14. *Boston Daily Evening Transcript,* December 21, 1935, Crawford file, Boston Athenaeum.

15. Charles Sumner, "Crawford's Orpheus, p. 455.

16. Ibid.

17. George S. Hillard, *Six Months in Italy,* vol. 2, pp. 261–262.

18. Charles Sumner, "Crawford's Orpheus," p. 455.
19. File, Metropolitan Museum of Art, New York City.
20. Thomas Hicks, *Thomas Crawford, His Career, Character, and Works, A Eulogy*, p. 29.
21. Crawford to Sumner, January 4, 1842, Pennsylvania Historical Society.
22. Hicks, *Thomas Crawford*, p. 22.
23. Ibid.
24. Julia Ward Howe to Louisa, September 12, 1843, Ward Papers, Harvard University Library.
25. Hillard, *Six Months in Italy*, vol. 2, p. 256.
26. Susan Hale, ed., *The Life and Letters of Thomas Gold Appleton*, p. 196. Appleton visited Rome in February 1834.
27. Mrs. Hugh Fraser, *A Diplomatist's Wife in Many Lands*, vol. 1, p. 33.
28. Louisa Hall Tharp, *Three Saints and a Sinner*, p. 70.
29. Ibid., p. 71.
30. Henry Wadsworth Longfellow to Cornelius Felton, 1842, Harvard University Library.
31. Louisa Hall Tharp, *Three Saints and a Sinner*, p. 76.
32. Edward L. Pierce, *Memoir and Letters of Charles Sumner*, vol. 2, p. 298.
33. Ibid, pp. 298 and 307.
34. Samuel G. Howe to Crawford, 1845 (?), Ward Papers, Harvard University Library.
35. Crawford to Greene, June 20, 1844, Brumbaugh Collection, Virginia Historical Society.
36. Ibid.
37. Ibid.
38. Ibid.
39. Fraser, *A Diplomatist's Wife in Many Lands*, vol. 1, pp. 12–13.
40. Julia to Louisa, Saturday, 1844, Ward Papers, Harvard University Library.
41. Julia to Louisa, November 1, 1844, Ward Papers, Harvard University Library.
42. Julia to Crawford, November 1, 1844, Ward Papers, Harvard University Library.
43. Mrs. Hugh Fraser, *A Diplomatist's Wife in Many Lands*, vol. 1, pp. 13–14.
44. George S. Hillard, *Six Months in Italy*, vol. 2, p. 441.
45. Philip Hone, *Diary of Philip Hone*, December 28, 1844, p. 724.
46. Julia to Louisa, November 1844, Ward Papers, Harvard University Library.
47. Pierce, *Memoir and Letters of Charles Sumner*, vol. 2, p. 331.
48. Files, Office of the Architect of the Capitol, Washington, D.C.
49. Crawford to Louisa, February 12, 1845, Rocca Collection, Archives of America Art, Wayne State University.
50. Ibid.
51. Pierce, *Memoir and Letters of Charles Sumner*, vol. 2, p. 332.
52. Julia to Louisa, April 21, 1845, Ward Papers, Harvard University Library.
53. Julia to Louisa, August 1, 1845, Ward Papers, Harvard University Library.
54. Julia to Lou (Louisa), May 1845, Ward Papers, Harvard University Library.
55. Files, Boston Athenaeum.
56. "Private Journal of John Langdon Sibley of Harvard University Library," 2 volumes, unpublished manuscript, Harvard University Archives, Sibley Librarian collection, Harvard University Library. From 1841 to 1846 Sibley was assistant librarian of Harvard.
57. Julia to Louisa, August 1845, Ward Papers, Harvard University Library.
58. Louisa to Julia, Rue de la Paix, September 18, 1845, Brumbaugh Collection, Virginia Historical Society.
59. Fraser, *A Diplomatist's Wife in Many Lands*, vol. 1, p. 15.
60. Hicks, *Thomas Crawford*, p. 39.
61. Hillard, *Six Months in Italy*, vol. 2, p. 264.
62. Christopher Pearse Cranch to John

Dwight, March 14, 1848, Dwight Papers, Boston Public Library.

63. Lenora Cranch Scott, ed., *The Life and Letters of Christopher Pearse Cranch*, p. 114.

64. Ibid.

65. Crawford to Robert Launitz, November 6, 1846, Boston Public Library.

66. Hicks, *Thomas Crawford*, p. 29.

67. Maude Howe Elliott, *My Cousin, F. Marion Crawford*, p. 11.

68. Franklin Dexter to William H. Prescott, December 7, 1852, Massachusetts Historical Society.

69. Ibid.

70. Ibid. Crawford has offered to make allegorical representations of *History* and *Poetry* in half life-size figures for $750 each for Prescott. Prescott's top limit was a total of $1,000.

71. Mr. Hicks' daughter bequeathed the statue to the Metropolitan Museum of Art in 1897.

72. Julia to Louisa, July 21, 1847, Ward Papers, Harvard University Library.

73. Fraser, *A Diplomatist's Wife in Many Lands*, vol. 1, pp. 29–30.

74. Emma Detti, *Margaret Fuller Ossoli & i suoi Corrispondenti (Margaret Fuller and her Correspondents)*, pp. 331–332.

75. Ibid., p. 336.

76. Ibid., p. 339.

Notes to Chapter 18: Equestrian Washington

1. Crawford to Captain M. C. Meigs, July 10, 1854, Office of the Architect of the Capitol.

2. Crawford to Charles Sumner, May 13, 1849, Brumbaugh Collection, Virginia Historical Society.

3. Crawford to Meigs, July 10, 1854, Office of the Architect of the Capitol.

4. Crawford to Louisa, January 3, 1850, Rocca Collection, Archives of American Art, Wayne State University.

5. Ibid.

6. Memorial to the General Association of Virginia for a Monument to Washington, *Journal of the House of Delegates*, Session 1848–1849, Document No. 63, pp. 235 ff., Virginia State Library.

7. Crawford to Sumner, February 15, 1850, Howe Papers, Harvard University Library.

8. Ibid.

9. Ibid.

10. Crawford to Louisa, January 8, 1850, Wayne State University.

11. Ibid.

12. Crawford to Louisa, January 11, 1850, Wayne State University.

13. Ibid.

14. Ibid.

15. Crawford to Louisa, January 26, 1850, Wayne State University.

16. Crawford to Louisa, January 12, 1850, Wayne State University.

17. Ibid.

18. Crawford to Louisa, January 26, 1850, Wayne State University.

19. Ibid.

20. Crawford to Louisa, January 20, 1850, Wayne State University.

21. Crawford to Louisa, February 17, 1850, and January 13, 1850, Wayne State University.

22. Crawford to Louisa, January 13, Wayne State University.

23. Crawford to Louisa, January 26, 1850, Wayne State University.

24. Ibid.

25. Ibid.

26. Crawford to Louisa, January 20 1850, Wayne State University.

27. Ibid.

28. Crawford to Louisa, January 28, 1850, Wayne State University.

29. Crawford to Louisa, January 30, 1850, Wayne State University.

30. Crawford to Louisa, February 2, 1850, Wayne State University.

31. Ibid.

32. Edward L. Pierce, *Memoir and Letters of Charles Sumner*, vol. 3, p. 46.

33. Ibid.

34. Crawford to Louisa, February 5, 1850, Wayne State University.

35. Ibid.

36. Ibid. Mills' original sketches are in the Virginia State Library.

37. Crawford to Conway Robinson, August 12, 1852, Virginia Historical Society. Crawford enclosed a copy of his letter to Robert Mills, dated July 31, 1851.

38. Crawford to Louisa, February 13, 1850, Wayne State University.

39. Crawford to Louisa, February 10, 1850, Wayne State University.

40. Crawford to Louisa, February 28, 1850, Wayne State University.

41. Crawford to George Washington Greene, Rome, 1840. Property of Dr. Thomas B. Brumbaugh, Emory University, Atlanta, Georgia. A copy is owned by the Virginia Historical Society and was printed in the *Virginia Magazine of History and Biography*, volume 66, pp. 448–453, issued by the Virginia Historical Society.

42. *Calendar of State Papers* for 1850, pp. 27–31, Virginia State Library.

43. Ibid.

44. Crawford to Louisa, February 28, 1850, Wayne State University.

45. Ibid.

46. Crawford to Louisa, March 6, 1850, Wayne State University.

47. Ibid.

48. Crawford to Louisa, June 10, 1850, Wayne State University.

49. Crawford to Louisa, June 17, 1850, Wayne State University.

50. Julia to Louisa, January 25, 1850, Ward Papers, Harvard University Library.

51. Julia to Annie, 1849, Ward Papers, Harvard University Library.

52. Julia to Louisa, January 25, 1850, Ward Papers, Harvard University Library.

53. Crawford to Louisa, July 2, 1850, Wayne State University.

54. Crawford to Louisa, February 17, 1850, Wayne State University.

55. Crawford to Louisa, June 23, 1850, Wayne State University.

56. Fraser, *A Diplomatist's Wife in Many Lands*, vol. 1, pp. 62–65. In the 1870s Villa Negroni was demolished to make room for the Piazza dei Termini and the Grand Hotel.

57. *Virginia Historical Register and Literary Notebook*, vol. 4, 1851, File, Virginia Historical Society.

58. Fraser, *A Diplomatist's Wife in Many Lands*, vol. 1, p. 32.

59. Ibid.

60. Mary Crawford later married Hugh Fraser, an English diplomat, the second secretary of the British Legation at Florence, and published her memoirs as *A Diplomatist's Wife in Many Lands*.

61. Crawford to Conway Robinson, August 12, 1852, containing a copy of Crawford's letter to Mills, July 31, 1851, Virginia Historical Society.

62. Meigs to Crawford, August 18, 1853, Office of the Architect of the Capitol.

63. Crawford to Meigs, October 16, 1853, Office of the Architect of the Capitol.

64. Ibid.

65. Franklin Dexter to William H. Prescott, December 7, 1852, Massachusetts Historical Society.

66. Crawford to Conway Robinson, August 12, 1852, Virginia Historical Society.

67. Crawford to Louisa, May 13, 1852, Wayne State University.

68. Crawford to Louisa, May 14, 1852, Wayne State University.

69. Crawford to Louisa, May 22, 1852, Wayne State University.

70. Crawford to Louisa, May 11, 1852, Wayne State University.

71. Ibid.
72. Ibid.
73. Julia to Louisa, July 20, 1852, Ward Papers, Harvard University Library.
74. *Virginia Historical Register and Literary Notebook*, vol. 4, 1851, Crawford File, Virginia Historical Society.

75. Launitz to Meigs, September 26, 1853, Office of the Architect of the Capitol.
76. Rand, McNally and Company, *A Week at the Fair Illustrating the Exhibits and Wonders of the World's Columbian Exposition with Special Descriptive Articles*, p. 158.

Notes to Chapter 19: Capitol Adornment

1. Captain M. C. Meigs to Jefferson Davis, July 27, 1855, Massachusetts Historical Society.
2. Edward Everett to Meigs, July 12, 1853, Office of the Architect of the Capitol.
3. Meigs to Powers, Meigs to Crawford (identical letters), August 18, 1853, Office of the Architect of the Capitol.
4. Ibid.
5. Meigs to Crawford, August 23, 1853, Office of the Architect of the Capitol.
6. Crawford to Louisa, June 11, 1853, Wayne State University.
7. Crawford to Louisa, July 12, 1853, Wayne State University.
8. Crawford to Louisa, June 11, 1853, Wayne State University.
9. Crawford to Louisa, June 23, 1853, Wayne State University.
10. Crawford to Louisa, July 7, 1853, Wayne State University.
11. Ibid.
12. Crawford to Louisa, August 4, 1853, Wayne State University.
13. Ibid.
14. Crawford to Louisa, August 7, 1853, Wayne State University.
15. Crawford to Louisa, August 22, 1853, Wayne State University.
16. Ibid.
17. Crawford to Meigs, October 20, 1853, Office of the Architect of the Capitol.
18. Meigs to Jefferson Davis (secretary of war), July 27, 1855, Massachusetts Historical Society.

19. Meigs to Crawford, August 18, 1853, Office of the Architect of the Capitol.
20. Crawford to Meigs, October 20, 1853, Office of the Architect of the Capitol.
21. File of letters relating to the sculptures of Randolph Rogers and Thomas Crawford on the Capitol Building, Office of the Architect of the Capitol.
22. Meigs to Crawford, November 28, 1853, Office of the Architect of the Capitol.
23. Meigs to Crawford, December 27, 1853, Office of the Architect of the Capitol.
24. Meigs to Crawford, October 20, 1853, Office of the Architect of the Capitol.
25. Meigs to Crawford, August 9, 1854, Office of the Architect of the Capitol.
26. Ibid.
27. Meigs to Crawford, June 12, 1854, Office of the Architect of the Capitol.
28. Crawford to Meigs, January 17, 1854, Office of the Architect of the Capitol.
29. Meigs to Crawford, April 4, 1854, Office of the Architect of the Capitol.
30. Meigs to Crawford, October 13, 1855, Office of the Architect of the Capitol. In Washington roughing out cost $2.75 an hour, as compared to $1 an hour in Rome.
31. In Rome Galliardi had made a marble

bust of Crawford that is now lodged with many others in an obscure hallway of the Capitol.

32. Lewis Cass, Jr., to Meigs, undated, Office of the Architect of the Capitol.

33. Crawford to Meigs, January 17, 1854, Crawford File, Office of the Architect of the Capitol.

34. Crawford to Meigs, May 15, 1854, Office of the Architect of the Capitol.

35. Crawford to Meigs, February 7, 1854, Office of the Architect of the Capitol.

36. Crawford to Meigs, February 17, 1854, Office of the Architect of the Capitol.

37. Crawford to Meigs, June 28, 1855, Office of the Architect of the Capitol.

38. Meigs to Crawford, April 4, 1854, Office of the Architect of the Capitol.

39. Crawford to Meigs, March 7, 1854, Office of the Architect of the Capitol.

40. Bagni di Lucca, "La Svizzera di Toscana," pamphlet in a series, "Le Cento Citte d'Italia" (Milano: Sansogno, no. 92, series initiated 1887).

41. Crawford to Louisa, June 20, 1854, Wayne State University.

42. Crawford to Louisa, June 14, 1854, Wayne State University.

43. Crawford to Louisa, June 20, 1854, Wayne State University.

44. Ibid.

45. Crawford to Meigs, June 13, 1854, Office of the Architect of the Capitol.

46. Ibid.

47. File, Pennsylvania Academy of Fine Arts, Philadelphia.

48. Crawford to Louisa, July 10, 1854, Office of the Architect of the Capitol.

49. Crawford to Louisa, September 9, 1854, Wayne State University.

50. Ibid.

51. Crawford to Louisa, September 28, 1854, Wayne State University.

52. Ibid.

53. Crawford to Louisa, September 30, 1854, Wayne State University.

54. Ibid, and Julia to Louisa, October 28, 1851, Ward Papers, Harvard University Library.

55. Crawford to Louisa, October 5, 1854, Wayne State University.

56. Ibid.

57. Meigs to Crawford, June 18, 1854, Office of the Architect of the Capitol.

58. Ibid.

59. Meigs to Crawford, July 23, 1855, Office of the Architect of the Capitol.

60. Ibid.

61. Report of the Commissioners of the Washington Monument, *Journal of the House of Delegates* Session 1855–1856, Document No. 22, October 16, 1855, Virginia State Library.

62. Meigs to Crawford, June 1, 1855, Office of the Architect of the Capitol.

63. Crawford to Meigs, March 19, 1856, Office of the Architect of the Capitol.

64. Crawford to Meigs, November 27, 1855, Office of the Architect of the Capitol.

65. "Crawford's Beethoven 'Inauguration' in the Music Hall of Boston," *Putnam's Magazine*, vol. 7, no. 40, April 1856, p. 448.

66. "The Athenaeum Exhibit at Boston," *Putnam's Magazine*, vol. 6, no. 33, September 1855.

67. Ibid.

Notes to Chapter 20: American Ghiberti

1. Thomas Crawford to Captain M. C. Meigs, June 28, 1854, Office of the Architect of the Capitol.

2. Crawford to Meigs, October 23, 1854, Office of the Architect of the Capitol.

3. Crawford to Meigs, May 8, 1855, Office of the Architect of the Capitol.
4. Ibid.
5. Meigs to Crawford, October 11, 1855, Office of the Architect of the Capitol.
6. Crawford to Meigs, July 10, 1855, Office of the Architect of the Capitol.
7. Ibid.
8. Crawford to Meigs, June 20, 1855, Office of the Architect of the Capitol.
9. Meigs to Jefferson Davis, January 11, 1856, Office of the Architect of the Capitol.
10. Crawford to Meigs, October 18, 1855, Office of the Architect of the Capitol.
11. Jefferson Davis to Meigs, January 15, 1856, Office of the Architect of the Capitol.
12. Ibid.
13. Crawford to Louisa, June 23, 1854, Wayne State University.
14. Crawford to Meigs, March 19, 1856, Office of the Architect of the Capitol.

Notes to Chapter 21: Terminus

1. Crawford to Louisa, August 15, 1855, Wayne State University.
2. Ibid.
3. Crawford to Louisa, August 14, 1855, Wayne State University.
4. Crawford to Jack Bigelow, September 4, 1855, Copy in Virginia Historical Society, Richmond, Virginia. The original letter is in the Thomas Brumbaugh private collection.
5. Crawford to Louisa, August 15, 1855, Wayne State University.
6. Crawford to Louisa, August 21, 1855, Wayne State University.
7. Crawford to Louisa, August 25, 1855, Wayne State University.
8. Crawford to Louisa, September 1, 1855, Wayne State University.
9. Crawford to Louisa, September 4, 1855, Wayne State University.
10. Crawford to Louisa, September 7, 1855, Wayne State University.
11. Ibid.
12. Mrs. Hugh Fraser, *A Diplomatist's Wife in Many Lands*, 2 volumes, vol. 1, pp. 82–83.
13. Ibid., vol. 1, pp. 73–74.
14. Crawford to Louisa, April 22, 1856, Wayne State University.
15. Crawford to Louisa, May 14, 1856, Wayne State University.
16. Crawford to Meigs, August 21, 1856, Office of the Architect of the Capitol.
17. "Crawford's Equestrian Statue," *Savannah Republican*, article dated Munich, October 30, 1855. File in Virginia State Library.
18. Ibid.
19. Crawford to Louisa, June 19, 1856, Wayne State University.
20. Ibid.
21. Ibid.
22. Crawford to Louisa, June 25, 1856, Wayne State University.
23. Ibid.
24. Ibid.
25. Crawford to Louisa, July 25 and 28, 1856, Wayne State University.
26. Crawford to Louisa, July 28, 1856, Wayne State University.
27. Ibid.
28. Crawford to Louisa, August 3, 1856, Wayne State University.
29. Crawford to Ritchie, August 1, 1856, Brumbaugh Collection. Copy in Virginia Historical Society.
30. Crawford to Meigs, September 17, 1856, Office of the Architect of the Capitol.
31. Crawford to Louisa, August 7, 1856, Wayne State University.
32. Crawford to Louisa, August 9, 1856, Wayne State University.
33. Crawford to Louisa, August 13, 1856, Wayne State University.
34. Crawford to Louisa, August 16, 1856, Wayne State University.

35. Ibid.
36. Crawford to Louisa, September 5, 1856, Wayne State University.
37. Crawford to Louisa, September 19, 1856, Wayne State University.
38. Ibid.
39. Crawford to Louisa, October 2, 1856, Wayne State University.
40. Crawford to Louisa, October 6, 1856, Wayne State University.
41. Crawford to Louisa, October 13, 1856, Wayne State University.
42. Crawford to Louisa, October 25, 1856, Wayne State University.
43. Crawford to Louisa, October 30, 1856, Wayne State University.
44. Crawford to Louisa, November 12, 1856, Wayne State University.
45. Ibid.
46. Crawford to Louisa, October 30, 1856, Wayne State University.
47. Crawford to Louisa, postscript to a letter of Jenny Campbell to Louisa, December 24, 1856, Wayne State University.
48. Crawford to Louisa, December 10, 1856, Wayne State University.
49. Crawford to Louisa, postscript to a letter of Jenny Campbell to Louisa, December 18, 1856, Wayne State University.
50. Crawford, postscript to letter of Jenny Campbell to Louisa, December 30, 1856, Wayne State University.
51. Jenny Campbell to Louisa, January 8, 1857, Wayne State University.
52. Ibid.
53. Crawford to Louisa, January 13, 1857, Wayne State University.
54. Ibid.
55. Crawford to Louisa, February 12, 1857, Wayne State University.
56. Edward Pierce, *Memoir and Letters of Charles Sumner*, vol. 3, p. 530.
57. Crawford to Meigs, April 1, 1857, Office of the Architect of the Capitol.
58. Henry T. Tuckerman, *Book of the Artists*, p. 318.
59. Samuel Osgood, *Thomas Crawford and Art in America. An Address before the New-York Historical Society*, April 7, 1875.
60. Crawford to Meigs, November 14, 1855, Office of the Architect of the Capitol.
61. Crawford to Meigs, November 14, Office of the Architect of the Capitol. The contract with Rinehart was dated October 4, 1864. The doors cost $50,495, exclusive of transportation, which brought the cost to the final figure of $56,495.
63. Meigs to Crawford, November 26, 1855, Office of the Architect of the Capitol.
64. Meigs to Crawford, June 1, 1855, Office of the Architect of the Capitol.
65. Meigs to Crawford, April 20, 1857, Office of the Architect of the Capitol.
66. F. C. Adams, *Account of Art in the United States Capital*, p. 761. See also Executive Document No. 101, 40th Congress, 3rd Session, House of Representatives, Office of the Architect of the Capitol.
67. Adams, *Account of Art in the United States Capital*, p. 761.
68. Report of the Secretary of the Interior for November, 1864, Office of the Architect of the Capitol.
69. Report of Captain W. B. Franklin, November 6, 1859, File, Office of the Architect of the Capitol.
70. George Washington Greene, *Biographical Studies*, p. 149.
71. Ibid.

List of Works

This list of works is not intended to be considered as a complete list of all the works of these three sculptors. The lack of information on many of the works and the proliferation of copies of some of them prohibit any complete list.

These works are listed in the order in which they were created, as closely as can be determined from the existing records.

Works of Horatio Greenough

Bunker Hill Monument, design and wooden model for an obelisk. The scale model was for a monument of 100 feet. The eventual monument was 200 feet high and influenced by Greenough's design.

Dead Abel, full size statue modeled in Thorwaldsen's studio in Rome, 1826, never executed in marble.

Josiah Quincy, bust, 1827–1838, now at Harvard University. Copies: Boston Athenaeum and the Massachusetts Historical Society.

Samuel Appleton, bust, 1827–1838, now in the Fogg Art Museum, Harvard University.

John Jacob Astor, bust, 1827.

John Quincy Adams, bust, 1828–1829, commissioned in 1829 for the Boston Athenaeum. Copy in the New-York Historical Society. Half life-size copy in the Boston Museum of Fine Arts.

Chief Justice John Marshall, bust, 1828.

John Adams, bust, 1829, now located in a church in Quincy, Massachusetts. Copies in the Boston Museum of Fine Arts and the New-York Historical Society.

Sarah Ladson Gilmor (Mrs. Robert), bust, 1829, modeled in Baltimore. Now in the possession of Mrs. Grover Cleveland Edwards of Inman, South Carolina.

George Washington, marble bust after Houdon, 1830. Commissioned by Mr. Roosevelt of New York. A copy made for Commander Biddle is now in the Boston Museum of Fine Arts.

Giulia Grisi, bust, 1830, modeled in Florence.

Chanting Cherubs, marble group, commissioned in 1829 by James Fenimore Cooper, completed in marble in 1830 in Florence. Now in the National Collection of Fine Arts, Smithsonian Institution.

James Fenimore Cooper, marble bust, 1830–1833. Copies: Boston Public Library, Boston Museum of Fine Arts, New-York Historical Society.

Self Portrait, marble bust, 1830–1831, modeled in Florence. Now in a private collection, 59 rue St. Dominique, Paris.

Thomas Cole, marble bust, 1831, modeled in Florence. Now in the Wadsworth Athenaeum, Hartford, Connecticut.

Kinlock of North Carolina, bust, 1831, modeled in Florence.

Arthur Brisbane of New York, marble bust, 1831.

Princess Christina di Belgioioso, plaster bust, 1831.

Marquis de Lafayette, life size marble bust, 1831. Copies in the Boston Museum of Fine Arts, the Pennsylvania Academy of the Fine Arts, and the New-York Historical Society.

Samuel Finley Breese Morse, marble bust, 1831, modeled in Florence. Now in the National Collection of Fine Arts, Smithsonian Institution. Plaster copy in the Metropolitan Museum of Art.

Cornelia Grinnell (Mrs. Nathaniel Parker Willis) of New York, statue, 1832. Now in the possession of Mrs. William Burnham of Brookline, Massachusetts.

John Thornton Kirkland, marble bust, 1832. Now in the Boston Athenaeum.

Medora, 1832, marble statute of a life-size recumbent female. Commissioned by Robert Gilmor, Jr. Now in possession of Mrs. Sumner A. Parker, The Cloisters, Baltimore, Maryland.

Napoleon I, bust, 1832, from the death mask. Commissioned for the Boston Athenaeum but subsequently given to the Boston Museum of Fine Arts.

George Washington, marble statue, 1832–1840. Now in the National Collection of Fine Arts, Smithsonian Institution.

Miles of New York, bust.

Elizabeth Cabot, marble bust, 1833, modeled in Florence. Now in the possession of Dr. George C. Shattuck, Brookline, Massachusetts.

Genius of America, 1833, statuette (2′6″ high), commissioned by Mr. Hoyt of New York. There is a sketch of this work in Prime's *Life of Samuel F. B. Morse.*

Genius of Italy, 1833, statuette (2′6″ high), commissioned by Mr. Hoyt of New York.

Nathaniel Parker Willis, marble bust, 1832–1834. Now in the possession of Mrs. William Burnham, Brookline, Massachusetts.

David, Singing to Saul, an incomplete study made in Florence, 1832.

Achilles, 1833, clay model (7′ high), unfinished.

Mary Frazier Curtis, marble bust, 1833, modeled in Florence. Now in the possession of Mrs. Louis Curtis, Brookline, Massachusetts.

Francis Alexander, marble bust, 1834–1835, modeled in Florence.

Madame Para, marble bust, 1834–1835, modeled in Florence.

Love Captive (*Cupid Bound*), marble statue (3′7″ high) of a young boy with wings, 1832–1836, modeled in Florence. Inspired by a poem of Petrarch, "Trionfo della Castita." Now in the Boston Museum of Fine Arts.

Ellen Adair White, marble bust, 1834, modeled in Florence. Now in the Mary Buie Museum, Oxford, Mississippi.

Angel and Child, marble group, 1835. Also called *Ascension and the Infant Spirit, Journey to Heaven Group*, and *Infant and Cherub.* Commissioned by the Perkins family of Boston. Now in the Museum of Fine Arts, Boston.

Sears Children, marble group, 1835–1837, modeled in Florence. Now in the Massachusetts Historical Society.

David Sears, marble bust, 1835. Now in the Somerset Club, Boston, Massachusetts.

Joseph M. White, marble bust, 1835, modeled in Florence. Now in the New-York Historical Society.

Carlo Botta, bust, 1836. One copy went to Marquis Gino Capponi; another to the poet Niccolini.

Alexander Hamilton, marble bust. Now in the Boston Museum of Fine Arts.

Young Augustus, bust. Copy of the figure in the Vatican galleries. Commissioned by Francis Calley Gray. Now in the Boston Museum of Fine Arts.

Aristides, marble statue. Copy of a statue in the Royal Museum in Naples. Commissioned by Mr. Halsey of New York. Another copy was commissioned by Edward E. Salisbury. One is now in the Yale University Art Gallery.

Washington in Modern Dress, statue. Commissioned by Mr. Halsey as a companion piece to *Aristides.*

Halsey, bust.

Thomson Children, marble group, 1837, modeled in Florence. Commissioned by Colonel Thomson of Boston. Now in the Somerset Club, Boston, Massachusetts.

Colonel Thomson, bust.

Young Griffin, marble bust. Commissioned by the Griffin Family of New York. Copy made for Colonel Thorn.

Evan Philip Thomas, marble bust, 1837, modeled in Florence. Now in the Maryland Historical Society.

Elizabeth Todhunter Thomas, marble bust, 1837, modeled in Florence. Now in the Maryland Historical Society.

Heloise, marble ideal head, 1837, modeled in Florence, Inspired by a character in a poem by Alexander Pope. Commissioned by Evan Philip Thomas of Baltimore; copy commissioned in Philadelphia.

Head of Christ (*Our Saviour*), marble ideal bust (33" high), 1837, modeled in Florence. Completed in marble in 1846. Copies in the Boston Public Library and the Fogg Art Museum of Harvard University. Both of these were gifts from Louisa Greenough.

John Warren, marble bust, 1837, modeled in Florence. Now in the Boston Athenaeum. Copy at Harvard University.

John Collins Warren, marble bust, 1837, commissioned in Florence. Now in the Fogg Art Museum, Harvard University.

John Warren, medallion, 1837, commissioned in Florence.

Ideal Head, American clay, 1838, modeled in Florence.

Marquis Gino Capponi, marble bust, 1838, modeled in Florence.

Jonathan Mason, marble bust, 1838, modeled in Florence.

Miniature copy of the Washington statue, 1838, modeled in Florence for the Capponi family.

Arno, marble statue of a greyhound, 1838, modeled in Florence. Purchased by Edward Everett.

Emily Marshall Otis (Mrs. William Foster Otis), marble bust, 1839, modeled in Florence. Now in the Boston Athenaeum.

Venus Victrix, marble statue (smaller than life-size) 1839, modeled in

Florence. Commissioned by John Lowell of Cambridge, Massachusetts. Now in the Boston Athenaeum.

Judgment of Paris, marble bas-relief, 1839. Commissioned by John Lowell of Cambridge, Massachusetts. Now in the Boston Athenaeum.

The Angel Abdiel, marble statue, 1839. Commissioned by E. E. Salisbury. Now in the Yale University Art Gallery.

The Angel Warning St. John, marble bas-relief statue, 1839–1841. Commissioned by E. E. Salisbury. Now in the Yale University Art Gallery.

Gibbs Monument, marble statue, 1839, modeled in Florence for the Gibbs family tomb, Saint Mary's Church, South Portsmouth, Rhode Island.

Benjamin Franklin, colossal marble bust, 1839. Now in the Boston Athenaeum.

Psyche, ideal head, marble, 1839. Commissioned by Francis Calley Gray of Boston.

James Freeman Curtis, marble bust, 1841. Now in the possession of Miss Mary Curtis, Hamilton, Massachusetts.

William Ellery Channing, bust, 1841, modeled in Florence for Count Mournieff.

Little Girl and Butterfly, statue of Ada, the three-year-old daughter of Count Revicksky, Austrian minister to Florence, 1841.

Countess Revicksky, marble bust, 1841.

Satan (Lucifer), marble ideal bust, 1842, modeled in Florence as a companion piece to *Head of Christ*. Now in the Boston Public Library. A plaster cast is at Harvard University.

Abdiel, marble bust, 1844. Completed in Florence for Mrs. Elizabeth H. Bartol of Boston. Now in the Art Institute of Chicago.

St. Bernard, marble statue of a dog for Colonel Thomas Perkins of Boston, 1844. Now in the Perkins family plot, Mt. Auburn Cemetery, Cambridge, Massachusetts.

David, statue, 1846, unfinished.

Dejected Artist, marble bas-relief, 1849, modeled in Florence for George Ticknor, Cambridge, Massachusetts. This statue is a classical female figure with a hand pouring oil into an expiring lamp.

Apollo, the Avenger, sketch for a statue, 1850, not executed.

Castor and Pollux, marble bas-relief, 1850. Now in the Museum of Fine Arts, Boston.

Bacchante and Young Faun, marble statue in bas-relief, 1850.

Castor Gemelli, sketch for a statue in bas-relief, 1850, not executed.

Genius of Italy for the Giuseppe Giusti Monument at Pescia, Italy, plaster bas-relief statue (See J. J. Jarves, *the Art Idea,* p. 261), unfinished.

Genius of Poesy, sketch of a classical figure for the Giusti Monument, never executed.

Venus, Contending for the Golden Apple, larger than life-size statue, 1850, plaster modeled in Florence, lost at sea.

Rescue Group, marble group, commissioned in 1837, completed in 1850. Now in the Capitol.

Homer, marble bust, 1851.

Cooper Monument, sketch made in Boston in 1851, never executed.

James Fenimore Cooper, design for a colossal bust for the projected Cooper Monument (see Gleasin's Pictorial Drawing Companion on file in the New York State Historical Association, Cooperstown, New York), 1852.

Equestrian Washington Monument, sketch made for monument to be placed in Union Square, New York City, 1852. Unfinished, although Greenough started to model the horse.

Works of Hiram Powers

Aaron Corwin, wax medallion, Cincinnati, 1823.

Marquis de Lafayette, plaster bust, for Frederick Eckstein, Cincinnati, 1825.

Luman Watson, bas-relief bust, Cincinnati, 1820s.

John Foote, plaster bust, Cincinnati, 1826 or 1827.

Katherine Foote (four-year-old daughter of John Foote), beeswax bust, Cincinnati, 1826 or 1827.

Miner Kilbourne Kellogg, wax bust, Cincinnati, 1828. Now in the Cincinnati Art Museum.

George Washington (from the death mask), bust, modeled in 1832; marble, Florence, 1838. Given to Nicholas Longworth. Now at the Cincinnati Historical Society.

Chief Justice John Marshall, bust, modeled in Washington in 1835; marble carved in Florence. Now in the Capitol.

Judge William Cranch, bust, modeled in Washington, 1835; marble, Florence.

Andrew Jackson, bust, modeled in Washington, 1835; marble, Florence. Copies: the Hermitage, Nashville, Tennessee, and the Metropolitan Museum of Art.

Daniel Webster, bust, modeled in Boston, 1836; marble, Florence. Now in the Boston Athenaeum.

Governor John Winthrop, bust, modeled in Boston, 1836; marble, Florence.

Governor John Davis of Worcester, Massachusetts, bust modeled in Boston, 1836; marble, Florence.

William Lawrence, bust, modeled in Boston, 1836.

Mrs. William Lawrence, bust, modeled in Boston, 1836.

Abbott Lawrence, bust, modeled in Boston, 1836; marble, Florence. Now in the Lawrence Scientific School, Harvard University.

Katherine Lawrence (Mrs. Abbott), bust, modeled in Boston, 1836.

Judge William Baldwin, bust, modeled in Boston, 1836; marble, Florence.

Professor John Farrar of Harvard, bust, modeled in Boston, 1836.

James M. Barnard, bust, modeled in Boston, 1836.

President John Quincy Adams, bust, modeled in Washington, 1837; marble, Florence, for Horatio Greenough. Now at the Adams family shrine in a church at Quincy, Massachusetts.

Colonel John S. Preston, bust, modeled in Washington, 1837; marble, Florence.

Mrs. John S. Preston, bust, modeled in Washington, 1837; marble, Florence.

Senator William C. Preston, bust, modeled in Washington, 1837; marble, Florence. Now at the University of South Carolina.

Martin Van Buren, bust, modeled in Washington, 1837. Now in the New-York Historical Society.

Senator Robert J. Walker, bust, modeled in Washington, 1837.

General Hunt of Texas, bust, modeled in Washington, 1837; marble, Florence. Now owned by the state of Texas.

Colonel Richard M. Johnson of Frankfurt, Kentucky, vice-president of the United States under Andrew Jackson when Powers modeled the bust in Washington, 1837.

General Edmund Pendleton Gaines, bust, modeled in Washington, 1837; marble cut in Florence for the Texas statehouse.

General MacComb, bust, modeled in Washington, 1837.

General Duff Green, bust, modeled in Washington, 1837; marble cut in Florence. Now at the University of North Carolina at Chapel Hill.

Anna Sarah Maxcy (Mrs. George Hughes, daughter of Virgil Maxcy), bust modeled in Washington, 1837.

Honorable Levi Woodbury, bust, modeled in Washington, 1837.

William J. Stone, bust, modeled in Washington, 1837; marble, Florence. Now in the Corcoran Gallery of Art, Washington, D.C.

Senator Thomas Hart Benton, bust, modeled in Washington, 1837.

John C. Calhoun, bust, modeled in Washington, 1837; marble, Florence, 1839. Commissioned in marble by Congress, 1849. Plaster copy now in the Yale University Art Gallery.

Anna Maria Calhoun (daughter of John C. Calhoun), bust, modeled in Washington, 1837.

Francis Granger, bust, modeled in Washington, 1837; marble, Florence. Now in the Memorial Art Gallery, University of Rochester.

LeRoy of New York, bust, modeled in 1837.

Mrs. William H. Wharton of Texas, bust, modeled in Washington, 1837.

George Tiffany of Baltimore, Maryland, bust modeled in Washington, 1837.

Robert Hamilton Bishop (president of Miami University), bust, modeled in Washington, 1837; marble, Florence. Now at Miami University, Oxford, Ohio.

Nicholas Longworth, bust, modeled in Cincinnati, 1837; marble, Florence. Now in the Cincinnati Art Museum.

Judge Jacob Burnett, bust, modeled in Cincinnati, 1837; marble, Florence. Now in the Cincinnati Art Museum.

Robert Todd Lytle, bust, modeled in Cincinnati, 1837; marble, Florence. Now in the Cincinnati Historical Society.

Anna Barker Ward (Mrs. Samuel Gray Ward), marble bust cut in Florence, 1838. Now in the Corcoran Gallery of Art, Washington, D.C. Copy owned by Mrs. William C. Endicott, Boston.

Louisa Greenough, marble bust, Florence, 1838. In possession of the Greenough family.

Richard Henry Wilde of New Orleans, bas-relief, Florence, 1839.

Horatio Greenough, Florence, 1839. Now in the Boston Museum of Fine Arts.

Genevra, ideal female bust, marble, 1838. Copies: Corcoran Gallery of

Art, Washington, D.C., and the Toledo Museum of Art, Toledo Ohio.

Proserpine, ideal female bust, marble, Florence, 1839. Copies: Albright-Knox Art Gallery, Buffalo, New York; Corcoran Gallery of Art, Washington, D.C.; Montreal Museum of Fine Arts, Montreal, Quebec, Canada; and the Newark Museum, Newark, New Jersey.

Loulie's Hand, marble, Florence, 1839. Now in the Fogg Art Museum, Harvard University. Gift of J. C. Ropes.

Charles Lowell of Boston, marble bust, Florence, 1839.

Honorable George McDuffie of South Carolina, marble bust, 1839.

Edward Everett, marble bust, Florence, 1841. Copies: Harvard University and the National Portrait Gallery, Smithsonian Institution.

John Slidell of New Orleans, marble bust, Florence, 1841.

Eve Tempted, marble statue, ideal female nude, Florence, 1842. Purchased by John S. Preston; sold to A. T. Stewart, New York. Now in the National Collection of Fine Arts, Smithsonian Institution.

Eve, marble bust, Florence, 1842. Copies: Mrs. C. Van Rensselaer, Albany, New York; George Tiffany, Baltimore, Maryland; Brooklyn Museum; Nicholas Longworth, Cincinnati, Ohio; and the Museum of Fine Arts, Boston.

Mrs. C. Van Rensselaer of Albany, New York, marble bust, 1842.

John Parker of Boston, marble bust, 1842.

Cornelius Low of New York City, marble bust, 1842.

Miles of New York City, marble bust, 1843

Dr. George Brimmer of Boston, marble bust, 1843.

George Calvert of Baltimore, Maryland, bust, 1843.

Joseph Bonaparte of Florence, marble bust, 1843.

The Greek Slave, marble statue, Florence, 1843. Six commissioned statues: Captain John Grant, London; James Robb, New Orleans; A. T. Stewart, New York City; Lord Ward, England; Prince Anatoli Demidov, Florence; and E. W. Stoughton, New York City. Copies: Corcoran Gallery of Art, Washington, D.C.; Newark Museum, Newark, New Jersey; Brooklyn Museum of Art; Pennsylvania Academy of Fine Arts, Philadelphia; Toledo Museum of Art, Toledo, Ohio; and the Yale University Art Gallery. Several miniature copies were made. Four may be seen in the United States; a 14″ marble in the Detroit Institute of Art and three, a 13½″ Parian Ware, a 12⅞″ Parian Ware, and a 10⅛″ alabaster, in the Newark Museum, Newark, New Jersey.

Greek Slave, marble bust, 1843. Copies: Addison Gallery of American Art, Phillips Andover Academy, Andover, Massachusetts; Berkshire Museum, Pittsfield, Massachusetts; Boston Public Library; and the Cincinnati Art Museum. Sketch: Corcoran Gallery of Art, Washington, D.C.

Captain John Grant of London, marble bust, Florence, 1844.

The Fisher Boy, marble statue, ideal boy, Florence, 1846. Copies: Metropolitan Museum of Art and the Museum of Fine Arts, Richmond, Virginia. One of the five copies made was sold to an Englishman named Stephenson.

The Fisher Boy, marble bust, Florence, 1846. Several copies.

Princess Mathilde Bonaparte Demidov, marble bust, Florence, 1846.

Maria Antoinetta, Grand Duchess of Tuscany, marble bust, Florence, 1846. Commissioned by Prince Anatoli Demidov. Ten to twelve copies were made; one is in the Worcester Art Museum, Worcester, Massachusetts.

Martha Endicott Peabody (Mrs. Dennis Rogers) of Salem, Massachusetts, marble bust, Florence, 1846.

Pair of Angels for altar of a cathedral in Cincinnati, Ohio. Commissioned in 1847 by Bishop Purcell.

David Urguart of New Orleans, marble bust, Florence, 1849. Now in the Dominican College Library, New Orleans.

Psyche, marble bust, ideal female, Florence, 1849, for William Haywood, Charleston, South Carolina. Eight copies; one in the Cincinnati Art Museum.

Mrs. Emily Ward, marble bust, Florence, 1849.

Francis Calley Gray of Boston, marble bust, Florence. Now in the Boston Athenaeum.

Alma Hammond L'Hommedieu, marble bust, Florence. Now in the Detroit Institute of Arts.

Margaret Fuller Ossoli, Florence, marble bust, 1849. Lost at sea.

John C. Calhoun, statue, fashioned after the portrait bust of 1837. Commissioned in 1845 for the city of Charleston, South Carolina. Plaster, 1847; marble, 1849. Destroyed during the Civil War. There is a parian porcelain copy 16¾″ high in the Gibbes Art Gallery, Charleston, South Carolina.

Colonel Wade Hampton of South Carolina, bust, 1849.

Catherine Hampton, bust, 1849.

Cyrus W. Field, bust, 1849.

Cornelius Vanderbilt of New York City, bust, 1850.

Thurlow Weed of Albany, New York, bust, 1850.

Sir Isaac Newton, marble bust, Florence, 1850. Now in the Virginia Museum of Fine Arts, Richmond, Virginia.

James Pennyman, bust, 1851.

Mrs. James Pennyman, bust, 1851.

Dr. W. B. Moffat of New York, bust, 1852.

Sir Henry Bulwer, bust, Florence, 1852.

Diana, marble bust, ideal female, Florence, 1853. Many copies; one in the Corcoran Gallery of Art, Washington, D.C., and another in the Wadsworth Athenaeum, Hartford, Connecticut.

Chanler of Boston (father of Winthrop Chanler), bust, 1853.

Daniel Webster, marble bust, 1853, for George Ticknor, Cambridge, Massachusetts. Now in the Boston Athenaeum.

America (Liberty), marble statue, 1854, designed for the Capitol but not commissioned by Congress. Copies: Corcoran Gallery of Art, Washington, D.C., and the Fogg Art Museum, Harvard University.

America, bust, 1866. Many copies; one in the Wadsworth Athenaeum, Hartford, Connecticut, another in the Metropolitan Museum of Art.

George Washington, marble statue after Houdon's bust, modeled in 1853, finished in 1855, for the Louisiana statehouse, Baton Rouge. Destroyed during the Civil War.

George Washington, marble bust after Houdon. Copies: Freemason's Lodge, Fredericksburg, Virginia; New-York Historical Society; Cincinnati Historical Society; and two copies (slightly different, one has drapery) are in the Philadelphia Museum of Art.

La Penserosa, marble statue, ideal female, 1856, for James Lenox of New York City.

La Penserosa, marble bust, 1856, for Edward Everett.

Felix Grundy, congressman of Nashville, Tennessee, marble bust, 1856.

Jared Sparks, marble bust, 1857. Copies: Boston Public Library; Harvard University; Peabody Institute, Baltimore, Maryland; Massachusetts Historical Society, Boston; and the Antiquarian Society, Worcester, Massachusetts.

Mrs. Edward C. Pickering (daughter of Jared Sparks), marble bust, circa 1857. Now in the Boston Public Library.

Alexander Hamilton, bust, for Hamilton Fish of New York.

Daniel Webster, bronze statue 8″ high, for the Massachusetts statehouse grounds, Boston.

California (*La Dorada*), marble statue, ideal female, 1858. William Backhouse Astor purchased the statue and sold it to A. T. Stewart, who gave it to the Metropolitan Museum of Art.

Mrs. James S. Wadsworth of New York, bust, 1858.

Elizabeth Gibson Powers, marble bust, Florence, 1859. Now in the Powers family collection.

Mrs. Louisa McCord, marble bust, Florence, 1859. Now in the Gibbes Art Gallery, Charleston, South Carolina.

Judge Langdon Cheeves of Charleston, South Carolina, marble bust, Florence, 1859.

Mary Singleton McDuffie (Mrs. Wade Hampton) of Charleston, South Carolina, marble bust, Florence, 1860.

Louisa Greenough Powers (Mrs. Alfred Ibbotson), marble bust, Florence, 1862. In the Powers' family collection.

Evangeline, marble bust, ideal female, Florence, 1859. Now in the Cincinnati Art Museum.

Heloise Durant Rose of New York, marble bust, Florence. 1864. Now in the Toledo Museum of Art, Toledo, Ohio.

Mrs. Bigelow Lawrence of Boston, marble bust, Florence, 1863.

Benjamin Franklin, life-size statue, marble, Florence, 1862. Now in the Capitol. A copy of this statue made for the New Orleans Central Public Library was destroyed by fire.

Benjamin Franklin, marble bust. Copies: Yale University Art Gallery and the Fogg Art Museum, Harvard University.

Thomas Jefferson, life-size statue, marble, modeled and commissioned in 1859; completed in 1863. Now in the Capitol. Some busts of this statue were made.

George Perkins Marsh, marble bust, Florence, 1864. Now at the University of Vermont in Burlington.

Mrs. George Perkins Marsh, marble bust, Florence, 1864. Now at the University of Vermont in Burlington.

Christ, ideal bust, marble, Florence, 1865, for William H. Aspinwall of New York.

Right Reverend William Ingraham Kip, Episcopal Bishop of California, marble bust, Florence, 1865.

Genevra (entirely different from the first *Genevra*, ideal bust, marble, Florence, 1865, for Ignatius Scott of Boston.

Edward C. Litchfield of New York, marble bust, 1866.

Elisa Litchfield of New York, marble bust, relief fondo, 1866. Now in the Brooklyn Museum of Art, Brooklyn, New York.

Chief Justice Salmon P. Chase, marble bust, 1866.

Honorable Robert Charles Winthrop of Boston, bust, 1868. Copy: Harvard University.

Endicott Peabody of Salem, 1868. Gift to Robert C. Winthrop.

Henry Wadsworth Longfellow, bust, 1869.

Reverend Henry Bellows of New York City, marble bust, Florence, 1869.

Anna Barker Powers (daughter of Hiram Powers), bust, 1869. In the Powers' family collection.

Clytie, marble bust, ideal female, Florence, 1867.

Faith, marble bust, ideal female, Florence, 1867. Now in the Boston Museum of Fine Arts.

Charity, marble bust, ideal female, Florence, 1868. Now in the Newark Museum, Newark, New Jersey.

Hope, marble bust, ideal female, Florence, 1869. Now in the Brooklyn Museum.

Judge Alphonso Taft of Cincinnati, marble bust, Florence, 1869. Now in the Taft Museum, Cincinnati, Ohio.

Alice Key Pendleton, marble bust, Florence, 1870. Now in the Corcoran Gallery of Art, Washington, D.C.

Edward Everett, life-size marble statue, Florence, 1870. Now at Harvard University.

Edward Everett, bust, fashioned after the statue. Many copies; one at Harvard University and one in the National Portrait Gallery, Smithsonian Institution.

Eve Disconsolate (Paradise Lost), marble statue, ideal female, modeled in 1859; completed in 1871. Copies: Cincinnati Art Museum and the Toledo Museum of Art, Toledo, Ohio.

Eve Disconsolate, marble bust, 1871. Many copies, one in the Rhode Island School of Design, Providence, Rhode Island.

Indian Girl (Last of the Tribe), statue, modeled in 1859, completed in marble in 1873 for Mr. Haight of New York. Now in the private collection of David Burliuk. Riverhead, Long Island, New York. Copy in the National Collection of Fine Arts, Smithsonian Institution.

Sidney Brooks of New York, marble bust, Florence, 1870.

Julius S. Morgan of London, marble bust, 1870.

General Philip Sheridan, marble bust, 1871.

Joshua Wolcott, marble bust. Now in the Newark Museum, Newark, New Jersey.

Works of Thomas Crawford

Bacchante, life-size statue, idealized female, cut in Thorwaldsen's studio
in Rome, 1836.
Commander Isaac Hull, marble bust, Rome, 1836.
Mary Hone Schermerhorn, marble bust, Rome, 1837. Now in the New-
York Historical Society, New York City.
Paris Presenting the Apple to Venus, statue, for Mr. Calhoun of New
Orleans. The plaster cast was destroyed.
Demosthenes, copy of the statue in the Vatican galleries, Rome, 1838.
Benjamin Franklin, study for a statue, Rome, 1839.
George Washington, study for a monument, Rome, 1839.
Ingraham of England, bust, Rome, 1839.
Carlo Botta (the historian), medallion. Presented by Crawford either to
President Martin Van Buren or to Mr. Butler of New York, who
gave it to the Library of Congress.
Orpheus and Cerberus, life-size marble group, Rome, 1838–1843. Now
in the Museum of Fine Arts, Boston, on permanent loan from the
Boston Athenaeum.
*Hercules Arrested by Diana and Diana in the Act of Carrying Away
the Golden-Horned Stag*, oblong bas-relief, marble, Rome, 1839,
for Prince Anatoli Demidov.
Battle of the Centaurs, round bas-relief, marble, Rome, 1839, for
Prince Anatoli Demidov.
George Washington Greene, marble bust, Modeled in Rome 1838, com-
pleted in 1840. In Longfellow's room in Boston in 1841; now in the
Longfellow House in Cambridge.
Charles Sumner, marble bust, Rome 1839–1842. Now in the Museum of
Fine Arts, Boston.
Sir Charles Vaughan, British minister to Washington, marble bust,
Rome, 1839.
John Kenyon, English poet, bust, modeled in Rome, 1839. Marble sent
to George Ticknor in 1841 at Kenyon's request.
Genius of Autumn, statue of a young boy with sickle and sheaf,
modeled in Rome, 1839. Marble for John Paine, New York City.
Centurion, statue, Rome, 1839, for John Paine, New York City.
Judge Edmund K. Pendleton, marble bust, Rome, 1839. Now in the
New-York Historical Society, New York City.
Four Winds, designs for bas-reliefs, commissioned in Rome, 1840, for
the Boston Athenaeum, never executed.

Anacreon, marble bas-relief, 1842. Now in the Boston Athenaeum.

Orpheus, marble head, Rome, 1841, for Mr. Homans, Boston.

The Infant Savior, sketch for a bas-relief, Rome, 1842.

Hebe and Ganymede, life-size statues, marble, Rome, 1842, for Charles C. Perkins. Now in the Museum of Fine Arts, Boston.

Ganymede, drawing, Rome, 1842, for Mrs. Cleveland of Boston.

Jefferson, design for a statue, 1843.

Washington, design for a statue, 1843.

William Ellery Channing, design for a statue, 1843.

Lead Us into Life Everlasting, bas-relief for the tombstone of Mrs. George Tiffany. Commissioned by George Tiffany, Baltimore.

Day and Night, copies of Thorwaldsen's statues, for George Tiffany, Baltimore.

Cupid in Contemplation, ideal statue, for George Tiffany, Baltimore. Copy in marble for Jonathan Phillips, Boston.

Venus as Shepherdess, marble bas-relief, after Thorwaldsen. Now in the Museum of Fine Arts, Boston.

Glory to God in the Highest and on Earth, Peace and Good Will Towards Men; The Wise Men; and *The Shepherds*, three religious sketches, were engraved and published in Rome in 1843 (see *Boston Transcript*, December 21, 1935, Boston Athenaeum File.)

Other religious sketches were:

Christ Disputing with the Doctors.
Christ Ascending from the Tomb.
Christ Raising Jairus' Daughter.
Christ Blessing the Little Children.
Christ at the Well of Samaria.
Repose in Egypt.
Eve Tempted.
Eve with Cain and Abel.

Christ, marble bust, circa 1843.

Charles Brooks of Boston, marble bust, Rome, 1843.

Vesta, ideal head, marble, Rome, 1843.

Pandora, ideal head, marble, Rome, circa 1843.

Io, ideal head, marble, Rome, circa 1843.

Bride of Abydos, statue, Rome, 1843, for John Parker, Boston.

Mercury, ideal bust, marble, Rome, 1843, for John Parker, Boston.

Psyche, ideal bust, marble, Rome, 1843, for John Parker, Boston.

Little David, marble statue, Rome, 1844.

Mathias Bruen of New York, marble bust, Rome, 1845.

David Triumphant, marble statue, Rome, 1845, for Mrs. Pickman, Boston.

Genius of Mirth (*Dancing Girl, Jenny*), marble statue, Rome, 1844, for Mr. Hicks, New York City. Presented by his daughter, Mrs. Anna Hicks Lord, to the Metropolitan Museum of Art in 1897.

Josiah Quincy, marble bust, Rome, 1845. Now at Harvard University. Plaster copies: Boston Athenaeum and the Massachusetts Historical Society.

Mrs. Charles C. Perkins, marble bust, Rome, 1846.

Psyche, drawing, Rome, 1846, for Mrs. Cleveland, Boston.

Leverett Saltonstall, Rome, circa 1846.

Louisa Ward Crawford (*Portrait of a Lady*), marble bust, Rome, 1846. Possession of Lawrence Terry on loan to the Museum of the City of New York.

Christian Pilgrim, marble statue, woman holding a bronze cross, Rome, 1847, for Mrs. Cleveland, Boston. Gift to the Boston Athenaeum by Mrs. Eliza Callahan Cleveland.

Daughter of Rodias, Holding the Head of St. John Under her Arm, statue, modeled in Rome, 1847.

Dying Mexican Princess, marble statue, Rome, 1848, for Mr. Hicks, New York City. His daughter, Anna Hicks Lord, gave the statue to the Metropolitan Museum of Art in 1897.

Dying Mexican Princess, marble bust, Rome, 1848.

Washington Allston, design for a statue, not executed.

Lord Byron, silver medallion. Now in the City Art Museum of Saint Louis, Missiouri.

Morning Star, life-size marble statue. Now at the Rhode Island School of Design, Providence, Rhode Island.

Henry Clay, bust (in contemplation of a monument).

Equestrian Washington, Rome, 1850–1857, bronze monument for Capitol Square, Richmond, Virginia. Crawford executed the figures of *Washington*, *Thomas Jefferson*, *Patrick Henry*, *John Marshall*, *George Mason*, and Washington's horse.

George Washington, marble bust, Rome, 1850s. Gift of the Lenox Library to New York Public Library. Now located at the entrance to the main reading room. Copy in the New-York Historical Society.

Babes in the Wood, marble group, recumbent figures of two children in period dress, Rome, 1851, for Hamilton Fish, New York. Given to the Metropolitan Museum of Art.

Children Holding a Bird's Nest Tenanted by a Bird, marble group, Rome, 1850s, for Mrs. C. Van Rensselaer, Albany, New York. Now in Hampshire House, 84 Beacon Street, Boston.

Boy Playing Marbles, marble statue, Rome, 1853, for Stephen Salisbury, Worcester, Massachusetts. Given to the Worcester Art Museum.

Flora, marble statue, larger than life-size ideal figure, Rome 1853, for Mr. Haight, New York City. Shown in Crystal Palace exhibition, New York City, 1854. Now in the Newark Museum, Newark, New Jersey.

Flora, marble bust, ideal, Rome, 1853, for Stephen Salisbury, Worcester, Massachusetts. Loaned to the Metropolitan Museum of Art for an exhibition in 1897 but returned to the owner. Now in a private collection.

The Hunter's Horn, Rome, 1853, for James Lenox, New York City.

Adam and Eve After their Expulsion, marble statues, smaller than life-size. Now in the Boston Athenaeum. Also made as statuettes.

Apollo with Pegasus, ideal group.

Peri, winged female figure, two marble copies, 1855. Life-size copy: Corcoran Gallery of Art, Washington, D.C.; larger than life-size copy: Pennsylvania Museum of Fine Arts, Philadelphia.

Beethoven, bronze statue 7″ high, Rome, 1854. Cast in Munich, 1855, for Charles C. Perkins. Gift to the New England Conservatory of Music, Boston.

Sappho, ideal marble bust, Rome, 1855. Now in Longfellow House, Cambridge.

Beethoven, plaster bust, Rome, 1857. Gift of Crawford to Charles C. Perkins. Now in the possession of the Perkins family.

Progress of American Civilization, fourteen figures for the Senate pediment, Senate wing of the Capitol. Central figure: colossal *America.* Others: Indian chief (hunter), Indian wife, Indian boy, soldier (in Revolutionary uniform), schoolmaster, schoolboy, mechanic, and merchant.

Justice and *History,* idealized colossal statues, marble, Rome, 1854–1856, recumbent classical draped female figures, above the senate entrance doorway.

Senate Doors. Plaster model completed by Crawford in Rome, 1855–

1856. Bronze casting supervised by William Henry Rinehart, 1860.

House Doors. Design completed by Crawford in Rome, 1855–1856.

Armed Liberty (*Armed Freedom*), colossal bronze figure, 1855–1862, for the dome of the United States Capitol. Plaster model (bronzed) in the National Collection of Fine Arts, Smithsonian Institution.

Indian Chief, life-size marble statue, recumbent male figure. Rome, 1856. Presented by Frederick de Peyster to the New-York Historical Society in 1875.

James Otis, bronze statue, 7'6", Rome, 1856. Commissioned for a memorial for Auburn Cemetery, Cambridge, Massachusetts. Now at Sanders Theater, Harvard University.

Revised Sappho, sketch for an ideal bust, Rome, 1856, for Mrs. Wadsworth, Boston.

Bibliography

GUIDE TO SOURCES

The basic source materials for this study were the letters of the three sculptors and those of their friends, patrons, and colleagues. These letters are scattered through multiple collections in a variety of archives which are listed here. Some of this correspondence has been published in private journals and memoirs and in biographies but most of it remains in manuscript form. The periodicals of the nineteenth century in America yielded valuable information in numerous articles, book reviews, and reports of art exhibitions. The biographies, memoirs, guide books, and travel books were informative of general attitudes and tastes of the period as well as of relevant events.

Manuscript sources for Horatio Greenough

Ann Arbor, Michigan. University of Michigan.
Baltimore. Maryland Historical Society. Robert Gilmor Papers. Robert Gilmor Journal. Volume 1, *Travels in Europe.*
Boston. Boston Athenaeum. Files and letterbooks.
Boston. Boston Public Library. Greenough File. Griswold and Chamberlain collections.
Boston. McLeans Hospital. Record on Horatio Greenough.
Boston. Massachusetts Historical Society. Proceedings of the Massachusetts Historical Society. Letters in the collections of Horatio Greenough, Washington Allston, Samuel Cabot, Thomas H.

Cabot, Richard Henry Dana, George S. Hillard, Thomas H. Perkins, William Hinckling Prescott, William Wetmore and Emelyn Story, Charles Sumner, and George Tickor. Of special importance to Greenough's aesthetics: Horatio Greenough to Richard Henry Dana, June 11, 1844, in the Dana Collection.

Cambridge, Massachusetts. Harvard University. Archive of Harvard University. Houghton Library. Letters in the collections of Horatio Greenough, Washington Allston, Ralph Waldo Emerson, Edward Everett, Margaret Fuller (Ossoli), Henry Wadsworth Longfellow, James Russell Lowell, John L. Motley, Charles Eliot Norton, and William Wetmore and Emelyn Story. Of special importance to Greenough's aesthetics: Horatio Greenough to Charles Sumner, November 16, 1830, in the Charles Sumner Autograph File.

Cambridge, Massachusetts. Longfellow House.

Florence. Accademia di Belle Arti. Files and two letters.

Florence. Archivio di Stato. Police records.

Florence. Biblioteca Nazionale. Carteggi Capponi. Twelve letters.

Haverford, Pennsylvania. Haverford College Library. Quaker Collection.

Nashville. Joint Universities Library (Peabody College, Scarritt College, Vanderbilt University). Eighty-one letters from Edward Everett to Horatio Greenough.

New Haven, Connecticut. Yale University Library. James Fenimore Cooper Papers. Henry Kirke-Brown Papers.

New York. American Academy of Arts and Letters. One letter.

New York. New-York Historical Society. Greenough File. Of special importance to Greenough's aesthetics: Horatio Greenough to Rembrandt Peale, November 8, 1831.

New York. New York Public Library. Greenough Personal File. William Cullen Bryant Papers. Of special importance to Greenough's aesthetics: Horatio Greenough to William Cullen Bryant, May 7, 1851.

Philadelphia. Historical Society of Pennsylvania. Greenough File. Peale Family Papers.

Portland, Maine. Maine Historical Society. Two important letters of Horatio Greenough.

Providence, Rhode Island. Brown University Library. One letter of Horatio Greenough, five letters of Louisa Greenough.

Shippenberg, Pennsylvania. Lincoln Library. Five letters of Charles

Sumner to Horatio Greenough. Of special importance to Greenough's aesthetics: Charles Sumner (Berlin) to Horatio Greenough, January 8, 1839. This letter is mistakenly dated 1839; it should read 1840.

Washington. Library of Congress. Greenough Personal File. Samuel F. B. Morse Papers.

Washington. National Archives, especially the Fiscal Division.

Washington. Office of the Architect of the Capitol. Files and correspondence.

Manuscript sources for Hiram Powers

The chief source of manuscript material for Hiram Powers is the collection in the Cincinnati Historical Society at Cincinnati. The repository contains some 200 letters from Powers to friends (Salmon P. Chase, Miner K. Kellogg, Charles King, Thomas Buchanan Read, and especially Nicholas Longworth) and about 700 letters from friends to Powers. This store of letters was recently acquired from the Powers family in Florence. I was the first person to read the letters after they were catalogued by Mrs. Clara Dentler for her commissioned biography, which is still unpublished but in progress. A sizable portion of the original Powers collections has recently been acquired from the Powers family by the National Collection of Fine Arts in Washington.

Boston. Boston Athenaeum. Files and letterbooks.

Boston. Boston Public Library. Powers File. Chamberlain, Dwight, and Griswold collections.

Boston. Massachusetts Historical Society. Powers File. Papers of the Dana family, Edward Everett, William Hinckling Prescott, William Wetmore and Emelyn Story, Charles Sumner, and Robert Winthrop.

Cambridge, Massachusetts. Harvard University. Houghton Library. Powers File. Collections of Edward Everett, George Washington Greene, James Russell Lowell, Charles Eliot Norton, and William Wetmore and Emelyn Story.

Cincinnati. Cincinnati Historical Society. Powers Collection.

Florence. Accademia di Belle Arti. Archive.

Haverford, Pennsylvania. Haverford College. Quaker Collection.

New York. Metropolitan Museum of Art. Files.

New York. New York Public Library. Powers File.

Philadelphia. Pennsylvania Historical Society. Greenough Letters.
Portland, Maine. Maine Historical Society.
Washington. Corcoran Gallery. Files.
Washington. Library of Congress. Galloway Maxcy Markoe Papers.
Washington. National Collection of Fine Arts.
Washington. Office of the Architect of the Capitol. Files and correspondence.

Manuscript sources for Thomas Crawford

Atlanta. Private collection of twenty Crawford letters. Professor Thomas B. Brumbaugh, Department of Fine Arts, Emory University.
Boston. Boston Athenaeum. Archive and Letterbooks.
Boston. Boston Public Library. Crawford File and collections of Chamberlain, Dwight, Folsom, and Griswold.
Boston. Massachusetts Historical Society. Collections of Thomas Crawford, Edward Everett, George Washington Greene, Norcross, William Hinckling Prescott, William Wetmore and Emelyn Story, and Charles Sumner.
Cambridge, Massachusetts. Harvard University. Houghton Library. Collections of Thomas Crawford, Edward Everett, Margaret Fuller (Ossoli), George Washington Greene, Samuel Gridley Howe, William Wetmore and Emelyn Story, Charles Sumner, and Ward family papers.
Charlottesville, Virginia. University of Virginia. William C. Rives papers.
Detroit. Wayne State University. Archives of American Art. Countess Eleanora Marion Crawford Rocca Collection (126 letters). This is the richest collection about Crawford's personal life in the final years, especially 1850–1857, the period of his work on the *Equestrian Washington* and his numerous works for the United States Capitol.
London. British Museum. *Handbook for Travellers in Central Italy, Rome and its Environs.* London, John Murray. Editions: 1843, 1850, 1855, 1856, 1862, 1869, 1875, 1894. This is the most complete set of Murray's guide in existence. It was the favored handbook for the English and American travelers of the period. It lists artists of all categories at work in Rome and gives the addresses of their studios. At first the Americans got short shrift. No Ameri-

cans are listed in the 1843 edition, but in 1869 most of the American artists resident in Rome were listed.

New York. Frick Art Reference Library.

New York. J. Pierpont Morgan Library. Ford Collection. Three letters.

New York. Metropolitan Museum of Art. Archive.

New York. New-York Historical Society.

New York. New York Public Library. Crawford File. William Cullen Bryant letters.

Philadelphia. Historical Society of Pennsylvania. Seven letters.

Portland, Maine. Maine Historical Society. Letter of Thomas Crawford to George Loring Brown.

Richmond. Virginia Historical Society. Several Crawford letters and clippings. Virginia Historical Register and Literary Notebook, volume 4, 1851. Virginia Historical Society Notes. *Virginia Magazine of History and Biography.*

Richmond. Virginia State Library. Virginia State Papers. Document 1: Governor's Message and Reports of Public Officers of the State, 1857. Document 22: Report of the Commissioners of the Washington Monument, 1855–1856. Document 63: Journal of the House of Delegates, 1848–1849. Information concerning Virginia Senate Bill 113, 1914: "Why the Houdon Statue of Washington Should be Copied."

Rome. Archivio di Stato. Police files.

Rome. Biblioteca di Stato.

Rome. French Academy. Archive.

Washington. Corcoran Gallery. Archive.

Washington. National Archives.

Washington. Office of the Architect of the Capitol. A rich collection of Crawford correspondence, particularly regarding his work for the United States Capitol.

Secondary Sources

Adams, F. C. *Account of Art in the United States Capitol.* Washington: U.S. Government Printing Office.

Adams, Henry, ed. *Powers' Statue of the Greek Slave.* Boston: Eastburn Press, 1848. Pamphlet.

Adams, John Quincy. *Memoirs, Comprising Portions of His Diary from 1795–1848.* Edited by Charles Francis Adams. Twelve volumes. Philadelphia: J. B. Lippincott, 1876.

Akers, Charles. "Sculpture in the United States." *Atlantic Monthly, a Magazine of Literature, Science, Art, and Politics.* Boston: Phillips, Sampson and Company, 1857– (hereafter cited as *Atlantic Monthly*). Volume 22, November 1868, pp. 558–564.

Alison, Sir Archibald. *Essays on the Nature and Principles of Taste.* Edinburg: Bell and Bradfute, 1790. Reprinted. Edinburgh: A. Constable and Company, 1812.

Allston, Washington. *Letters on Art and Poems.* Edited by Richard Henry Dana, Jr. New York: Baker and Scribner, 1860.

Almanacco Romano. Rome: Tipografia Chiassa, 1855.

American Sculptors: 19th Century. New York Public Library, 1931.

"Americans in Italy." *New England Magazine.* Boston: J. T. Buckingham, 1831–1835. Volume 1, July 1831, pp. 50–54.

Angeli, Diego. *Le Cronache del Caffè Greco.* Milan, 1930.

Anglo-Tuscan Advertiser and Florence Record of Literature, Science, and Art. Three numbers. Florence, 1848.

"Apollo and the Mohawk." *Art News.* New York: Art News, Inc., 1901. Volume 57, September 1958, pp. 30–33.

Appleton, Thomas Gold. *Life and Letters.* Edited by Susan Hale. New York: D. Appleton and Company, 1885.

Arthos, John. "Hawthorne in Florence." *The Michigan Alumnus.* Ann Arbor: University of Michigan Alumni Association, 1934. Volume 59, February 21, 1953, pp. 118–129.

"The Artists in America." *The Crayon, A Journal Devoted to the Graphic Arts.* New York: Stillman and Durand, 1855–1861 (hereafter cited as *The Crayon*). Volume 7, February 1860, pp. 44–51. References to Horatio Greenough, pp. 50–51.

"The Athenaeum Exhibit at Boston." *Putnam's Monthly Magazine of Literature, Science, and Art.* New York: G. P. Putnam and Company, 1853–1870 (hereafter cited as *Putnams' Monthly Magazine*). Volume 6, September 1855, p. 331. Volume 7, April 1856, p. 448.

"The Athenaeum Exhibition of Painting and Sculpture." *The Dial, A Magazine for Literature, Philosophy, and Religion.* Boston: Weeks, Jordan, and Company, 1840–1844 (hereafter cited as *The Dial*). Volume 1, 1841, pp. 260–263. Volume 1, number 2, October 1840, pp. 260–263, compares busts of Webster by Clevenger and Powers.

Babcock, Martha Amory. *The Domestic and Artistic Life of John Singleton Copley.* Boston and New York: Houghton Mifflin and Company, 1882.

Bagni di Lucca, La Svizzera Toscana. Pamphlet number 92 in a series initiated in 1887, "Le Citte D'Italia." Milan: Sansogno.

Baker, Paul R. *The Fortunate Pilgrims, Americans in Italy 1800–1860.* Cambridge: Harvard University Press, 1964.

Ball, Thomas. *My Threescore Years and Ten.* Boston: Roberts Brothers, 1891.

Barzun, Jacques. *Romanticism and the Modern Ego.* Boston: Little, Brown, and Company, 1943.

Beazley, John Davidson, and Bernard Ashmore. *Greek Sculpture and Painting to the end of the Hellenistic period.* Cambridge, England: University Press, 1932.

Beck-Friis, Johann. *Il Cimitero Acattolico di Roma* [The Protestant Cemetery in Rome]. Malmo, Sweden: Allhams Forlay, 1956.

Beer, Henry A. *Nathaniel P. Willis.* Boston and New York: Houghton Mifflin Company, 1885.

Bellows, Henry. "Seven Sittings with Powers, the Sculptor." *Appleton's Journal, A Magazine of General Literature.* New York: D. Appleton and Company. 1869–1881 (hereafter cited as *Appleton's Journal*).

Bellows, J.N. "Horatio Greenough, the Sculptor." *The Knickerbocker, New York Monthly Magazine.* New York: Morris, Phillips, 1833– (hereafter cited as *The Knickerbocker*). Volume 7, 1836, pp. 343–346.

Benedict, Erastus C. *A Run Through Europe.* New York and London: D. Appleton and Company, 1860.

Benjamin, Asher. "The Builder's Guide." *North American Review.* Boston: Gray and Bowen; New York: Carvell, 1815–. Volume 52, April 1841, pp. 301–320.

Benson, Eugene. *Art and Nature in Italy.* Boston: Roberts Brothers, 1882.

Berenson, Bernard. "Americani dell' Ottocento." *Corriere della Sere.* Milan, 1876–. February 10, 1959.

Berrian, William. *Travels in France and Italy in 1817 and 1818.* New York: T. and J. Swords, 1821.

Beyle, Marie-Henri [Stendhal]. *Promenades dans Rome.* Sceaux: Jean-Jacques Pauvert, 1955.

Beyle, Marie-Henri [Stendhal]. *Rome, Naples et Florence.* Sceaux: Jean-Jacques Pauvert, 1955.

Bigelow. "Foreign Correspondence: Rome." *The Crayon.* Volume 6, 1859, pp. 183–185.

Bonfigli, F. Salverio. *The Artistical Dictionary: or Guide to the Studios in Rome.* Two editions. Rome: Tipografia legale, 1857 and 1858.

Bowra, C. M. *The Greek Experience.* Cleveland and New York: The World Publishing Company, 1957.

Boynton, Henry. "Hiram Powers." *New England Magazine.* New series. Boston: Warren Kellogg, 1884–1917. Volume 20, July 1899, pp. 519–533.

Brand, C. P. *Italy and the English Romantics, The Italianate Fashion in early nineteenth century England.* Cambridge, England: University Press, 1957.

Breckinridge, Issa Desha. *A Memorial to Joel T. Hart, the Kentucky Sculptor.* Edited by Issa Desha Breckinridge and Mary Desha. Cincinnati: R. Clarke and Company, 1884.

Brooks, Charles. *Diary in Europe, 1842.* Manuscript. Houghton Library, Harvard University.

Brooks, Van Wyck. *The Dream of Arcadia.* New York: E. P. Hutton, 1958.

Brooks, Van Wyck. *The Flowering of New England.* New York: Everyman, 1957.

Brown, Glenn. *History of the United States Capitol.* Two volumes. Washington: U.S. Government Printing Office, 1900.

Browning, Elizabeth Barrett. *The Complete Poetical Works of Elizabeth Barrett Browning.* Boston and New York: Houghton Mifflin Company, 1900.

Browning, Elizabeth Barrett. *Letters of Elizabeth Barrett Browning.* Edited by Frederic G. Kenyon. Two volumes. New York and Boston: Macmillan and Company, 1899.

Brumbaugh, Thomas Brendle. "The Evolution of Crawford's Washington." *Virginia Magazine of History and Biography.* Richmond: Virginia Historical Society, 1893–. Volume 70, pp. 3–29.

Brumbaugh, Thomas Brendle. "The genesis of Crawford's Washington, a letter from Thomas Crawford to George Washington Greene [in 1840]." *Virginia Magazine of History and Biography.* Volume 66, 1958, pp. 448–453.

Brumbaugh, Thomas Brendle. *Horatio and Richard Greenough; a critical study with a catalogue of their Sculpture.* Ann Arbor: University of Michigan Press, 1956.

Bryant, William Cullen. *Letters of a Traveler*. New York: Putnams, 1851.

Buckingham, J. T. "The Art of Sculpture." *New England Magazine*. Volume 5, December 1833, pp. 480–485.

Buckley, Theodore, ed., *Aristotle's Treatise on Rhetoric . . . also the Poetic*. London: George Ball and Sons.

Bulfinch, Ellen Susan, ed. *The Life and Letters of Charles Bulfinch, architect, with other family papers*. Boston and New York: Houghton Mifflin and Company, 1896.

Burke, Edmund. *A Philosophical Enquiry into the Origin of Our Ideas of the Sublime and the Beautiful*. London: Montrose, 1803.

Butcher, S. H. *Aristotle's Theory of Poetry and Fine Arts*. New York: Macmillan and Company, 1894. Reprint (fourth edition), New York: Dover Publications, 1931.

Byron, George Gordon Noël. *The Works of Lord Byron with his Letters and Journals and his life by Thomas Moore*. Six volumes, London: John Murray, 1833.

"Canova." *The Dial*. Volume 3, April 1843, pp. 454–458.

Carrarese, Alessandro. *Lettere di G. Capponi E. Di Altri A Lui*. Six volumes. Florence: LeMonnier.

Chandler, Charles Lyon. "The Life of Joel R. Poinsett." *Pennsylvania Magazine of History and Biography*. Philadelphia: Historical Society of Pennsylvania, 1877. Volume 59, January 1935, pp. 1–31.

Chanler, Mrs. Winthrop. *Roman Spring, Memoirs*. Boston: Little, Brown and Company, 1935.

"The Chanting Cherubs, Horatio Greenough's Marble Group for James Fenimore Cooper." *New York History*. Albany: New York Historical Association, 1919. Volume 38, April 1957, pp. 177–179.

"Chauncey B. Ives." *Cosmopolitan Art Journal*. New York: Cosmopolitan Art Association. Volume 4, December 1860, pp. 163–164.

Clark, Kenneth. *The Nude: A Study in Ideal Form*. New York: Pantheon, 1956. A. W. Mellon Lectures in the Fine Arts for 1953, Bollingen Series.

Clement, Clara Erskine. *Painters, Sculptors, Architects, Engravers, and their Works*. Boston: James R. Osgood and Company, 1873.

Cooper, James Fenimore. *Correspondence*. Two volumes. New Haven: Yale University Press, 1922.

Cooper, James Fenimore. *Excursions in Italy*. London: Roberts Bentley, 1838.

Cooper, James Fenimore. *Gleanings in Europe, by an American.* Two volumes. Philadelphia: Carey, Lea and Blanchard, 1837.

Cooper, James Fenimore. "Greenough's Chanting Cherubs." *Harper's Magazine.* New York, 1850. Volume 58, 1878–1879, pp. 657–672.

Cooper, James Fenimore. *Home as Found.* Philadelphia: Lea and Blanchard, 1838.

Cooper, James Fenimore. *Letters and Journals.* Edited by James Franklin Beard. Six volumes. Cambridge: Belknap Press of Harvard University Press, 1960. Especially volume 2.

Cooper, James Fenimore. *Letter to his countrymen.* New York: J. Wiley, 1834.

Crane, Caroline Marsh. *Life and Letters of George Perkins Marsh.* New York: Charles Scribner's Sons, 1888.

Crane, Susan. "Edward Sheffield Bartholomew." *The Connecticut Magazine.* Hartford: The Connecticut Quarterly Company, 1895–1908. Volume 2, July–September 1896, pp. 203–214.

Crawford, Francis Marion. *Ave Roma Immortalis.* Two volumes. London: Macmillan, 1905.

Crawford, Jane. "The Sculptor in his Studio." *United States Magazine and Democratic Review.* Volume 12, June 1843, pp. 567–568.

"Crawford's Beethoven." *The Crayon.* Volume 2, September 12, 1855, p. 166.

"Crawford's Beethoven Inauguration in the Music Hall of Boston." *Putnam's Monthly Magazine.* Volume 7, April 1856, p. 448.

"Crawford's Equestrian Statue." *Savannah Republican.* Savannah, Georgia. Letter dated Munich, October 30, 1855. Crawford File, Virginia State Library, Richmond, Virginia.

Crosby, Nathan, compiler. *Annual Obituary Notices of Eminent Persons.* Boston, 1848. "Thomas Crawford," pp. 106–112.

Crowinshield, Clara. *Diary: A European Tour with Longfellow, 1835–1836.* Edited by Andrew Hulen. Seattle: University of Washington Press.

Curtis, George William. "American Travelers." *Putnam's Monthly Magazine.* Volume 3, June 1855, pp. 561–576.

Curtis, George William. "Letter from Italy." *The Harbinger.* New York: G. P. Allen; Boston: Crosby and Nichols, 1845–1849. Volume 5, July 3, 1847, pp. 49–50.

Curtis, George William. "Letter from Rome." *The Harbinger.* Volume 4, February 13, 1847, pp. 145–146.

Deiss, Jay Joseph. *The Roman Years of Margaret Fuller*. New York: Thomas Crowell, 1969.

DeMare, Marie. *G. P. A. Healy, American Artist*. New York: D. McKay and Company, 1954.

Detti, Emma. *Margaret Fuller e suoi correspondenti*. Firenze: LeMonnier, 1942. Especially "Extracts from the Letters of Lewis Cass, Jr., American Minister to the Papal States . . . to Margaret Fuller."

Dewey, Orville. "Mr. Powers' Statue." *The Union Magazine of Literature and Art*. New York and Philadelphia: Sartain, 1847–1852. Volume 1, October 1847.

Dewey, Orville. *The Old World and the New: or, A Journal of Reflections and Observations made on a Tour of Europe*. Two volumes. New York: Harper and Brothers, 1836.

DeZurko, Edward Robert. *Greenough's Theory of Beauty in Architecture*. Pamphlet. Houston: Rice Institute, 1952. Volume 39 of a 47 volume series.

Dix, John A. *A Winter in Madeira and a Summer in Spain and Florence*. New York: W. Holdredge, 1850.

Donald, David. *Charles Sumner and the coming of the Civil War*. New York: Knopf, 1960.

Dunlap, William. *History of the Rise and Progress of the Arts of Design in the United States*. Edited by Bayley and Goodspeed. Three volumes. New York: G. P. Scott and Company, 1834. Review in *North American Review*, volume 41, 1835, pp. 146–170.

Dupres, Giovanni. *Thoughts on Art and Autobiographical Memoirs*. Translated by E. M. Peruzzi. Edinburgh and London: William Blackwood and Sons, 1884.

Dwight, Theodore. *The Roman Republic of 1849*. New York: R. Van Dien, 1851.

Eastlake, Sir Charles. *Contributions to the Literature of the Fine Arts*. London: John Murray, 1870.

Eastlake, Lady, ed. *Life of John Gibson, R.A.* London: Longmans, Green and Company, 1870.

Elliott, Maud Howe. *My Cousin, F. Marion Crawford*. London: Macmillan, 1934.

Elliott, Maud Howe. *Three Generations*. Boston: Little, Brown and Co. 1923.

Elliott, Maud Howe. *Uncle Sam and His Circle*. London: Macmillan, 1938.

Emerson, Ralph Waldo. *The Complete Works of Ralph Waldo Emerson*. Twelve volumes. Boston and New York: Houghton Mifflin, 1876, 1883. "Art," volume 3, first series. "Society and Solitude," volume 7.

Emerson, Ralph Waldo. *The Complete Works*. Twelve volumes. Boston: James Osgood and Company, 1873. "Beauty," and "Nature," and "The Transcendentalist," volume 6. "The Conduct of Life," volume 1.

Emerson, Ralph Waldo. *The Complete Journals of Ralph Waldo Emerson with annotations*. Edited by Edward Waldo Emerson and Waldo Emerson Forbes. Ten volumes. Boston and New York: Houghton Mifflin Company, 1912. Volume 8, 1849–1855.

"The Eulogy of Thomas Crawford." *The Crayon*. Volume 5, April 1858, p. 113.

Everett, Alexander. "Greenough's Statue of Washington." *United States Magazine and Democratic Review*. Volume 14, June 1844, pp. 618–621.

Everett, Edward. "American Sculptors in Italy." *Boston Miscellany of Literature and Fashion*. Boston: Bradbury, Soden, January 1842–February 1843. Edited by Nathan Hale, Jr., and H. T. Tuckerman. Volume 1, January–June 1842, pp. 2–9.

Everett, Edward. *A Defense of Powers' Statue of Webster, An Address, June 1859, to a meeting of the General Committee of a Hundred on the Webster Memorial*. Pamphlet. Boston: William White, 1859.

Everett, Edward. "Italy." *North American Review*. Volume 12, January 1821.

Exhibition of Powers Works. Pamphlet. Cincinnati: Cincinnati Art Museum. Powers File, New York Public Library.

"Extracts from the Correspondence of Charles Willson Peale relative to the establishment of the Pennsylvania Academy of Fine Arts." *Pennsylvania Magazine of History and Biography*. Volume 9, number 2, July 1855, pp. 121–133.

Fairman, Charles Edwin. *Art and Artists of the Capitol of the United States of America*. Washington: U.S. Government Printing Office, 1927.

Felton, Cornelius C. "Chanting Cherubs of Greenough." *North American Review*. Volume 41, 1835, pp. 167–169.

Felton, Cornelius C. *Familiar Letters from Europe*. Boston: Ticknor and Fields, 1865.

Ferguson, James. *Principles of Beauty in Art*. American edition. Two volumes. Edited by Robert Patterson. Philadelphia: M. Carey, 1806.

Field, Henry. "The Italian Revolutions in 1848. "*New England Magazine*. February 1849.

Fielding, Mantle. *Dictionary of American Painters, Sculptors and Engravers*. Compiled by James F. Carr. New York: James F. Carr, 1965.

"The Fine Arts." Editorial notes. *Putnam's Monthly Magazine*. Volume 9, September 1857, p. 110.

"The Fisher Boy." *Art Union Bulletin, A Bulletin of Foreign Literature, Science, and Art*. Edited by John Holmes Agnes. New York and Philadelphia: Leavitt, Trow, and Company, 1847–1857. Volume 1, December 18, 1847.

"The Fisher Boy." *Metropolitan Museum of Art Catalogue of Sculpture, 1908*. New York: Metropolitan Museum of Art publication.

Fitch, James Marston. *American Building*. Boston: Houghton, Mifflin Company, 1948.

Fitch, James Marston. "Horatio Greenough and the art of the machine age." *Columbia University Forum*. New York: Columbia University, 1959. Volume 2, no. 4, Fall 1959.

Flagg, Jared B. *Life and Letters of Washington Allston*. New York: Scribners, 1892.

Florentia [pseudonym]. "Crawford and his last work." *Art Journal*. London, 1855. Volume 17, p. 41.

Fraser, Mrs. Hugh. *A Diplomatist's Wife in Many Lands*. Two volumes. London: Hutchinson and Company, 1911.

Freeman, James E. *Gatherings from an Artist's Portfolio*. Two volumes. New York: D. Appleton Company, 1877.

Frothingham, Octavius Brooks. *Transcendentalism in New England*. New York: G. P. Putnam's Son's, 1876.

Fuller, Margaret Sarah (Ossoli). *At Home and Abroad, or Things and Thoughts in America and Europe*. Edited by Arthur B. Fuller. Boston: Crosby, Nichols and Company, 1856.

Fuller, Margaret Sarah (Ossoli). *Life without and life within: or Reviews, narratives, essays, and poems*. Edited by Arthur B. Fuller. Boston, Brown, Taggard, and Chase; New York, Sheldon and Company: 1859.

Fuller, Margaret Sarah (Ossoli). *Memoirs of Margaret Fuller*. Edited by Ralph Waldo Emerson, William E. Channing, T. W. Higginson, et al. 2 volumes. Boston: Phillips, Sampson, and Company, 1852. Especially volume 1, pp. 266–267.

Fuller, Margaret Sarah (Ossoli). *The Writings of Margaret Fuller*. Selected and edited by Mason Wade. New York: Viking Press, 1941. Especially volume 2, pp. 211, 226–227.

Gale, Robert Lee. *Thomas Crawford, American Sculptor*. Pittsburgh: University of Pittsburg Press, 1964.

Gale, Robert Lee. "Thomas Crawford, dear Lou, and the Horse." *Virginia Magazine of History and Biography*. Volume 68, 1960, pp. 171–192.

Gales and Seaton. *Register of Debates in Congress*. Washington: U.S. Government Printing Office.

Galt, John. *The Life and Studies of Benjamin West*. Philadelphia: M. Thomas, London: T. Cadell and W. Davies, 1816.

Garbett, Edward Lacy. *A Rudimentary Treatise on the Principles of Design in Architecture*. London: John Weale, 1850.

Gardner, Albert Ten Eyck. "Hiram Powers and 'the hero.'" *Metropolitan Museum of Art Bulletin*. New York: Metropolitan Museum of Art, 1905. New series. Volume 2, October 1943, pp. 102–108.

Gardner, Albert Ten Eyck. "A Relic of the California Gold Rush (Hiram Powers)." *Metropolitan Museum of Art Bulletin*. New series. Volume 8, December 1949, pp. 117–121.

Gardner, Albert Ten Eyck. *Yankee Stonecutters, The First American School of Sculpture, 1800–1850*. New York: Columbia University Press, 1945.

Gibbs, George. *The Gibbs Family of Rhode Island*. New York: privately printed, 1933.

Gibbs, Robert W. *A Memoir of James de Veaux of Charleston, S.C., A Member of the National Academy of Design*. Columbia, S.C.: I. C. Morgan's Letter Press Print, 1846.

Gillespie, William M. *Rome: As Seen by a New Yorker in 1843–1844*. New York and London: Wiley and Putnam, 1845.

Gillespie, William M. "A Week Between Florence and Rome." *American Whig Review*. Volume 1, June 1845, pp. 613–616.

Goethe, Johann Wolfgang. *Essay on Art*. Translated by Samuel Gray Ward. Boston: J. Monroe and Company, 1840.

Goethe, Johann Wolfgang. *Fragments on Italy*. London: G. Ball and Sons, 1892.

Goethe, Johann Wolfgang. *Italian Journey 1786–1788*. London: G. Ball and Sons, 1892.

Goethe, Johann Wolfgang. *Second Residence in Rome*. London: G. Ball and Sons, 1892.

Gray, John C. "Foreign Travel." *North American Review*. Volume 9, 1819, p. 11.

"The Greek Slave: Sculpture." *Eclectic Magazine*. Boston: 1844–1907; New York and Philadelphia: Leavitt, Trow and Company, 1844–1850. Volume 5, August 1845, p. 568.

Greeley, Horace. *Glances at Europe in a series of letters from Great Britain, France, Italy, and Spain*. New York: Dewitt and Davenport, 1851.

Greene, George Washington. *Biographical Studies*. New York: G. P. Putnam, 1860. Especially the section on Thomas Crawford, pp. 121–154.

Greene, George Washington. "Crawford, the Sculptor." *The Knickerbocker*. Volume 17, February 1846, p. 174.

Greene, George Washington. "Letters from Modern Rome." *The Knickerbocker*. Volume 15, June 1840, pp. 488–496. Volume 17, February 1841, pp. 174ff.

Greene, George Washington. "Letters from Rome." *The Knickerbocker*. Volume 18, November 1841, pp. 371–378. Volume 19, April 1842, pp. 293–301; May 1842, pp. 412–415. Volume 20, July 1842, pp. 11–14.

Greenough, Frances Boott, ed. *Letters of Horatio Greenough to his Brother, Henry Greenough*. Boston: Ticknor and Company, 1887.

Greenough, Henry. *Appelles and his contemporaries, A Novel*. Boston: Ticknor and Fields, 1860.

Greenough, Henry. *Ernest Carroll, or Artist-Life in Italy*. Boston: Ticknor and Fields, 1858.

Greenough, Henry. "Greenough, the Sculptor." *American Magazine of Useful and Entertaining Knowledge*. Boston: J. L. Sibley, 1834–1837. Letter to William Dunlap for his *History of the Rise and Progress of the Arts of Design*.

Greenough, Horatio. "Etchings with a Chisel." *United States Magazine and Democratic Review*. Volume 18, February 1846, pp. 118–125.

Greenough, Horatio. *Form and Function, Remarks on Art*. Edited by

Harold A. Small. Berkeley and Los Angeles: University of California Press, 1947.

Greenough, Horatio. "Fourier et Hoc Genus Omne." *The Crayon.* Volume 1, June 18, 1855, pp. 371–372.

Greenough, Horatio. "Fragment." *The Crayon.* Volume 1, February 7, 1855, p. 89.

Greenough, Horatio. "The Shin Piece." *The Crayon.* Volume 1, May 9, 1855, p. 294.

Greenough, Horatio. "A Sketch." *The Crayon.* Volume 1, April 18, p. 243.

Greenough, Horatio. "Remarks on American Art." *United States Magazine and Democratic Review.* Volume 13, July 1843, pp. 45–48.

Greenough, Horatio. *The Travels, Observations, and Experience of a Yankee Stonecutter.* New York: G. P. Putnam and Company, 1852.

"Greenough, the Sculptor." *Putnam's Monthly Magazine.* Volume 1, March 1853, pp. 317–321.

Hale, Edward Everett. *Ninety Days Worth of Europe.* Boston: Walker, Wise and Company, 1861.

Hamlin, Talbot Faulkner. *Benjamin Henry Latrobe.* New York: Oxford University Press, 1955.

Hamlin, Talbot Faulkner. *Greek Revival Architecture in America: Being an Account of Important Trends in American Architecture and American Life Prior to the War between the States.* London and Oxford: University Press, 1944.

Hawthorne, Nathaniel. "The Artist of the Beautiful." *United States Magazine and Democratic Review.* Volume 14, June 1844.

Hawthorne, Nathaniel. *Passages from the French and Italian Notebooks.* Unexpurgated manuscript edition. Edited by Norman Holmes Pearson. Three volumes. Yale University, New Haven, Connecticut.

Hawthorne, Nathaniel. *Passages from the French and Italian Notebooks.* Two volumes. Boston: James R. Osgood, 1870.

Hawthorne, Nathaniel. *The Marble Faun, or the Romance of Monte Beni.* Two volumes. Boston: Ticknor and Fields, 1860.

Hawthorne, Sophia. *Notes in England and Italy.* New York: G. P. Putnam and Sons, 1869.

Hazelton, George Cochrane. *The National Capitol: its architecture, art, and history.* New York: J. J. Little and Company, 1897.

Headley, Joel Tyler. *Italy and the Italians in a Series of Letters*. New York: J. S. Platt, 1844.

Headley, Joel Tyler. *Letters from Italy*. New York: Wiley and Putnam, 1845. Review, "Italy . . . Headley's Letters," in *American Whig Review*, volume 2, July 1845, pp. 100–104.

Headley, Joel Tyler. *The Power of Beauty*. New Yorks: J. S. Taylor, 1850.

Healy, George Peter Alexander. *Reminiscences of a Portrait Painter*. Chicago: A. C. McClurg and Company, 1894.

Henderson, Helen. *The Pennsylvania Academy of Fine Arts and other collections of Philadelphia*. Boston: L. C. Page and Company, 1911.

Hewins, Amasa. *A Boston Portrait Painter Visits Italy: the Journal of Amasa Hewins, 1830–1833*. Edited by Francis H. Allen. Boston: Boston Athenaeum, 1931.

Hicks, Thomas. *Thomas Crawford: His Career, Character and Works. A Eulogy*. New York: Appleton and Company, 1859.

Hillard, George Stillman. "Letter on the Chanting Cherubs" (signed Tyro). *New England Magazine*. Volume 1, July 1831, pp. 20–26.

Hillard, George Stillman. "Mr. Greenough's New Group of Statuary." *New England Magazine*. Volume 8, 1835.

Hillard, George Stillman. *Six Months in Italy*. Boston: Ticknor, Reed, and Fields, 1853.

Hillard, George Stillman. "Thomas Crawford, A Eulogy." *Atlantic Monthly*. Volume 24, July 1869, pp. 40–54.

"Hiram Powers." *Cincinnati Mercury*. September 3, 1819. Powers File, Clippings, Cincinnati Historical Society.

"Hiram Powers' Greek Slave." *International Monthly Magazine of Literature, Science and Art*. New York: Stringer and Townsend, 1850–1852. Volume 2, number 1, December 1850, p. 8.

"Hiram Powers." *Tuscan Athenaeum*. English weekly published in Florence from October 30, 1847, to January 22, 1849. Volume 1, number 8, December 18, 1847.

"Hiram Powers." *United States Magazine and Democratic Review*. Volume 14, February 1844, pp. 202–206.

Hogarth, William. *The Analysis of Beauty*. Oxford: Clarendon Press, 1855. First edition, 1753.

Hone, Philip. *A Diary of Philip Hone*. Edited by Allan Nevins. New York: Dodd, Mead, 1936. Manuscript: New-York Historical Society.

Hopkinson, Vivian G. *Spires of Form, A Study of Emerson's Aesthetic Theory*. Cambridge: Harvard University Press, 1951.

"Horatio Greenough." *American Quarterly*. Fall 1858, pp. 338–343.

"Horatio Greenough." *Boston Courier*. December 12, 14, 1833.

"Horatio Greenough." *Boston Daily Advertiser and Patriot*. October 25, 1833.

"Horatio Greenough." *Boston Mercantile Journal*. December 1, 1833.

"Horatio Greenough." *The Crayon*. Volume 1, 1855.

"Horatio Greenough." *New York American Reviewer*. April 30, 1831.

"Horatio Greenough." *New York Review*. New York: E. Bliss and E. White, June 1825–May 1826. October 1825, pp. 396–398.

Hosmer, Harriet Goodhue. *Harriet Hosmer, Letters and Memories*. Edited by Cornelia Carr. New York: Moffat, Yard and Company, 1912.

Howe, Julia Ward. *Margaret Fuller (Marchesa Ossoli)*. Boston: Roberts Brothers, 1883.

Howe, Julia Ward. *Reminiscences*. Boston: Houghton Mifflin and Company, 1899.

Howe, Samuel Gridley. *Letters and Journals*. Edited by Laura E. Richards. Two volumes. New York and London: D. Appleton-Century Company, 1935.

Hull, Isaac. *The Papers of Isaac Hull, Commander of the United States Navy*. Edited by Gardner Weld Allen. Boston: Boston Athenaeum, 1929.

Hurley, Lewis R. "The life experiences of a painter-poet, Thomas B. Read." In *Confessions of a school-master and other essays*. Philadelphia: J. B. Lippincott, 1914.

Il Mercurio di Roma. Rome: Tipografo dello Scienze, 1843.

James, Henry. *William Wetmore Story and His Friends*. Two volumes. Boston: Houghton Mifflin and Company, 1903.

Jarves, James Jackson. *Art Hints, Architecture, Sculpture, and Painting*. New York: Harper and Brothers, 1855.

Jarves, James Jackson. *The Art Idea, Confessions of an Inquirer*. New York: Hurd and Houghton, 1864.

Jarves, James Jackson. *Art Studies: The "old-masters" of Italy: Painting*. New York: Derby and Jackson, 1861.

Jarves, James Jackson. *Art Thoughts: the Experiences and Observations of an American Amateur in Europe*. New York: Hurd and Houghton, 1869.

Jarves, James Jackson. "A Day at Pompey." *Harper's Magazine*. New York: E. P. Allen, 1850. Volume 11, November 1855, pp. 721–743.

Jarves, James Jackson. "Holy Week at Rome." *Harper's Magazine*. Volume 9, June 1854, pp. 721–743; July 1854, pp. 471–479; August 1854, pp. 317–327.

Jarves, James Jackson. *Italian Rambles*. New York: G. P. Putnam and Sons, 1883.

Jarves, James Jackson. *Italian Sights and Papal Principles Seen Through American Spectacles*. New York: Harper and Brothers, 1856.

Jarves, James Jackson. "Sights and Principles Abroad." *Harper's Magazine*. Volume 8, March 1854, pp. 471–479; April 1854, pp. 617–624; May 1854, pp. 744–758.

Kellogg, Miner K. *Justice to Hiram Powers, An Address to the Citizens of New Orleans*. Pamphlet. Cincinnati, December 3, 1848.

Kemble, Frances Anne. *A Year of Consolation*. Two volumes. New York: Wiley and Putnam, 1847.

Kemble, Frances Anne. *Journal of a Residence in America*. Two volumes. Brussells: A. Wahlen, 1835.

Kip, William Ingraham. *The Catacombs of Rome*. New York: Redfield, 1854.

Kip, William Ingraham. *The Christmas Holidays in Rome*. New York: D. Appleton and Company, 1846.

Kirkland, Caroline Matilda. *Holidays Abroad: or Europe from the West*. Two volumes. New York: Baker and Scribner, 1849.

Klenzo, Camillo Von. *The Interpretation of Italy during the Last Two Centuries*. Chicago University Decennial Publications, volume 17. Chicago: Chicago University Press, 1907.

Langdon, William Chauncey. "Recollections of Rome During the Italian Revolution." *Atlantic Monthly*. Volume 52, October 1883, pp. 503–507; November 1883, pp. 658–664; December 1883, pp. 746–753.

LaPiana Angelina. *La Cultura American e L'Italia*. Turin: C. Einaudi, 1938.

Larkin, Oliver. *Art and Life in America*. New York: Rinehart, 1949.

Latrobe, J. H. B., ed. *The Journal of Benjamin Henry Latrobe*. New York: D. Appleton and Company, 1905.

Lester, Charles Edwards. *The Artists of America*. New York: Baker and Scribner, 1846.

Lester, Charles Edwards. *The Artist, the Merchant, and the Statesman of the Age of the Medici and of our own Time*. Two volumes. New York: Paine and Burgess, 1845.

"Letter from an Artist in Italy." Author anonymous. *New York*

Review and Athenaeum Magazine. New York: E. Bliss and E. White, 1825–1826. October 1825, pp. 396–398.

Lester, Charles Edwards. *My Consulship*. Two volumes. New York: Cornish Lamport and Company, 1853.

"Letter of Thomas Crawford to George Washington Greene." *Virginia Magazine of History and Biography*. Volume 66, 1958, pp. 448–453. Crawford File, Virginia Historical Society, Richmond, Virginia.

Letters and Papers of John Singleton Copley and Henry Pelham, Massachusetts Historical Society Collections, volume 71. Boston: Massachusetts Historical Society, 1914.

"Letters of Thomas Crawford." *Virginia Historical Register and Literary Notebook*. Richmond: Macfarland and Fergusson, 1848–1853 (hereafter cited as *Virginia Historical Register*). Volume 4, 1851.

Lippincott, Sara Jane Clarke [Grace Greenwood]. *Haps and Mishaps of a Tour in Europe*. Boston: Ticknor, Reed, and Fields, 1854.

Lippincott, Sara Jane Clarke. *Stories and Sights of France and Italy*. Boston: Ticknor and Fields, 1867.

Lockett, Annie Hoge. "Hiram Powers: Clockmaker's Apprentice." *Bulletin of the Historical and Philosophical Society of Ohio*. Cincinnati: Historical and Philosophical Society of Ohio, 1943–1963. Volume 12, October 1954, pp. 282–292.

Longfellow, Fanny Appleton. *Selected Letters and Journals*. Edited by Edward Wagenknecht. New York: Longmans, Green, 1956.

Longfellow, Henry Wadsworth. *Italian Sketch Book*. Manuscript edition. Longfellow Collection, Houghton Library, Harvard University.

Longfellow, Henry Wadsworth. *Outre-Mer: A Pilgrimage Beyond the Sea*. Two volumes. New York: Harper and Brothers, 1835.

Longfellow, Samuel. *Life of Henry Wadsworth Longfellow, with extracts from his journals and correspondence*. Boston and New York: Houghton Mifflin and Company, 1887.

Louisiana Historical Quarterly. New Orleans: Louisiana Historical Society, 1917. Volume 2, 1919, pp. 272–275. Letters concerning Hiram Powers' Statue of Washington made for the state of Louisiana before the Civil War.

Lowell, James Russell. *Leaves from My Journal in Italy, Fireside Travels*. Boston; Ticknor and Fields, 1864.

Lowell, James Russell. *Letters*. Edited by Charles Eliot Norton. Two volumes. New York: Harper Brothers, 1894.

Lyman, Theodore, Jr. *The Political State of Italy.* Boston: Wells and Lilly, 1820.

Mabee, Carleton. *The American Leonardo, A Life of S. F. B. Morse.* New York: Knopf, 1943.

McCausland, Elizabeth. *George Inness, an American Landscape Painter, 1825–1894.* New York: American Artists Group, 1946.

Manuele Artistico ed Archaeologico riguardante gli Stabilimenti, Professori d'Ogni Genere Artisti e Negozianti, residenti in Roma. Rome: Alessandro Monaldi, 1845.

Marraro, Howard. "American Travelers in Rome." *Catholic Historical Review.* Washington, D.C.: The Catholic University of America, 1916. Volume 29, January 1944, pp. 470–509.

Mathiessen, Francis Otto. *The American Renaissance, Art and Expression in the Age of Emerson and Whitman.* London and Toronto: Oxford University Press, 1941.

Memes, John Smythe. *Memoirs of Antonio Canova, with a critical analysis of his works and an Historical View of Modern Sculpture.* Edinburgh: A. Constable and Company, 1825.

Metropolitan Museum of Art. *19th Century American Paintings and Sculpture, An Exhibition in celebration of the hundredth anniversary of the Metropolitan Museum of Art, April 16 through September 6, 1970.* Introduction by John K. Howatt and John Wilmerding. Text by John K. Howatt, Natalie Spassky and others. New York: Metropolitan Museum of Art, 1970.

Metzger, Charles E. *Emerson and Greenough, Transcendental Pioneers of an American Aesthetic.* Berkeley and Los Angeles: University of California Press, 1954.

Migliarini, A. M. "Powers, the Sculptor." *The Knickerbocker.* Volume 18, December 1841, pp. 523–529. Translated from *Giornale Arcadico.*

Milizia, Francesco. *Le Vite de' piu celebri architetti d'ogni nazione e d'ogni tempo precedente da saggio sopra architettura.* Nella Stamperia di Paolo Giunchi Komarek a spese di Venanzio Monaldini libraro, 1768.

Milizia, Francesco. *The Lives of Celebrated Artists ancient and modern: with historical and critical observations on their works and on the principles of the art.* Translated by Mrs. Edward Cressey. Two volumes. London: J. Taylor Architectural Library, 1828.

Milizia, Francesco. *Memorie degli architetti antichi e moderni.* Parma: Stamperia reale, 1781.

Milizia, Francesco. *Principi di architettura civile.* Rome: Salomoni, 1800.

Miller, Perry. *The Life of the Mind in America from the Revolution to the Civil War.* New York: Harcourt Brace and World, Inc., 1965.

Minot, William, Jr. "Greenough." *North American Review.* Volume 52, 1841, pp. 310–311.

Missirini, Melchior. "Observations of Canova, recorded by A. M. Missirini." *The Dial.* Volume 3, April 1843, pp. 458–483. Translated from Missirini's *Della Vita di Antonio Canova.* Prato: Fratello Giachetti, 182.

Mitchell, Maria. *Life, Letters, and Journals.* Edited by Phoebe Mitchell Kendall. Boston: Lee and Shepard, 1896.

Morse, Edward Lind, ed. *Letters and Journals of S. F. B. Morse.* Two volumes. Boston and New York: Houghton Mifflin Company, 1914.

Motley, John Lothrop. *The Correspondence of John Lothrop Motley.* Edited by George William Curtis. Two volumes. New York: Harper and Brothers, 1889.

"Mr. Page's Portrait of Hiram Powers." *The Art Union.* New York: Journal of the American Art Union, 1884–1885. Volume 1, April 1884, p. 90.

Murray, John. *Handbook for Travellers in Central Italy.* London: John Murray, 1853–. Annual editions. The most complete set is in the Library of the British Museum. See reference under London in list of manuscript sources for Thomas Crawford.

Murray, John. *Handbook for Travellers in Northern Italy.* London: John Murray, 1846–.

Murray, John. *Handbook for Travellers in Southern Italy.* London: John Murray, 1853–.

Negro, Silvio. *Seconda Roma 1850–1870.* Milan: Ulrich Hoepli, 1943.

Nicholson, James M. "Mrs. Cohen's Fancy Dress Party." *Maryland Historical Magazine.* Baltimore: Maryland Historical Society, 1906. Volume 15, 1919, pp. 348–358. Nicholson's letter to his mother, Rebecca Lloyd (Mrs. Edward) Shippen, February 2, 1837.

Noble, Louis L. *The Course of Empire, Voyage of Life and other Pictures of Thomas Cole.* New York: Cornish Lamport and Company, 1853.

Norton, Charles Eliot. *The Correspondence of Thomas Carlyle and Ralph Waldo Emerson, 1834–1872.* Two volumes. Boston: James R. Osgood and Company, 1883.

Norton, Charles Eliot. "Italy in 1855–1856." *The Crayon.* Volume 3:

March 1856, pp. 85–87; April 1856, pp. 118–120; May 1856, pp. 151–155; June 1856, pp. 179–181; July 186, pp. 206–209; August 1856, pp. 246–247; September 1856, pp. 274–276; October 1856, pp. 306–309; November 1856, pp. 338–340; December 1856, pp. 371–372.

Norton, Charles Eliot. *Notes of Travel and Study in Italy.* Boston: Ticknor and Fields, 1850.

"Notable Examples of American Art in the Collection of Mrs. (Hicks) Lord." *The Curio.* New York: W. R. Wright, September 1887– February 1888. Volume 1, November 1887, pp. 97–104. Illustrations of *The Dying Mexican Princess* (p. 104) and *Genius of Mirth* (p. 97).

Notizie e Guida de Firenze e de' suoi Contorni. Florence: Presso Guglielmo Piatti, 1841. Two editions.

Nye, W. A. R. *Historical Account of the Washington Monument in Capitol Square, Richmond.* Pamphlet. Richmond, 1869.

Osgood, Samuel. "American Artists in Italy." *Harpers Monthly Magazine.* Volume 41, August 1870, pp. 420–426.

Osgood, Samuel. *Thomas Crawford and Art in America, An Address Before the New York Historical Society*, April 7, 1875. New York: John F. Trow and son, 1875.

Parrington, Vernon Louis. *Main Currents in American Thought.* Three volumes. New York: Harcourt Brace, 1927. Especially volume 2, *The Romantic Revolution in America.*

Peabody, Ephraim. "Italy." *North American Review.* Volume 78, April 1854, pp. 449–500.

Peale, Rembrandt. *Notes on Italy, Written During a Tour in 1829 and 1830.* Philadelphia: Carey and Lea, 1831. Review entitled "Review of Peale's Notes on Italy," in the *American Quarterly Review.* Philadelphia: Adam Waldie, 1827–1837. Volume 9, June 1831, pp. 512ff.

Peale, Rembrandt. "The Skies of Italy." *The Crayon.* Volume 4, December 1857, pp. 370–371.

"Persico's Columbus." *United States Magazine and Democratic Review.* Volume 15, July 1844, pp. 95–97. An illustration of Persico's *Columbus* was the frontispiece of the September 1844 issue of this magazine.

"Personal Reminiscences of Thorwaldsen." *Putnam's Monthly Magazine.* Volume 1, January 1853, pp. 93–97.

Pierce, Edward L. *Charles Sumner, Memoir and Letters*. Four volumes. Boston: Roberts Brothers, 1877.

Plato. *Dialogues*. Translated and edited by Benjamin Jowett. Five volumes. Oxford: Clarendon Press, 1876. "Lysis," volume 1, "Gorgias," "Phaedrus," volume 2; "Philebus," volume 4; "The Republic," volume 5.

Plon, Eugene. *Thorwaldsen, Sa Vie and Ses Oeuvres*. Paris: E. Plon et Cie, 1874.

Plowden, Helen Haseltine. *William Stanley Haseltine, Sea and Landscape Painter, 1835–1900*. London: F. M. Muller, Ltd., 1947.

Powers, Ellen Lemmi. "Recollections of My Father." *The Vermonter*. White River Junction, Vt.: Vermont Historical Society, 1895. Volume 12, February–March 1907, pp. 46–51, 72–85.

"Power's Greek Slave." *Putnam's Monthly Magazine*. Volume 4, December 1854, p. 666. A poem.

Powers, Hiram. Letter. *Virginia Historical Register*. Volume 4, 1851, pp. 55–56.

Powers, Hiram. Letter (to his brother about California). *The Literary World*. Boston: James R. Osgood and Company, 1847–1853. March 1851.

Powers, Hiram. "Letters of Hiram Powers to Nicholas Longworth." *Historical and Philosophical Society of Ohio Quarterly*. Cincinnati: Historical and Philosophical Society of Ohio, 1906. Volume 1, April–June 1906, pp. 33–59.

Powers, Hiram. "The New Method of Modelling in Plaster for Sculpture." *Putnam's Monthly Magazine*. Volume 2, August 1853, pp. 154–155.

Praz, Mario. "Impressioni Italiane di Americani nell'Ottocento." In *Studi Americani*. Rome: Edizioni di Storia e letteratura, 1955.

Preston, William C. *Reminiscences*. Edited by Minnie Clare Yarborough. Chapel Hill: University of North Carolina Press, 1933.

Prezzolini, Giuseppe. *Come Gli Americani Scoprirono L'Italia, 1750–1850*. Milan: Fratelli Treves, 1933.

Prime, Samuel Iraneus. *The Life of Samuel F. B. Morse*. Two volumes. New York: D. Appleton and Company, 1875.

Prinsen, Val C. "An Artist's Life in Italy in 1860." *Magazine of Art*. London, Paris, New York: Cassell, Petter, Galpin and Company, 1878–1904. Volume 28, July 1904, pp. 417–421.

Putnam, George. *The Tourist in Europe . . . During a Tour, 1836*. New York: Wiley and Putnam, 1838.

Quigley, Isabel. "Americans in Italy." *The Spectator*. London: E. C. Wesley, 1828–1967. March 6, 1953, pp. 272–273; March 13, 1953, pp. 311–312; March 20, 1953, p. 346.

Quincy, Josiah. *History of the Boston Athenaeum*. Cambridge: Metcalf, 1851.

Rand, McNally and Company. *A Week at the Fair Illustrating the Exhibits of the World's Columbian Exhibition with Special Descriptive Articles*. Chicago: Rand, McNally and Company, 1893.

Read, Thomas Buchanan. "Letters." Edited by Alice E. Smith. *Ohio State Archaeological and Historical Quarterly*. Columbus, 1937. Volume 46, pp. 68–80.

"Recollections of a Voyage to Italy in the Year 1800." *The Port Folio*. Philadelphia: H. Maxwell, 1801–1827. Volume 14, September 1822, pp. 107–236.

Report of the Board of Trustees of the Massachusetts General Hospital, 1866. Boston: Eastburn Press, 1867.

Reynolds, Sir Joshua. *Discourses*. London: Seeley and Co., 1905.

Richardson, Edgar P. "Americans in Arcadia." *Art News*. Volume 49, January 1951, pp. 20–21.

Richardson, Edgar P. *Washington Allston, A study of the romantic artist in America*. New York: T. Y. Crowell, 1967.

Richardson, Edgar P., and Otto Wittmann. *Travellers in Arcadia: American Artist in Italy, 1830–1875*. Detroit: The Detroit Institute of Arts, The Toledo Museum of Art, 1951.

Rippy, James Fred. *Joel E. Poinsett, Versatile American*. Durham, North Carolina: Duke University Press, 1935.

Robinson, C. S. "A Morning with Hiram Powers." *Hours at Home, A Popular Monthly of Instruction and Recreation*. New York: 1865–1870. Hereafter cited as *Hours at Home*. Volume 6, November 1867, pp. 32–37.

Rogers, Samuel. *Italian Journal, 1814–1821*. Edited by J. R. Hale. London: Farber and Farber, 1939.

Ross, Marvin C., and Anna Wells Rutledge. "William Henry Rinehart's Letters to Frank B. Mayer." *Maryland Historical Magazine*. Volume 43, June 1948, pp. 127–138.

Rostenberg, Leona. "Margaret Fuller's Roman Diary." *Journal of Modern History*. Chicago: University of Chicago Press, 1929. Volume 12, June 1940, pp. 209–220.

Rusk, Ralph Leslie, ed. *Letters of Ralph Waldo Emerson*. Six volumes. New York: Columbia University Press, 1949.

Rusk, William Sener. "Benjamin Henry Latrobe and the Classical Influence in his Work." *Maryland Historical Magazine*. Volume 31. June 1936, pp. 126–154.

Rusk, William Sener. "New Rinehart Letters." *Maryland Historical Magazine*. Volume 31, June 1936, pp. 225–242.

Rusk, William Sener. "Notes on the Life of William Henry Rinehart, Sculptor." *Maryland Historical Magazine*. Volume 19, 1925–1926, pp. 309–338.

Rusk, William Sener. *William Henry Rinehart, Sculptor*. Baltimore: N. T. A. Munder, 1939.

Ruskin, John. *The Seven Lamps of Architecture, Lectures on Architecture and Painting*. New York: J. Wiley, 1849.

Ruskin, John. *The Stones of Venice*. New York: Merrill and Baker, 1851.

Rutledge, Anna Wells. "Robert Gilmor, Jr., Baltimore Collector." *The Journal of the Walters Art Gallery*. Baltimore: The Trustees of the Walters Art Gallery, 1938. Volume 12, 1949, p. 19.

Rutledge, Anna Wells. *William Thornton, Benjamin Henry Latrobe, Thomas U. Walter, the classical influence in their works*. Baltimore: John Hopkins University Press, 1933.

Scherer, Margaret. *The Marvels of Ancient Rome*. Edited by C. R. Morey. New York: Phaidon Press, 1955.

Schuyler, Eugene. *Italian Influences*. New York: Scribner and Sons, 1901.

Scott, Leonora Cranch. *The Life and Letters of Christopher Pearse Cranch, by his daughter Leonora Cranch Scott*. Boston and New York: Houghton Mifflin and Company, 1917.

"The Sculptor of Albany" [Erastus Dow Palmer]. *Putnam's Monthly Magazine*. Volume 7, April 1856, pp. 194–200.

"Sculpture in the United States." *Atlantic Monthly*. Volume 22, November 1868, pp. 558–564.

Sedgwick, Catharine Maria. *Letters from Abroad to Kindred at Home*. Two volumes. New York: Harper and Brothers, 1841.

Shaffer, Robert. "Emerson and His Circle, Advocates of Functionalism." *Journal of the Society of Architectural Historians*. New York: Van Rennsselaer Polytechnic Institute, 1941. Volume 7, July 1948, pp. 17–20.

"Shobal Vail Clevenger." *United States Magazine and Democratic Review*. Volume 14, February 1844, pp. 202–206.

Silliman, Benjamin. *A Visit to Europe in 1851*. Two volumes. New York: G. P. Putnam and Company, 1854.

Silliman, Benjamin, and C. R. Goodrich, eds. *The World of Science, Art, and Industry Illustrated from Examples in the New York Exhibition, 1853–54*. New York: G. P. Putnam and Company, 1854.

"Sketches." *The Crayon*. Volume 7, November 1860.

Slater, Joseph, ed. *The Correspondence of Emerson and Carlyle*. London and New York: Columbia University Press, 1964.

Sloan, James. "Rambles in Italy." *Analectic Magazine*. Volume 12, July 1818, pp. 11–36.

Sloan, James, and Theodore Lyman. *Rambles in Italy in the Years 1816 . . . 1817*. Baltimore: N. G. Maxwell, 1818.

Spiller, Robert E., Willard Thorp, Thomas H. Johnson, and Henry Seidel Canby. *American Literary History of the United States*. Three volumes. New York: Macmillan, 1949.

Staël-Holstein, Anne Louise Germaine de. *Corinna, or Italy*. New York: D. Longworth, E. Sargeant, and Ward, 1808.

Stebbins, Emma, ed. *Charlotte Cushman: Her Letters and Memories of her Life*. Boston: Houghton, Osgood and Company, 1878.

Statistici de Roma. Rome: Dei Pipi di Angelo Agani, 1834, 1842, 1855.

Stern, Madeleine B. *The Life of Margaret Fuller*. New York: E. P. Dutton and Company, 1942.

Story, William Wetmore. *Browning to his American Friends, Letters between the Brownings and the Storys and James Russell Lowell, 1841–1890*. New York: Barnes and Noble, 1965.

Story, William Wetmore. *Cástel Sant' Angelo and the Evil Eye*. Philadelphia: J. B. Lippincott and Company, 1877.

Story, William Wetmore. *Conversations in a Studio*. Two volumes. Boston: Houghton Mifflin Company, 1890.

Story, William Wetmore. *Excursions in Art and Letters*. Boston: Houghton Mifflin Company, 1891.

Story, William Wetmore. *Graffiti d'italia*. New York: Scribner and Company, 1868.

Story, William Wetmore. *The Proportions of the Human Figure*. London, 1884.

Story, William Wetmore. *Roba di Roma*. Two volumes. London: Chapman and Hall, 1864.

Story, William Wetmore. *Vallambrosa*. Edinburgh: William Blackwood and Sons, 1881.

Stowe, Harriet Beecher. *Sunny Memories of Foreign Lands.* Boston: Phillips, Sampson and Company; New York: J. C. Derby, 1854.

Sumner, Charles. "Crawford's Orpheus." *United States Magazine and Democratic Review.* Volume 12, May 1843, pp. 451–455.

Swan, Mabel Munson. *The Boston Athenaeum as an Early Patron of Art.* Boston: Boston Athenaeum, 1940.

Taft, Lorado. *The History of American Sculpture.* New York: Macmillan Company, 1903.

Taliaferro, Robert, ed. *Mr. Hunter's Oration delivered at the inauguration of Crawford's Equestrian Statue at Richmond.* Richmond: Macfarlane and Fergusson, 1858.

Taylor, Joshua C. *William Page: the American Titian.* Chicago: University of Chicago Press, 1957.

Tharp, Louisa Hall. *Three Saints and a Sinner.* Boston: Little Brown, 1956.

"Thomas Crawford." *Cosmopolitan Art Journal.* New York: Cosmopolitan Art Association, 1856–1860. Volume 2, December 1857, pp. 27–28.

"Thomas Crawford." Domestic Art Gossip. *The Crayon.* Volume 7, November 1860, pp. 323–325.

"Thomas Crawford." *The Living Age.* Boston: Littell, Son and Company, 1844–1941. Reprinted from the *Boston Courier,* volume 56, January 1858, pp. 274–280.

"Thomas Crawford, Obituary." *The Crayon.* Volume 4, December 1857, p. 380.

"Thomas Crawford's Engravings, Illustrated." *Boston Evening Transcript.* December 21, 1935. Crawford File, Boston Athenaeum.

"Thomas Crawford's Works for the Senate pediment and bronze doors, Sketchings." *The Crayon.* Volume 2, July 11, 1855, p. 26.

"Thomas Crawford's Works for the United States Capitol on exhibit." *The Crayon.* Volume 4, February 1857, pp. 53–54.

Ticknor, Anna Eliot, ed. *The Life of Joseph Green Cogswell as Sketched in his Letters.* Cambridge: privately printed at Riverside Press, 1874.

Ticknor, George. *Life, Letters, and Journals of George Ticknor.* Edited by George S. Hillard, Mrs. Anna Eliot Ticknor, and Anna Eliot Ticknor. Two volumes. Boston: J. R. Osgood and Company, 1876.

Ticknor, George. *The Life of William Hinckling Prescott.* Boston: Ticknor and Fields, 1864.

Tinto, Mario. *La Vita di Lorenzo Bartolini.* Rome, 1936.

Townsend, Harry J., ed. *A Memoir of Thomas Buchanan Read.* Philadelphia, 1889.

Treves, Giuliana Artom. *Anglo-Fiorentini di Cento Anni Fa.* Florence: Sansoni, 1953. English edition: *The Golden Ring, The Anglo-Florentines, 1847–1862.* Translated by Sylvia Spigge. London: Longmans Green, 1956.

Trollope, Adolphus. *What I Remember.* Two volumes. London: Bentley, Richards, 1887. Especially volume 1.

Trollope, Frances. *The Domestic Manners of the Americans.* New York: Knopf, 1949.

Trollope, Frances. *A Visit to Italy.* Two volumes. London: Bentley, Richards, 1842.

Tuckerman, Henry T. *Artist-life, or Sketches of American Painters.* New York: D. Appleton, and Company, 1847.

Tuckerman, Henry T. *Biographical Essays.* Boston: Phillips, Sampson and Company, 1857.

Tuckerman, Henry T. *Book of the Artists: American Artists Life.* New York: G. P. Putnam and Son, 1867.

Tuckerman, Henry T. *The Criterion.* New York: Hurd and Houghton, 1866.

Tuckerman, Henry T. "A Day at Ravenna." *The Knickerbocker.* Volume 19, 1839, pp. 28–33.

Tuckerman, Henry T. "The Funeral of Thomas Crawford." *The Living Age.* Boston: Littell, Son and Company, 1844–1941. Volume 56, January 1858, p. 280. A poem, reprinted from the *New York Evening Post.*

Tuckerman, Henry T. *Isabel, or Sicily, A Pilgrimage.* Philadelphia: Lea and Blanchard, 1839.

Tuckerman, Henry T. "The Italian Question." *Putnam's Monthly Magazine.* Volume 1, number 1, January 1868, pp. 105–111.

Tuckerman, Henry T. *The Italian Sketch Book.* Philadelphia and Boston: Key and Biddle, 1837.

Tuckerman, Henry T. *Leaves from the Diary of a Dreamer.* London: W. Pickering, 1853.

Tuckerman, Henry T. *A Memorial of Horatio Greenough, Memorial Selections from Writings and Tribute.* New York. G. P. Putnam. 1853.

Tuckerman, Henry T. *Sketches of Eminent American Painters.* New York: D. Appleton and Company, 1849.

Tuckerman, Henry T. "Two of Our Sculptors: B. P. Akers and E. S. Bartholomew." *Hours at Home*. Volume 2, April 1866, pp. 525–532.

Usher, Leila. "Benjamin Paul Akers." *New England Magazine*. Volume 11, December 1894, pp. 460–468.

Viator [pseudonym]. "Can there be a new architecture? *Putnam's Monthly Magazine*. Volume 6, August 1855, pp. 334–335.

Vindication of Hiram Powers in the Greek Slave Controversy. Cincinnati: The Great West, 1849. Correspondence between James Robb and Hiram Powers, published by Powers' friends to vindicate him.

A Visit to Rome in 1764. Pamphlet. Cambridge: The Fogg Art Museum and the Harvard College Library, 1956.

Wade, Mason. *Margaret Fuller Ossoli, Whetstone of Genius*. New York: Viking Press, 1940.

Wade, Mason, ed. *The Writings of Margaret Fuller*. New York: Viking Press, 1941.

Ward, Samuel G. "The Greek Slave." *Massachusetts Quarterly Review*. Boston: Coolidge and Wiley, 1847–1850. Volume 2, December 1847, pp. 54–62.

Ward, Samuel G. "Notes on Art." *The Dial*. Volume 3, July 1843.

Warfield, Ethelbert Dudley. *Magazine of Western History*. Cleveland and New York: Magazine of Western History Publishing Company, 1884–1894. Volume 2, September 1885, pp. 524–533.

Wharton, Edith. *Italian Backgrounds*. New York: Scribner's Sons, 1907.

Wharton, Edith. *Italian Villas and Their Gardens*. New York: Century Company, 1910.

Whipple, Evangeline E. *A Famous Corner of Tuscany*. London: Jarrolds, Ltd., 1928.

Whiting, Lillian. *The Florence of Walter Savage Landor*. Boston: Little, Brown, and Company, 1905.

Whiting, Lillian. *Italy, the Magic Land*. Boston: Little, Brown, and Company, 1907.

Willis, Nathaniel Parker. *Pencillings on the Way*. New York: Morris and Willis, 1844.

Winckelmann, Johann Joachim. *The History of Ancient Art*. Translated by G. Henry Lodge. Two volumes. Boston: J. R. Osgood and Company, 1883.

Winsor, Justin. *A Memorial History of Boston, 1630–1881*. Four volumes. Boston: J. R. Osgood and Company, 1883.

Wittmann, Otto, Jr. "Americans in Italy; Mid-Century Attitudes a Hundred Years Apart." *College Art Journal.* New York: College Art Association of America, 1941–1960. Volume 17, Spring 1958.

Wright, Nathalia. *Horatio Greenough, the First American Sculptor.* Philadelphia: University of Pennsylvania Press, 1963.

Wright, Nathalia. "Horatio Greenough, Boston Sculptor." *Old-Time New England, the Bulletin for the Preservation of New England Antiquities.* Boston: Boston Quarterly, 1910. Volume 45, January–March 1955, pp. 55–60.

Wright, Nathalia. "Horatio Greenough, Boston Sculptor and Robert Gilmor, Jr., His Baltimore Patron." *Maryland Historical Magazine.* Baltimore: Maryland Historical Society, 1906–1967. Volume 51, March 1956, pp. 1–13.

Wright, Nathalia, ed. "Letters by Horatio Greenough in the Library." *Boston Public Library Quarterly.* Boston: Boston Public Library. Volume 11, April 1959, pp. 79–93.

Wyeth, Samuel Douglas. *The Federal City, or Ins and Abouts of Washington.* Washington: Gibson Brothers, 1865.

Wynne, George. *Early Americans in Rome.* Rome: Rome Daily American Press, 1966.

Wynne, Nancy, and Beaumont Newhall. "Horatio Greenough, Herald of Functionalism." *Magazine of Art.* Washington: American Federation of Arts, 1909. Volume 32, 1939.

Young, William, editor and compiler. *A Dictionary of American Artists, Sculptors and Engravers from the beginnings through the turn of the twentieth century.* Cambridge: William Young and Company, 1968.

Index